Farmation

D1261062

Consider Your Call

Consider Your Call

A Theology of Monastic Life Today

DANIEL REES
and Other Members of the
English Benedictine Congregation

Foreword by
CARDINAL BASIL HUME
Archbishop of Westminster

CISTERCIAN PUBLICATIONS
Kalamazoo, Michigan

First published in 1978 by
The Society for Promoting Christian Knowledge
Holy Trinity Church
Marylebone Road
London NW1 4DU

First published in the USA by
Cistercian Publications 1980
Kalamazoo, Michigan

Printed in Great Britain at
The Camelot Press Ltd, Southampton

ISBN 0 87907 820 0

Contents

CONTENTS

Community

Commission Members

Dom Daniel Rees (*Chairman*)
R. R. Dom Gregory Freeman
   (*Representative of the Abbots*)
Dom Wilfrid Sollom (*Secretary*)
Dom Gregory Floyd

Dom Philip Jebb
Dom Sylvester Mooney
Dom David Morland
Dom Kevin Seasoltz
Dame Maria Boulding (*Editor*)

Contributors and Consultors

R. R. Dom Basil Hume
   (*now Cardinal*)
Dom Aelred Burrows
Dom Aldhelm Cameron-Brown
Dom Francis Davidson
Dom Finbarr Dowling
Dame Anne Field
Dom Edmund Flood
Dom Stanislaus Hobbs
Dom Dominic Milroy
Dom Louis O'Dwyer
Dom Edmund Power
V. R. Dom Luke Rigby

Dame Frideswide Sandeman
Dom Placid Spearritt
A group at Stanbrook
Dame Scholastica Daly
   and a group at Holme Eden
Dame Ethelberta Smith
   (*now Abbess*)
   and a group at Talacre
Dame Edith Street
   and a group at Colwich
Sister Teresa Gillin and
   Sister M. Gregory Forster
   with a group at Pennant Hills

Foreword

It may seem strange that a book of this kind is offered to the general public, since it has the appearance of a piece of self-searching by a very specialized group of people. If monks and nuns want to talk to each other about their peculiar vocation, most people would be inclined to say that they have a perfect right to do so, but that the conversation is not likely to be of interest to anyone else.

Christian monasticism, however, is not entirely a specialist affair. It is true that only a few of Christ's followers are called to be monks and nuns, but their way of life is no more and no less than an attempt to live out their Christianity in all its implications. All Christians are called to holiness through perfect love. There are many ways of following this call, but, in so far as we all hear and try to respond to it, we shall find that we have a good deal of experience in common.

Many of the issues raised in this book, therefore, although discussed in relation to monastic life, are issues which concern all Christians today, and indeed all men and women who care for the values on which our society is built. Christians search for God in prayer and worship him in the Eucharist. They listen to his word in Scripture, liturgy, and life. They are concerned for the dignity of human work and its integration with the life of the individual and the human community. They seek to establish human groups where the healing love of Christ may be shared, where relationships may be truly Christian, and where persons matter. Questions of authority, responsibility, obedience, and true freedom of spirit confront the Christian conscience in many walks of life. People seek to regain a Christian and human relationship to the earth and its resources, to tools and time and the rhythms of living; they seek a creative way of life, peace, and wholeness.

The search for solutions and balance in all these things is of vital importance to our society, both in its sickness and in its hopes. If national and international society is to be healthy, human life must be sound and good at its roots. Because the monasticism inspired by St Benedict has

xi

traditionally cared for these vital issues, it can speak to the modern world in terms that will not need too much translation.

None the less, it would be dishonest to represent monasticism as primarily a panacea for social ills or a philosophy possessing all the answers. It is a venture of faith, and if it makes a social contribution it does so by aiming off-target, by fidelity to its call to seek first the Kingdom of God. The lordship of God and man's duty to love and worship him are the springs of the monastic life, and human affairs are valued rightly only when seen in the light of the eternity to which we are called. It is the business of Christ's Church to be both a preliminary presence of God's Kingdom on earth and a prophetic sign of that ultimate salvation open to all men which is to be realized in the life to come. The Church must preach this good news by many forms of contact and exchange with persons of all beliefs and cultures. A monastery may be a place where such exchange regularly occurs.

This book is not an academic exercise; it is written out of the experience of men and women who have lived the monastic life for years, grappled with its realities, and freely shared with one another. I recommend it in the belief that it will have something to say not only to monks and nuns but also to Christian laymen and laywomen, and to all who are concerned for our common humanity.

CARDINAL BASIL HUME
Archbishop of Westminster

Preface

The spur behind the production of this book must ultimately be traced to the mandate to renew themselves which the Second Vatican Council issued to all religious congregations in the decree *Perfectae Caritatis* (28 October 1965). The general criteria which were there prescribed for renewal were a return to the sources (that is, the gospels, the spirit of the founder and the sound traditions of the particular religious order) and adaptation to the changed conditions of our times (*PC* 2). More precise guidelines for implementing this renewal were issued in the post-Conciliar document *Ecclesiae Sanctae*, part ii (6 August 1966), among whose requirements was that the general laws (constitutions) of every religious order be revised by its general chapter after an ample and full consultation of all its members. This instruction continued with a very emphatic injunction that the renewed constitutions should not be purely juridical in character but should also express the evangelical and theological principles concerning religious life and its incorporation in the Church, and 'an apt and accurate formulation in which the spirit and aims of the founder should be clearly recognized and faithfully preserved'.

The General Chapter of the English Benedictine Congregation appointed various commissions to execute these requirements. At first, provisional Constitutions were drafted where the legal provisions were intercalated by expositions of spirituality extracted from *A Statement on Benedictine Life*. The latter was a manifesto of monastic aims adopted by a Congress of all the abbots held in Rome in September 1967. Since this Congress is a federation of representatives of many different species of Benedictine life, its *Statement* was inevitably very general in character and could not be taken as an adequate expression of the differing traditions and interpretations of monastic theology to be found among its members.

So in the General Chapter of 1969 the English Benedictine Congregation set up a Commission on the Theology of the Monastic

Life with the purpose of drafting a document that would make explicit those theological principles and particular emphases which lie behind our own Congregation's manner of conceiving the monastic life and indicate how they can be pointers for its future. It was still intended at that time to blend this theological statement with the Constitutions which were being revised concurrently. But the Commission soon objected that a theological investigation could hardly be pursued if it had to shape itself to a predetermined juridical framework, and urged that the two processes of theological reflection and canonical revision be carried out independently of one another. Their plea for autonomy was accepted by the authorities of the English Congregation, but does not necessarily preclude any eventual interaction between their document and the new Constitutions, though it remains to be seen what form such relations will take.

This book has, therefore, been eight years in the making and is rather a belated arrival on the field of literary efforts at monastic renewal. The two American Benedictine Congregations had made their contributions before we had begun: *Renew and Create* was issued by the American Cassinese in June 1969, and the Swiss-American Benedictines issued *Covenant of Peace* at about the same time. Just as quick off the mark and also 'an indirect consequence of the Second Vatican Council's call to renewal' (the Bishop of Exeter in his Preface) was the reappraisal of their principles by Anglican religious communities entitled *Religious Communities in the World of Today* (London, SPCK, 1970). (The author of the commentary accompanying this statement, Canon A. M. Allchin of Canterbury, was kind enough to come to one of the earliest meetings of our Commission and help us with his experience of procedure.) The English Benedictines, however, have been forced to go at a much slower pace than most others, chiefly because most of the Commission's members were already fully occupied by other duties. But it could be that such a tardy achievement would have its own advantages of a longer perspective, the test of post-Conciliar experience and the closer influence of the monastic workaday world.

Two special features of the English Congregation were reflected in the composition of this Commission. First, we have three houses in the United States and, in spite of the difficulties of travel and getting together, representatives of these houses made a contribution out of all proportion to their relative numbers; one of them was responsible for drafting the general scheme of the topics discussed in this book. Second, the English Congregation is anomalous in the monastic world in that it includes as integral members several houses of nuns. These nuns have also fully participated at every stage of the book's production, not only in its final literary expression (which is very largely their work) but also in the theological wrangles that accompanied its gestation.

The procedure that we followed always began with the submission of a draft paper by an individual member of the Commission on one of the items enumerated in the general scheme. This would be discussed and amended over and over again at meetings of the Commission; it was not infrequent for a chapter to pass through seven different drafts before its final acceptance. The papers were also circulated to every member of the Congregation, and a great volume of comments and criticisms was received and attended to. The final result therefore can no longer be attributed to the original author of the chapter, but is very much a corporate production.

Although this book has been written under the patronage of the English Benedictine Congregation, none of the views here expressed should be taken to reflect that Congregation's official and final standpoint. We hope, however, that our investigations have been pursued in the spirit which animates the Congregation, one of freedom combined with care for inherited responsibilities.

Throughout its long genesis this book has owed much to the encouragement received from the Abbot President, Dom Victor Farwell, who has always taken a great interest in our proceedings, granting us full liberty and much material support. The same must be said of the Abbots and Abbesses of the Congregation generally, who as a body have even sometimes worked along with the Commission in discussing thorny topics, and have invited distinguished speakers from outside to come and address us. We are also indebted to Abbot (now Cardinal) Basil Hume who piloted the composition of one of our papers, and to Abbot Gregory Freeman who has been a tireless and comprehending liaison between the Commission and the Abbots. Finally we would like to thank all the numerous people, both inside and outside the Congregation, who have read our papers and given us considered and helpful verdicts.

Acknowledgements

Thanks are due to the following for permission to quote from copyright sources:

The Reverend Walter M. Abbott, s.j. and The America Press: *The Documents of Vatican II*, edited by Walter M. Abbott and Joseph Gallagher

Ave Maria Press: *The Pentecostal Movement in the Catholic Church* by E. O'Connor

Blond & Briggs Ltd: *Small is Beautiful* by E. F. Schumacher

Burns & Oates Ltd: *The Rule of St Benedict*, edited and translated by Dom Justin McCann

William Collins Sons & Co. Ltd: *Between Man and Man* by Martin Buber

Darton, Longman & Todd Ltd: *Method in Theology* by B. Lonergan; *A New Pentecost?* by L. J. Suenens; *Theological Investigations*, vols 4, 6, and 8, by Karl Rahner (by permission also of the Seabury Press); *The Climate of Monastic Prayer* by Thomas Merton (by permission also of Cistercian Publications, Inc., Kalamazoo, Michigan)

The Trustees of Ealing Abbey: *The Rule of St Benedict for Monasteries*, translated and edited by Dom Bernard Basil Bolton

Victor Gollancz Ltd: *Unpopular Opinions* by Dorothy L. Sayers

The Editor, *Monastic Studies*: Article by Ambrose Wathen, in *Monastic Studies*, 11

Pantheon Books (A Division of Random House, Inc.): *Leisure, the Basis of Culture* by Josef Pieper, translated by Alexander Dru. All rights reserved

SCM Press Ltd: *The Crucified God* by Jürgen Moltmann (by permission also of Harper & Row, Inc.); and *The New Being* by Paul Tillich (by permission also of Charles Scribner's Sons)

The Seabury Press: 'The Institution of Religious Celibacy' by G. Lafont in *The*

Future of the Religious Life, edited by Peter Huizing and William Bassett (*Concilium*, vol. 97, 1974)

The Tablet: Article by David Goodall in *The Tablet*, 9 October 1976

Times Newspapers Ltd: Article by Martin Jarrett-Kerr in *The Times*, 5 June 1971; reproduced from *The Times* by permission.

Extracts from the Jerusalem Bible, published and © 1966, 1967, and 1968 by Darton, Longman & Todd Ltd and Doubleday and Co., Inc., are used by permission of the publishers.

Quotations from the Revised Standard Version of the Bible, copyrighted 1946 and 1952 by the Division of Christian Education of the National Council of the Churches of Christ in the USA, are used by permission.

Abbreviations

AA	*Apostolicam Actuositatem*, Decree on the Apostolate of the Laity by Vatican II
AAS	*Acta Apostolicae Sedis*
AG	*Ad Gentes*, Decree on the Church's Missionary Activity by Vatican II
CBQ	*Catholic Biblical Quarterly*
CD	*Christus Dominus*, Decree on the Bishops' Pastoral Office in the Church by Vatican II
CSCO	*Corpus Scriptorum Christianorum Orientalium*
CSEL	*Corpus Scriptorum Ecclesiasticorum Latinorum.*
DV	*Dei Verbum*, Dogmatic Constitution on Divine Revelation by Vatican II
EBC	English Benedictine Congregation
GS	*Gaudium et Spes*, Pastoral Constitution on the Church in the Modern World by Vatican II
IGLH	*General Instruction on the Liturgy of the Hours*
JB	Jerusalem Bible
LG	*Lumen Gentium*, Dogmatic Constitution on the Church by Vatican II
NEB	New English Bible
NRT	*Nouvelle Revue Théologique*
PC	*Perfectae Caritatis*, Decree on the Appropriate Renewal of the Religious Life by Vatican II
PG	Migne, *Patrologia Graeca*
PL	Migne, *Patrologia Latina*
PO	*Presbyterorum Ordinis*, Decree on the Ministry and Life of Priests by Vatican II
RB	The Rule of St Benedict. RB (Bolton) = *The Rule of St Benedict for Monasteries*, tr. Dom Bernard Basil Bolton, O.S.B. (Ealing Abbey 1970). RB (McCann) = *The Rule of St Benedict*, ed. and tr. Abbot Justin McCann (Burns & Oates 1952).

RM	The Rule of the Master
RSPT	*Revue des Sciences philosophiques et théologiques*
RSV	Revised Standard Version of the Bible
SC	*Sacrosanctum Concilium*, Constitution on the Sacred Liturgy by Vatican II
ST	The *Summa Theologiae* of St Thomas Aquinas
UR	*Unitatis Redintegratio*, Decree on Ecumenism by Vatican II
ZAW	*Zeitschrift für die alttestamentliche Wissenschaft*
ZNW	*Zeitschrift für die neutestamentliche Wissenschaft*

References to the Rule are given according to the numeration in Dom Cuthbert Butler's Critico-Practical Edition, *Sancti Benedicti Regulam Monasteriorum: Editionem Critico-Practicam adornavit D. Cuthbertus Butler: Editio Altera MCMXXVII* (Freiburg im Breisgau, Herder).

References to the Documents of Vatican II followed by the words 'ed. Abbott-Gallagher' indicate that the translation edited by Walter M. Abbott, s.j., and Joseph Gallagher, published by Geoffrey Chapman 1966, has been used.

Introduction

What is a monk?

Many people within monastic life or closely related to it would deprecate the attempt to answer the question, 'What is a monk?', reflecting that monasticism as a way of life has its own strength and consistency which are unaffected by the failure of its followers to produce a formula which at best can only embody and stabilize the experience of living, and at worst may be misleading and remote from real life. Living comes before self-definition, because self-definition is the outcome of a synthesis between (1) the ideas, ideals, and objective historical developments which have shaped and determined the present situation, and (2) self-conscious reflection on these data by persons who are themselves involved in and influenced by the historical process on which they are reflecting. Hence it need be matter for neither alarm nor despondency if those committed to a certain way of life are unable to articulate a self-definition, or, as is more usually the case for monks today, are unable to agree among themselves which of the plethora of self-definitions available is valid.[1]

Some suggestions must, however, be made if monasticism is to be discussed in more than purely pragmatic terms, and if we are to enhance our appreciation of what we are living in order the better to celebrate and thank God for it. Two basic questions can be asked, and the answers affect deeply both the theory and the practice of monastic life.

1. Is Christian monasticism to be approached as one manifestation of a much older and more widespread adventure of the human spirit which is manifested also in pre-Christian and non-Christian monasticism; or is Christian monasticism primarily a manifestation of Christianity itself and to be understood only in terms of the gospel?

2. Within the context of Christian monasticism, is the primary reality the individual monk in search of union with God (the community being understood to be his necessary environment); or is the primordial and

I

typical reality the monastic community (composed, obviously, of individual monks seeking God)?

The alternative approaches

Monasticism is not a specifically Christian phenomenon; it is born of aspirations inherent in the human spirit. It has emerged in the great world religions, particularly Hinduism and Buddhism, as a way of life embraced by those whose desire for God is an overriding passion, and organized to promote the search for union with God. The mystery of God, self-revealing and self-giving, transcends conceptual formulation. It can be in part disclosed by signs, but no single range of signs is adequate. The tradition crystallized in the Old Testament is a privileged but culturally limited complex of signs. The signs provided by those cultures in which the great non-Christian religions have flourished are also needed that the one mystery may be more fully expressed. This is particularly true in the area of monasticism where Hinduism and Buddhism especially have through their contemplative wisdom, compassion, and simplicity expressed values which Christians too recognize and honour. It must be acknowledged, however, that non-Christian monasticism has often been marked by a rejection of the world and its values as alien to the monk's quest and perhaps as deceitful and illusory.

Christianity is the way of life of those who have been called, and have responded to the call, to share in the life of God through incorporation into Jesus Christ and fellowship in his Spirit. It is not primarily a search for an absent God, but a response to his loving initiatives and a celebration of his saving presence in history, in the Church and in the believer. Moreover the ennoblement of all human experience through its assumption by Christ who became like to us in all save sin, and the promised transformation of all created things through the power of his resurrection, make it impossible for the Christian to reject the world that God has so loved.

It follows, therefore, that from the Christian point of view monasticism is ambiguous. It has flowered within Christianity but its genuine values need to be discovered and reinterpreted in the light of God's presence in Christ within the community of mankind. There is no doubt that the desire for communion with God has been in both ancient and modern times a spring of Christian monastic vocations, and that Christian prayer can legitimately be described in terms of the search for

God. But these phrases have taken on newness of meaning in the light of the gospel, for God has come to seek and to save what was lost.

A venerable and persistent tradition in monastic theology, represented in the pre-Benedictine era by St Basil, St Gregory of Nyssa and St John Chrysostom, holds that to be a monk is simply a wholehearted way of being a Christian; monasticism is integral Christianity. Although there is obviously much truth in this view, particularly in the sense that the monk himself becomes unable to separate his Christian vocation from his monastic calling, it leaves the difficulty of explaining how the Christian monk differs from the Christian layman. The end of all Christian life is the glorification of God by perfect charity, and the most essential means to its attainment are in some degree binding on all: every Christian must seek to follow Christ in obedience to the will of the Father, must pray, exercise faith and hope and love, make use of the sacraments, and live in the Spirit. Neither in the end nor in these primary means is the monk essentially different from any other Christian. Moreover, the traditional appeal to such gospel passages as the story of the rich young man in an attempt to find scriptural warrant for monastic life is now seen to have been oversimplified, since it is possible that these stories illustrate the call to detachment from property and even from marriage which may in some circumstances become imperative for any Christian at least for a time.

However, although our appeal to Scripture may now be marked by more nuances, we can still find in the gospels certain indications which provide a starting-point for the development of Christian monastic life. The Lord spoke of those 'who have made themselves eunuchs for the sake of the Kingdom of heaven',[2] and the gospels give glimpses of a fully and permanently dedicated group of people who had left all things to follow him. Experience of the Kingdom takes some people that way, inviting them to a deliberate simplification of their lives. Christian monasticism is born of a radical and charismatic option in favour of the new presence of God in his word and in his saving mysteries. It implies an exclusive and (normally) lifelong dedication to the Kingdom of God, and the adoption of a disciplined life-style comprising celibacy, renunciation of personal ownership, obedience, prayer and praise, habitual listening to God's word in meditation and *lectio divina*, work, silence, and usually a life in community with others. The monk's choice is stabilized by vows. His solidarity with the rest of God's people is always a spiritual reality and may be expressed in apostolic work. His way of life and his vows give to his Christian life a certain sign-value. Monasticism should be a witness to the Kingdom. Sadly, a monastic community, especially a large one, can become a counter-witness if it substitutes other values for the gospel, suffers from corporate pride, and fails to live up to its vocation. But when it is faithful it is a sign of the holiness of the Church, not in the sense that monks are necessarily holier than anyone else but because their profession is a public testimony to the all-sufficiency of God, to the power of his grace, to the destiny beyond death that he is preparing for those who love him and to the breaking through of the eschatological realities into this present age. A monastic community is like a sacrament in which the mystery of salvation is revealed and communicated.[3]

Consideration both of the New Testament bases of the monastic vocation and of its relationship to the calling of the Christian layman raises the second question: is the specifying reality the individual monk seeking God, striving for contemplation *solus cum Solo*; or is it the presence within the Church and the world of a community of Christian monks, with all that their presence entails of salvation-experience and witness? The New Testament texts provide indication both of the highly personal and unique character of each man's encounter with the Lord, and of the raising of the mystery of communion with one another in the Lord to a new power. There is much support in both tradition and contemporary monastic experiments for the idea that the monk is a marginal person, one who has deliberately withdrawn to the fringe of society to live in prayer and poverty for the sake of freedom to deepen certain fundamental human experiences in fellowship with God,[4] and to identify with those who are willy-nilly on the fringe. The ecclesiology of Vatican II has, however, probably helped many monks to become more explicitly aware of the deeply sacramental character of their life and rule, and hence to arrive at a richer understanding of the mystery of community. It may also happen that in the life of an individual monk there is progression. He may not begin with a fully developed picture of communal salvation and then look round for a community in which his ideal can be realized; all vocations are highly personal and intimate, and he may begin to follow his call in a very individualistic spirit, discovering only gradually and with increasing experience the sacramental values of community life. On the other hand, no Christian and monastic community life can be sustained unless each member has a continuous and growing personal contact with the risen Lord and responds in personal faithfulness. The two emphases appear to be opposed only if wrongly stated; in reality each requires the other.

4

A sharp dichotomy is therefore to be avoided in framing the basic questions; they require answers that allow for 'both . . . and'. It is also clear that to try to isolate any pure timeless 'essence of monasticism' apart from incarnate living is a mistake. It may be noticed that while the two questions discussed above are distinct they are interlinked. The monk who is more impressed by the ideal of monasticism as solitude and search may be (though he need not be) more aware of the relevance of non-Christian monastic contributions than one who prefers to think in terms of Christian community. The latter is likely to regard his monasticism as above all an experience and a flowering of the Christian vocation, even though he may honour non-Christian monastic movements and many contemporary forms of search for community living as a *praeparatio evangelica*.

A subsidiary question suggested by the foregoing discussion is that of the relationship between monastic life and the various forms of religious life that abound in the Church of the West. It may not be wise to attempt to demarcate monasticism in such a way that it is clearly differentiated today from these forms of religious life; such attempts can become narrow, artificial, and defensive. Historically it is not correct to speak of monastic life as one species within the genus, 'religious life', because in fact all types of Christian religious life in the West are in some way developments from the monastic ideal. They have arisen in response to particular needs in the Church and the world and have adapted monastic practice, in greater or lesser degree, for their own purposes, even deliberately discarding monastic elements such as stability, choral office, and community life when these would have been a hindrance. Vatican II presented religious life in relation to the nature and purpose of the Church,[5] describing the Church as the direct recipient of all the graces and charisms of the religious life.[6] Monasticism, which arose in response to no specific apostolic challenge, shares with various forms of religious life the role of witnessing to the eschatological tension of the Church and of showing forth the prophetic character of Christ, but it also has its own ways of realizing and signifying the Church's mystery, especially in its power to constitute, through the close Christian fellowship of the monastery and the exercise of hospitality, a sign of that *koinonia* which was so marked a feature of early Christianity. There is much to be said for the view that a monastery constitutes in itself a small local church, an *ecclesiola*, in the sense that it is a community that enjoys fellowship in the Spirit of the risen Christ.[7] It was conceived in ancient monasticism as the ideal representation, in miniature, of Christ's Church. It may happen that, prescinding from questions of historical origin, monasticism today does not find itself markedly different from other institutions in the Church that are not highly specialized. This discovery need not point to any crisis of identity; it may suggest that the meaning of monasticism is to be sought in the centre rather than on the periphery of the Church's life. To say this is not to deny the usefulness of attempts to differentiate the monastic from other vocations when confusion of roles may have occurred through historical circumstances. Awareness of the possibility of such confusion can clarify discussion of questions concerning the priesthood, the *opus Dei*, the Eucharist, and similar matters.

Tentative answers to the question, 'What is a monk?' may be valid up to a point, but monks can become smug and their thinking too facile if they travel far along the road of attempting to prove the relevance of monasticism to either the Church or the modern world, or if they are preoccupied with the notion of 'witness'. The monk is not in search of any immediately demonstrable 'relevance'; he is not 'for' anything. His way of life is a venture of faith, not in the sense that he is beyond the reach of doubts, but in the sense that having to struggle with doubt and emptiness and the forces of death within himself he is reaching beyond them to the ultimate reality of the living God. He has disengaged himself from certain secular concerns not because he is aloof or self-sufficient or immune to loneliness, but because he wants to admit his loneliness and to find the meaning of it in his need to be open to the gift of God and the gift of others. He is in search of a liberation of the spirit, a 'mindfulness', a freedom from enslavement to propaganda, half-truths, and the majority opinions that close a man against experience of the transcendent Creator Spirit.

Towards monastic renewal

Openness to the new and unexpected action of the Holy Spirit implies not that the monk has discarded or played down all traditional forms of observance, worship, and asceticism inherited from the monastic past, but that he has assimilated and interiorized them, recognizing them as necessary but remembering that they are means. Such an appreciation, however, presupposes that external observances and structures are truly at the service of the spirit and that fidelity to tradition is understood not as a paralysing rigidity but as true responsiveness to a living inspiration. External forms may therefore need to change and evolve if genuine

6

faithfulness is to be maintained. Benedictine monachism, like the Church itself, is in constant need of renewal.

This renewal is an inherent quality of monastic life, as indeed of all life, a normal process of growth and adaptation which may at times also demand remedial measures. It is not an operation applied from outside to the living organism, but the working out of the individual and communal conversion to God (*metanoia*) characteristic of Benedictine monasticism in the context of a changing world and a changing Church.[8] However, renewal may be envisaged along either of two lines, since Benedictine monachism is related to forms of monasticism outside the Christian tradition but is also an expression of the life of the Christian Church.

Vatican II encouraged dialogue between Christians and representatives of other religions with a rich spiritual heritage, and the Secretariat for Non-Christian Religions was set up to promote exchanges. Asian spiritual classics are increasingly familiar in the West, and with the help of contributions from psychology, anthropology, and the studies of comparative religion an intertraditional vocabulary of religious experience is becoming available. It must be admitted that much of the enthusiasm in the West for Eastern spirituality is dangerously superficial, especially when the contacts are made only through books and by Christians who have only a shallow acquaintance with the riches of their own tradition. But contact between persons steeped in their own faiths can be very fruitful, and in this dialogue monks, both Christian and non-Christian,[9] have a special part to play. Communion at a level deeper than that of discussion can be achieved through exploration in common of monastic experience within the different traditions. Initiatives like that of the Bangkok meeting in 1968 pointed the way. Of perhaps more lasting significance is the presence of Christian monastic foundations in India and South-East Asia in proximity to non-Christian monks.[10] Contacts of this kind may be a source of renewal and enrichment for Christian monasticism, but they may also serve a larger purpose in contributing to the urgent task of salvaging and deepening the spiritual patrimony of mankind, built up by many generations of saints and men of God. In helping to preserve and develop this heritage monks are keeping the way open for modern technological man to recover an awareness of his own inner depths, his personal integrity, and his transcendent freedom. 'We are witnessing the growth of a truly universal consciousness in the modern world. This universal consciousness may be a consciousness of transcendent freedom and vision, or it may simply be a vast blur of mechanized triviality and ethical cliché.'[11] Monastic renewal is in this perspective more than a purely domestic affair.

On the other hand Benedictine monachism finds its meaning and identity within the mystery of Christ and the Christian Church, and its inner renewal is therefore bound up with the purification and revitalization of the Church itself. The renewal of the Church called for and inspired by Vatican II is in its most intimate reality not a matter of structural or disciplinary changes but a deeper participation in the paschal mystery of Christ. In the glorification of Jesus the Spirit was set free to renew the face of the earth. Since Benedictine life is a way of participating in the life of Jesus through the Spirit, and since the monk by his baptism and profession is dead to sin and alive to God in Christ Jesus, the general renewal of the Church and monastic renewal have a common source and goal.

A study devoted to Benedictine renewal might therefore develop from either of two positions: (a) it might begin from the universal monastic phenomenon, and attempt to reflect on the values we have in common with monks of every age and many different religions who have also sought God in prayer and silence, in solitude and community life, in conversion and purity of heart; or (b) it could take the Christian Church as its context, and work out the particular applications of the Church's renewal in our monasteries. In this book the latter alternative has generally been followed. But it must be borne in mind that the alternatives, 'broad phenomenon of monasticism' and 'Christian Church', are far from exhaustive. The post-Christian Western world is the scene of many very genuine movements that search for experience of God, prayer, sharing, and community life; these are often monastic in character but without conscious relation to any monastic tradition or contact with any monastic group. It may be that when Western monasticism has begun to learn from, assimilate, and transform these secular forms of search it will be better able to appreciate Eastern monastic contributions.

The place of theology in monastic renewal

Monastic *life* is the primary reality with which we are concerned. Monastic *work* is an overflow and expression of the vigour of that life.

Monastic *theology* is an activity engaged in by persons committed to and experienced in monastic life, when they stand back a little to reflect on and criticize their experience in the light of faith. But monastic theology is not only born from monastic life; it should also, if it is truly a living activity, have its effect on the way in which that life is lived and understood in daily practice. Vatican II indicated two main requirements for the renewal of religious: a return to the sources, particularly the Scriptures and their rule, and an adaptation to present conditions.[12] The task of monastic theology is not primarily to suggest concrete measures but to provide an adequate basis of theological understanding on which such measures can be taken. Practical reform without theology is blind.

The dearth of monastic theology today is a matter for wonder to many both inside and outside Benedictine monasteries. There are probably several reasons for it. During the last few centuries theology has tended to be impoverished by an exclusively cerebral approach, or by a cleavage between scientific theology and the richness of the spiritual and mystical tradition of the Church. There has also been a failure on the part of Catholic theology to keep up with contemporary anthropology. Within the monastic tradition itself there has probably been a certain failure of nerve, a kind of inferiority complex on the part of an older, more sapiential style of theology when confronted with the professionalism of much modern non-monastic theology. And there has often been a failure on the part of monastic theologians to grasp the relative character of some elements in monastic tradition that have been conditioned by the social and cultural ethos of an earlier day.

Renewal in monastic theology needs therefore to proceed along a number of different lines. We need thorough historical research, an investigation of the scriptural adumbrations of monasticism, the rules, commentaries and other works of monastic writers of the patristic period, the history of Christian monasticism in East and West, and a study of the development of monastic theology and legislation. We also need to rethink Christian monachism in the light of contemporary ecclesiology, concentrating particularly on the Church as Sacrament of Christ, Body of Christ, and People of God. We need to think seriously about the theological give-and-take between the values of creation and those of revelation,[13] asking ourselves what we can learn from modern sensitivity to such realities as freedom, the dignity of the human person, professional integrity, and social responsibility. These considerations should lead us to re-examine critically, in the light of modern theology and anthropology, some of those themes which, taken for granted in

9

earlier periods of monastic theology, do not ring true to us today, such as the notions of 'contempt for the world' and the 'angelic life', and the understanding of life according to the evangelical counsels in a way that fails to do justice to the universal call to holiness addressed to all Christians.

All these studies deserve the most expert attention possible and the use of the best means of investigation made available by the various modern sciences. Yet a return to the sources needs to be kept strictly attuned to the real issues that immediately confront us at the present time. Honest discussion is required among present-day monks and nuns, and between them and men and women of other religious institutions, and of the Church and the world outside the monasteries. This book is no more than a modest attempt to consolidate what has been done so far in the English Benedictine Congregation; since this Congregation comprises both monks and nuns it has been possible throughout to draw on the experience of both. While acknowledging the value and necessity of speculative theology, this book is intended as an exercise in practical theology, and is wholly oriented to serving the continuing renewal of monastic life.

Part of the Christian mystery, and of the life of the Church on earth, is expressed in the paradox: 'You would not be seeking Me unless you had already found Me.'[14] All theology is a search, and practical theology in the context of monastic renewal is bound to be problem-oriented to some extent. But in the person, work, and promises of Jesus Christ we know that the answer to our problems, or the object of our search, is already freely given. It is therefore also the task of monastic theology to witness to that answer, and to do so not in any spirit of human self-sufficiency but in expectant faith.

PART ONE

►▼◄

THE WORLD AND THE CHURCH

I

The Contemporary World

This first chapter is empirical and descriptive. It abstains from reference to the Scriptures and traditional theology, and attempts simply to identify some of the features of modern life that condition the world in which the Church and monasticism exist. The broad perspective of these early chapters on world and Church is necessary before particular elements in monasticism can be considered. Without it there is a danger of posing monastic questions too narrowly, through failing to recognize that many issues with which monks and nuns are concerned today are not specifically monastic but are related to general human and Christian experience in the modern world.

The contemporary world presents to an objective eye an ambiguous array of positive and negative forces. On the one hand, the desire for social justice and for peace and brotherhood, the search for a meaning in life which transcends our present experience, the technological advances, and the immense possibilities for constructive progress are sufficiently evident. On the other, the fear of mass destruction, the social and cultural disintegration, the violence and injustice, and the threat of the exhaustion or irreversible pollution of the earth's resources are equally striking. The world has a face of hope and a face of despair, and it is amid this complexity that the Christian and the monk live. The question they may often ask is: How should I regard this world? With optimism or with apathy?

The individual Christian or monk does not, however, stand alone: he is a member of the Church, the pilgrim People of God who are being led through history by the Holy Spirit. The answer to his question, indicated by Vatican II, is one of realistic optimism, an optimism based not simply on human expectations or human achievements but on the promises of God and the redemptive work of Christ. The contemporary world is, indeed, plagued by evils and problems of every sort, owing to the blindness and selfishness of men and the sheer limitations and ambiguities of human existence. But it also contains the seeds of hope, of constructive human development in this world, and of faith in the presence of God. The renewal that the Holy Spirit has inspired in the Church today is a renewal of human values and Christian hope, the purpose of which is to guide men to fashion their future in holiness, justice, and peace, and to point to a total fulfilment which lies beyond human history.

In order to understand more precisely the contemporary secular scene which forms the background to monastic life, it will be helpful to consider some of the movements and influences which are to be found within it.

First, the most obvious characteristics of the secular scene today are its complexity and fragmentation. Technology has expanded the scope of the humanly possible with regard to our knowledge and control of man and his environment, and yet there is little wisdom and agreement about how, or to what end, this capacity for self-determination is to be directed. Modern communications, together with social and economic interdependence, have created a new sense among men of belonging to *one* world; yet national divisions, ideological strife and economic inequality and exploitation form a vicious circle from which there seems no escape. The proliferation of knowledge in the humanities and the natural sciences has brought about so vast an increase in the bulk of information available to man about himself and his world that specialization has become inevitable, yet this specialization has caused a fragmentation of knowledge, so that communication, mediation, and integration between the sciences, or even within a single discipline, have become extremely difficult.

Second, the very success of the empirical sciences in the western world has led to a concentration on the material fulfilment of man's needs; this, combined with the ruthlessness and impersonalism of modern industrial societies, has created a vacuum of meaning which established religious institutions and traditional philosophies of life seem unable to fill. There results widespread disillusion, especially among the young, expressing itself in a variety of ways: the confused search for liberation through sex, drugs or mysticism and the hunger for spiritual experience; the attempt to create a more human world by destroying the existing establishment through revolution; the apathetic refusal to face any of these problems.

Third, the advances in historical criticism, comparative religion, psychology, sociology, and anthropology, advances of great promise in themselves but largely made in a climate where no common philosophical or moral values are acknowledged, have helped to create an atmosphere of relativism. Many people are sceptical about any absolute claim made on behalf of truth or moral values: there is no consensus about the existence of God, the nature of man, or the meaning of life. In such a climate any absolute commitment can seem dishonest or impossible. Even dedication to cultural achievement or professional work may lack any secure point of reference. Although political institutions retain their power and influence, evidence of their corruption or their failure leads to disillusionment and cynicism. Distrustful of existing institutions and fearful of being smothered, people drift. For many, the only credible value is responsible commitment in personal relationships. But this is to place on friendship, sexual love, and marriage a weight they cannot bear alone.

Fourth, there is a powerful sense, whether correct or not, of living in a *new* age, radically different from previous historical eras. This has caused a breakdown of 'tradition' as a mediating vehicle of human wisdom and has led to exclusive concentration on the present moment and the future. It has also contributed to individual insecurity and a lack of cohesion in social groups of every kind, which is reflected in a movement away from traditional institutions and a search for new forms of community living to provide an authentic framework of existence.

Fifth, amid all this uncertainty and insecurity, there is a strong right-wing reaction, an attempt to halt the tide of moral permissiveness and social anarchy through the enforcement of traditional values by discipline, law and order. But at best this is a holding operation, offering no enduring solution to contemporary problems; at worst it can relapse into totalitarianism and the oppression of minority groups.

Meanwhile the developing countries, though affected by these western conditions, are struggling with their own problems as well. Efforts to eliminate subhuman conditions by increased production are more than cancelled out by population growth. The passing of the colonial era, while making way for the self-conscious assertion of national identities, has in many places also left the new nations open to the dangers of political immaturity and instability. The intelligentsia, potentially the seed-bed of national leaders, may be confused and uncertain of its identity as on the one hand it revolts against the European culture to which it is nevertheless educationally indebted, and on the other finds itself out of touch with its ancient indigenous cultural roots.

From this very summary description of the contemporary scene three dominant characteristics may be noted: crisis, complexity, and the quest for solutions. That the modern world is in a state of crisis is evident enough, but an accurate analysis of this crisis is extremely difficult because of the multiplicity of factors involved, many of them mutually contradictory. An informed awareness of these factors, however, is essential for any renewal in the Church, whether in monasteries or elsewhere. Otherwise we are in grave danger of 'updating' the Church on the basis of a narrow or superficial understanding of what the signs of the times demand.

Some monks become clearly aware of all these problems after entering the monastery, and hence discover new dimensions of meaning in their monastic life. Others, having lived amid or very close to these problems, enter the monastery almost because of them, not in order to escape from them but because a dedicated life of prayer and work in union with God seems the best contribution they can make to the solution of problems too big to be handled by human resources alone. In either case, it is in the context of this kind of world that monastic communities live, and it is the task of such communities to grow in their own form of life so that they may fulfil their specific role in the life of the Church and in its mission to the world. Monks must be ready to share the sufferings of Christ and of the world, since only by passing through suffering can they share Christ's risen life and communicate it to others. In the measure of its fidelity to this call a monastic community will be a living sign of hope in the world. It can offer help especially to people who are seeking, however obscurely and unknowingly, a genuine community life and an experience of God, for it is through the presence of love among the brethren that Christ's work among men assumes a tangible form in the world. This faith and charity offer the possibility of the realization of essential human values and point to a hope and a meaning that will be fulfilled in the final coming of God's Kingdom.

2

The Mystery of the Church

In the world, and yet not of the world, stands the Church of Christ, the sacrament of the world's salvation. In this chapter we move into a completely different realm of discourse: the standpoint is explicitly that of faith; the thought and language rely on biblical imagery. If the reader experiences a jolt in passing from Chapter 1 to Chapter 2, it may be salutary. The very abrupt change of style may illustrate the fact: the universe of modern man and the universe of Scripture are extremely different. Chapter 3 will suggest the relationship between them.

During the twentieth century the self-awareness of the Catholic Church has moved through three major stages, concentrating on the Church as (1) the preliminary and earthly form of the Kingdom; (2) the Body of Christ; (3) the new People of God. Since Vatican II Catholic ecclesiology has stressed the role of the Church as the sacrament of universal salvation and the subordination of its mission to the coming of the eschatological Kingdom of God.

The Church as mystery and sacrament
of salvation

a) The plan of God

Lumen Gentium insists in its first chapter that the Church is a mystery, *the* sacrament of Christ. This means that the Church is more than the sum total of the individuals who belong to it. It is more than a community of people who share a view of life and history. God is so present to the Church that it can truly be called the temple of the Holy Spirit. And the Lord Jesus is so intimately associated with its life and work that it can be called the Body of Christ.

In his First Epistle St John simply says that God is love.[1] Therefore one must seek to understand love in order to come to some understanding of God, and one must abide in love to abide in God. God is a community of love in which the three divine Persons share the divine nature in love for one another. But love is dynamic, eager to give of itself. So God seeks to diffuse his life and his love. From this desire to share he creates the world. To share himself he brings man into being and forms him in his own image. The divine community of love constantly creates a community of love on earth. Many words are used to express God's intention for man: he would save man, redeem man, sanctify man. But perhaps the most comprehensive description is that God would unite man with himself in a community of love.

Human history seen through the eyes of faith is salvation history. It is the account of God's bringing man from isolation into a community alive with the presence and life of God himself. This is the plan of God which is called by St Paul 'the mystery hidden for ages and generations'.[2] For St Paul the mystery is the benevolence of God towards man in sharing his life through his Son; it is God's intention, hidden from all eternity, for which man is gradually prepared by repeated divine interventions in human history. The mystery is revealed in Christ and realized in us.

The fullest expression of this is found in the prologue of the Letter to the Ephesians, where the author enumerates the various aspects of the divine plan for man. These include (1) our adoption as children of God in union with Christ; (2) our redemption and the remission of our sins through the blood of Christ; (3) the gift to us of the indwelling Holy Spirit; (4) the praise and glory given to God. These points need examination.

(1) God's eternal plan is that we should become sons in his Son. Through union with Christ we are to have access to God our Father as his children. It is only when Christ, the beloved Son of God, reaches out and joins us to himself that we receive the gift of adoptive sonship.[3]

(2) The second aspect of God's plan reminds us that it is to a race estranged from God that Christ came. By sin man refuses to live the life which God wants to share with him. So he brings about discord and alienation: he is alienated from God, from his true self and his destiny, and from his brothers. The work of Christ, then, is one of reconciliation. It is a work of restoration to the unity which man destroyed by sin. It is 'a gathering together into unity of the children of God who were scattered abroad'.[4] To reconcile us to his Father Christ overcame our proud disobedience by a filial obedience manifested in the loving surrender of

18

life itself.[5] Accepting this perfect sacrifice, the Father raised Christ from the dead so that he might share his risen life with all men.[6]

(3) We have been joined to Christ and have become sons in the Son of God by receiving the Holy Spirit who gives us a share in the love and life of God.[7] St Paul calls the Holy Spirit whom we have received 'the first instalment of our inheritance'.[8] A seed has been sown. We have entered into a life-giving union with Christ that brings with it an outpouring of the Holy Spirit. Yet it is only a first instalment. We still look forward to, and long for, the full inheritance that will be ours when the work of redemption is completed.

(4) The ultimate reason for the mystery of Christ is the praise and glory of God.[9] The gathering of all creation under the headship of Christ is for the honour of God. It is through the communion of all men with each other in Christ that praise and glory are given to God. The resurrection of Christ both glorifies God and gives eternal life to us. But this eternal life consists in knowing the one true God, and Jesus Christ whom he has sent; in being with Christ so that we may contemplate the glory that was given him before the creation of the world.[10]

b) The Church as sacrament of salvation

The Church is the present realization of the mystery. The kingdom of God has been perfectly embodied in the risen humanity of Christ. In acknowledging his creaturely condition as man and his utter dependence on God as his Father, Christ offers an eternal sacrifice of praise. But that condition of sonship which he shares with the rest of humanity through the gift of his Spirit has been only partially realized in us. To the extent that the Church has responded to the gift of Christ's Spirit, it is truly an effective sign of his presence in the world. But to the degree that the Church is still struggling to be delivered from alienation and isolation, it is in need of reformation and renewal.

The notion of sacrament is fundamental to an understanding of Christianity. All religious activity is designed to achieve some kind of union between the divine and the human. Whatever means are employed for this purpose have a sacramental character. They are external signs by which God encounters man and man encounters God. The human condition requires some form of outward, visible expression of the mysterious, invisible, holy reality. We need to encounter the transcendent at some definite point. In the person and ministry of Jesus Christ the transcendent has appeared decisively in our history. Christ is pre-eminently the sacrament of God because, in his single personality, there reside the fulness of God and the completeness of man. He is that unique point where divine initiative and human responsiveness perfectly meet. This is true of the historical Jesus, but when we speak of Christ as the sacrament of God, as the point of encounter between God and man, we are speaking primarily of the risen Lord, the Lord who sits at the right hand of the Father interceding for us.[11]

Christ is the sacrament of God, and in an analogous way the Church is the sacrament of the suffering, dying, and risen Christ. The sacramental life of the Church exists to dramatize publicly what has already taken place in history, what is to occur in the future, and what is actually happening here and now. The Church is the visible, outward sign of the redemptive love and mercy of the Father in Christ. And the Church is the place where man responds, through word, work and worship, to the divine initiative in Christ. Given this larger sacramental context, we see the seven sacraments as acts of Christ in his Church. They are privileged points of encounter with the risen Lord.

Perhaps the most important and prophetic statement among the declarations of Vatican II was that the Church is a 'kind of sacrament or sign of intimate union with God, and of the unity of all mankind. It is also an instrument for the achievement of such union and unity.'[12] In other words, the emphasis has shifted away from the conception of the Church as the ark of salvation in which the individual believer seeks refuge, though this conception is not rejected. The self-identification of the Church here articulated is rather in terms of a visible, tangible manifestation in history of the structure of that salvation which God wills for all men, those who never become visible members of the Church or even hear of it as well as those who do.

In view of the tiny minority of the human family, past and present, who have come into effective contact with the Church, and in the light of the signs of the times in so far as they enable us to foresee the Church of the future, it would appear that visible membership is the extraordinary rather than the ordinary means of salvation. For those who do effectively encounter the Church such visible membership is a necessary expression of faith, but this does not seem to be the case for the majority of men. Yet God's universal saving will is certain, and union with the Body of Christ is the one way of salvation for all, since that union is the very meaning of what it is to be saved.

The Church is therefore much more than a necessary means for the few. It is the sacramental sign of the salvation of all, the embodiment of saving grace in history, the manifestation of God's unrestricted saving purpose. Within the huge complexity of the historical process grace is everywhere at work, giving the world a secret orientation to the glory of God, but this grace and divine self-communication break through in the Church, so that the Christian community can both consciously become aware of it and bear witness to God's purpose for all men.[13]

To the extent that the Church is a true sacrament of encounter with Christ it can effectively engage in dialogue with the world. Part of the message which Christianity brings to the world is that full humanity is possible in Jesus Christ. If it were not for God's promises, we would not even be aware of this potentiality. The Church exists, with its sacramental liturgy and its proclamation of the word, for the nourishment of eschatological hope, for the strengthening and celebration of this hope in the community of those who believe in the Lord Jesus, and for the proclamation of this message to the world. In the life of the Church Christians proclaim and worship the God of man's future, the God who has power to transform a history without salvation into a saving event.

Salvation is conditioned by man's response of faith to the word, for the Church as mystery and sacrament of salvation is intelligible only to men who have faith. Nevertheless it is important that the credibility gap between sign and reality should not be wide. In the way of life of the individual Christian and in that of the ecclesial community it should be evident that membership of the Church is not merely a way of ensuring that salvation will be achieved, but also a real communal experience of salvation in Christ through the Spirit. The Church 'is only truly a sign when it allows the Holy Spirit to centre it upon Christ and not upon itself'.[14]

The Church as the Body of Christ, formed by the Spirit

Since God's plan is to draw men into communion with his trinitarian mystery through the establishment of fellowship with them even on earth, it follows that the mystery of the Church derives from the mission of the Son and the mission of the Spirit.[15] The Church as both fellowship and sacrament is grounded in the Spirit.[16]

Theological tradition and liturgical practice have drawn attention to the role of the Spirit in forming the Body of Christ – mortal, eucharistic, and mystical. The New Testament writers show Christ in his glorified manhood as the one who has totally assimilated the Spirit and can therefore become the principle of the gift of the Spirit to men.[17] He is shown as 'yielding his spirit' in the moment of death,[18] and more explicitly as launching the Church on its mission by breathing his Spirit on the apostles.[19] St Luke puts the paschal gift of the Spirit in a different perspective, stressing the unity of the Church and the universality of its mission by his description of the Pentecost event.[20]

The Church is therefore presented in the New Testament and especially by St Paul as the People of God formed by the Spirit into the Body of Christ. Although the expression 'body and members' was already current in the Greek-speaking world as a way of referring to the state and its citizens, it is used by St Paul as far more than a metaphor. He never speaks of the 'Body of Christians' but always of the 'Body of Christ', with reference to the personal body of the Lord, dead and risen and now the germ-cell of the new creation. The faithful can be described in this way because of the extraordinarily intimate union they have entered into with the person of Christ.

This union can be partially understood in the light of the biblical notion of solidarity that identified the father with his progeny, the representative with the represented, the first-fruits with the whole crop: the one could act for the many, while the many were present and personified in the one. But St Paul's doctrine of the incorporation of the faithful into Christ goes much further. Christ is the new Adam, and through the law of solidarity his death and resurrection are efficacious for all: 'Since one died for all, therefore all died.'[21]

The unity of the Body is not only derived from the Spirit but also furthered by the Spirit's action; it is not a static unity but a process of growth, for the Body is to be built up 'to mature manhood, to the stature of the fulness of Christ'.[22] To this end the Spirit lavishes his charisms on the members of the Church, graces extremely varied in their function but one in their source and their ultimate purpose.[23] Because Christians are one in Christ they are committed to selfless love for one another and cannot be indifferent to each other's lot.[24] No matter what his status in the Christian community or how modest his talents, each has something to contribute to the growth of the Body of Christ.

The organic unity of the many in one living structure is expressed also by the New Testament imagery of the Church as a temple of God. Both individually and collectively Christians are the temple in which the Spirit dwells.[25]

The fellowship with Christ and one another into which Christians have entered by becoming Christ's Body is manifested sacramentally. Baptism is the initial incorporation[26] and has practical consequences which St Paul points out to the Corinthians, who, having become living members of Christ's risen Body, have no right to use their own bodies for immoral unions.[27] What is begun at baptism is perfected through the Eucharist.[28] Christians are men who have come into bodily sacramental contact with the Lord, not once only but repeatedly, as often as they fulfil the injunction of Christ to eat the Bread and drink the Cup in remembrance of him.[29] And because the Spirit is one, as Christ is one, the partaking of the 'one bread' deepens the union of Christ's members with one another. All sacramental activity and all the visible, material, social structures of the Church exist to further the action of Christ through his Spirit in the hearts of men.[30]

The gift of the Spirit is for the New Testament writers the radically new reality, the decisive mark of difference between the old covenant and the new, the inauguration of a new relationship between God and his people.[31] As Israel had to trust in God and depend completely on him, so also, St Paul stresses, the new Israel is 'in Christ', but the relationship transcends that between Israel and Yahweh under the old covenant. The Church is established on the foundation of Christ and draws all its life, strength and stability from him. Christ, who is the *Kyrios* gloriously reigning in heaven, rules and empowers his people on earth through the Spirit whom he sends, and this Spirit could be given only when Jesus was glorified.[32]

The 'seal of the Spirit',[33] the 'anointing' with the Holy Spirit,[34] is the gift of the last days, the most powerful pledge for both the Church as a whole and the individual Christian that in the Body of Christ the good things of the kingdom are already given. The Spirit is the first instalment of our inheritance, the pledge of glory, and the guarantee of authentic sonship. He works in the Body of Christ to inspire prayer and to lead the members to holiness. Yet he is also the principle of unrest, of unfulfilled longing, the one who 'groans' within the Church and the Christian as we wait in hope for that resurrection of our bodies which membership of Christ's glorified Body promises. 'We too, even although we have received in the Spirit a foretaste of what the new life will be like, groan inwardly, as we wait longingly for God to complete his adoption of us, so that we will be emancipated from sin, both body and soul.'[35] The Spirit thus makes most poignant the tension which the Church must always experience as it stands midway between what is achieved and what is still to come.

St Paul's captivity epistles concentrate more explicitly on Christ's headship of the Church. This theme is developed in two ways. First, because he is the Lord incarnate, Christ occupies a position of absolute authority over his Church. In this sense he is likewise Head of the whole cosmos.[36] But, secondly, Christ as Head of redeemed humanity is not only above and distinct from mankind; he is also the life-giving Head of the Church, his Body.[37] A further development of this theme is found in Ephesians: marriage is to be patterned on the union between Christ and his Church.[38] The idea of intimacy and love suggested by the image of the Church as bride of Christ is thus added to the ideas of vital growth and organic dependence of the members upon the Head. Christ and redeemed humanity form one living whole. Only through a loving and ever deepening union with their Head can the members of the Body fulfil their vocation to build themselves up in love.

The Church as the People of God

Looked at as the People of God the Church appears above all in its temporal and social dimensions. It is a community of persons gathered into unity by God's Spirit, advancing towards a destiny. God's mercy to men, however, did not begin with the coming of Christ nor is it confined to Christians; it has been operative from the beginning of human history. God chose

> to make men holy and save them not simply as individuals . . . but by making them into one single people, a people which acknowledges him in truth and serves him in holiness. So he chose the race of Israel to be a people for himself. With them he established a covenant. He led this people onwards step by step, manifesting himself and his will in their history and making them holy. . . . But all these things were done by way of preparation, as a type of that new and perfect covenant which was to be ratified in Christ, and of that more luminous revelation to be given through God's Word made flesh.[39]

The coming of Christ is the climax of God's merciful action in the world. The New Testament describes Jesus as the fulfilment of Israel's hope for salvation, a fulfilment which is not national liberation but freedom from sin and participation in God's life.[40] The Church is the new People of God, in continuity with the old Israel but united with God by a new covenant ratified in the blood of Christ.[41] The redeeming death of Christ and the gift of the Spirit of sonship have established an entirely new relationship between God and his people.[42] Assertion of the continuity between Israel and the Church must therefore be balanced by recognition of the overwhelming change brought about by Christ. The Church is not simply the people of Israel which has received its Messiah. God's entry into human history is so mysterious an act that it transcends all the promises made to Israel and initiates a new creation: the new People of God in Christ Jesus.[43]

Even as the new People of God, the Church is still a community of weakness wandering through the desert towards its promised land, the heavenly Jerusalem. The period from Pentecost to the parousia is one of struggle and frustration. Repentance and renewal must always be part of the Church's life as it seeks to live out its vocation within the covenant. The weakness of the Church can tempt us to discouragement and cynicism, yet it is precisely in human weakness that the power of Christ is revealed.[44] In the constant experience of its own weakness and of God's grace the Church becomes aware of its need of a radical conversion to the gospel.

Since the People of God is a pilgrim people its final consummation will be achieved only in the glory of heaven when all things are perfectly restored in Christ.[45] But this promised restoration which we await 'has already been inaugurated in Christ, is carried forward through the mission of the Holy Spirit, and through him continues in the Church'.[46] During the present era the Church must pray, work and suffer for the final completion of the redemptive mystery.

The Church and the Kingdom

The proclamation of the Kingdom was the heart of Christ's preaching and ministry. He spoke of it as something future and taught men to pray for its coming, yet the Kingdom was also a present reality in his own person. His miracles revealed his power to break the rule of Satan and to bring men under the reign of God; his parables revealed something of the nature of the Kingdom and challenged the hearers to a decision in face of the imminence of its coming.

Rising from the dead and enthroned as the Lord to whom all power in heaven and on earth belongs, Jesus commissioned the leaders of his Church to proclaim and spread the Good News of the Kingdom among all nations, endowing them with the power to teach with authority, to forgive sins, and to cast out demons. The Church is not simply identical with the Kingdom of God, but its mission is to be 'a seed and a beginning of the Kingdom on earth',[47] and a prophetic sign of the consummation of that Kingdom in heaven.

The future Kingdom is most dramatically and symbolically revealed in the Church's central act of worship, the Eucharist. In the Eucharist the holy, priestly People of God celebrates in faith the new covenant in the blood of Jesus. The celebration of the Eucharist is a sign, a ritual anticipation, and the sacramental preparation for eating and drinking at the Lord's table in his Kingdom.[48]

The eucharistic assembly is a pledge of the coming Kingdom because it is, here and now, a sign of the present growth of the Kingdom. The Eucharist is the pattern and ideal for the life of the Church as a community. For the Kingdom of God comes into being wherever men accept one another as Christ accepted us, wherever men bear one another's burdens as Christ bore ours. The Church will be a credible sign of the Kingdom if its life is truly eucharistic, if it lives a life of fellowship, of healing and of service.

The Church also has a prophetic responsibility to be the sign of the future Kingdom by reminding the world that its designs cannot be perfectly achieved within the confines of human history. The Lord alone can bring unity to mankind, gather all things together under his headship, and hand over the perfected creation to the Father.[49]

The Church's mission, then, consists not only in announcing the Kingdom but also in manifesting through its life and work what the kingdom is about and what is to be the final destiny of mankind. Hence the mystery of the Church as the sacrament of the Kingdom among men has bearing on both the present and the future. The Church is a sign of the nature and present reality of the Kingdom in its work for the healing of the divisions within the human family by ministering to man in his needs, and by the communion of its members with Christ and one another especially as manifested in its eucharistic life. But it is also a prophetic sign of the final Kingdom by its refusal to embrace without reservation the standards and values of the world, for much of the world's activity is contrary to the spirit of the gospel. By prophetic chastisement, exhortation, and its own repentance, the Church gives witness to its belief that the Kingdom of God will be brought to perfection beyond human history and only by the initiative of God.

3

The Mission and Relationship of the Church to the World

The atmosphere of this chapter is again that of Chapter 1, but an effort is made to suggest how dialectic can be converted into dialogue. The chapter ends with some preliminary considerations on the role of monastic communities in this task.

The mission of the Church

a) The mission of Christ

The Church has a mission in the world because it is the sacrament of Christ in the world. Since the Church is missionary because of its relationship to Christ, it is the mission of Christ himself which must first be considered.

Christ has a mission, or is the one sent, in two senses. In the first sense, he was sent into the world by the Father in order to proclaim a message, namely the coming of the Kingdom of God. Christ was seen as a missionary, a teacher, and a prophet because he had a message to proclaim, a message which was not his own but that of his Father by whom he was sent.

In the second sense, Christ not only proclaims the Good News of salvation, he *is* that Good News. He is the one sent because God's plan of establishing his Kingdom is revealed and fulfilled in Christ's person and his redemptive work. The historical Jesus of the synoptic gospels proclaims who God is, namely the Father, and how men should respond to this revelation by conversion of heart and faith in God's word. The risen Christ of the early Christian preaching is himself the revelation of God; his life, death, and resurrection are the very acts of merciful love by which men are saved.

b) The mission of the Church

Similarly, the Church has a twofold mission.

First, the Church is missionary because it has a message to proclaim, the Good News that God has saved the world in his Son. The Church is the servant of the word of God and its mission springs from Christ's command to go out into the whole world and preach the gospel to all creation.[1] Through the gift of the Spirit the Church is enabled to reflect more deeply on the meaning of Christ and to remain faithful to the authentic revelation of God.

Second, the life of the Church is to *be* a mission in the sense of being a sign of Christ in the world, a sign which expresses visibly the meaning of God's self-revelation and man's response. Thus in his prayer after the last supper, Jesus asks the Father 'that they may be one, so that the world may know that you have sent me'. Here the love and unity among the brethren is a sign to the world of the Father's love for men, and provides the evidence for the authenticity of Christ's mission. The Spirit is sent not only to illuminate and guarantee the gospel message but also to form those who believe into a community. The life of the community of believers, its faith and love, are to reveal and make visible in the world the inner life of God: 'I have given them the glory you gave to me, that they may be one as we are one, with me in them and you in me.'[2]

These two 'missions' of the Church are intimately united: the missionary activities of the Church flow from the nature of the Church. Thus the 'apostles', the 'twelve', are both the foundation of the new Israel and those sent to witness to the resurrection of Christ and proclaim the gospel. Similarly, the apostolic community in Jerusalem shared their goods, adhered to the teaching of the apostles and broke bread together; they also preached God's word to the Jews and pagans, so that these too might believe and be saved. Thus 'apostolic' covers both senses of the term 'mission', the inner building up of the community and the proclamation of the gospel. It is this interdependence of the preaching and life of the Church which provides the theological foundation for the missionary character of contemplative communities; it also demands that every Christian be open to the world, since the mission to the world is part of the Church's life.

A sacrament is an effective sign of a reality which is present and operative, but not fully revealed or fulfilled. This means that the reality of which the Church is a sign extends beyond the bounds of the Church both in the future and in the present. This is an important consideration for the understanding of the Church's response to the world: the Church must take the 'signs of the times' seriously, testing and discerning whether they be of God, and so to be obeyed, or whether they need to be criticized and transformed.

The world

a) The meaning of the term 'world'

The most fundamental sense of 'world' is the complex of physical and human phenomena which is the context, framework, and horizon of human experience. It is the dimension in which human life, in all its manifold variety, is situated; it includes human culture and history, and the details of everyday life, as well as the physical universe. According to this sense of the term, man's present existence is essentially a 'being-in-the-world'; to be out of the world would be to cease to share in the human condition, to stand outside the conditions of historical existence.

If the world is not merely regarded as the external material universe but includes human history and activity, then the world is dependent in two ways on human creativity. First, it is dependent in the obvious sense that man can determine and fashion himself and his environment according to his own intentions, an aspect of the world especially evident today. Second, the world is dependent on human intelligence in that the very notion of *one* world, one horizon or perspective forming the framework of human life, is a rational discovery of man. Men naturally strive to create and sustain a unifying understanding of the world, in order to give sense and purpose to the complexities of human experience and natural phenomena. This may take various forms, including those of religious myth, Marxist ideology, or Christian faith. Each 'faith' presupposes a different understanding of the world and makes the claim that its world is *the* (real) world. It is on this fundamental level that the Christian attitude to the world must be analysed.

b) The Christian understanding of the world

The Christian understanding of the world, in the sense outlined above, is centred on the person and work of Christ. In the New Testament the term 'world' has a variety of meanings: (1) it may refer to the totality of created being, the cosmos; (2) it may mean 'this age', this *aion*, in contrast to the new age inaugurated by the death and resurrection of Christ and awaiting fulfilment at the parousia; (3) finally, it can signify the world as hostile and opposed to God and the gospel, the 'flesh' closed in on itself, proud, lustful, and self-sufficient. But in each case the interpretation of the world is determined by the person and meaning of Christ: (1) Christ is Lord of the cosmos; (2) it is his person and actions which show this age to be too narrow to embody the full plan of God; (3) it is rejection of him and his message which bars a man from life in the Spirit and encloses him in the values of the 'flesh'.

Human history, the destiny and experience of each individual, and indeed the sum of all that exists only stand revealed for what they are in the light of Jesus Christ. Thus it is faith in Christ which forms St Paul's understanding of his own past and present experience, of the history of Israel, and of the whole of man's history, reaching back to creation and Adam and reaching forward to the coming of Christ in glory.

This new vision of the world, springing from faith in Christ, may be characterized as an *enlargement of horizons*. First, the promises of God, limited to Israel under the old covenant, now embrace through Christ, at least in principle, the whole of humanity; this provides the foundation for the brotherhood of all men and the new commandment of love. Second, the scope of human history, instead of being circumscribed by the fact of death, is enlarged to include the resurrection of the dead and the final establishment of the Kingdom of God, when sin, suffering, and death shall be no more. Third, through Christ men are set in a new relationship to God and to one another. As sons of God in the Son of God they have access to the Father; as brothers of Christ they are formed into a new human fellowship (*koinonia*), in which their means of communication with one another is the Spirit of God.

It is only in the light of this new enlargement of horizons that the negative characteristics of the 'world' make sense. The new perspective of man and the world opened up by Christ demands a total revaluation of human life, and it is the refusal to make this and the acceptance of too limited a perspective which constitutes living 'according to the flesh'. In this sense it is by the gospel of Christ that man and the world are both saved and judged.

From this view of the world a number of important conclusions follow. First, it is *this* historical world of which the horizons are extended; it is not some other world, spiritual, immaterial, ahistorical, which is brought into being through Christ. Christian salvation is historical not only in the sense that it came about through a series of historical events, but also in the sense that it concerns the plan of God for this actual world. This point is extremely important in any consideration of the Christian attitude to the world or the relation between the Church and the world, for it provides the theological basis for both Christian involvement and Christian detachment.

Second, Christian perfection, according to the New Testament, does not consist in separation from the world in a local or physical sense, but rather in conversion of heart, justice, and love. The Kingdom of God in this world is not some separate entity but rather the presence of revolutionary values based on a new understanding of man and the world. Separation from the world means the critique of false value systems, whether these lead to the enslavement of man here and now or to the denial of a broader horizon than that of this life.[3]

Third, the Christian perspective of the world is a perspective of faith. It is the acceptance of a horizon, in theory and practice, which is only partially perceived and partially attained. In the New Testament 'living in the flesh' not only has the negative connotation of opposition to God, but also describes the present condition of human life, in which neither the process of salvation nor the process of judgment is yet complete. The dark shadow of human existence, the pain, war, loneliness, sin, and death, are as much a part of experience as the knowledge of God and the experience of human brotherhood.

The Church and the world

a) The Church as a community and a way of life

Our understanding of the world is formed through communication and interaction with the community which surrounds and sustains us; a view of the world can scarcely exist apart from a community and a way of life which are based on that world-view and give practical and conceptual expression to it. An individual can no more form such a view in isolation than he can create a private language.

The Church, understood as the community of believers and the Christian way of life, embodies the conviction that God has saved the world in Christ and will finally transform it into the Kingdom of God. The structure of the Church, the doctrines of faith, liturgical prayer, and the practical following of Christ in daily life are all different expressions of the perspective in which man and the world are seen. The Church is necessary for the believer since it is through the beliefs and way of life of this community that he can make Christ's perspective of the world his own; it is necessary for the whole of mankind since it embodies the truth about the world and man.

b) Critical transformation of the world [4]

The Church as the community of believers does not exist in isolation from the other communities, the other 'worlds', which make up human history. The visible Church, like other human institutions, is intimately connected with these other 'worlds', and intimately involved in the whole process of human history. It is itself subject to the conditions of historical existence and inevitably bound to change and develop. It is also subject to influence from the worlds outside it, which modify and shape it. Its members as citizens, scientists, workers, or thinkers belong to other communities as well as to the community of the Church.

The interaction between Church and world (understood as the sum of those 'worlds' which are not the Church) does not take place on the external plane only, from the outside, as though the history of the Church were some separate process from secular history. The more important relationship between the Church and the world is the inner relationship between the community of believers and the worlds around it. The Church possesses its identity in itself, yet it is dependent for the expression of that identity on movements of thought, on cultural and political phenomena, and on historical events outside itself.

Every department of the Church's life gives evidence of this interdependence. The inner structure of the Church, its manner of government, its language of prayer and piety, its articulate reflection on its faith (theology) – all these require human forms of expression while yet possessing their *raison d'être* in the relation of the Church to Christ. Only if suitable human forms of expression are found will the knowledge of salvation become available to people of every age and culture. The Church's relationship to the world and human history is not therefore accidental to its inner nature but rather forms an essential part of it. Its life and mission require the continual reassessment of this relationship, so that the Church may be the sacrament of Christ in the world. The process of discrimination, rejection or transformation of non-Christian categories of thought and practice is an enduring task for the Church and forms the basic inner relationship of the Church and the world. It is this which constitutes the work of critical transformation of the world.

Since the Church is also a 'being-in-the-world' the process of transformation naturally involves self-criticism, experimentation, and the painful abandonment of cherished habits, since the synthesis of faith and the world made in a past age may have to be radically modified in the light of changes in the secular scene. The greater the secular development, the more radical, and the more difficult, will be the Church's self-examination. This is not a matter of accommodation to the values of the age, nor an attempt to 'sell' Christianity at the expense of the scandal of the cross or the mysteriousness of God. It is rather that the Church's own self-understanding, the possibility of faith, prayer, and Christian love, and the Church's fulfilment of its mission to the world all demand this critical transformation, so that the Church as a 'being-in-the-world' may be true to its own self. The rigid attempt to defend 'orthodoxy' at the expense of such a process entails in the end the loss of that very orthodoxy. It is to fall victim to the illusion that the Church is in some magical way above history. On examination the 'orthodoxy' which is being defended may turn out to be the result of some past historical transformation of the world, which now itself requires transformation if its own inner dynamism is to be preserved.

The external relation of the Church to the world is the expression of this inner relation and takes its character from it. In the mission of the Church, and in its relation to the world, the external interaction must flow from a more radical confrontation within the Church itself. The authentic witness of the Church to the gospel demands that its members come to grips with the world and 'worlds' in which they live. It entails, in other words, the appropriation of Christian tradition in the light of their own experience as men of a particular age and culture.

c) The mission of the Church in the world

1. The present and the future

The Christian perspective of man and the world implies a new understanding of human life and human history here and now, and also opens up a horizon beyond the scope of human development. In consequence, the proclamation of the gospel involves the proclamation of both the *presence* and the *coming* of the Kingdom of God. It means both a sharing in the efforts of men to fashion a more just and human society and the proclamation in word and practice of a horizon broader than that of this world, a hope for total communion with God and other men which this age cannot realize. To make the gospel either an other-worldly recipe for heavenly blessedness or synonymous with social justice, technological progress, or personal fulfilment would fail to do justice to the full scope of the Christian understanding of man and the world.

In practice, however, these two aspects of the Church's mission are related in such a way that one cannot effectively be performed without the other. The Sermon on the Mount does not offer a code of ethics for heaven or for some closed ecclesiastical world; it states how men should live in the present age. Yet it is precisely by making these values his own that a person becomes a member of the Kingdom of God. Similarly, it is part of the message of the gospel that no human society or culture is permanent or absolute but that all are provisional and relative when compared with the Kingdom of God. Yet this does not imply that Christians can take a neutral stance with regard to social or political problems. The critique of all human values, ideologies, and societies, as falling under the judgement of God, is an empty gesture unless it includes opposition to both 'establishments' and revolutions which lead to human oppression or a narrow, materialist philosophy of life. Again, Christian virginity has its ultimate rationale in an experience of communion with God which is the pledge of a future fulfilment when this age passes away. Yet the test of its authenticity is precisely its growth in the love of men. It is evident from these examples that the proclamation of the *coming* of the Kingdom of God must be accompanied by the acceptance of and search for its *presence* in history if the gospel is to have meaning and credibility.

2. Mission and life

The organic connection between the life and mission of the Church comes out most clearly in the proclamation of the gospel to the world. The decision of the early Church, for example, that the observance of the Jewish law was neither a condition nor a necessary consequence of belief in Christ or membership of the Church was made in a missionary context, yet it clearly affected the life of the Church and its own self-understanding as the new People of God in contrast to the Jews. Similarly today, the urgent missionary problem of how to preach the gospel to people who already possess a deep religious tradition, such as Hindus, Buddhists, or Moslems, raises basic questions about what is essential in the existing Christian tradition and what is an accidental historical consequence of Graeco-Roman influence. Clearly, the life and mission of the Church cannot be separated.

If the above analysis of the inner relation of the Church and the world is accepted, then it is clear that the very same conditions obtain for the living of the gospel as for its proclamation. Critical transformation of the world and self-reflection are required for an authentic integration of faith and secular experience, and for the authentic preaching of the gospel. This is not primarily the task of the Christian as an individual: it is rather the Christian community which must embody this creative mediation between the Christian tradition and the contemporary world.

d) The contemporary situation

The dominant characteristics of the contemporary world, namely complexity, crisis, and the search for solutions, have a profound effect on the inner relationship between the Church and the world. In large measure they determine the scope of the Church's task today. There are, however, important factors springing from the recent history of the Church itself which must be briefly examined.

The defensive and negative attitude of the Christian Churches, and of the Catholic Church in particular, towards various secular movements in the last 300 years, however understandable historically, has meant that the task of critical transformation and self-reflection has not for the most part been steadily and perceptively undertaken for centuries; in fact it has not even been generally admitted as a task until recently. The result of this long period of defensive withdrawal is that now, in the post-conciliar era, when the floodgates have been opened, the Church is singularly ill-equipped to meet the challenge of critical transformation, which is essential for both its life and its mission and indeed for the genuine preservation of that orthodoxy with which the post-Tridentine Church was so preoccupied. It would be illusory to imagine that a series of internal ecclesiastical reforms, however necessary and desirable in themselves, directed to bringing the Church 'up to date', would resolve this crisis, since it is a crisis of human values and faith, affecting the whole of society as well as the Church. Thus renewal necessarily implies a re-examination of the relation of the Church to the world, for the sake of both the world and the Church.

This renewal is not only a matter of the individual Christian's appropriation of his faith as the integrating factor of his 'world'. It is rather a question of the Christian community, as a community, renewing

35

its own identity, beliefs, and form of life, so that it provides a framework in which to integrate Christian faith with what is good in contemporary ideologies, values, and life-styles. Unless the Christian community fulfils this mediating role the individual Christian is in no position to integrate the various worlds of his own experience through his faith. This is one of the key problems of both the life and the mission of the Church today. For it is often the case that the established religious institution, by its structure, attitudes, and behaviour, is an obstacle to this process of integration, an obstacle which obscures the witness to the gospel in the world and alienates the critical believer from both the Church and his own faith.

This analysis may be briefly illustrated by some examples. Christian theology has always consisted in articulate reflection on revelation by means of rational categories mostly taken from outside the Church. Today, however, the proliferation of secular thought-forms makes the task of creating a language of faith which is both contemporary and true to tradition extremely difficult. Christian tradition has often failed to provide criteria by which to assess the legitimacy of any given critical transformation. Again, on the social plane the search for justice is a basic Christian duty; the gospel must not be reduced to an illusory world of 'private morality'. This entails concrete involvement in secular ideologies and social and political movements in the world, since the problem is one that affects the whole of society.

In the present very complex situation, perhaps the most urgent need is for Christian communities to be open to all the tensions and options of this situation, and sensitive to the promptings of the Holy Spirit. For the creative disclosure of God's purposes for the proclamation of the gospel and the following of Christ demands an awareness of the truth of the present crisis and a readiness to wait as well as to act.

e) The monastery and the world

This general analysis of the relation between Church and world applies to monastic communities, as they are part of the Church and set in the contemporary world. It applies not only to the external relationship of the monastery to the world, but also to the actual form of monastic life (which essentially implies continual conversion), to the way in which this life is understood by those who live it and presented to those who do not, and to the monks' attitude to secular developments. For there are important questions facing monks in their renewal today which are not specifically monastic but are common to all Christians, and, in some measure, to all men. The search for experience of God, the desire to fashion more genuine forms of community life, the tension between exacting professional work and responsibilities to the group with which one lives, the attempt to find a new style of exercising authority, the emphasis on the worth of the human person – all these and many others are not limited to monastic communities but are to be found throughout the Church and secular society. Certainly, monastic tradition and the history and character of individual communities will give a particular orientation to these questions, as they will also determine the right solution they demand. But monastic tradition, like orthodoxy, can be understood in too narrow and static a way; to preserve its inner dynamism and its full scope it must be renewed and transformed in the light of the contemporary situation.

In practice this means that the scope of renewal must not be limited to exclusively monastic or Benedictine questions – the Rule, the vows, the divine office, etc. – as though the other areas of Christian faith and human values could be safely assumed; in fact, all the issues mentioned above concern monks as much as they concern other Christians and non-Christians. There is a danger of superficiality if questions are defined in exclusively monastic terms: liturgical changes, for example, may be carried out and thought to embody genuine renewal, when in fact there is no reflection or consensus in the community about the meaning of common prayer or the Eucharist. Crises in individuals or communities are often described and dealt with in narrowly monastic terms, when in fact their roots lie elsewhere. It is vital to discover the right categories in which to analyse such situations; otherwise the wrong questions will be asked and inadequate solutions found.

It is not only the life of monastic communities but also their mission which requires this basic openness to, and awareness of, the contemporary scene. Whatever influence a monastery has on the world through its apostolic works, schools, parish work, hospitality, or scholarship, the value of this influence is in direct proportion to the manner in which monks themselves have faced the questions which occupy the people with whom they come in contact. Monasteries need this awareness both in their external apostolate and, more fundamentally, in their corporate identity as communities living a certain form of life, for it is on this level that the mission of a monastic community is really to be found. The style of life, the form of government, observance, and attitudes of mind all come into play here and all require radical re-examination and common reflection, so that amid the sense of meaninglessness felt by so many today, a monastery may be a Christian community where men may experience God and be able to communicate that experience to others.

Part One has examined the dialectic between the Church and the contemporary world. Benedictine monachism has an affinity with both poles in the dialectic, because while the charism of Christian monasticism belongs within the mystery of the Church, monastic communities are made up of people who by upbringing, education, and sympathy are children of the modern age.

In the conviction that monasticism as lived in the English Benedictine Congregation has, therefore, a special role to play in the encounter of Church with world, we move on in Part Two to consider specific areas of monastic experience and renewal.

PART TWO

►▼◄

THE MONASTIC LIFE

4
The Rule

All law, and especially law in a Christian context, should be a pattern and means of growth. A strong case can be made that the Rule of St Benedict has assisted Christian growth throughout the course of its history. Its expressed intention, repeated several times, is to aid personal progress to the point where laborious advertence to the letter is transcended. In the context of God's gracious relationship with men, law is never primary but always the corollary of covenant and promise. The Rule of St Benedict is most truly understood in this perspective. The life for which it legislates is a life of love in response to the covenant of baptism, and the Rule points to a promised land beyond itself, even on this earth.

Whatever its literary antecedents, the Rule is generally recognized to be a highly creative piece of work which has shaped all Western monasticism, and influenced most forms of Christian religious life outside the monastic tradition. It has also affected history to a degree that can scarcely be estimated: during about six formative centuries most of the people who did anything constructive in Europe were either monks themselves or owed something of their training and culture to monastic communities where the Rule was a living reality and an educative power.

Through its wisdom, simplicity, and equilibrium, its grasp of essentials and flexibility in their precise application, the Rule has continued to be a source of inspiration perennially fresh, so that each new surge of life and reform within monasticism has tended to rediscover it, and to think out anew its own relationship to the Rule. Hence the centrality of the present chapter, which explores the principles that can serve us in our understanding of the Rule's normative value for us today.

Introduction

When we make our vows we not only proclaim our conversion, but we also define the terms of our engagement by using the formula:

'according to the Rule of our Holy Father Saint Benedict and the Constitutions of the English Congregation approved by the Holy See'. But also, because the life that is then being undertaken is of its nature a joint enterprise, this engagement is clearly not only a personal obligation, but one which is incumbent too on the local community within which the profession is made. Yet in fact the practice of our communities, with the full support of the Constitutions and house customs, diverges from the Rule very frequently.

Different explanations have been proffered to justify this anomaly. It has been maintained that our profession of the Rule means no more than that we acknowledge it as our spiritual ancestor, and now a rather remote one. The holders of this view claim that the gulf which divides us both from the mind of St Benedict and from the situation for which he was legislating is now so wide that it is futile to look to the Rule even for the general criteria of monastic self-examination, let alone for a solid framework for community life today. More common, perhaps, is the opinion that affirms some continuity, albeit a faint one, between our present monasteries and those which St Benedict had in mind, and that our obligation is to the spirit rather than to the letter of the Rule. Finally there are those who feel that a spirit disengaged from its letter is far too elusive to constitute a norm in any real, objective sense and can too easily become a subterfuge for self-chosen practice. They would maintain that our endeavour should be to observe the Rule both in its entirety and in its details, except in the instances, numerous though they be, where to do so is no longer practicable. St Benedict, they would say, has in his masterly idea for community life created a sensitive organism, and any amputation, except where really necessary, would injure irreparably both the vitality and still more the equilibrium which is generally conceded to be its outstanding quality. And hitherto the usual avenue for monastic reform has been a return to the observance of the Rule in its completeness, as thus conceived.

All three of these differing estimates of the weight to be given to the Rule in our lives and in our present discussions have serious disadvantages. The first, which by referring it to the irrevocable past altogether minimizes its import, entails the sacrifice of our Benedictine identity in every meaningful sense, and our utter inability to respond to the call of the Vatican Council to return to the spirit of our founder. The second standpoint, though rightly distinguishing between spirit and letter, confines its interest to the interior disposition of the legislator, and therefore tends to depreciate the concrete and social expression of his intention in particular activities, observances, and other items of behaviour. The third attitude, which would admit modifications of the Rule only under grave necessity, seems to underestimate the number of instances in every monastery where such adaptations have already occurred, so that, with the best will in the world to preserve St Benedict's actual practice, the resultant pattern of life is an uneasy combination of things new and old, lacking the very internal consistency which it was seeking to maintain. This tends to reduce monastic fidelity to a rearguard action and can lead to a growing sense of insecurity as one literal observance after another has to be abandoned under pressure of circumstances.

Within the Rule two different classes of material can be distinguished: St Benedict's spiritual teaching and his detailed prescriptions for monastic life. The former has perennial relevance, and indeed a privileged and normative position in monastic theology and practice for all who profess allegiance to St Benedict's Rule. It is the expression of his ideal, and the theology of that ideal with its roots in revelation. But it is inseparable from the embodiment of his teaching in the basic structural principles which give his monastic society its essential form, and which provide the framework for the monks' relationships with God and with one another. St Benedict's detailed practical provisions, on the other hand, are accidental to the effective embodiment of his ideal; they are of the same nature and occupied with the same particulars as are monastic constitutions and customaries. And just as these are frequently changed in the course of history, so too St Benedict's more specific injunctions can be modified, though it might well be wise to retain as many as possible as practical signs of our attachment to the Rule.

However, since St Benedict's monastic wisdom and his particular precepts frequently interpenetrate, it follows that even those of his provisions which are today patently anachronistic nevertheless deserve careful and sympathetic attention. The real alternatives facing us are not: spirit with letter versus spirit without letter, since the former is not feasible and the latter is too vague. The real alternatives are: an insistence on the letter which cramps or destroys the spirit, *versus* a reinterpretation of the letter to preserve the spirit and even allow it to grow. But this latter course means more than a simple quantitative division in the text of the Rule.[1]

Characteristics of the Rule

The first stage in examining the place which the Rule, as the embodiment of the spirit of our founder, should occupy in the life and in the obligations of St Benedict's monasteries and monks is to study it from within, to discover its own estimation of itself. It should always be borne in mind that in Benedictine tradition the concepts of 'spirit of the founder' and 'Rule' have a very different meaning from that usually given to them. St Benedict's spirit is not to be found in a religious family which formed around him so that his personality became the starting-point of its growth. Instead, his influence was diffused by means of a document which gradually found acceptance in Western monasteries. It should be remembered too that previous to St Benedict the many monastic rules, which often coexisted in the same house, were not intended to be juridical codes in the modern sense or to ensure uniformity of behaviour within a community, but were personal writings which transmitted the experience of great monks who had been raised up by the Holy Spirit to create a line of spiritual sons.[2] And rules of this kind only receive their full meaning in the context of a living community and through the interpretation of a living spiritual father.

St Benedict assigns to the Rule a function in the life of his community which is characterized by four notes: it is a function which is indispensable and central, but at the same time one which is subordinate and open to development.

a) Indispensable

Living according to a Rule is an integral part of St Benedict's definition of a cenobite, *militans sub regula vel abbate*,[3] and the phrase *sub regula* in that definition is a precision added by St Benedict (along with the Rule of the Master) to definitions almost identical in their phraseology which were current among his sources and had become classic in Latin monasticism.[4] The Master and St Benedict therefore not only introduced a new element, the Rule, into that definition of cenobitism which they had inherited from Cassian and others, but they also granted to this element a certain priority: they mention the Rule before the abbot.[5] The abbot's authority was now to be organically linked with that of the Rule, of which he was the guardian and interpreter. Furthermore, St Benedict and the Master were clearly speaking about a fixed and written Rule, not the living oral tradition, the *disciplina*, by which Cassian's monks had ordered their community life.

Conversely, St Benedict's description of the Sarabaites, the living antithesis of his own monks, repeatedly criticizes their independence of any rule; this is further proof that he ascribes a certain value in its own right to life according to a rule, whether that rule be his own or any other: 'They have not been tested by any rule or by the lessons of experience . . . their law is their own good pleasure; whatever they think or choose to do, they call holy, but what they like not they regard as unlawful.'[6] Here again his emphasis on the absence of the rule is in striking contrast to his sources, since for Cassian the outstanding vice of the Sarabaites was their possession of private property.[7]

b) Central

In St Benedict's intention the Rule is not only a *sine qua non* in the life of his community; it is also a reality which has constantly to be adverted to, the point of universal reference. 'In all things let all follow the Rule as master, nor let anyone rashly depart from it.'[8] The highest authorities in the monastery are subject to it: 'The abbot himself should do all things in the fear of God and observance of the Rule.'[9] At the end of Chapter 66 St Benedict enjoins that the Rule be frequently read aloud in the community in order that no one may plead ignorance (this injunction is commonly held to refer to the Rule as a whole, not simply to the prescriptions about enclosure which immediately precede it). The Rule is also the clearest exposition of the terms of the life to which the monastery's recruits engage themselves,[10] one which must be repeatedly inculcated 'so that they may know on what they are entering'.[11] The candidate who comes to monastic life studies the Rule and examines how it is lived in the monastery to see if he can identify with it, if his way is to be found therein; to become a monk is equivalent to taking upon oneself the yoke of the Rule. Even those duties of kindness to old men and children which, St Benedict recognizes, might well be trusted to the generous instincts of human nature, he also provides for by the Rule. The same is true of many humbler and apparently indifferent details of monastic observance which, one would have thought, could have been left entirely to the judgement of the abbot.

c) Subordinate

Yet although its solicitude extends to every aspect of the monastery's life, St Benedict is far from intending that the Rule should dominate the mental horizon of his monks finally and exclusively. In his last chapter he twice asserts that he has issued only a little rule for beginners,[12] not one that can be invoked on every question as providing the last word. And yet every Christian, and therefore every monk,[13] is morally bound to strive after 'the full observance of justice', which is precisely what St Benedict disclaims having established in his Rule.[14]

The greater realities which tower over the Rule in the life of the monk are found in the Prologue where St Benedict offers his pattern of religious life to those who wish to respond to the call given them by the gospel[15] and by the Spirit.[16]

1. The gospel

The Rule can justly claim to be the practical interpretation of the gospel for us, while never supplanting this Good News in the life of the monk. The Rule applies the demands of the gospel to the monastic way of life, a life which, though a very particular calling, is at the same time a universal phenomenon, found both within Christianity and outside it, for the single-minded quest for the Absolute which is the perennial characteristic of monasticism has been identified by Christian monks with their life in Christ according to the spirit of the gospel. And therefore if there are changes in our understanding of the New Testament today, there will clearly have to be changes too in our understanding of the Rule which is related to it. It is true that Catholic exegetes are no longer united in recognizing certain passages of the New Testament long accepted as proof texts providing an explicit evangelical foundation for the religious life (namely the episode of the rich young man, Mark 10.17–22; the logion on eunuchs for the sake of the Kingdom of heaven, Matt. 19.10–12).[17] Indeed many exegetes now believe that the radical sacrifices for the sake of the Kingdom mentioned in these classical passages are those to which every Christian is liable should his particular calling and situation require it. Religious find in the New Testament more solid justification for their way of life in the sustained and total response to the gospel made by the apostles who 'left all to follow Christ', a radical attitude which in the post-resurrection era found expression in the voluntary common life, the *koinonia* of the primitive Church which so impressed St Benedict,[18] as it had St

Pachomius and St Augustine before him. It is thus the gospel as a whole which should be the ever-present and overriding reality in the mind of the monk, and which therefore should be, as nearly all religious founders have explicitly recognized in their legislation,[19] the rule which outshines all other rules. 'The fundamental norm of the religious life is a following of Christ as proposed by the gospel; such is to be regarded by all communities as their supreme law.'[20]

2. The Spirit

Because of the many examples of holiness it has inspired in the course of its history, the Rule can also claim to be an objective expression of one of the Holy Spirit's charisms given for the building up of the Church. The training the Rule sets out to give is ordered to awakening sensitivity to the Holy Spirit.[21] For this reason it seeks to maintain its followers in the closest contact with the inspired writings of Scripture and in the attitude of receptivity that comes from the practice of silence. Moreover fraternal unity in the pursuit of the common life can be effected in monasteries only by the same agent who was at work in the apostolic life of the early Church, the Spirit of Christ.[22] But there is a great variety among the gifts of the unifying Spirit.[23] St Benedict himself welcomed their diversity[24] and intended both the Rule and the abbot to protect and nurture the personal charism of the individual, which might sometimes even lead outside the framework of life provided by the Rule,[25] as in the case of hermits and missionaries, since the Spirit with a sovereign liberty 'blows where it wills'.[26] Shrewdly, however, St Benedict requires as the first objective of monastic formation that the spirits be tested to see whether they proceed from God[27] and serve for the building up of the Body of Christ.

Thus St Benedict's Rule is a training in responsiveness to these two realities, the gospel and the Spirit, which both possess a universal and final authority which the Rule itself cannot claim. The Rule cannot supplant either of them as the overriding norm in the personal and corporate lives of those who have professed allegiance to it. Usually it brings the monk to them.

d) Open to development

St Benedict also anticipates that differing circumstances of time and place will make necessary a margin of freedom in his legislation. Recognizing his inability to make provision for every contingency, he has built into his Rule express authorization for certain changes in its details where these would better serve his general intention.[28] It would be not only reasonable but also consonant with the mind of St Benedict to extend this concession in order to justify in terms of the Rule itself other modifications of its more specific injunctions. For it is quite often the case that a material observance which once served St Benedict's purpose admirably might even impede that purpose when circumstances are changed. Indeed a discretionary power over the whole range of observances seems to be vested in the abbot when he is commanded by the Rule to 'temper all things so that the strong may still have something to long after, and the weak may not draw back in alarm'.[29] Thus flexibility is found in the very fabric of the Rule, though St Benedict reiterates the value of conformity to an objective, regular pattern of common observance. Unlike the Rule of the Master, St Benedict takes pains not to stifle spiritual liberty by over-precise legislation; he avoids trying to foresee every possible contingency, seeking rather to educate the consciences of the abbot, his officials, and his monks so that each may be able by the light of God's grace to understand the demands of the present moment and to conform to them spontaneously. 'It is in this emphasis on inner principle, rather than in any enforcement of a definite organisation, that we find the secret of its [the Rule's] power. An organisation would have waxed old and perished; an inner principle can adapt itself to changing needs.'[30]

Having considered these four characteristics of the Rule, we conclude that St Benedict would regard as an aberration any tendency to justify either legalism or its opposite – antinomianism – by an appeal to the Rule.

Legalism he has precluded by situating the Rule firmly in the context of the gospel. Just as the monastic course is embarked upon *excitante nos Scriptura*,[31] so throughout its continuation the monks walk *per ducatum Evangelii*.[32] He stands therefore in the same line as St Antony,[33] St Augustine,[34] St Francis,[35] and many others whose conversion hinged on hearing a verse of the New Testament.[36] St Benedict therefore would discountenance any attitude that would erect his Rule into the equivalent of the law, in the Pauline sense of that word, for his Rule partakes of the gospel's own spirit of liberty. Many of its provisions require us to see Christ in the abbot, the sick and the poor, and therefore depend on the act of faith, one of whose essential notes is freedom. It is also by re-echoing repeatedly the gospel's assertions of our total dependence on God's grace and by carefully disclaiming any pretence to proffer a system of 'works', in themselves availing for salvation, that the Rule rejects its contemporary heresy of Semi-Pelagianism.[37]

But at the same time St Benedict intends the Rule to live up to its name without any equivocation. It must not merely lay down such norms as are expedient for the order and smooth running of any organization; it must also be the appointed form of life by which the monks implement the self-offering made to God with their vows. Stability therefore should follow from the Rule's regular observance, a stability which is not just a matter of physical location but is reflected both in one's settled interior resolution and also in a sustained level of conduct and in constancy in the service of one's brethren. Obedience to the Rule provides a ready instrument for the renunciation of self-will and caprice in favour of a more devoted service of God and of one's brethren; and the text, 'If you love me, keep my commandments',[38] finds an echo in St Benedict's frequent assertion that the motive of true obedience is the love of God.[39] Finally, conversion, which in the New Testament is the right response on man's part to the gospel, should also follow from abiding by the Rule whose primary concern is to confront the monk with the gospel as forcefully as possible.

The Rule's place in history

To obtain a just estimate of the Rule one should consider not only its own self-assessment, but also its place in history and especially in the line of development where it claims to be situated, that of the monastic tradition. Viewing it in this perspective too, one must conclude that the Rule has some elements which are the product of historical accidents, but others which are of perennial value.

a) Even though St Benedict in drafting his legislation was far-seeing and had in mind other monasteries than his own, he was bounded by a particular cultural context. In many instances he was legislating at that level of detailed prescription which is today the competence of constitutions and declarations, documents which require periodic change. Had he written a century later, many of his concrete regulations would doubtless have been different. His own environment, its categories of thought, and his sense of what was socially fitting have inevitably been unconscious assumptions behind many of his pronouncements and have perhaps influenced the whole literary style of the Rule. He was himself convinced that he was tempering to an age of monastic decadence the lofty demands of the classical era of monasticism.[40] This fact might well seem to give his Rule only a relative value, but it also makes it a conspicuous example of the spirit in which adaptation to new times should be conducted. Furthermore, the modest lack of self-sufficiency with which St Benedict regarded his Rule and his frequent expressions of dissatisfaction with contemporary monastic performance combine to implant in his Rule a dynamic character, spurring the generous on to higher things, which they would find in the practice and teachings of the early monastic fathers.[41]

Opening the Second Vatican Council, Pope John XXIII declared: 'The actual deposit of faith, that is, the truths which are contained in our venerable teaching, is one thing; but quite other is the form in which they are enunciated.'[42] So, if it is true of the texts of the Church's Magisterium that the realities which they convey are greater than any conceptual expression which might be given to them, then the same applies *a fortiori* to ancient texts regulating the lives of communities within the Church. The Rule and its formulations are indeed to a very great degree historically conditioned, and often too by forces which today have ceased to operate and perhaps in some instances are even, and with just cause, held in reprobation.[43]

b) But when all this has been conceded it does not follow that the Rule's only bearing upon the lives of modern Benedictines is that of a document from which we can trace our historical descent, but from which we are otherwise completely isolated by the forces of change. There are good reasons for believing that the Rule can still have directive force in the lives of monks today.

(1) In the growth of the monastic tradition the Rule has earned for itself a position that is by common consent a definitive one. While St Benedict as legislator for the monastic life had indeed a long line of predecessors, there is no historical successor of the same stature. St Benedict is especially acclaimed today for having transmitted very faithfully the common tradition which he derived from his sources, although he has expressed this in memorable words and pieced it together in a masterly synthesis. What is striking is that St Benedict's Rule has never been superseded by the works of another writer in the same way as St Benedict himself subsumed all his predecessors, but that all subsequent monastic regulations have presented themselves in

subordinate fashion as glosses to his Rule. The medieval convention of literary servility by way of glosses and commentaries to ancient Christian writers goes only part of the way towards explaining this phenomenon, as does the prohibition of new rules by Canon 13 of the Fourth Lateran Council (1215). And although this homage, which extends over fourteen centuries and is found in the East and in the New World as well as in Europe, does not guarantee that the Rule will always prove adequate, it is testimony to inherent qualities which cannot be confined to the sixth century.[44]

(2) Further evidence that the Rule retains its relevance for monks of the twentieth century is its frequent, sober, and pointed use of the Scriptures, the inspired word of God who speaks to men of all ages.[45] St Benedict does not usually cite Scripture merely to give support to his own pronouncements, but in all important matters allows texts of the Bible to determine the course he will prescribe. Nor does he intend that the Rule should be a résumé or digest that would replace the gospel or try to improve upon it. Both by its contents and by the life it inculcates the Rule is designed by St Benedict to lead the monk to the gospel and to help him understand what the Lord addressing him through the gospel requires of him. In this respect, as in so many others, the Rule seeks to be a starting-point rather than a conclusion. In this way too it anticipates the first requirement for the appropriate renewal of the religious life, namely a continual return to the sources of all Christian life.[46]

(3) The Rule also illustrates and seeks to develop among its disciples an attitude not only to God but also to persons and things which has a value as permanent as Christianity itself, though the ceremonial forms of some of its expressions are today outmoded. Reverence is to be accorded to everyone whom the monk encounters, together with a delicate awareness of differences of personality and an especial tenderness towards human frailty. One of the greatest mutations to be observed between the Rule of the Master and that of St Benedict is that the legislator's interest shifts from the objective to the subjective level, chiefly because St Benedict owes far more to St Augustine. The preoccupation is no longer with a high standard of monastic performance but with the material and spiritual well-being of the persons engaged in it, what has frequently been termed St Benedict's 'sense of subjectivity'.[47] Although one should not expect to find all modern values anticipated by St Benedict, this aspect of his Rule should

be emphasized today when the whole idea of a rule exalted above persons is repugnant to so many. Likewise the Rule is pervaded by a respect for tools, materials, buildings, food, weather, daylight, and all created things as objective realities which one must not only accept, but positively recognize as sacred and God-given.[48]

(4) Another sign that the Rule was not the creature of its immediate surroundings in time and place, but frequently rose above them, is the number of passages where its ruling on concrete questions, not to speak of the general attitude which it enshrines, challenges the preconceptions of its age.[49] And yet these expressions of social protest are so casual, almost *obiter dicta*, that it is impossible to regard the Rule as a document of reaction against prevalent contemporary social assumptions, and therefore in an inverse way just as much a creature of them.

(5) The Second Vatican Council prescribed that 'wholesome traditions' should be loyally recognized and safeguarded.[50] It is widely held today that St Benedict obtained his dominant position in western monasticism not only because of the inherent genius of the Rule, but also because of his success in recapitulating all the previous monastic traditions, bringing them all to a single head in his body of teaching and making them more widely available.[51]

But tradition is the past living in the present; it does not mean a subjection to the standards of the past, nor merely an accurate transmission of something that remains identical throughout the whole process. Tradition (*paradosis*) is of its nature a process of vital communication directed towards the future, and it must therefore adapt itself to its changing recipients. This especially has to be the case where the tradition concerned is a way of life, not only if it is to pursue the course of legitimate development, but even if it is to retain the same role it has played earlier.

Conclusion

St Benedict's Rule, then, is an amalgam of two components: (*a*) spiritual teaching and general directions which seek to communicate to the disciple an attitude of openness to God's Spirit, of attentiveness to his word, of love for the fraternity, and of abandonment to God's providence through obedience and community of property; (*b*) his practical code which sought to give effect to the institutional requirements of such an attitude in terms of the world with which St Benedict was acquainted.

As far as the detailed juridical prescriptions in (*b*) are concerned, it seems reasonable to conclude, both from the mind of St Benedict as revealed in the pliability of his Rule and from the mind of the Church today, given official expression in the decree *Perfectae Caritatis*,[52] that we have full liberty to change any or all of them with reference to legitimate authority. In effect this has already long been the case. The modifications introduced by successive editions of the Constitutions have substantially altered, sometimes almost beyond recognition, nearly every concrete provision of the Rule. Hitherto the rationale of these changes has often been the questionable one that they are no more than minor adaptations of St Benedict's regulations which, wherever practicable, should be observed in their integrity.

But one should not by any means conclude that these very specific sections of the Rule are valueless. St Benedict wished to ensure by them that his monastic theology, with its general directives and the basic requirements for its implementation, should be given detailed and practical shape and not left in an abstract or elusive condition. The picture which the Rule hands down of his monastery and of its organization is a working model for us, constructed to the scale of the simple world of the sixth century, a model in which we can see his principles at work. Communities should be familiar with the Rule in its integrity, for each element in St Benedict's construction, however archaic it may seem today, deserves the most careful and appreciative examination in order to discover its function in the working of the whole complex and to find, where necessary, its modern counterpart. Very special attention too should be paid to the manner in which St Benedict formulates, delivers, and justifies his concrete regulations – the care for detail, the firmness, the discretion, the serenity, and the humanity – which ranks among the clearest indications of the spirit of his Rule.[53] In this way we will be better imbued with the spiritual attitudes intended by monastic tradition, having learned them, so to speak, from within our picture of a world which tried to incarnate them.

St Benedict's spiritual teaching delineates a distinctive way of responding to the gospel call that is not bound up inextricably with a single period of history, but seems to emerge spontaneously wherever Christianity strikes root. Its rejection would entail a forfeiture of our right to the name of Benedictines. But here too organic development, such as has already occurred in the general understanding of Christian truth in which this teaching has its context, is not to be excluded. For example, the virtues of Christian brotherhood, of corporate poverty, and of service to the world register today far more than previously both in the general Christian conscience and in the teaching of the Magisterium, and inevitably require some form of expression in spirituality. Sometimes too St Benedict seems to have been altogether reticent, providing no adequate treatment of some matters which awaken concern today, such as the place of recreation in the equilibrium of the monk's life or the positive values of virginity and sexuality.

It cannot be denied that the task of distinguishing in the Rule between those elements which still affect us directly and vitally and those which comprise a code of monastic legislation with a primarily contemporary reference is an operation of great delicacy and risk, since the frontiers between the two cannot be easily drawn. Acceptance of a principle does not eliminate disagreements about its application. Some will want to class as obsolete and expendable items which seem to others to belong to the very essence of monasticism. The issues may be blurred by the interference of non-theological factors, such as, on the one side, restlessness and the fear that the clock may be put back, or, on the other, instinctive resistance to change and fear that the roots of our life are being tampered with. But failure to make the necessary distinction will lead either to the attitude that all the contents of the Rule are equally above question and therefore that, for all important purposes, to discuss them would be superfluous; or to the contrary opinion that the whole Rule must share the fate of its outmoded sections and is no longer able to inspire or provide viable directions for a definite way of life in which the grace received at baptism may grow to maturity. Vatican II's Decree on Ecumenism pointed to a difference of level between various truths of the faith: 'In Catholic teaching there exists an order or "hierarchy" of truths, since they vary in their relationship to the foundation of the Christian faith.'[54] The reference here is to doctrine, but by analogy the same principle applies to the incarnation of doctrine in life, and can point the way to a more discriminating approach to the Rule of St Benedict.

Community

Introduction

The understanding of human community today: psychological and sociological aspects

A human person is unique, a world of mystery in himself. At the same time he is radically needy, because he cannot realize himself as a human person except through relationships with others. In the depth of his being he is oriented to a union of knowledge and love with God, in whose image he is created, but he can arrive at this destiny only through accepting and living a large number of other relationships involving knowledge and love of human persons.

Contemporary psychology and personalist philosophies have helped to show not merely that a man needs to love and to be loved, to know and to be known, if he is to realize his potential as a human being, but also that he needs to achieve a fully human relationship with some kind of community of which he forms a part. He needs a 'place' in a more than geographical sense; he cannot become himself without knowing that he 'belongs' to some kind of human group, whether he lives under the same roof as its other members or not. Growth to maturity entails, among other things, acceptance both of one's inalienable responsibilities and of one's need for support; or, in other words, maturity includes the capacity for both right independence and right dependence. Mature membership of any community therefore implies that each person should know that he is respected and accepted as he is, that he will receive the support and the concessions he needs, and that the contribution he can make will be needed and appreciated.[1]

Throughout a considerable stretch of man's history these needs have been met, to some extent, by the sociological structures provided by civilized life. Membership of a city-state or a village community could be a genuine and supportive form of human 'belonging'. Within the

57

Christian Church the parish system grew up on a similar pattern, reflecting and baptizing the structure of human groups for large numbers of believers. In some parts of the world this is still true. But in the West the social upheavals resulting from the industrial revolution began a disintegrating process which is today affecting many of the developing countries as well: technology and urbanization have meant for millions of people a loss of roots in village communities without providing any satisfactory substitute. Within the Church, no adequate alternative to the parish structure has yet emerged to meet the needs of people whose living patterns are determined by mobility, commuting, and conurbanization. On the one hand communications are swifter and easier, and the development of the mass-media has produced a new understanding of global issues; on the other, the size of these issues and the conditions of modern life can generate a sense of depersonalization and of loneliness amid the crowd. The result is a widespread search, both outside the Christian context and within it, for new forms of community life through which persons may have room to grow in a human way within a loving, caring fellowship.

At the same time, modern secular developments have affected the understanding of community life within traditional monasticism. It was argued in Chapter 3 that the interaction of Church and world is a two-way process, a process that takes place continually not only at the level of external exchange but also in the inner relationship between the Church, involved in the flux of history, and the other human 'worlds' around it.[2] These 'worlds' need the Church and the Church must critically transform them in the light of the gospel, but equally the Church needs the 'worlds' of human thought, culture, political experiment, and so on to experience and express its own identity. An instance of this latter process is the influence exerted on the Church's life by evolving secular thought about democracy, universal enfranchisement, responsible citizenship, accountability of governments to the governed, and the principles of co-responsibility and subsidiarity in healthy society. It would be strange if the monastic ideal of community life had remained immune to the influence of these ideas, some of which found expression in the message of Vatican II under the name of collegiality. The impact on monastic communities of increased sensitivity to community values in the world around them may be twofold: monastic consciences are troubled when secular idealists seem to have higher standards of caring, sharing, and concern in community life; but also monks and nuns are helped to a greater appreciation of the community life that is part of their own Christian and monastic inheritance by seeing its relevance for so many of their contemporaries.

The communal structure of salvation:
Christian monastic life as participation in Christ's life through the Spirit

The Church is a mystery of community. From the beginning of the story of salvation God formed a people to be the hearer of his word and the partner in his covenant of love. In the fulness of time this people brought forth its Messiah, who was God's definitive Word of self-communication to men. Through the passover of Jesus God's people, dead and reborn, is formed by the Spirit into the Body of Christ, and stands as the effective sign of God's purpose for all men.[3]

Throughout the Old Testament the God of Israel had revealed himself as one who wished to have dealings with men. The Wisdom hymns,[4] though obscure in their literal reference, at least suggest that divine perfection is to be understood in terms of self-giving and communication rather than as remoteness or inaccessibility; Wisdom 'delights to be with the sons of men' and 'passes into holy souls, making them friends of God'.[5] Parallel to these developments in the idea of Wisdom was that of Yahweh's Word as a personified reality.[6] These powerful images served the New Testament writers, especially John and Paul,[7] in their attempts to express what God, the undivided God of Israel, had done in the person and work of Jesus Christ.

Thus it could be seen that the communal structure of Christian salvation resulted from no arbitrary decision on God's part but reflected something of his nature. At the height of New Testament revelation God is seen as a God of self-communication, first of all within his trinitarian mystery and then in his giving of himself to us. He is the kind of God who gives and shares, and so at the end of the first century St John could write that the purpose of evangelization was *koinonia*, fellowship: 'that you may have fellowship with us', for 'our fellowship is with the Father and with his Son, Jesus Christ'.[8]

St Luke's portrait of the first Christian church in Jerusalem shows that the instinctive reaction of these Christians to the Easter events was to want to share with one another. They were the new messianic people, the people of the promises; God had given himself and shared his life with them in the life, death, and resurrection of his Son and the sending of his Spirit. The logical response seemed to be to live together, sharing their goods, their joy, their work, their meals, their prayer and praise, their Eucharist.[9] Although as a practical programme the experiment may have been short-lived, the ideal it represented continued to haunt early monastic founders,[10] who consciously harked back to it as to a nostalgic memory of how things were at the beginning of the post-Easter Church, and could be again in monastic communities.

Similarly the memories of the earthly ministry of Jesus, crystallized in the gospels, showed him both as the revelation of God to man, inasmuch as he incarnates the ultimate divine self-giving, and also as the revelation of what human relationships are meant to be. The historical Jesus whom the Church remembers is a man who could stand alone: he could face solitary struggle in the desert, spend nights alone on the mountain in prayer, hand himself over to his enemies with the request that his followers be allowed to go free, and die abandoned by nearly all of them. Yet he was also a man consumed by a relationship of intimacy and love with one whom he called his Father. He was open and sensitive to every human being who crossed his path, not only as a good giver but as one who welcomed and made much of whatever they had to offer, whether material things or their feeble intellects and slow-witted questions. He was the centre of a group of friends and disciples with whom he shared his life, his thoughts, and his mission. His human relationships reveal how it is possible for a man wholly surrendered to God and uniquely himself to be open, trusting, loving, vulnerable, and courageously committed to other human beings. They also reveal that our vocation to be sons of God in him who is the Son of God includes the vocation to be brothers of men.

Monastic life, in the perspective in which this book has chosen mainly to view it,[11] is a way of living out this Christian vocation to sonship and brotherhood in God's family, by the commitment of the human person to God and to other human persons in a community life of giving and sharing, where relationships of love and trust can be formed and persons can grow truly human. It is a life that demands both openness to the brethren and openness to the Spirit, for the unity towards which it grows, though incarnate in the give and take of daily life, springs not from human goodwill alone but from the action of God. The Spirit of sonship who is given to us creates Christian community, as on a larger scale he builds the whole Body of Christ. Such unity cannot be attained simply by human effort; in Jesus's prayer for unity it seems to be identified with the revelation of the glory of Father and Son: 'The glory which you have given to me I have given to them, so that they may be one even as we also are one.'[12] It is a gift from God, a sign of his presence and glory. Christian community life is the celebration of the presence of the risen Christ among us through his Spirit.

Experience of Benedictine community life

a) Acceptance of self and others

In Jesus Christ, and through the gift of his Spirit, the Father has accepted each of us. We know this in faith, and St Paul's vigorous teaching on the indwelling Spirit who impels us to the instinctive cry, 'Abba!'[13] shows that it is an experienced reality. But we experience 'being accepted' in a particular way when the Father's love comes to us through the attitudes of our brethren. The monk who in his community experiences an accepting love like this finds in it the strength and encouragement to accept himself, in a deep, peaceful act of radical obedience. Acceptance of his own being and make-up, with its strengths, weaknesses, flaws, and individuality, is a man's primary obedience to the Creator, and it is also the necessary foundation for acceptance of others in their differentness from himself. Because in Christ he is accepted, he can accept others; because in Christ he has been welcomed, he can welcome his neighbour.[14] Such acceptance is not a facile permissiveness, a pseudo-tolerance or a 'couldn't-care-less' attitude; it is more even than the (often prudent) decision to turn a blind eye. It is a positive way of loving that affirms the other in his being, and rejoices that the other is the person he is; it is the love that enables a man to 'live and let live' in a genuinely creative way.

b) Healing, forgiveness, and trust

True tolerance in monastic communities is therefore a matter of caring, of being willing to be involved with people when love requires it, and of respect and fidelity to other persons throughout the lifelong stretch of the relationship. St Benedict compares the patient, caring love of the abbot for a monk in trouble with the unwearying and resourceful care of a good doctor,[15] but he surely did not mean to limit this kind of concern to the abbot alone: the involvement of the community also is required, at least through their prayers.[16] Apart from the rather extreme case here envisaged, any monk or nun may be in special need sometimes, and in general need always, of the healing love of a caring community. All are wounded in some way by the experiences of life, and all look to Christ the healer for their wholeness. But there are many incidents in the gospels where appeal is made to Christ on behalf of one who needs healing by his family or friends who bring him to the healer: the sick person is 'carried' by those who love him[17] and the act of carrying is performed in hope. Every monastic community, as well as every superior, knows what this means. St Benedict enjoined that his monks were to 'bear with weaknesses, whether of body or character, with the utmost patience',[18] but this 'bearing' need not be interpreted as mere stoical endurance. Community life can be, and is meant to be, a healing experience.

Healing is lifelong, and no Christian can say at any point that he no longer needs the healing love of God or his neighbour; the wholeness in holiness to which Christ calls him is never complete until he dies. But some degree of inner healing seems to be necessary for many people before they can be free enough to share in community life without fear. A person carrying inner wounds is liable to be preoccupied with shielding them, and incapable of the openness and trust that full community life implies. A wounded person is usually afraid. To have experienced the healing love of God, particularly as mediated by the community, is to be delivered, in some degree at least, from the fear of being hurt again. To put it otherwise: it is paradoxically necessary to have been healed before one can dare to be vulnerable.

The openness and sensitivity shown by Christ to every person who approached him implied a willingness to be hurt. When sinful human beings live together, paying God and each other the compliment of trying to do everything they have to do in as human a way as possible, they get hurt, not merely by external circumstances but by one another. St Benedict regarded this mutual hurting as something so inevitable in community life that he built in mutual forgiveness as a daily task: the *Our Father* was to be said aloud at Lauds and Vespers to remind the monks that they ask God to measure his forgiveness by their own willingness to forgive;[19] making peace with one's adversary was regarded as a tool to be used before nightfall;[20] and a generous attitude of self-humbling was required of any monk who saw that one of the seniors was annoyed with him.[21] Many modern Anglo-Saxons have been conditioned to hate receiving apologies even more than making them, and to shrug off a proffered apology with a brief indication that the matter is of no consequence. It is true that in community life a smile or a relaxed attitude on both sides often puts the situation right more effectively than a formal apology. But there can be cases where community life demands, and makes possible, a deliberate asking, granting, and accepting of forgiveness in the presence of God. If there has been a wound, the power of God's forgiving and healing love can then act and create deep peace, and both parties are set free.

In refusing to withhold anything he has to give, even to the point of sending his only Son,[22] God has trusted men, and continually trusts them, far more than they are ever prepared to trust him. When men fail him, and God forgives, it is not a grudging decision to make no further reference to the incident, but a loving and joyous re-acceptance that entrusts them with more than they had before.[23] In the redemptive mystery Christ offers us the possibility, and demands of us the venture, of becoming, through grace, fully human. But to do this we have to become Christlike by growing into the profound, risky, demanding, freeing human relationships of love and trust. A monastic community is not primarily functional; its work is not its *raison d'être*. It exists in order . to realize a certain quality of human, Christian life. It must therefore be a community that gives scope for the kind of personal relationships in which the presence and power of God are revealed, a living community in which the trust and love for God implied by monastic profession are reflected in trust and love between the members. This is true of Christian community anywhere, but in a Benedictine community the stability vowed by the monks implies a lifelong commitment to one another which both makes possible, and requires, continual deepening in trust.

c) *Sharing in word and Spirit*

Human community is not just an aggregate of individuals; it is constituted by some kind of common meaning, or shared understanding.[24] There must be a field of common experience, convergent or at least complementary interpretations of that experience, and basic agreement about the community's goals. In the case of Christian community this common understanding is created by God's . word. The word of God proclaimed and received on Sinai constituted the Israelites God's holy people.[25] Similarly, it was God's word, proclaimed and received, which constituted the primitive community of Christians as the new Israel,[26] and this same word proclaimed and heard in the Church of every age not only reminds Christians of their identity and their destiny but also, as the powerful and life-giving word of God,

summons them to conversion of heart and obedience. St Benedict is in
the tradition of Israel and the Church when he stresses the importance of
listening to the word of God, and the necessity of silence, humility, and
obedience as the dispositions required for its effective reception.[27] This
listening, receptive attitude to the word is created in the Christian by the
indwelling Spirit, but listening is not a purely individual matter. In
monastic life the monks must listen as a community to the word of God
which brings them into unity and peace.

The proclamation of the word in the Eucharist and the *opus Dei* is the
most vital occasion for the members of a monastic community to listen
together to what God may be saying to them. But the word will not
penetrate the whole of monastic life unless there are also other ways of
sharing insights and understanding. The strength and unity achieved in
prayer, the sharing of ideas derived from *lectio divina* and experience, the
sharing of work and life, the bearing of one another's burdens, common
participation in the joys and sorrows of the members, and shared
reflection on events in the community's life – all these are occasions and
means by which the Spirit can lead a community forward into new
understanding and love, and so form its members into Christ's Body.

The ideal of Christian sharing pervades the Rule. It underlies St
Benedict's vehemence against private ownership or *proprietas* in any
form,[28] his provisions about common prayer and common meals,[29] and
his conception of excommunication as the worst penalty a monk can
suffer, short of definitive expulsion from the monastery.[30] Faithful and
generous sharing in the common life is a way in which members of a
community can minister the Spirit to one another and build up one
another in faith.[31]

Mutual encouragement in this strong sense is essential in community
life. When tempted to disbelief and despair a monk needs the support of
a faithful and hopeful community;[32] to the extent that he is rooted in a
strong community he will be able to proclaim a message of joy, hope,
and faith to the contemporary world.[33] The early Christian communities
knew very well what it meant to be filled with the Holy Spirit, and they
remembered the Lord's promise: 'You shall receive power when the
Holy Spirit comes upon you, and you shall be my witnesses.'[34] They
expected the presence and power of the Spirit to be manifest, and had no
inhibitions about regarding as normal a Christian community life that
rejoices in present union with the Lord. According to the New
Testament the gift of the Spirit is something that can be recognized.[35]
Christ does not promise his disciples a joyless existence, a never-ending

trudge through spiritual deserts, but a peace the world cannot give and a joy no man shall take from them. Openness to these gifts implies expectant faith, and the experience of sharing within monastic community life builds up the faith of all.

d) The experience of tensions and paradox

The Church's life in this world, poised as it is between what is achieved and what lies ahead, is paradoxical. Christ has come in his incarnation, yet he is still to come in glory. He is with the Church, and yet he goes on ahead, summoning all men into the future. The Church as the sacrament of Christ is consequently both incarnational and eschatological,[36] and monastic life, situated within the Church, necessarily experiences this tension. This is true not only of the life of individuals, but also of community life itself. There may be tension between the desire for solitude and the call to sharing, or between the duty of contributing fully to community life and the demands of outside work or ministry. At a deeper level there is a tension between the real love among the members of a community and their frequent want of tact or sensitivity in their dealings with one another; this is an instance of the fundamental tension between what the community is and what it would be. In the Communion of Saints these tensions will have been resolved, but in the earthly sacrament of that Communion they are a matter of daily experience. But they are healthy, serving to remind the members that their life together on earth is a preparation for, and a sign of, fellowship of a higher order in eternal life.

5

Communication and Co-responsibility

In the next few chapters particular elements in Benedictine community life, such as the abbot, the vows, and the recruitment of new members, will be examined in detail. The purpose of this chapter is to raise certain general questions and indicate principles that bear on the structure and life of a Benedictine community.

Principles

The most radical reason why the monks of a community are together is that they have all been called to share in the life of God. The one Spirit of which all are given to drink[1] is the Spirit of communication, self-giving, and unity.[2] But his action flows through the channels of human exchange and shared human responsibility among the brethren.

This underlying theological principle, the communication of the Spirit, provides the basis for the common life and fraternal unity. In more particular terms, its application may be guided by four different principles. First, there is the principle of *solidarity*, which states that in every area of life, from the most spiritual to the most mundane, all that the community does is the concern, and, in differing measure, the responsibility of each individual monk, even when it is a question of work that goes beyond the immediate confines of the monastery. Second, there is the principle of *pluralism*, which recognizes the ultimate worth of every individual person and that it is right, within certain bounds, for there to be variety and diversity within the framework of the community. Third, there is the principle of *authority*, which expresses the underlying need for and validity of the exercise of leadership in the monastic community, above all in the case of the abbot, but also at other levels of the monastery's life and work. Fourth, there is the principle of *subsidiarity*, which states that what is within the competence of a person or body of persons should not be taken over by a higher authority. This principle governs the delegation of authority, the responsibility of an individual or group within the monastery for a particular task, and the legitimate exercise of free intiative at every level in the community.[3]

These principles do not of themselves define any actual type of monastic community, nor will they all be applicable in the same manner or to the same degree. But they should be borne in mind in the ensuing brief survey of different areas of monastic life, since their right application is a major factor in the achievement of communication and co-responsibility in a monastic community.

Application

a) Structures

In the course of monastic history there has been great variety in the type of structure of Benedictine monasteries, ranging from the large, hierarchically organized medieval monasteries to the small, more flexible communities, whether of the early monastic period or of the present day. Certain basic elements found in the Rule – the role of the abbot, the existence of some form of council of seniors, the stability of the individual monk in a particular community, the role of the whole community in reflection and deliberation on important issues – all these have assumed a great variety of forms in the course of Benedictine history. For this reason the framework provided by the Rule should be regarded not as an inflexible system but rather as a model to be embodied in different ways in different periods according to the needs of the time.

At the present day this means that renewal may affect not only monastic ideals or monastic activity (e.g. prayer and work) but also the structures of monastic government, the correlation between the basic elements outlined in the Rule. For example, the size of a monastic community is a major factor determining the best manner in which it can be structured and governed. In a small community important issues can be discussed effectively by everyone and there may be no need for a council, while in a large community intermediate structures will be necessary. This clearly affects the role of the council and the chapter in each case. It would be futile to impose what is suited to a small community on a large one or vice versa. Again, in a larger monastery, particularly one with diverse works and monks resident away from the monastery, changes may be necessary both to guarantee communication and unity within the community and to permit smaller groupings for the sake of closer fraternal relations (on the model of St Benedict's deaneries). In another sphere, it is evident that with the growing complexity of modern life, including monastic life, the abbot may become so involved in administrative work or activities outside the monastery that his basic spiritual role may be obscured and his personal contact with every member of the community may become tenuous. Such a situation may call for structural changes in order to give the abbot more time and freedom for his most essential work. This point illustrates how a type of government inherited from the past may have been suited to earlier conditions but does not meet contemporary needs. Continual revision of the structure and style of government and organization may therefore be needed for the sake of the well-being of the community.

b) Prayer

The unity of a Benedictine community is not grounded in its structure or organization, or even in its activities, but rather in its fellowship with God. For this reason it is in the love and prayer of the brethren that communication and sharing are most necessary and valuable.

Communication in prayer is provided for above all in the sound tradition of the office in choir and the conventual Mass. St Benedict also makes provision for prayers for the brethren absent from choir on essential work, or outside the monastery,[4] and they in their turn are to remember their brethren at home.[5] When members of the community are sent out on the authority of the abbot for the wider interests of the Church, their obedience should be recognized as a sacrifice of that support derived from the mutual self-giving of community life which is experienced by the monks at home. On the other hand, since prayer in common is central to the life of the monastery, the stresses and strains that can be felt by individuals praying in choir should be seen as a burden to be borne in the community's interests. Acceptance of this burden is often a real encouragement to others.

Apart from the tradition of choir office, there may be other forms of prayer which are more flexible and provide greater scope for spontaneity. There is evidence of a growing movement in the Church towards freer types of prayer,[6] a desire to give more explicit form to belief in the presence of the Holy Spirit. But unconventional or new forms of prayer need freedom and time to achieve their right expression and to allow their value to be tested. It would be tragic if something intended as a means of sharing and communication in a community were to become a source of dissension; hence there is a need for loving tolerance and mutual respect.

c) Communication and deliberation

1. The historical background

Some form of consultation of the brethren by the superior is found in the earliest traditions of cenobitic monasticism, particularly among the followers of St Basil.[7] It was, however, confined for the most part to a consultation of the seniors only, and there is little trace before the sixth century of genuine deliberation by the whole community. When this latter form of consultation appeared in the Rule of the Master[8] it was, owing to certain secular influences of the day, concerned mainly with economic matters, and was understood as the exercise of that co-responsibility which devolved on the monks as co-proprietors of the monastery's temporal goods. The Master therefore provides for a consultation of all the brethren, but confines it to decisions about temporalities. He has no separate council of seniors.

In the Rule of St Benedict this consultation of all the brethren is similarly provided for,[9] but not explicitly limited to the concerns of economic administration. St Benedict also adds a more supernatural motive to the obvious common-sense motive for consultation: not only should human prudence, confirmed by the scriptural recommendation to 'do everything with counsel',[10] lead the abbot to listen to the opinions of all without exception, but it may also happen that God has revealed the best course to the youngest. Both St Benedict and the Master understand the assembly to be an occasion for pooling ideas and knowledge for the benefit of the abbot, whose authority to decide is in no way diminished.

St Benedict differs from the Master by legislating for a council of seniors in addition to the plenary assembly. This matter is dealt with in a kind of appendix to his chapter on consulting the brethren. The council of seniors is envisaged as dealing with matters of lesser importance, and the provision for it may be the result of St Benedict's experience of life in a large community where consultation of all on every issue was impracticable. It is however characteristic of St Benedict to assume that in his complex task the abbot will have both the right and the need to rely on the the discreet assistance of experienced members of the community; they appear in other chapters of the Rule in the capacity of deans, senpectae, spiritual seniors, and novice master.[11]

2. Deliberation today

In the modern western world most people have been educated to an independence of mind and judgement and a breadth of knowledge not to be found in the generality of monks in the sixth century. Moreover most monks today are involved in some sort of pastoral work, which means that they, like the abbot, are called upon in the regular course of their lives to bring forth things new and old from their store.[12] The abbot has not lost that prime and central position as teacher and leader assigned to him by St Benedict, but just as skilled craftsmen may contribute to the well-being of the monastery if the abbot sees fit, so it is appropriate for the thinkers, preachers, teachers, and officials of the community to share their wisdom and experience with their brethren.

Similarly, in matters calling for common deliberation, the individual members of a community may be better informed than in St Benedict's day. While all the principles laid down in Chapter 3 of the Rule on accepting the abbot's decision and not pressing one's own opinion intemperately still apply as strongly as ever, there is now a need for more responsible assent on the part of the community.

At least two conditions are necessary for such responsible assent. The first is the availability and communication of information regarding the affairs of the monastery. Naturally there will be occasions when information is necessarily reserved by the abbot to himself, or to the council or some other competent body, but secrecy should be kept to the absolute minimum; otherwise the monks cannot play a responsible role in the deliberations and decisions of their own community. Such sharing of information is particularly necessary in a large community with diverse activities and outside work. Everyone should be able to see that what each member of the community is engaged upon is in a proper sense the concern of the whole community. It is therefore important that all monks working outside should make frequent visits to the monastery, in order to share what they are doing with their brethren, for the sake of mutual building-up in faith.[13] Those who work within the enclosure should also have opportunities to share their concerns: the head-master, the bursar, the housemasters, teachers (especially of religious instruction), and younger monks in subordinate positions. It may be possible to have discussions on the various works of the monastery, in order to improve them and to encourage and help those involved in them. This underlines the joint responsibility of the whole community for all that is done, and gives all its members access to the wisdom of those who have practical experience in special fields. A genuine sense of solidarity, human interest, and co-responsibility is impossible if people are ignorant of what is going on in large areas of the life and work of the community. It must be borne in mind, however, that the right to information is not unlimited; it has to be reconciled with other existing rights. The right of privacy, which protects the good name or the sensibilities of an individual, and the rights of professional secrecy, must be respected. Whenever personal or public good is at stake, discretion must be exercised in the preparation of news.

Second, responsible assent by a community demands a measure of consensus, which in turn requires (though it is not guaranteed by) discussion and common reflection. The abbot still has the initiative, particularly in chapter, but since today the chapter's consent is required for certain decisions he no longer has the unfettered power to decide accorded to him in the Rule. He should make it his aim not only to hear all but to carry a general agreement on the merits of the case. There would therefore appear to be a need for general discussions before individual points are brought up for decision, and the gathering together of the community for self-reflection should be a regular part of monastic life and not something which occurs only in an annual chapter.

The *council* can and should exercise a unitive role in the life of the community. It has a two-way function, and should not be considered exclusively as either the abbot's council or the community's delegation. Two factors determine its character. One is the position of the abbot as the person ultimately responsible for decisions and policy. This responsibility entitles him, in his need for all the pertinent advice and information, to look on the council as an advisory body which will support him in his guidance of the community. The second element is the community's responsibility for its activities and policy and the need for all its members to participate in deliberation and decision-making. This gives the council its representative quality, which requires that its membership cover the main areas of life and opinion in the community. The present manner in which the council is chosen, one half being elected by the community and the other half appointed by the abbot, illustrates and provides a sound basis for its dual character. In the choice of councillors both abbot and electors should keep in mind the double function of the council and be careful not to seek persons who will merely reflect their own views and interests. If these two aspects of the council's task are realized in practice, it can build up unity in the monastery. To this end it is desirable that there be as much communication between council and community as is consistent with the demands of discretion.

Common reflection is not only needed for particular decisions, but more fundamentally forms part of a general process of education and growth affecting all the members of a community. The basis of the monastic life is the common search for God, which demands a strong shared faith and commitment to clear monastic principles. In a time of rapid change especially, this requires a continuous process of reflection on the basic realities of Christian and monastic life. Without it, practical decisions affecting any part of a community's life and work lack their proper foundation. The task of reflection in common is difficult and demanding; there are numerous obstacles and frustrations which may tempt individuals or the community to abandon the effort. But in the long run it is essential.

On occasions deep divergences can appear within a community, even on points which seem to touch the roots of its vocation. Not only is the meaning or utility of certain observances challenged, but the status of all the elements is called in question. Agreement can no longer be presupposed even about what monastic life is. Much personal anguish ensues. In a time of rapid evolution it is impossible to abstain, in the name of loyalty, from critical evaluation of these issues oneself, or to suppose that critical discussion of them by others is a sign of disloyalty, disobedience, or lack of generosity.

It is helpful to distinguish between levels of doubt or disagreement. (a) There can be disagreement about the behavioural expression of the community's beliefs and values. This is a normal and healthy tension; it can stimulate the community to reflect upon itself and so can promote growth. (b) There can be doubt or disagreement on the beliefs and values themselves. It may be only partial, or again it may be capable of resolution by patient search and personal growth. There are various possible reactions to the discovery that other members of one's own community differ from oneself on matters that seem to touch the nerve of monasticism.

First, there can be rejection of the others' point of view. People can close their minds, and take it as axiomatic that certain beliefs and values are beyond question; it follows that 'the others' must be mistaken, if not dishonest or perverse. This approach is likely to be unfruitful, but it is not as unreasonable in community life as it would be in a debating society.

The persons concerned have more justification for feeling aggrieved, because after committing themselves to a joint enterprise they now find their flanks exposed, and they rightly consider that the points at issue are more than a matter of opinion. A moderate demonstration of strong feeling can occasionally do good; it shows that people are concerned about their lives and about the contribution that others make to their lives.

Second, there is the policy of politeness and common sense. One can reflect that charity is the highest law, that one has to go on living for the rest of one's life with the people from whom one differs, and that one's own cool-headed objectivity (or theirs) is unlikely to survive a confrontation. Therefore a confrontation had better be avoided. There are still plenty of neutral areas in which one can meet and exchange views; mutual kindness and courtesy can continue; and one can simply recognize the existence of minefields and avoid stepping on them.

This second approach is not wrong. It may be the best that can be done in certain circumstances, and it may be charitable, but it is not the highest charity and it is sub-monastic. We cannot be content with mere politeness. We are called to tend towards reconciliation in love and trust, and this is the third way. It presupposes that all those concerned are seeking the guidance of the Spirit in prayer. This seeking is not to be reduced to a mere weighing of the pros and cons in the presence of God; the latter procedure may be useful, but it may also rouse passions and increase confusions. To turn prayer into an anticipation or prolongation of the human debate is not conducive to clarity of mind. What is to be sought in prayer is not so much direct light on the content of the decision as the freedom of heart and openness to the Spirit that will enable one to face contentious issues without passion or prejudice, sensitively attuned to whatever guidance God may give and prepared to learn.[14] Those with divergent views can then meet, utter their convictions, formulate the ideals and values they are concerned to promote, admit their fears and suspicions, listen to one another, and try to understand the values for which their opponents are concerned. An impartial outsider who can sketch the whole picture sympathetically but dispassionately may do the community valuable service; a visitation or a good retreat may be useful in this way. It is very important to avoid premature polarization of opinions and persons. To tie labels like 'conservative' or 'progressive' on to oneself or others is to limit people; life is richer and more complex than this. To narrow and harden the positions is to do injustice to persons who do not want to be driven into this or that camp, and such hardening makes progress towards agreement much more difficult.

But all the same, no unanimity may be achieved. Pseudo-problems may be disposed of, but the process of clarification may reveal the divergences on real issues to be deeper than anyone had previously realized. It may be possible for those at variance to pray together; certainly each can pray to see the others and the others' world-view through the eyes of Christ. One can pray to be led into the love of the Creator who rejoices in the diversity of the things he has made. One can pray for grace to accept others in their differentness from oneself. But still the question remains: can we still go on living together as a community if we fundamentally disagree about what we are doing?

It must be admitted that there are cases when the answer is No. Absolute disagreement about the very existence of the community is not compatible with the maintenance of the common life. In the case of an individual it leads to the 'death' of the person *qua* community member; if generalized it leads towards the death of the community. In either case death may be a gateway to rebirth.

But there are also cases where the contestants, even if they agree on almost nothing else, do agree that monastic life is worth preserving, that it is the bearer of such values as charity and prayer which ought to be fostered, and that it gives glory to God. So they are implicitly agreeing that they are vowed to something that is deeper, broader, and more mysterious than their own particular understanding of it, and that a great deal of patience, charity, tolerance, and trust are needed if the virtualities of this something are to be deployed. They are acknowledging that their differences are not ultimately irreconcilable; the meeting-point may be beyond the vision of any of them, but they can believe that there is one. Human problems are often messy and do not admit of immediate answers; to be able to live with a certain amount of ambiguity and tension is a mark of maturity, and indeed if we wait for the disappearance of all conflicts before beginning to live fully we shall never live at all.[15] Even if we never come to embrace our adversary's point of view we experience our finiteness; we are forced to give up any illusion that we have a monopoly of truth and we experience the need for a bond of unity in Christ which transcends any merely human unity achievable either by agreement or by agreement to differ. The peace Christ gives is beyond anything we can establish, and beyond the understanding of this world. We do not create it, we are invited to enter into it. We are radically incomplete and needy, but we have been promised membership of the mature, fully-grown Body of Christ, beyond the clash of divergent views and doctrines, in the unity of faith and knowledge.[16] For this ultimate unity, this 'full stature of Christ', every contribution is needed. We grow towards it by speaking and living the truth in love; and in it, we may believe, every true insight will be found again.

d) *Personal relationships*

Over and above the contacts provided for by common prayer and deliberation, monks need to relate and communicate as persons in ordinary free human exchange. A monk owes it to his brethren and to himself not to be always absent at times of recreation or holidays. For monks should not be less human than lay people, and they need to guard against the dangers of institutionalism; they need to love and to be loved. 'We know that we have passed from death to life *because* we love the brethren.'[17] Significantly, St Benedict constantly uses the word *frater* for members of the community (about ninety times in all). When he uses 'monk' (about thirty times) it is mainly in contexts where he is stating general principles;[18] for the contacts of daily life he prefers the relational word. Mutual love and service were for the cenobitic tradition represented by St Pachomius a principal way in which the *kenosis* of Christ, who became the Servant of all, was reproduced among monks. St Benedict, especially by the picture he gives of fraternal relationships in his Chapters 71 and 72, shows himself to be of the same mind.[19]

This mutual love provides the context for understanding the particular Benedictine characteristic of peace: the individual monk has a positive contribution to make to the peace of the whole community, and this peace is an important part of the community's contribution to the life of the world. Lack of interior peace is an attack on the fabric of the community, as was so clearly shown by St Benedict in his severity against murmuring.[20] But peace should also be pursued and cultivated between individuals and groups within the community, and peace is more than a good-mannered benevolence or the avoidance of positive opposition; it involves the sense of feeling free to talk openly about what one feels. To paper over divisions which in fact exist is not to work for peace, even though there may be a time when it is better to be silent than to speak.[21] The love which the brethren owe to each other must include real friendships between individual monks; the vice of 'particular friendships' only appears when these are divisive of the community.[22] But the responsibility for this divisiveness can rest as much upon the community (or a group in the community) as upon those who are friends. True friendship cannot but build up the love of those in contact with it.

6

The Abbot

Many questions arise today about the place of the abbot. Can true Benedictine life exist without an abbot? Is his office one of the historically conditioned items of the Rule or is it essential to monasticism? What is the nature of his authority and what is its basis? Is there a sense in which his commands are the will of God? In what sense is he to be thought of as Christ's representative in the monastery? Can he still be expected to function as teacher of the community?

Some of these questions overlap with points raised in other chapters, e.g. The Rule *and* Obedience. *Moreover, the discussion in the present chapter on the nature of the abbot's function today is closely related to that on* Communication and Co-responsibility *which precedes it. But an attempt is made here to approach these questions, so vital to community life, in the light of the special grace of service with which monastic tradition has claimed that the abbot is endowed, and to suggest how modern conditions affect his ministry.*

The abbot as normative of Benedictine life

There can be little question about the absolute priority that St Benedict gives in his Rule to the place of the abbot. After the first chapter, dealing with the different kinds of monks (where the *fortissimum genus* of the cenobites is defined as 'those who serve under a rule and an abbot'), St Benedict immediately treats of the abbot in one of the most carefully devised chapters of the Rule.[1] This teaching is amplified near the end of the Rule in Chapter 64 on the election of the abbot. The abbot is also implicitly proposed as the model and example for the other officials of the monastery in the sense that many of the features in St Benedict's portrait of the ideal abbot recur in those he draws of subordinate officials.[2] Such an extensive treatment, dealing with both his actions and his attitudes, finds no parallel among any of the earlier monastic legislators, with the exception of the Rule of the Master, which is often taken as the immediate source of St Benedict's teaching. To jettison the office and idea of the personal rule of the abbot in the name of historical development would therefore be to depart from the very nature of the monastic life as set out by St Benedict.

The abbot in the monastic tradition before St Benedict[3]

St Benedict made a synthesis of a monastic tradition which was as pluralist as modern monasticism has recognized itself to be. Two currents in the fourth and fifth centuries are of special importance:

a) In many places of the Christian East, ranging from Cappadocia to Upper Egypt, there emerged spontaneously and independently cenobitic groups which were rooted in the normal life of various local churches. This type of monasticism did not originate from eremitical movements and had its own *raison d'être* without further eremitical implications, because of the very reality of the fraternal communion which it embodied and realized. This fraternal communion of ascetics could sometimes be within the framework of the local church. Its spirituality reflected the gospel, being based on the renunciation of self-will and service to the community of brothers. To this tradition belong St Gregory of Nyssa, St Basil, and St Pachomius.

In the mind of St Basil the superior is the product of the community. He is an element of the structure by which it achieves unity. He has the charism of being the 'eye' of the community; his office is to discern the will of God for the community by taking cognizance of what God requires of each member.[4]

Similarly the *koinonia* set up by St Pachomius in Upper Egypt is primarily a union of brothers. The role of the superior is highly esteemed but is situated *within* this brotherhood, and is on the level of communion of life rather than on that of hierarchical authority.[5]

Seen in the light of this tradition the abbatial function is necessary for fostering and preserving the *koinonia*, and is *expressive* of it. Essentially different from that of the hierarchical pastor (the bishop), the authority of the abbot belongs to the realm of the monastic search for God in community.

b) Alongside but independent of this cenobitic tradition a different type of monastic community and of spiritual fatherhood developed among the hermits of Lower Egypt. Tradition represented St Paul and St Antony as going out into the desert alone. But experience soon proved that whoever aspired to the difficult life of the desert needed to place himself first in apprenticeship to an experienced monk who was a 'bearer of the Spirit'. The function of the spiritual father in this desert tradition should probably be seen as continuing that of the teachers (*didaskaloi*) of the early Church, mentioned by St Paul along with the apostles, prophets, evangelists, and pastors.[6] Originally these teachers functioned in virtue of special charisms, but later they held hierarchical teaching positions in the Church and prepared catechumens for baptism. The most famous examples of these ecclesiastically deputed *didaskaloi* are Origen and the other teachers in the school at Alexandria.

Among the hermits the question of official deputation by the Church did not arise, but the spiritual father was above all a veteran and an experienced teacher. In this *educative* situation the bonds which united master and disciple were temporary. A man came to the master in order to be formed by him, and obedience had a special character primarily directed to this end. If authority was absolute, this was not the effect of a charism in the master expressing the will of God. It was a means accepted by the disciple for his own formation.

In the West monasticism arose not so much from the spontaneous appearance of brotherhoods within local churches as from the initiative of bishops, as in the instance of St Martin of Tours. But the definitive influence here was Cassian's. Before coming to Gaul, Cassian had passed all his monastic life in the semi-eremitic environment of Lower Egypt, and when presented with the task of reforming western monasticism he simply transposed the institutions of the desert 'school' into a framework of stable common life. In his way of thinking the *cenobium* is primarily a school of formation. Its educative activity, like that of the Church itself, ultimately serves the purpose of bringing human persons closer to the divine Persons. Of course the whole of monastic life grows within a community framework, but this framework becomes more and more dispensable for the individual monk as he becomes more proficient.[7] The superior is no longer the centre of the fraternity, the 'eye of the body', but a teacher whose task is to instruct individual monks.

The other important innovation of Cassian was his insistence on conformity to the 'true monastic tradition'; just as the Church has its dogma and its discipline, monasticism too has its tradition and its human custodians. No one has the right to direct others unlesss he has first subjected himself to this living magisterium.[8]

This teaching of Cassian was taken to its logical conclusion by the Rule of the Master, for whom the abbot is above all a teacher commissioned by Christ. As such he is Christ's representative and plays in the monastery a role closely parallel to that of a bishop in the Church at large; he is a successor of the apostles and endowed with their authority.[9]

This second, *educative* tradition concerning the abbot, deriving from Lower Egypt by way of Cassian and the Master, greatly influenced the teaching of St Benedict, although he significantly refrained from simply reproducing the Master's views.

The abbot in the Rule of St Benedict

St Benedict's concept of the abbot owes much to these two currents in earlier monastic tradition. But in his Rule the abbot appears not only as the unitive centre of the community, and not only as a teacher; he is the representative of Christ inasmuch as he is the recipient of the obedience of one who hears the call of God and follows the counsels.

The notion of the abbot as standing in the place of Christ is certainly not St Benedict's original contribution, for the Rule of the Master puts far more emphasis on it than does St Benedict. The latter's originality is to be seen rather in the tempering, balancing and enriching of the doctrine he derived from the Master. St Benedict makes little or no allusion to the hierarchical-sacral-episcopal analogy so stressed by the Master in justification of the abbot's claim to an authority derived from Christ.[10] He also balances and broadens the inheritance he received from the 'educative' tradition by a richer understanding of Christian community and of the abbot's place in it; where he differs from the Master his contributions are often of Basilian, Pachomian or Augustinian inspiration. He rejects the Master's arrangement whereby each retiring abbot designated one of the brethren to replace him in a kind of 'apostolic succession', and reverts to the traditional cenobitic practice whereby the community bears the responsibility for choosing its new abbot. Further, the position of the abbot is modified by the fact that other officials, such as the prior, novice master, and cellarer, have a genuine responsibility and authority within the community which they did not have in the Rule of the Master.

Although St Benedict's 'first directory' for the abbot, found in Chapter 2, is closely dependent on the corresponding chapter in the Rule of the Master, he provides a 'second directory' in Chapter 64 in which his originality, personal experience, and concern for the human problems involved are more clearly discernible. Omitting the Master's detailed description of the 'ordination' of the new abbot,[11] St Benedict supplies an extended treatise on the personal qualities and attitudes that must characterize his dealings with the brethren whom he rules, insisting on mercy, discretion, prudence, and avoidance of any excess, especially excess of rigour. The abbot's authority is to be exercised with compassion, gentleness, and peace; he is to temper the severity of both his commands and his corrections with an understanding of the weakness or fear of the monks who might otherwise 'recoil in alarm' (*refugiant*, an echo of the end part of the Prologue which is also proper to St Benedict). The reminder that he must not be 'turbulent', together with the reference to the bruised reed that is not to be broken, evokes the Servant of Second Isaiah.

The first Christian community at Jerusalem, as described in the Acts, with its love, joy, prayer, and sharing of goods, is certainly the model for St Benedict's ideal of community life, as it was for all early monastic legislators. But although he nowhere alludes to it explicitly, it seems clear that another model was before his mind – that of the fellowship of Christ with his disciples. He gives a composite portrait of the abbot in which the Isaian Servant, the compassionate Christ seen by St Matthew's Gospel as the antitype of the latter, the patient shepherd, the skilful physician, the ideal overseer of the Pastoral Epistles and Cassian's merciful, discreet 'ancient' fuse into one figure who makes present to the brethren the charity of Christ. These allusions, together with the citation of Romans 8.15 to justify the abbot's title, constitute an assertion of a truth discernible only by faith: 'The abbot *is believed* to be the representative of Christ in the monastery.'[12]

Everything therefore must be done with the consent of the abbot.[13] He must act in accordance with the law of God and the Rule,[14] but otherwise no limits are set to his competence as long as he gives no just cause for murmuring[15] and remembers constantly that he has to give an account to God for the souls of all those entrusted to his care.[16] He must therefore give consideration to the varying strengths and qualities of individuals,[17] and to the needs of the old and the sick.[18] He should strive to be loved rather than feared and to profit his brethren rather than to preside over them;[19] and if a monk finds a command impossible, or even hard, to carry out, he must have every freedom to put the point to the abbot.[20] He must be flexible, adaptable, and patient. In his teaching of the brethren he must not only be learned in the divine law but must also himself be living by the Holy Spirit who is the source of the doctrine he teaches: *ut sciat et sit unde proferat nova et vetera*.[21]

In the difficult task of caring for souls the abbot is answerable to God rather than to the community,[22] and all authority delegated to officials remains strictly under his control; he alone appoints such officials and determines the extent of their competence. However, the abbot is the master of a school of disciples (*magister*), not the lord of slaves (*dominus*), and St Benedict is very far from seeing obedience as sheer submission to the will of another, or mere execution of his commands. The abbot must do all things with counsel, listening even to the youngest.[23] Indeed, after Chapter 2 on the abbot, St Benedict deals immediately with the question of calling the brethren to council.

To sum up, it may be said that St Benedict presents in his picture of the abbot a father who must take responsibility for the lives of all; one around whom the life of the community revolves; one who must show love, gentleness, and discretion, but must also show firmness and must command.[24] The abbot in St Benedict's Rule still definitely stands above the community as a teacher; the full force of Eastern cenobitic spirituality which envisaged the abbot rather as the centre of the community never reached western monasticism. Nevertheless, St Benedict's ideal surpasses and unites the earlier concepts of the abbot in that it combines the fraternal stability of the 'unitive' tradition and the teaching function of the 'educative' tradition. The temporary relation of disciple to teacher is replaced by a permanent relation of obedience which is given a special quality and depth by the monk's stability in the community. The purpose of this obedience is to liberate a man from the limitations and deceptions of self-will, and to lead him to integrity of heart in his response to God. For a Christian, obedience to Christ embodies his new relationship to God as son; so a monk's obedience to the abbot gives concrete expression both to his obedience to Christ and to his filial relationship to God.[25]

To what extent this whole conception of the abbot's authority as that of Christ's representative has been modified by later thinking about authority and community will be discussed later in this chapter, but before considering the pressures exerted by history upon theory it is well to note a characteristic of the scriptural exegesis practised by St Benedict. For him, as also for the Master, the Scriptures, and particularly the New Testament, are the medium through which the Lord himself speaks directly to the believer. The monk is to walk in the Lord's ways *per ducatum Evangelii*[26] and the gospel is therefore valid for him personally; he must hear it in faith and seek to shape his life upon it. This process of actualization is the main concern of the Master and St Benedict. Scripture is used to bring the claims, the grace, and the love of God before the monk or the community; it is interpreted with personal immediacy as the legislator strives to illuminate with the help of biblical texts the believer's present reality before God.[27] Since St Benedict's understanding of the abbot's authority in the community is one of the fruits of this kind of scriptural interpretation, and since the concern for confronting the believer in his existential situation with the power of the Word is prevalent today, the Rule's doctrine of the abbot, even if it needs rethinking, is more than a relic of a remote age devoid of any but historical interest.

Development in the position of the abbot since the time of St Benedict

In his provisions for the election of an abbot,[28] St Benedict makes it clear that the monastery is an integral part of the Church at large and that abuses and failings of observance can become the responsibility of the bishop of the diocese or of neighbouring abbots or even of the local Christians. Although this is left very vague in the Rule, the development through the Middle Ages of the system of visitations within congregations certainly had the effect of limiting the discretionary power of the abbot; and the practice of exemption, while it freed the abbot and the monastery from local interference, brought them firmly within the scope of canon law.

But apart from these elements of outside control which have their roots in the Rule, there were two other important developments, quite unforeseen by St Benedict, which had a radical effect upon the relations between the abbot and his community. The first was the steadily increasing importance of the abbot in the affairs of Church and State which made of him a great lord with responsibilities far beyond the enclosure or the interests of the monastery. This separated him more and more from his brethren and meant that in fact the community had less and less say in his appointment, and his appointment had anyway less and less to do with their daily or spiritual lives. Eventually the interests of abbot and community could diverge so far that some checks had to be placed on the abbot's freedom to dispose of the goods of the monastery;

from this arose the monastic chapter's power of veto in certain matters. As a result of the abuses of the commendatory system there arose congregations (for example, St Justina of Padua) where the monasteries were ruled by temporary superiors appointed by a general chapter of the congregation. An element of centralization that had been characteristic of the Cluniac reform some centuries earlier, and which was to be usual among the later orders, was thus adopted as part of normal Benedictine practice in certain reforming congregations which enjoyed considerable influence.

The other great development not foreseen by St Benedict was the situation where all choir monks normally went on to be ordained priests. This made of all monks men who had to be in their own way 'masters of the spiritual life' and gave to many of them personal and inalienable responsibilities which could be quite independent of the judgement and jurisdiction of the abbot. This had the further consequence that a monk could quite normally have as 'spiritual director' some monk other than the abbot. There is a certain basis for this development in the Rule: St Benedict had the realism and humility to know that there could be times when the relationship between the abbot and a monk in trouble might be strained, and when a more effective approach to the latter might be made by a tactful 'senpecta' or experienced senior.[29] Again, he enjoins that a monk's secret sins should be revealed 'to the abbot only, *or to some spiritual senior*'.[30] He presumably knew from experience that in a community where trust and humility abound this kind of ministration can go on without any prejudice to the abbot's authority. Historical development has, however, taken the matter much further: canon law has put considerable barriers in the way of an abbot's hearing the confession of one of his monks, or even discussing the state of his conscience with him. This, combined with other factors, has produced the regrettable result that the abbot has sometimes been the last person to hear of the spiritual difficulties of his monks, which is quite alien to St Benedict's idea.

Characteristics of the tradition in the English Benedictine Congregation

For nearly 300 years the structure of the English Benedictine Congregation was modelled on that of the Congregation of St Justina. General Chapter was a self-perpetuating body appointing a prior to each house for a fixed period of time to rule over only the resident part of his community, for all those – and they were a large proportion of each house – who went on the Mission came under the jurisdiction of the President and the Provincials of Canterbury and York. That this was an abnormal arrangement to meet an abnormal situation was ultimately recognized by the constitutional changes at the end of the nineteenth century which established the monasteries as abbeys electing their own abbots and abolished the provincial system.

As a result of this lack of prelacy among the superiors, the short period of their appointment and the smallness of the communities there has remained in all the houses of the EBC, as compared with many monasteries and congregations, a strong tradition of closeness of life and relations between the abbot and his brethren. This is combined with a very healthy independence of mind and judgement among the individual members of each community, since they all either have had already, or may have in the future, experience of fending for themselves on the Mission.

Through the twentieth century the EBC has kept the tradition of electing its abbots for periods of eight years (it should be noted that St Benedict nowhere explicitly legislates for life abbots), and this can be seen as consonant with the growing practice of our age both within the Church and outside it. Yet in the abbeys of the EBC there have been enough instances of abbots re-elected for the remainder of their effective working lives to indicate a stability of purpose in the communities. At the same time the abbots themselves have been able to set a personal character upon their houses during their period of rule, and this is a great strength of the Congregation. The relative permanence of superiors in office, combined with the stability of the members of a community, can provide the context for the growth of very deep relationships of love and trust.

The nature of the abbot's function today

An abbot today has to face a far more searching scrutiny of his credentials, and a far more formidable task, than did his predecessor in the time of St Benedict. Although the fundamental nature of his office has not changed, many factors have intervened to affect our understanding of community, our concept of authority, and the circumstances in which the abbot has to exercise his ministry. A brief review of some of these factors is necessary before the abbot's role as Christ's representative, which includes his ministry as the unitive centre of the community and as its teacher, can be discussed in a modern context.

Christian understanding of *community* is rooted in the New Testament teaching on *koinonia*, and particularly in St Paul's doctrine of the work of the Spirit in forming the Body of Christ.[31] This aspect of the Good News has special relevance for a monastic community whose real work is the building up of the Body in love, a work for which every monk's gifts are needed. Moreover, advances in psychology and philosophy, evolving political ideas and social changes have helped monastic minds to an enhanced appreciation of the community life inherited from tradition. These changes in outlook have already been discussed.[32] The universal availability of education today also affects our understanding of community life by bringing with it the supposition that everyone in a monastic community is (or will be, or should be, but certainly thinks he is) intellectually an adult. The result is that paternalism has become very suspect. In the so-called Dark Ages and even in the medieval period spiritual fatherhood might take the form of paternalism, a benevolent and protective attitude which, even though inspired by love and a desire to serve, did not always leave room for the subjects to grow to adult responsibility. Spiritual fatherhood is a perennially authentic notion, built into the Rule and into Benedictine life and tradition. But paternalism was a form that it assumed in cultures and ages very different from our own, and it is a form no longer valid.

Understanding of Christian *authority* has also evolved. In addition to the kind of evolution already discussed, it may perhaps be said that the Church today is more acutely aware of the identification of authority with service. It would be absurd to represent this as a new insight: the example and express teaching of Jesus the Servant[33] and St Paul's view of authority as a special charism of service within the Body[34] show that it is as old as the gospel; and the adoption of the title *Servus servorum Dei* by St Benedict's near-contemporary, Pope St Gregory, shows that the evangelical ideal of authority was not forgotten. Yet it is probably true to say that today, when the image of the Church as a power-structure has either vanished or is under heavy fire, we have recovered an earlier sensitivity to the New Testament teaching on authority, and, as has already been pointed out, certain features of EBC history have helped this sensitivity.

Finally, the *circumstances* in which an abbot today has to exercise his ministry are vastly different from those envisaged in the Rule. The sheer complexity of modern socio-economic life demands special skills of anyone whose work includes administration, as the work of any abbot must to some degree. The complexity is not, however, confined to the temporal and administrative aspects of the abbot's task; he also has to function in a Church and a monastery where many of the ancient certainties are questioned, where the effort to distinguish the essential from the accidental demands great wisdom and patience, and where the search for new forms in which to express the perennial values of monasticism seems unending.

Against the background of all these changes in the thinking and the circumstances of those who live the Benedictine life, an attempt can now be made to consider the traditional understanding of the abbatial office indicated earlier in this chapter.

a) The abbot as Christ's representative

Although St Benedict's treatment of the abbot as Christ's representative contrasts with that of the Master by its brevity and restraint, and although he tones down the hierarchical character of the Master's abbot, there can be little doubt that the doctrine of the abbot as the one who stands in Christ's place was of prime importance for St Benedict and has served his followers ever since as the basis for their understanding of the abbot's position. Yet the doctrine presents a strong challenge to modern ideas of authority. Facile interpretations of St Benedict's mind are rightly rejected, as, for instance, the simple identification of the abbot's commands with the will of God. But the doctrine itself, if understood with the faith that St Benedict requires, retains its central importance for those who are called to cenobitic monastic life in the modern Church. A characteristic of St Benedict's use of Scripture already mentioned is a key to understanding: in the Scriptures and especially in the New Testament the Lord himself is addressing us here and now, and our response must be an effort to understand our whole monastic existence in the light of the Bible, to hear what the Bible has to say to us. Given this 'existential' approach, the doctrine of the abbot's position can be examined both in the context of personal relationships and in that of the community's power to choose its abbot.

The nature of monastic obedience will be discussed in detail below,[35] but it must be noted here that there is a considerable difference between the obedience envisaged in the Rule and 'executive' obedience. The latter is directed to getting a job done. St Benedict's concept of obedience is much more a matter of the listening ear, the ready heart. He situates it firmly within the baptismal, Christian vocation of the monk, linking it closely with the paschal mystery: that is to say, with the redemptive obedience of Christ and with our adoption as sons of God through the gift of the Spirit. For any Christian who is called to work out his baptismal vocation in monastic life, obedience and its correlative – authority – must be kept within this perspective.

If monastic obedience is to be in this sense the implementation of a Christian's baptismal commitment, the community in which it flourishes must be a living community in which the Spirit of the risen Christ has free play. Through the varied distribution of his charisms the Spirit enables men in such a community to grow truly human through deep relationships with God and their fellow human beings. Within this rich variety of gifts – charisms of service that make for growth, unity, and fulness of life – is the charism of authority, which is always presented in the New Testament as a special and important form of service.

It is evident that for any man who in response to the invitation of the gospel and guided by the Spirit seeks to work out his obedience and sonship to God through effective obedience to Christ, there must be in the way of life to which God calls him scope for doing so in faith and in a fully human manner. His obedience to Christ must be an affair of love and trust, and it must be *incarnate*. St John, in his First Letter, exposes the fallacy of completely discarnate love of God: if any man says, 'I love God', but does not love his brother, he is a liar, because if he does not love his near and visible brother, how can he love the invisible God? And further, if he sees his brother in need and closes his heart against him, how can he say he loves him? So love of God must be incarnate in earthly love of the brethren, or it is bogus.[36] So far St John. But we could cross out 'love' and substitute 'obedience', and the statements would be equally true. The heart of prayer and of following Christ is free, loving, personal surrender to the whole will of God. But if such obedience remains in the realm of theory, if it is merely a matter of protestations made in prayer and never incarnate in daily life and real relationships, its authenticity is suspect. And so, St Benedict explains, men whom God calls to this way of life, who 'hold nothing dearer than Christ', see obedience as their 'good'; they deliberately choose the 'narrow way' and live in monasteries, not merely enduring authority but 'wanting to have an abbot over them'.[37] A man with this vision and vocation *needs* an abbot, because of God, because of Christ. In this sense the abbot is truly for him a sacrament of Christ whom he obeys, just as his brother is a sacrament of Christ whom he loves. In the new covenant all human relationships are Christified: compassionate relationships with people less fortunate than ourselves, fraternal relationships on a horizontal plane, but also relationships with those set over us, which are no longer purely functional, no longer tolerated as a necessary evil, but transfigured by the believer's awareness of the sacramental presence of Christ. In St Benedict's picture of life for his monks, Christ stands at the head of every avenue.[38]

An apparent discrepancy remains, however, between this 'sacramental' view of the abbot and the democratic manner of his election: if a monk participates in the election of a particular man, how does that person then become, for him and for his brethren, the holder of an authority derived from Christ, and even Christ's representative?

It is true, but insufficient, to say that since God calls a man to realize his Christian vocation as a Benedictine monk at a certain time and in a certain monastery, and since the abbot is an essential factor in the enterprise, the abbot – indeed, *this* abbot – is part of the monk's vocation. It is also true that a Benedictine community exists within the wider community of the Church, in which Christ is present through his Spirit. The abbot's election, although democratically organized, is subsequently ratified by the Church's authority; this is part of the justification for St Benedict's application to monastic obedience of the text, 'He who listens to you listens to me',[39] which is apostolic and ecclesial in its literal reference. But we must go further than this, for an abbatial election is far more than a merely administrative act. The principles of obedience and sacramentality are valid both for personal life and for the life of the community. As an individual the Christian is enmeshed in a network of secondary causes and circumstances that are not under his control, but he knows that all these 'given' elements are not layers of insulation between him and God; God's will, power, providence, and love touch his life at every point, and it is in a realistic acceptance of his situation that he discerns and obeys the divine will. But obedience and abandonment to God's will are not to be simply equated with passive acquiescence; a person is often called to act and choose intelligently, imaginatively, courageously, and creatively within this overarching will of God. He has to consider the possibilities, and see what can be done with the available material. When he does this in the fear of God, he can be confident that God chooses and wills *through* his choice and will. To shoulder the responsibility of choosing humanly can be a significant act of obedience.

The same is true of the life of a monastic community which seeks to obey God and believes in the sacrament of Christ's presence in human relationships. The mesh of circumstances is even more complicated, but God's will is over the community's whole life, touching it at every point. The monastic vocation itself is the gift of his grace to every member of the community, and so the Lord is present in the fact that these particular people make up the community at this particular time and are endowed with certain specific charisms that enrich the community's life. Within the given set of circumstances the community must act in obedience to its Benedictine vocation, taking prayerful and realistic account of the possibilities open to it and acting freely and vigorously. But the Benedictine vocation includes the *desire* to have an abbot, and so when the community gathers to reflect upon itself and seek God's will in an abbatial election it is performing a crucial act of obedience in co-operating with God and acting within his plan.

Such an action of human dignity and responsibility is very harmonious with sacramental truth. In sacramental activity we are free and human. It is true that we always receive more than we bring, because Christ comes to meet us and takes up our imperfect faith and love into his own perfect response to the Father; nevertheless the more truly human our approach, the more sacramental.

It does not therefore require a great leap of the mind to say that in the measure in which the members of a community choose their abbot 'in the fear of God',[40] bearing the full responsibility of intelligent human choosing in conscious obedience to God's will, in that measure the abbot elected is the bearer of God's grace, the sacrament of God's coming to meet them in Christ.[41]

b) The abbot as the unitive centre of the community

The authority of the abbot is thus from Christ and for the community, and Christ is himself the love and binding force among the brethren. The abbot's authority needs therefore to have that element of poverty which Christ showed throughout his life, which allows the eye of faith to look beyond him to the Father. The abbot stands in the place of Christ, but Christ is not only the Lord; he is the first-born among many brethren.[42]

So the abbot is truly a brother to his monks, and on this relationship all the brotherhood depends.

It follows that the abbot must himself obey God and must lead the community to that obedience, for Christ is the Son who came to do the will of the Father. The common will to obey is expressed in the abbot's own obedience to the Rule. Among the most significant of St Benedict's departures from the Rule of the Master is the delicate balance he provides for between the abbot with his personal charism of leadership, the Rule which mediates the wisdom of tradition, and the living community in which the Spirit is at work. Thus St Benedict's teaching on the central position and authority of the abbot is always set within the framework of the Rule; the abbot has the power and duty to interpret it but he is not himself above it and must make all his decisions 'in the fear of God and observance of the Rule'[43] which for him as for the brethren is indispensable and central; *all* are to 'follow the Rule as master'.[44]

The abbot's duty is both to express and to foster the life and unity of the brotherhood. He must express them to the world outside as well as to the community, but he must not let the demands of the Church or the world at large lead him to neglect his primary work in the monastery. His unifying task within the community is to stir the love of its members. This entails promoting an informed concern among all of them for the community's goals and bringing the community to a deepening self-awareness. Consultation and dialogue are therefore of the essence of his function: he needs to know all the movements of thought, the strains, and the aspirations that are to be found in the community and in individual monks. He needs to be sensitive to the creativeness of the Spirit among them, and to rejoice in the diversity of gifts and insights. Yet his business is to bring the community to a consensus, and this not only in chapter but in its life generally.[45] If the monks are to respond to the presence of the Spirit within and among them in full openness and confidence, they also need a human centre of cohesiveness and unity, and they must find it in the abbot.

The desired consensus must not, however, be simply equated with unanimity of opinion; true and rich unity of life is not found in a community of yes-men. The human ferment of disagreement, in which every member speaks the truth in love as he sees it, is part of the process by which truth is hammered out and God's will honestly sought. But a distinction must be made between the periods before and after the abbot's decision: disagreement is very healthy and proper before it, but once it is made there must be loyal acceptance (which does not necessarily imply theoretical agreement) out of love for the community. Nor is the common mind, which the abbot strives to bring into being, to be equated with the emergence of a majority view. Such a view does not have the status of a community consensus unless the abbot endorses it, and he must never become the 'possession' of any one group in the monastery, even though it be the majority. He fails in his office unless he is building up all the monks in the life of the Spirit.

His unifying responsibility is exercised also in his appointment of all the officials of the monastery, and in his effort to ensure that through them the community is doing its work in accordance with the mission God has entrusted to it. This is not simply a matter of efficiency; it is essential to the life and peace of the community that the abbot should see that in the actions of its members the body works as one. In all this there is need for dialogue and consultation, but ultimately the co-ordinating responsibility is the abbot's.

c) The abbot as educative guide in the life of the Spirit

This aspect of the abbot's office may be considered under two headings.

1. Initiatory and illuminative

St Benedict states that only the abbot should bring matters forward for discussion in chapter.[46] With the contemporary emphasis on dialogue and co-responsibility, this means that the abbot needs to be responsive to the promptings of the Spirit and the suggestions of the brethren in his guidance of the community, but even when new ideas originate in other minds than his, it is still his duty to lead the community forward, and to retain final authority in the initiatives taken by the brethren. He must listen, but not abdicate.

The abbot may not be the wisest, holiest, or most learned member of the community, yet he must still teach by word and example, and the brethren have the right to expect – indeed, to expect more especially today – that the abbot, confident in the power of the Spirit, will bring forth things new and old in his spiritual teaching and his counselling of his monks. On the one hand the election of a particular man to the abbatial office implies that the brethren see in him a trustworthy custodian and exponent of the accumulated wisdom of the community's tradition. On the other hand, the abbot more than anyone else needs to listen to what the Spirit is saying to the churches: what he is saying to this little flock within the universal Church, and what he is saying *today*, not merely what he was saying yesterday or the day before. This does not mean an uncritical acceptance by the abbot of everything that is being done and said in the modern Church, still less an undiscerning attempt to apply everything he hears to monastic life. But it does mean that he must be a man of God; that, however pressing the other demands of his office, he must have time to pray, read, and reflect; that he must be sensitive enough to the Spirit to be able to receive effective inspiration from the present life of the Church and communicate this inspiration to his monks. Making allowance for the inevitable mistakes, he must not fear that fire which Christ would have kindled on earth.[47]

The abbot must, moreover, be obedient to the promptings given by the Spirit through the events and persons around him. He should be prepared to recognize in members of his own community his equals or superiors in various fields, even in spiritual wisdom, and he should show respect for each member with his special gifts and talents. Illuminative leadership in the complex business of decision-making today does not imply that the abbot must know all the answers. The best service he can render to the community may often be his effort to keep in touch with and co-ordinate the rapidly expanding knowledge of the experts, to evaluate the factors involved in any issue and present his evaluation clearly to the community, and then to stand firm as a focus of unity as the brethren share with him the laborious task of sifting, absorbing, and acting upon the best knowledge available.

2. Corrective

The community as a whole has the right to look to the abbot for corrective guidance. There will also inevitably be failings and weaknesses in individuals, and the abbot owes it as a service both to them and to the community at large to give correction where needed to protect the community from what might be damaging or destructive. In an age when such abundant literature and educational opportunities are available to monks, it can happen that the traditional teaching role of the abbot (i.e. his relation as master to disciples) may often be exercised in the way of negative guidance, as when, using the gift of discernment of spirits,[48] he recognizes that a monk's enthusiasms or projects are unsound and may stem from pride, idiosyncrasy, or want of judgement.

The Rule also makes it clear that although correction is the responsibility of the abbot,[49] it can sometimes be exercised through the tactful mediation of the brethren, and through their prayers.[50] True Christian freedom of spirit is, however, to a considerable degree self-corrective, in its determination not to accept again the yoke of slavery to sin.[51]

Conclusion

Perhaps no man can possess the ideal balance of qualities for such an office, but there have been sufficient instances within the EBC to show that it is not unrealistic to look for a man who is open to the movements of the Spirit and well versed in the law of God; one who can maintain the truth without fear; who can order what is good for the community and the individual without losing that discretion which is the mother of the virtues; who can maintain in the community that peace which is the seed-ground of holiness.[52]

If the abbot knows that such considerations have been in the minds of his brethren at his election he can face his task with confidence and without losing courage. The brethren for their part can continue to confirm the act of faith they made at the time of the election, in spite of the inevitable imperfections that fall short of the ideal. They can show that perseverance in fidelity which all those in authority need if they are to fulfil their task. Much stress has been laid in this chapter on the duty of the abbot to recognize, respect, and foster the God-given charisms of every member of the community. But since Christian authority too is a charism of service within the Body of Christ, the monks have a correlative responsibility to foster the charism which the Spirit has given to the abbot. This implies respect, love, loyalty, support, and openness on the monks' side, for without these things the abbot cannot, as St Benedict recognizes,[53] exercise his authority as he is called to do.

It is a demanding programme on both sides, and when people are busy and tired there is pressure on all, monks and abbot alike, to opt for the least demanding, the mechanical, the less-than-human, in attitudes and relationships. But we have Christ's invitation and power to enable us to grow truly human, and we have a Rule that indicates how it can be done.

7

Freedom and Availability
for God

The Spirit forms Christians into communities, but the same Spirit called Jesus into the desert and on to the mountain, and calls every man to a personal transformation in Christ. So after the preceding chapters on the 'sharing' aspects of monastic life, this one turns to their indispensable complement, without which community would collapse into mere togetherness: the call to personal freedom for God in purity of heart.

Freedom as a basic human value

a) Aspects of freedom

Whatever is experienced as an authentic human value in man's striving towards fulness of life and fellowship with God is in some way relevant within the special vocation to Christian monastic life. One such fundamental human value, sought by men in every age, found at new depth in Christian life, and held in honour by contemporary thought, is the right to freedom. It can be thought of negatively, in terms of freedom *from* what diminishes us, whether that be external constraint or the internal pressure of fear or insecurity. More positively, freedom implies a confrontation with real possibilities between which one can choose; it implies the possibility of loving what one does and doing it because one loves it. But basic to the freedom to act is the more fundamental freedom to *be*, to possess one's being in fulness and integrity. Here it is close to the ideal of human maturity, and none of us is born free in this sense: we can only achieve freedom at the cost of a long process of growth, self-discipline, and courageous endeavour. These forms of personal freedom imply the further stage of becoming free for things or persons beyond oneself, whether this means freedom for creative work, or availability for other persons in love and service, or the ultimate freedom and availability for God who creates our freedom.

b) *Man's drive to seek solitude*

Man is a social animal, but as soon as he rises above the struggle for mere biological survival he begins to understand that some measure of aloneness is also necessary if he is to be fully human. He needs not only the support of the group but also occasions for confronting his God and himself, some chance to be alone with God from time to time, whatever he may mean by 'God'. The choice necessary to achieve creative freedom involves the choice of some measure of solitude. Some of the oldest civilizations of the world provided instances of this human phenomenon: in India, centuries before Christ, hermits were seeking the forests. Later, at the height of Greek civilization, there was explicit recognition of the value to the community of the 'contemplative' philosopher who stood apart from the general scramble for immediate goods in order to dedicate himself to the search for truth or wisdom. And in the popular memories of proto-history recorded in Genesis 4–11 there is a mention of an individual who, long before a Chosen People existed or salvation history had really begun, somehow rose above the general involvement with sin to some kind of fellowship with God: 'Enoch walked with God and was seen no more, because God took him.'[1]

Man knows a divine discontent; the created spirit is open to reality as such, to infinite reality, and what is confined, familiar, comfortable does not satisfy it. The beginnings of the fulfilment it seeks are already present: 'the experience of infinite longing, radical optimism, discontent which cannot find rest, anguish at the insufficiency of material things, protest against death, the experience of being the object of a love whose absoluteness and whose silence our mortality cannot bear. . . .'[2] These beginnings are brought to absolute fulfilment by grace, and hence we experience through them both grace and nature.

Freedom for the covenant

a) *A people called out and set apart*

Man's experience of God as the ultimate reality he confronts on every level of his life, as the horizon of absolute mystery against which all his most fully human responses are made, becomes explicit in his response to that event of self-communication by God called revelation and grace.

And so the urge to break free from confined and familiar surroundings, in order to seek an encounter with something or someone transcending both them and man himself, comes to be understood as a personal response to a word of summons. Abraham was called out by God, away from an accustomed environment and into a relationship of obedience, friendship, and grace.[3] The same symbolic calling-out was repeated when at the exodus God formed Abraham's descendants into the people of Israel, setting them apart and establishing them in a covenant-relationship with himself, within which they might be available for the experience of God and his self-communicating word, and be prepared for their mission.[4]

Israel's memories of this crucial event were shaped by the experience of the desert which had been its setting. The desert was not, for the most part, a nostalgic memory; it was thought of as a fearful place, a dry, weary land without water,[5] a place of danger and hardship, and the scene of Israel's sin.[6] But the desert march had been an essential stage in the story of salvation. There Yahweh had tested and trained them, and humbled them that he might know what was in their heart,[7] and there he had sworn irrevocable fidelity to them in the covenant of love. The prophets came to see the desert experience of the nearness and the demands of God as formative.[8] As individuals they sought the desert again as a place of encounter and union with God and of renewed faithfulness,[9] and their example was followed by a line of holy men which eventually included the monks of Qumran and John the Baptist. Sometimes a non-geographical 'setting apart' was demanded of a prophet: Jeremiah was called to celibacy as a sign to Judah of the rapid passing of the contemporary way of life.[10]

b) Christ, the new covenant

Christ is the new covenant. Before taking up his messianic work he was 'driven' by the Spirit into the desert,[11] there to relive the test his people had lived through, but to conquer where they had failed. As true Son of God and Servant, withdrawn from the support of men and the secure routines of life, he there fought out a symbolic conflict and affirmed in practice that it is not on bread alone nor on the kingdoms of this world that man lives. He returned from the desert to a ministry of intense, crowded activity in which he was heroically available to all who needed him, but he repeatedly sought mountain solitudes to renew the vital links of prayer with his Father.[12] When the crowds tracked him down in his solitude, he did not send them away.[13] Yet his mission was to be accomplished not through popular acclamation but in loneliness, in ultimate rejection by his own people who would not receive him. Only when 'lifted up from the earth'[14] could he draw all men to himself. On the cross he endured abandonment and apparent uselessness, vitally involved in the affairs of men, loving God and men more than ever before, yet withdrawn and obedient to his Father's will. The love that transformed that day's work from a brutal travesty of justice into a redemptive sacrifice won him the 'many' for his inheritance[15] and in his blood the new covenant was consummated. In his resurrection and ascension he broke through 'the flesh' inasmuch as his mortal state had been a barrier to his total availability to all, and opened a 'new and living way' of access to God for all men.[16]

c) The paschal freedom of Christians, the new Israel

Christ's work was an act of deliverance, of setting free. The cures and exorcisms of his public ministry had been anticipatory victories over the 'Strong One' who held men's souls and bodies captive.[17] But only by sharing his exodus to freedom could the whole people he had won for himself be led out to the freedom of the sons of God. Christ's priestly prayer indicates that a dedication like his own was to be demanded of the new covenant people: 'For their sake I consecrate myself, so that they too may be consecrated in truth.'[18] The apostles were the nucleus of the new Israel. They were to be the *ekklesia*, the people called into a covenant relationship with God through the indwelling Spirit, called to listen to the word and the testimony of the Spirit in the Church,[19] and to be sent to witness in their turn.[20] The *ekklesia* as a whole was to be 'a chosen race, a royal priesthood, a consecrated nation, a people set apart'.[21]

The new freedom was experienced at an intimately personal level as well. The apostles' confident boldness (*parrhesia*) in speaking the word undismayed by human power[22] echoed the old Greek ideal of the free citizen's right to speak his mind freely, but it found new meaning in the Christian experience of liberation. But *parrhesia* also means the right of free access to God: we can draw near with confidence to the throne of grace;[23] even if our hearts condemn us we can still have this confidence[24] because through Christ we have access in one Spirit to the Father.[25] Both these aspects of freedom – the free approach to men and the free access to God in prayer – were the gift of the Spirit. So overwhelming was the experience of this gift for the first Christians that they thought of freedom as an interior thing, a re-creation at the heart of the person, and could be almost shockingly tolerant of social structures that to us appear incompatible with human and Christian freedom. It does not seem to have occurred to them that slavery was wrong in itself. No doubt the supposed imminence of the parousia acted as a deterrent to social reform inspired by the Christian ethic, but in any case they were not sufficiently evolved to think in this way. It took Christianity about eighteen centuries to get rid of slavery from the social order. St Paul did not seem to regard it as a scandal; he maintained that everyone should stay in the state in which the call had found him.[26]

d) Individual calls to freedom and availability under the new covenant

As under the old covenant a reality of the life of the whole covenant-people had been exemplified in a special way in individuals (the prophets), so under the new covenant the aspect of being 'separated unto' was manifested in individual calls. The apostles immediately chosen by Christ were required to leave all things in their accustomed way of life as a condition of the *vita apostolica*. Paul significantly sought the desert for a time after his conversion,[27] and his missionary career was inaugurated by the Holy Spirit's demand: 'Set Barnabas and Saul apart for me.'[28] An apostolic vocation, however active, has a certain loneliness about it.

A different instance of this kind of personal call was the fourth-century rush for the desert. Some Christians saw the routines of social life as an impediment to the spirit; they heard and took with the utmost literalness the invitation to leave all and follow Christ, and in the desert they struggled for freedom, fighting their holy war against adversaries not of flesh and blood. The enemy's onslaught was now made through the evil tendencies in the Christian's own heart, and the monk's fight for freedom was a sharing in Christ's warfare and a new kind of witness to the power of his resurrection.

This is only one particular manifestation of the grace of the Spirit; the monasticism of the desert heavily emphasized one special path along which the Christian may search for freedom, a path for the few. The aberrations and imbalances of the movement are well known: the exaggerated emphasis on corporal macerations, the spirit of rivalry, and the sometimes neurotic externalization of interior passionate struggles. But the sanest current in the desert tradition always recognized the difference between means and end, and the variety of means by which a Christian or a monk may attain the real goal. Hence there remained a hard core of Christian heroism, holiness, and sanity which may be best illustrated in the doctrine of *purity of heart*, as preserved by Cassian:

> The end of our profession is the kingdom of God ... but the immediate aim or goal (*skopos*) is purity of heart. For without purity of heart no one can enter that kingdom. We should fix our gaze on this goal and walk towards it in as straight a line as possible. If our thoughts wander away from it even a little, we should bring our gaze back to it, and use it as a kind of test. ... It is for this end – to keep our hearts continually pure – that we do and endure everything, that we make light of parents and home and position and wealth and comfort and every earthly pleasure. If we do not keep this mark continually before our eyes all our travail will be futile waste that wins nothing, and will stir up in us a chaos of ideas instead of single-mindedness. ... To this end everything is to be done. Solitude, watches in the night, manual labour, nakedness, reading, and the other disciplines – we know that their purpose is to free the heart from injury by bodily passions and to keep it free. ... They are not perfection but the means to it. ... It should be our main effort, the immovable and steadfast purpose of the heart, to cleave to the things of God and to God himself.[29]

But this purity of heart, a freedom from attachment to whatever is not God, is the condition for monastic prayer:

> Every monk who looks for the perfect way aims at uninterrupted prayerfulness. As far as it is possible to a frail man, he struggles for imperturbable peace and purity of mind. ... When the mind is freed from lust, established in tranquillity, and does not waver in its intention towards the one supreme good, the monk will fulfil the precept of St Paul, 'Pray without ceasing'. ... Then, whatever thought the mind receives, whatever it considers, whatever it does, will be a prayer of true purity and sincerity.[30]

The ideal sketched here is one of personal freedom won through self-denial, a total availability for God who is to be sought and served in all things. It is true that some parts of the desert tradition speak as though such heights are attainable only by the solitary[31] or by those committed to extreme forms of outward asceticism, but spiritual teaching of such depth, strength, and centrality cannot be confined to the followers of one particular type of monastic life. Whatever be his way of life and degree of solitude, a monk is a man who has 'gone apart' in some sense from the multiplicity of human possibilities to dedicate himself to a search for God in purity of heart.

This view is supported by the ancients' habit of describing monastic life by a range of images almost all derived from Scripture. The monastery is the house of God, the primitive Jerusalem community, the *ecclesiola*; the monk is a witness to God or to Christ, an athlete, a slave in the service of his divine Master, a soldier fighting for the heavenly King, a pilgrim journeying towards the heavenly Jerusalem, the true philosopher. There is nothing esoteric about this stock of images; they all express a Christian's freedom from entanglements for the sake of meeting God in some aspect of the covenant relationship. Dedication to the monastic life, whether implicit as in the earliest forms of Christian monasticism or made explicit by vows, is a disengagement for the sake of unimpeded search for God, and is rooted in the baptismal dedication.[32] The degree of actual withdrawal from the affairs of the earthly city may vary enormously without the essential spiritual reality necessarily being affected.

St Benedict and the call to freedom

St Benedict was unambiguously legislating for cenobites, but in the cultural situation of his day the monastic engagement could still be expressed (and, as his strictures on gyrovagues show, needed to be expressed) by an effective isolation of the community from the outside world: all necessary resources were to be located within the enclosure, as far as possible, and monks who returned from journeys were not to pass on to their brethren anything they had heard outside.[33] Literal fulfilment of these injunctions is neither practically possible nor spiritually desirable today. But St Benedict's principles on the search for God, for which the monk's renunciations free him, are clear and valid still.

The Prologue evokes the personal call from God which has always been the initial stage in the setting apart of an individual or a people for a relationship with God, an experience of God, and a mission within the covenant of grace. From his state of torpor and routine a man is called to light, to life, to work, and to the Kingdom.[34]

The work is a spiritual craft which demands a guarantee of perseverance: 'Now the workshop in which we are diligently to carry out all these tasks is the monastic enclosure and stability in the community.'[35] The novice is repeatedly required to pause during his probation, to consider the Rule and its implications, and to reiterate his decision. A stable choice is being built up, so that he may eventually make his vows with his eyes open and in full freedom.[36] This stable, lifelong dedication implies a break with many distractions and alternative possibilities and is St Benedict's first requirement for a thoroughgoing monastic response to God.

A more interior kind of breaking free is demanded by the ancient monastic doctrine of compunction. Detachment from deliberate sin is the most elementary form of freedom for God and is significantly linked with prayer in Chapter 4: 'To apply oneself frequently to prayer; to confess one's past sins to God every day in prayer with tears and sighs; to amend those sins in future.'[37] In Lent the brethren 'should lead lives of great purity' (the desert ideal again), which will be done 'if we keep ourselves free from sin and apply ourselves to prayer with tears, to reading and to heartfelt compunction'.[38] With regard to the oratory: 'If anyone wants to pray privately, let him just go in and pray, not in a loud voice but with tears and earnestness of heart.'[39]

The most radical demands for disengagement are found in St Benedict's teaching on humility, where the monk's painful exodus towards a total freedom in love and in the Spirit is described. The elementary freedom from attachment to sin and the deeper freedom that follows it spring from an awareness of God as the horizon of the monk's being, the ultimate reality of his life. He is to 'shun forgetfulness' with all that this suggests of living on the surface of things in self-delusion and dispersion of his being. Such a 'fear of God' is the result of encountering God in prayer as well as the monk's further freedom for prayer through deepening humility.[40] He is called to disentangle himself more and more completely from his most dangerous addiction – self-will. He is stripped of *proprietas* in all its forms, whether attachment to material property[41] or delight in fulfilling his own desires (second and third rungs), or ambition and self-esteem (fifth, sixth, and seventh rungs), or singularity (eighth rung), or self-assertiveness and arrogance (ninth, tenth, and eleventh rungs), and he is freed at last from servile fear. With all these forms of self-sufficiency left behind, he is free for perfect love. 'Where the Spirit of the Lord is, there is freedom.'[42]

This process of deliverance relentlessly described by St Benedict in Chapter 7 is no other than the ongoing paschal conversion to which the monk is committed by his second vow. The process of stripping and freeing is essentially rooted in union with the paschal Christ: 'The third rung of the ladder of humility is that a man subject himself to his superior in all obedience, imitating the Lord, of whom the apostle says, He was made obedient even unto death.' And at the fourth rung 'they go on with joy to declare, In all these things we are more than conquerors, through him who has loved us.' It is by 'persevering in the monastery until death' that he will 'share by patience in the sufferings of Christ' in order to share also in his Kingdom.[43] The monk is bound to make himself 'a stranger to the standards of the world'[44] and in so doing is a sign to the pilgrim People of God,[45] but the other facet of his disengagement is a longing for eternal life, for the eternal Easter.[46] In purity of heart he is free to live the covenant reality without reservations, free to keep a 'Sabbath of the heart' to the Lord.

On the basis of this thoroughgoing asceticism, St Benedict makes prayer the climate of monastic life. Silence, at first a discipline,[47] becomes an inner receptivity, a waiting on God and a listening to his word, a freedom immediately prerequisite for prayer.[48] St Benedict gives little or no formal instruction on 'mental prayer' because his whole ascetical programme disposes his monks for it and because their habitual awareness of God as their Father is expected to find free expression in prayer.

What has been described (in terms of Israel, Christ, the Christian people, the individual Christian, and the monk) is a paradigm; it sketches a steady and rectilinear course from slavery to freedom, from the tyranny of sin, self-will, egoism, self-deception, and fear to the freedom of God's children in love, holiness, and truth, to the life of the new man in Christ. But in fact no one's progress is simply rectilinear, in life or in prayer. It is a matter of many invitations of grace, some accepted, some ignored, some accepted timorously and half-heartedly, some accepted and then afterwards nullified by our inconstancy. It is *hard* to accept the invitation to freedom in the risen Christ, to walk freely in the Spirit, because the invitation opens up vistas too big for us and we feel safer clinging to our prison bars, where at least we know where we are. Some degree of imprisonment can be experienced as a security. No doubt it was hard for some of the people whom Jesus set free from bondage of body or spirit to accept their freedom, to pick up their stretchers and walk, or to relinquish a whole way of life as a blind beggar. To step into such liberation may have been experienced as acute personal risk rather than as euphoria. And apparently Peter did not altogether enjoy walking on the water.

Like anything else that Christ gives, freedom is at once gratuitous and costly. It is a fearful thing to fall into the hands of the living God. Legalism, Pharisaism, and scrupulosity are some of the forms of the insurance policy we take out against him. We can, without falling into grave sin, lose some of the freedom we had. But repentance and the patient mercy of God keep the way open, making it possible for us to grow in freedom all our lives.

Practical use of St Benedict's model

Translation into modern terms of St Benedict's concrete prescriptions regarding enclosure and withdrawal from the world must on the one hand take into account the enormous changes in the cultural context of monasticism since his day, and on the other ensure a practical observance that keeps real and effective the monk's renunciations for the sake of freedom as demanded by the Rule's teaching on asceticism and prayer. The task of translation may be considered under different aspects, according to whether we are thinking of the individual's freedom within his own community, the relationship of the community to the modern world, or the relevance of monastic freedom to the Church today.

a) Freedom within the monastery

Personal fidelity to the monastic ascesis as enjoined by the Rule is a *sine qua non* for freedom. But there must also be respect on the community's side for the uniqueness of each individual and his personal vocation if each monk is to have room to grow, to be himself, and to reach the fulness of Christian maturity in responsible freedom. Christian *parrhesia* at the level of freedom to speak one's mind must be an aspect of community life: on the firm basis of stability the individual's certainty of being loved and accepted by his community can free him to speak with confidence to his abbot or his brethren. But the same *parrhesia*, the gift of the Spirit, means freedom of access to God; when he wants to pray he is 'just to go in and pray' with the freedom of God's sons.[49] The Mass formula makes the same point: 'Let us pray with confidence . . . Our Father. . . .' The spirit of adoptive sonship pervades the Rule, and to live it implies freedom for God and freedom to approach him. But since for the monk, as for the first Christians, this *parrhesia* is essentially an interior gift, the monk who is honestly unable to change unsatisfactory structures can accept them and be as unworried as were the early Christians about the conditions in which this freedom is to be lived. He does not have to wait for the perfect monastic set-up before he can begin to experience it.

However, the environment may help or hinder. Of major importance is a satisfactory balance in the life of the individual monk or nun between work commitments and leisure for prayer or *lectio divina*. The tempo of life has changed greatly in the last two or three centuries and the effects are as perceptible in the monastery as elsewhere. Monastic communities have however a duty to maintain critical freedom with regard to modern standards in this as in other areas, and to resist the ever-increasing pressure. They can provide creative criticism of the tendency to swamp the individual and leave him without time fully to *be*. Both superior and community have a responsibility to make serious efforts to distribute the community's work-load equitably, and even sometimes to restrain over-active members of the community from assuming too many tasks. We can recognize that in the familiar situation of overwork there is a modern form of aceticism that measures up well to the classical requirements for authentic penance: it is not self-chosen, not conducive to narcissism or pride, and is directly related to charity and the service of others. We can further recognize the power of God's grace to compensate the overburdened individual for lack of time and quiet. But these considerations do not absolve us from the effort to find a just balance.[50]

Silence is another indispensable factor. How much the actual practice of silence has varied in different times and places and with different interpretations of the Rule is clear from monastic history, and the type of work and service undertaken by the community or the individual monk will obviously condition practical observance in this matter. But there must still be islands of silence in the life of anyone who is trying to be free for God. Some adequate measure of release from sheer noise and from distracting preoccupation with duties is necessary if the interior silence that is the condition of prayer is to become a felt need and a habitual possibility. Activism can get such a grip on a person that he is unable to 'let go' in his own mind and quieten his anxiety or feverish planning about his work. Exterior silence can help here, but an interior ascesis is needed. A man who lives in habitual peace and interior silence is helping to create peace in his community. Shared silence can be a very creative thing.

b) The eremitical ideal

The paradox of the covenant as a call to an encounter with God and to an indispensable mission is made at its sharpest in the vocation of the monk-hermit. 'The hermit is not alone with himself: for that would not be a sacred loneliness. Holiness is life. . . . The solitude of a soul enclosed within itself is death. And so the authentic, the really sacred solitude is the infinite solitude of God Himself, Alone, in Whom the hermits are alone.'[51] An eremitical vocation granted by God to a member of a cenobitic community has a value of inspiration and sign for all: it asserts unequivocally God's right to distribute his graces as he will, and to demand sacrifice of both hermit and community. It entails an act of faith in the invisible but powerful value of a life wholly freed for prayer. The hermit's vocation forces us to consider the application of St Paul's doctrine on the diversity of grace and of mission, a diversity which is like the differentiation of function within the human body, where specialization dominated by a unifying life-principle makes for richness and more intense life and growth.

Some degree of the eremitical grace is commonly active in the lives of many monks and nuns who are not called to a definitive and permanent adoption of the hermit's way of life. A personal grace can lead a cenobite periodically to seek a relative degree of solitude for the sake of stricter silence and more prolonged prayer, and such ventures should be encouraged.[52] A sabbatical period for prayer or study can be a great help to one who has been heavily burdened with work. The custom of annual retreats can also be extremely useful. Flexibility needs to be maintained, however, with regard to the type and length of a retreat; its didactic function can be distinguished from its value as a time of silence and prayer, and the differing needs of individuals and communities taken into account.

Freedom to respond to these personal calls is opposed only to the collectivity of the herd, not to the building of true human community.[53] The man who can stand alone before God is also the man who has most to contribute to the community.

c) The relation of the monastery to the modern world

The pluralism within the monastery that determines the individual's measure of solitude is operative also at the level of the community's degree of contact with the world. However much this may vary according to the demands of the apostolate and the community's vocation, two fundamental spiritual facts remain: entrance into the monastery is a real choice, freely made, of a certain way of serving God which excludes some human possibilities of development; but, on the other hand, the monastic vocation is a reality lived in Christ and in the heart of the Church, and hence the monk's physical and even psychological withdrawal from the world is for the sake of a spiritual involvement with it at a deeper level. So we have to live with a tension. In practice, fidelity to both terms of this monastic and Christian tension means that contact and withdrawal must be balanced in such a way that (1) the witness of the monastic life can be seen and heard by those capable of responding to it; (2) all members of the community have access to such information about the contemporary scene that their fellow human beings are truly 'present to them in a deeper way in the heart of Christ';[54] (3) guests, whether Christian or non-Christian, who through temporary association with a monastic community seek some contact with God or spiritual values can be welcomed. St Benedict called the monastery 'a school of the Lord's service'[55] and we may extend the idea and assume that experience of prayer should be diffused from it. He also recommended that special honour be shown to poor men and pilgrims;[56] in a welfare state and a post-Christian society the poor may be those deficient in other than material goods, and the pilgrims may be those in search of truth. Within the EBC there are widely differing interpretations in this matter, the most obvious divergence being that in the case of the nuns disengagement for the sake of freedom is effected by strict enclosure. This kind of pluralism in observance allied with an underlying unity at the spiritual level is characteristic of healthy Benedictine life.

1. 'Fuga mundi'?

The origins of the term *fuga mundi* are obscure, but it appears to be associated with the desert tradition. It became a consecrated phrase but, like its more extreme medieval variant, *contemptus mundi*, it carries overtones which are unbiblical, foreign to the Rule, and misleading to the modern mind. Since the ideology compressed into the phrase *fuga mundi* was an attempt to relate the monastic vocation to the contemporary (Hellenistic) ideals, it seems better to discard the phrase and make the same attempt in our own idiom.

The modern equivalent would seem to be the need in today's world for 'marginal' persons and communities who can stand somewhat apart from the pursuits of society, loving its members but not wholly identified with its outlook.[57] This marginal aspect of monasticism will be prophetic only if it includes something of the tension already suggested between, on the one hand, the renunciations implied by monastic vows, and, on the other, our heightened awareness of the grace-laden goodness of the world which God so loved that he sent his Son to redeem it. Full recognition of the incarnational values of human experience and human responsibility for the world helps to make more clear-cut the choice demanded by the monastic vocation, which cannot be wholly accounted for in terms of this present age.

2. A reminder to the world

Thus one consequence of a monk's freedom of heart should be a critical and creative freedom in his attitude to those false systems of values so immensely powerful in contemporary society. We *can* become dulled and institutionalized, accepting contemporary standards uncritically, but we need not do so. If we remain rooted in basic human values, but understand them in the light of Christian revelation, if we stay in touch with things as they are, not accepting contemporary standards blindly but remaining open to the signs of the times and the unpredictability of God, we are in a position to exercise the critical freedom expected of 'non-conformist' communities towards such things as materialism, acquisitive living, compulsive and reckless consumption of things, and exploitation of persons, towards such mental tyrannies as advertising, and in general towards the sinful structures that hold the world back from its true destiny.[58] We can help by maintaining a true sense of values. An example may illustrate this. We live in a comparatively affluent section of a world where about two-thirds of our brothers and sisters are hungry. The question of how to help them troubles the consciences of most monks and nuns. Whatever chances to offer material help may be within our reach must be seized, and it is right that we should have disturbed consciences. But it may not be irrelevant to reflect on the experiences of some western missionaries in developing countries such as India whose people are the object of compassionate concern in the West: the physically hungry of the East sometimes genuinely pity the spiritual poverty of materialistic western society. Not on bread alone does man live. There is a hunger for the word of God,[59] for silence and for prayer, and to keep it keenly alive may be our contribution. Many people today are seeking centres of reflection and peace. Such seekers may not be explicitly Christian and yet may hope to find the depth of living they are searching for in Christian monasteries.

d) The relevance of monastic freedom to the Church

Personal dedication is a human value readily appreciated today; it implies faith in some reality beyond oneself which is honoured and is known to be worthy of the sacrifices entailed. Dedication to monastic life implies faith in God and his word. There are two ways in which this faith can have a special relevance to the modern Church.

First, it can serve the Church for the furtherance of theological understanding. During the centuries before the rise of scholasticism, Christian theologizing was largely a contemplative, meditative activity, carried on especially by monks and fed directly from the sources of Scripture and liturgy. In the Christian East it has tended to remain so, but in the West after the twelfth century the live centre of theology shifted from monastery to university. Theology became a highly professional discipline and the monastic contribution dwindled in importance. This state of affairs continued until the nineteenth century. But under the influence of the liturgical movement, the rediscovery of the Bible within the Church and the patristic revival, the possibilities and richness of a more contemplative style of theology have been rediscovered, and although this kind of theology is in no sense the prerogative of monks, there is an affinity between it and the monastic tradition. 'Do not be conformed to this world, but be transformed by the renewal of your mind, that you may prove what is good and acceptable and perfect.'[60] A monk has put some distance between himself and the clamour of the world in order to listen with open ear and open heart to the word of God. He is vowed to a lifelong conversion. He lives on the mysteries of word and sign, savoured and prayed. He is therefore favourably placed to grow towards a deep sapiential theology, and this not for himself alone, but in the heart of the Church:

> The tradition which comes from the apostles develops in the Church with the help of the Holy Spirit. There is a growth in insight into the realities and words that are being passed on. This comes about in various ways: it comes through the contemplation and study of believers who ponder these things in their hearts. It comes from the intimate sense of spiritual realities which they experience. And it comes from preaching. . . .[61]

The Church has great need of this contemplative theology, and not least as a means of meeting and sharing with Orthodox, Anglican and other Christians whose traditions have more in common with this older type than with post-Tridentine theology in the West.

Second, faith is the condition for fruitfulness, particularly where efforts for renewal are concerned. The Christian Church needs prophets and men of faith no less than does secular society. Monasticism's relative independence of the hierarchy means that its leaders and spokesmen can serve the Church by prophetic criticism, by favouring forgotten causes, or by indicating ways forward, in a manner which may be difficult for bishops. Much discussion and thought, alteration of structures, updating of customs, and new experiments may be needed, but unless they are nourished from the deep roots of faith they will be sterile. Hence the monastic vocation has a special relevance to the Church's renewal, since it cannot be wholly justified at the bar of reason but is possible only as a sustained act of faith. The monk's sacrificial freeing of himself by an initial breaking away in response to God's word, his surrender to the continuing process of paschal conversion, and his effort to hold himself in freedom and availability for the encounter with God are acts of faith-as-belief and faith-as-fidelity. This faith is upheld by God's gracious faithfulness, like that of Moses who 'held to his purpose like a man who could see the Invisible'.[62]

8

Vocation and Growth
in Community

All this discussion of the various aspects of monastic life presupposes the grace by which God calls a man or woman to love and serve him in the monastic way. That is to say, it presupposes vocation: mysterious, intangible, but real. Vocation is very difficult to talk about; partly because it cannot be objectified, partly because it is highly personal and no two vocations are alike, and partly because there is little or no conceptual theological framework for studying it. Modern thought has contributed something to the psychology of vocation, and plenty of canon law on the subject, but little theology.

However, the Old and New Testaments provide a rich variety of existential descriptions of human persons encountering the God who calls. Most monks and nuns are aware of the abiding relevance of these stories to their own lives; their understanding of their vocation is shaped by the power and mystery of the archetype — vocation as portrayed in Scripture.

This chapter therefore begins by examining the biblical accounts of vocation, and then considers their relation to the monastic vocation and the help that can be given to a newcomer as he responds to it in a Benedictine community.

God and man: vocation and response

a) God's call to man

In the Old and New Testaments there is no theorizing about 'vocation', but there is a variety of concrete descriptions of people being seized by God. In these encounters some of the constant characteristics of the monastic call are already present: the unpredictable freedom of God's elective love, an assurance of his faithfulness, a demand for faith and obedience from his servants, a summons to personal growth, and a promise of eventual transformation by grace.

Sometimes God's call came to men in the kind of setting where he might be expected to intervene: to Moses alone in the desert, and to Isaiah probably in the temple.[1] But in other cases the manner of its coming was more disconcerting. For Gideon the occasion was a time of national disaster: 'And the angel of the Lord appeared to him and said to him, "The Lord is with you, you mighty man of valour"... and the Lord said, "Go in this might of yours and deliver Israel from the hand of Midian; do not I send you?"'[2] Ezekiel was with the exiles in Babylon when he received his bizarre vision and his mission to 'a nation of rebels'.[3] Hosea apparently had to learn his vocation and the meaning of it through the personal shame and anguish of his marital tragedy.[4] The greatest of all Old Testament vocations is recounted with simplicity and with no description of the circumstances: 'Now the Lord said to Abram, "Go from your country and your kindred and your father's house to the land that I will show you."'[5]

Sometimes a man would hear the call in the commonplace circumstances of his work. Amos was 'a herdsman, a dresser of sycamore trees' and was about his ordinary business when the Lord said to him, 'Go and prophesy to my people Israel.'[6] Simon and Andrew, James and John were at their daily work, fishing or mending nets, and Levi-Matthew was at his tax office when Christ said, 'Come.'[7] For Paul the circumstances were anything but ordinary; Christ swept him off his feet and reduced him to temporary blindness.

But whatever the manner of his calling, God is never more clearly God than in these stories of his call to men. A sense of his holiness, his otherness, and his fearfulness pervades the narratives.

b) Man's response to God

Men react as individuals; there is no stereotyped pattern for the response any more than there is for the call. Shuddering awe in the presence of the Holy One was the immediate reaction of Moses, and especially of Isaiah who was overwhelmed by a sense of his own impurity.[8] But the Holy One does not paralyse his servant, and Isaiah's second movement of response was alacrity: 'Here I am! Send me.'[9] Others were less eager. Moses produced a series of objections, and Jeremiah's natural timidity made him shrink from the demand.[10] The probably fictional account of Jonah's mission delightfully describes the strenuous efforts of God's servant to escape the honour; the prophet-elect 'fled to Tarshish from the presence of the Lord' while the heathen sailors prayed 'and offered sacrifice to the Lord, and made vows'. But the Lord was not to be thwarted.[11]

One of the greatest prophets of the Old Testament so far effaced himself before God and his mission that no better name can be assigned to him than 'Second Isaiah'. No story of vocation is given here; there is only his 'voice crying' and proclaiming the abiding, powerful efficacious word of Yahweh.[12]

For the first apostles the immediate impact of the call must have been a fascination with Christ: ' "Rabbi, where do you live?" He said to them, "Come and see." They came and saw. . . .'[13] The human friendship grew, but there were moments when something like Isaiah's awareness of the Holy One must have broken in on the apostles: 'When Simon Peter saw it, he fell down at Jesus's knees, saying, "Depart from me, for I am a sinful man, O Lord." '[14] But Paul did not know this slow growth through a period of human friendship to the fulness of Easter faith; his call was violent and sudden[15] and his conviction all the stronger that he was an apostle 'not from men nor through man, but through Jesus Christ and God the Father, who raised him from the dead'.[16] Paul knew himself to have been set apart before he was born,[17] like Jeremiah and the Servant.[18]

Human freedom remains intact, and human personalities never emerge more clearly in all their variety and uniqueness than in these stories of men called by God. Often he calls them by their personal names, and always he calls them to a decision.

'Go . . .' and 'say. . . .' The words occur frequently. The call usually implied communication and always service. But God's first call was 'to be with him',[19] since it was God's good news that the one called had to bring to others. 'No longer do I call you servants . . . but I have called you friends, for all that I have heard from my Father I have made known to you. You did not choose me, but I chose you.'[20]

c) Common features in vocation narratives

1. God's elective love

Through all the freedom of God's dealings with men and all the diversity of their responses there are certain constants. The first of these is the primacy of God's elective love. Israel was called to be God's people 'not because you were more in number than any other people . . . but because the Lord loves you'.[21] Jesus too chose freely: 'He went up into the hills and called to himself those he wanted.'[22] In the story of one who did not answer the call, the point is made even more clearly: 'Jesus, looking upon him, loved him, and said to him, "Go, sell what you have and give to the poor . . . and come, follow me." '[23] On any man he calls, God has first looked with love.

2. God's assurance of his faithfulness

The summons is invariably followed by some kind of assurance. Moses objected, ' "Who am I that I should go to Pharaoh and bring the sons of Israel out of Egypt?" God said, "But I will be with you." '[24] Gideon pleaded, ' "Pray, Lord, how can I deliver Israel? Behold, my clan is the weakest in Manasseh, and I am the least of my family." And the Lord said to him, "But I will be with you." '[25]

3. God's demand for faith and obedience

On the basis of this call of grace and assurance of God's faithfulness there is in every case a demand for unconditional faith and obedience, and for active collaboration in God's plan of salvation. Occasionally the call may have involved a temporary commitment only, as perhaps in the case of the judges, but usually it was a demand for lifelong service. A man might waver and fear after years of commitment to Yahweh,[26] but the demand and the grace were still held out to him and the only way forward was through a deeper dedication. Some of the prophets probably ended as martyrs, and heroic perseverance was asked of them all.

This persevering fidelity was a strange blend of inner constraint and freedom. Amos spoke of his preaching as the inevitable reaction to the word he had received, inevitable as the clutch of fear at a man's heart: 'The lion has roared, who will not fear? The Lord God has spoken, who can but prophesy?'[27] Jeremiah spoke still more vividly of the intolerable agony of resistance:

> If I say, 'I will not mention him,
> or speak any more in his name,'
> there is in my heart as it were a burning fire
> shut up in my bones,
> and I am weary with holding it in,
> and I cannot.[28]

Paul explained, 'For necessity is laid upon me. Woe to me if I do not preach the gospel!'[29] Yet God demands free, loving service,[30] and a man called like this cannot be himself unless he responds.

4. Personal growth and transformation by grace

In obedience to the call he can become the person he is called to be. The grace and the calling are uniquely personal, and the newness of life is often signified by a change of name; Abram becomes Abraham, Jacob is called to be Israel, and Simon will be called Peter. God's call is creative, as his unique love for the man he calls is creative. Abraham, led on by grace, becomes the friend of God.[31] Paul forgets his qualifications as a Hebrew born of Hebrews, forgets all that lies behind and strains forward to what lies ahead, to attain the prize of the upward call of God, and to grasp Christ who has grasped him.[32] The Christian is reminded to 'walk worthily' of the God who is even now calling him to the Kingdom.[33] Transformation by grace is promised: 'To him who conquers . . . I will give a white stone, with a new name written on it which no one knows except him who receives it.'[34]

d) Response of one: destiny of many

Vocation also means a call to the service of other people at some stage in the unfolding of God's covenant. This aspect of vocation, however, is not a different reality from the highly personal mystery of grace in an individual's response to God, in the sense that there would inevitably be a divergence or a fundamental tension between the 'inner' and the 'outer' demands of God's call. Ultimately there is no tension. A human person says 'Yes' to God in a matter that seems to affect only himself, but the repercussions of his choice are felt far beyond his own life. He serves the economy of salvation precisely by being or doing what God is asking him to be or do, and on his obedience may hinge the destinies of many in ways entirely unknown to him. The point is of the utmost importance in reconciling a call to monastic life with a desire to serve the salvation of the world, and the vocation narratives in Scripture make it clear. Paul sets in close parallelism his own call to the apostolate and that of the whole Church to holiness: 'Paul, called to be an apostle, set apart for the gospel of God . . . to all God's beloved in Rome who are called to be saints. . . .'[35] Similarly the call of all Israel could be enacted in the experience of a prophet. The faithful response of one can mould the destinies of many. Abraham's 'Yes' to God was laden with consequences far beyond anything he could have suspected.[36] Much more significantly, God waited on one person's consent to her vocation before sending the promised Redeemer. In the story of Mary's call the classic elements are present: an assurance that 'the Lord is with you', the preliminary disclosure of the plan, the giving of a sign, and her consent in graced freedom: '*Fiat*'. But from that moment she had to go forward in partial ignorance and total trust, not knowing where that first consent would lead her.

Christ himself is the Elect.[37] Consecrated from his mother's womb to be the light of the nations,[38] he yet had to choose freely to walk the Servant's way. The story of his rejection of the alternatives presented by the tempter in the desert may well be a schematized account of his reiterated choices; this is suggested by his calling Peter 'Satan' for presenting to him once again the possibility of swerving.[39] Finally, his decision in Gethsemane was the climax of a life during which he had room to grow in understanding of his vocation and in free, adult dedication to the Father's will; 'although he was Son, he learned obedience through the things he suffered'.[40]

In him is formed the body of the elect, the *ekklesia*, the new people founded on the apostles whom Christ called, the people called in baptism to holiness. They are chosen in the unfathomable freedom of God's predilection:

> Consider your call, brethren; not many of you were wise according to worldly standards, not many were powerful, not many were of noble birth; but God chose what is foolish in the world to shame the wise, God chose what is weak in the world to shame the strong, God chose what is low and despised in the world, even things that are not, to bring to nothing things that are.[41]

Entry into community

a) The call to monastic life

The call into the life of the risen Christ works itself out in an endless variety of forms. In following Christ and in being conformed to him we do not lose our individuality; we find it. In Christ is our true identity. The incarnate Word is the norm of human living, the 'first-born of all creation' and the 'perfect man' in whom all individual personalities find their freedom and fulfilment.[42] This traditional Christian awareness is in accord with a significant movement in modern psychology which tends to concentrate more on the mature fulfilled personality as the norm than on neurotic deviations.[43]

There is no limit to the number of ways in which the creative freedom of God's Spirit can call men to live and grow in Christ. The baptismal call into a life of grace itself creates the possibility of a further call which is rooted in baptism but which makes the response to grace specific. One instance of this is the call to monastic life. However it becomes known to a person, it may be for him who receives it the only way to realize the full implications of his baptism, and it demands a free personal response.[44] Like the whole dispensation of grace it is mysterious, but unnecessary obscurity has been introduced by thinking of vocation as a *thing*. A vocation has been supposed to be some mysterious piece of equipment which an individual has, or does not have, or even loses. (Of course, he can fail to respond, or cease responding, and in this sense 'loss of vocation' is a real possibility.) It would probably be nearer the truth to say that he *is* a vocation: he is a graced, called person, and being unique as a person he is uniquely graced and called. His business is therefore to find out whether through commitment to monastic life he can respond with his whole being to the God whose love is calling him.

The most necessary means of finding this out is prayer for God's guidance on the part of both candidate and community. Beyond this, the Rule and Benedictine tradition do not seem to have evolved much theory. The approach has always tended to be pragmatic: there is to be a trial period during which the novice seriously gives himself to the life, is instructed in the Rule, and has plenty of time to consider his undertaking.[45] The practical question must be, Can he live it? Or, since this does not mean merely enduring it, Can he *grow* through this way of life to become the person God is calling him to be?[46]

Moreover, a candidate for Benedictine life enters not an order primarily, nor a congregation, but a monastery, a particular community with its own call, its own grace, and its own traditions. The pragmatic test is, therefore, Does he fit in *here*? But there is more discernment required than this. The community has to help him to find out not merely whether he is called but in some sense why he is called, how his own unique personal contribution is relevant and assimilable, and how to integrate what he brings with what he finds and will receive. St Benedict seems to have been open to this idea; he deals humbly with the question of generation gaps, mentioning that God often reveals what is better to the younger,[47] and he envisages the possibility that a visiting monk may have been sent by the Lord to open the community's eyes to some deficiency.[48] The principle can surely be extended and applied to the influence that any new member of the community will inevitably exert. The novice will be changed by the community's life, but the community will be changed too. If it is prepared to be so changed, retaining its identity and the vitality of its traditions but open to the new influx of life and ideas that come with new recruits, the community is living out its stability and conversion at a communal level and opening itself to the grace of God. But these attitudes clearly demand strong faith on both sides, and a readiness to see any signs that God may give.

St Benedict mentions a few signs for the novice master's guidance: he is to try to discover whether the novice is truly seeking God and is eager for the *opus Dei*, obedience, and humiliations. He is to tell the novice about the hard and rough road along which we travel to God.[49] A modern list of hints on 'discernment of vocations' would probably be a good deal longer and have a more logical rationale. St Benedict's approach is pragmatic as usual, but he provides indications that can be readily translated into modern terms. The signs he gives should become more evident as life goes on; the fact that they are mentioned in Chapter 58 does not mean that they are relevant only for novices.[50]

b) 'Whether he is eager for the opus Dei . . .'

The term *opus Dei* seems originally to have meant the whole 'work' of the monastic calling, the monk's laborious, ascetical struggle to return to God in Christ.[51] If this is what St Benedict meant in the signs he gives in Chapter 58, the criterion, 'whether he is zealous for the work of God', could perhaps suggest keenness, an ardent desire that this 'work' of attaining to holiness through co-operation with the grace of God should go forward at all costs. But it is more likely that St Benedict was using the term *opus Dei* in the more specialized sense of 'liturgy' that he gives it elsewhere.

The *opus Dei* in this latter sense is also indispensable to the Benedictine way of life. The liturgy is the work of God both in the sense that it is something he accomplishes in the world today and in the sense that it is the Church's labour of love for him. In the divine office God's manifestation of himself continues. The Christian people proclaims what God has done, is doing, and will do. There the risen Christ is in our midst praying with us and inviting us to a total surrender of ourselves, our time, and our talents to the glory of the Father.

The call to Benedictine life is a call to prayer, to faith, and to community. The person whose growth and response to God are to be realized in this way of life needs an ability to nourish his prayer and faith from Scripture and the liturgy, even though this may take some years to acquire. He has to be able to be himself in and through a community, to pray in a community, and to open up to the mystery of worship through Christ and with him and in him. The paschal Christ, who is present where two or three are gathered in his name, draws us through the liturgy more deeply into his covenant of love. Into this covenant we were grafted at baptism, and monastic profession is in continuity with the baptismal commitment. But the covenant is renewed in the Eucharist, and in a more general sense in the liturgy as a whole. A monastic community and its members individually must be able through worship to find their own way more deeply into the covenant commitment. An aptitude for growing towards this is one of the signs of a person's call to Benedictine life.

c) '. . . for obedience . . .'

Monastic obedience means the total surrender of the whole human person, with all his powers of loving and giving, to God. The monastic vows express the commitment of the whole man to God: 'Suscipe me, Domine'. A desire for this unqualified handing over of self is one of the clearest of the indications that a person is called to the life, but the desire and intention are actualized in concrete practical obedience.

An understanding of mature obedience is therefore one of the most important objects of training, and growth towards it begins, but will not be completed, in the novitiate. The most basic question to be faced in training for obedience is probably 'Why is it so important?' Formation must help the monk to see that obedience is not merely a discipline necessary for smooth co-ordination, still less the opium of monastic communities, but a mystery at the heart of the redemption and of Christian monastic life.

It is important at various levels. There is an obedience of the mind, a willingness to learn from the abbot or the spiritual tradition of the community.[52] There is an ascetical value in obedience, for it directly attacks the main obstacle to prayer and holiness, our self-will.[53] There is a mystical level at which obedience is above all a sharing with Christ, an identification with him, and a diffusion of his obedience throughout his Body.[54] There is a community level, at which obedience is a willingness to submit in faith to Christ's presence in the Church and in a community gathered in his name.[55] And there is an eschatological level: just as celibacy and poverty anticipate the life and reality of the Kingdom not yet fully revealed, so does religious obedience. Obedience is a union of wills, and finds its ultimate meaning in the Christ of Easter who 'lives unto God'.[56] So the monk who has 'received the Spirit of the adoption of sons'[57] lives 'no longer for himself but for him who for our sake died and rose again'.[58] Christ in his mortal life obeyed in pain, struggle, and labour, but risen he lives unto God. The direction of his obedience has not changed, only the conditions of its exercise; the same is true for his followers.[59]

Obedience is not 'blind'. Critical faculties, usually very well developed in young people today, are neither bad nor irrelevant to monastic life. On the contrary, they play an indispensable part in genuine human obedience; the owner must learn to use them constructively as a precision tool in the service of love. Such use must be distinguished from the 'spirit of criticism' which is destructive. A monk or novice may clearly see the defects or limitations in superiors or in the conditions of monastic life, and at the same time lovingly accept it all, in so far as it cannot be changed, because this is the context in which God calls him to respond, and the family to which he has committed or will commit himself by the vow of stability. So Christ also could accept the manifold limitations of his human situation.

In Chapter 58 of the Rule there is great stress on the novice's open-eyed, fully conscious, long-matured, free choice. These provisions are remarkable for the sixth century and very significant today when so much value is attached to man's need and right to choose freely, to commit himself from the core of his personality because he loves, and to find meaning and authenticity in so doing. Authentic and fully human obedience always springs from the free centre of the person and is united with Christ's free response to his Father. Because our freedom is created freedom we do not lose it but grow more free in surrender to God who gives it.

d) '. . . for humiliations . . .'

The day of fictitious humiliations provided by superiors in the belief that they would generate humility in monks or novices is happily past. Such methods may often have entailed injustice and a lack of respect for human persons, and they can be the more freely discarded when the real hardships and humiliations inherent in monastic life are recognized.

Chapter 72 of the Rule suggests an ideal of heroic charity in mutual obedience, genuine unselfishness, and humility, and the patient bearing of one's own weaknesses and those of one's neighbours. Cheerful obedience with alacrity,[60] calm and steadiness in trying situations,[61] adapting oneself to varieties of temperament and character,[62] willingness to admit oneself wrong,[63] and readiness to serve in any capacity[64] – all these are examples drawn from daily life of the self-denial demanded. The word *patientia* in its strong sense of endurance occurs in important contexts in the Rule: the monk under strain is to 'hold fast to patience with a silent mind',[65] the brethren are to bear one another's weaknesses 'with the greatest patience'[66] and, most significantly, it is by persevering in the monastery until death that they will 'share by patience in the sufferings of Christ' so that they may also share his glory.[67]

These passages suggest that the faith to see these apparently trivial everyday things as a humble share in the mystery of the cross is part of the grace of monastic vocation. *Conversatio morum* is, like obedience, a vow whose meaning is best understood in the light of the paschal mystery; it is by living it patiently in everyday 'humiliations' that monks grow towards the 'largeness of heart' and 'unspeakable sweetness of love' promised at the end of the Prologue.

Situations that are less than ideal and the general unsatisfactoriness of things can thus be essential elements in the humiliations for which the monk is to be 'eager'. It is true that the lifelong growth and formation of a monk will be promoted if as far as possible he is given scope to do and to do well things for which he is gifted and perhaps professionally trained. To use a highly trained or gifted member of the community as a stop-gap, in an unsuitable job, for a long period and perhaps from a point early in his monastic life, is not likely to promote either his personal growth or the good of the community in the long run. At the same time, leaving all things in order to follow Christ, and willingness to accept unromantic humiliations in a Christlike spirit, may sometimes involve a monk in patiently bearing the apparent waste of his personal gifts when his community's life-style, or economic conditions, or shortage of personnel make it impossible for such gifts to be directly used. This can be a very crucifying self-denial to one whose gifts – musical, artistic, literary, intellectual, or any other kind – are intimately part of his spiritual life. But even if such an apparent frustration is inevitable, it remains true that the gifts have helped to make the person what he is and still condition his dedication to God; hence his gifts, though he cannot use them directly, are not ultimately wasted.

e) Novitiate and novice master

1. Organization of novitiate

The novitiate serves a double purpose: both to find out whether a person is called to grow to his full stature in Christ through living the monastic life, and, if he is, to help him to get well started in his response. There is no blueprint for an ideal Benedictine novitiate. Many current ideas and practices with regard to novitiate training have been uncritically adopted from canon law and the model of the modern religious orders. Monks should beware of creating artificial categories which then have to be uncomfortably adapted or even discarded. The best novitiate for us is one that will ground a person in the essentials of monastic life, give him a real introduction to the life and spirit of the house he has entered, open up to him the prospect of growth in this community and establish him in generous, faithful response to his call.

Novitiate structures must therefore be geared to the particular house, and the application of general principles will be to a considerable extent determined by the community's situation. Such factors as, for example, the average number of novices at a time will influence the choice of the best structures.

'Open' or 'closed' novitiate?

One area in which discernment is required is that of deciding how far the novitiate should be 'open' or 'closed' to contact with the rest of the community. The most obvious advantage of an open novitiate is that it makes real mutual knowledge between novice and community much easier. This can be good for the community, which is in a better position to exercise its co-responsibility in admitting novices to profession, and is obliged in daily contacts to act responsibly in conduct towards them. The novice on his side gains experience of the life and work of the community that will later be definitively his own, and he also has opportunities for forming personal friendships. An open novitiate may also make it possible for a novice to find a positive role in the community quite early. If he is to feel accepted and needed it is not enough that he should have opportunities for friendly social conversation with the older monks; he must have a job and render some definite service. It is possible otherwise to inhibit a novice's growth by waiting too long before using his talents. Further, contact with the larger group can preclude some of the tension, artificiality, and infantilism that have sometimes characterized closed novitiates, and may ease the novice's transition to a new status at profession. Finally, a community whose novices scarcely ever number more than one or two has little choice but to adopt a considerable degree of openness in its novitiate policy.[68]

On the other hand, while rigid apartheid is obviously undesirable, there is a good deal to be said in favour of retaining some measure of the traditional seclusion. The experience of learning to live at close quarters with his contemporaries can be invaluable to a novice, but it can be a painful experience and one that he could well evade by disappearing into the larger group of the professed community if allowed to do so. If he can make a success of living with his fellow-novices he is well initiated into the art of living community life. Again, few novices complete their course without personal crises and explosions, and these can be more fruitfully dealt with in relative seclusion. It is also desirable that beginners who as yet lack the stability and security of commitment by vows should not be too deeply involved in community problems which at this early stage are likely to have a disturbing or even destructive effect. Above all, a relatively secluded novitiate gives more opportunity for reflection on some of the deep essential realities of monastic life. The novice has come from a world where Christian values are often obscured, into a life which makes no sense except in faith. He needs to be brought up against himself, more deeply perhaps than before, and to base his decision about his vocation on the most fundamental realities. There is some danger of his escaping from self-knowledge and confrontation with God if he can too easily involve himself in the more superficial aspects of the community's affairs. In a climate of prayer, silence, faith, obedience, and reflection he has more chance of coming to grips with the real monastic issues and making a mature and responsible choice.

Formation team or novice master?

Another example of the discernment needed in finding the best novitiate structures is the choice between a formation team and a single novice master. The most obvious advantage of a team is the possibility it provides for tapping all available resources. One man cannot be all things to all men. A good teacher may not be a good spiritual guide, and a good organizer may be neither, but a team may include a teacher, an expert spiritual director, a man with a flair for organization, and perhaps others. Different types of people enter our monasteries and their varied needs may be more satisfactorily met by a team. From the novice's angle there can be something claustrophobic in finding that his contacts are virtually limited to one man where formation is concerned. There is moreover a certain precedent for the team method in tradition which has long recognized the role of zelator or assistant novice master. The use of a formation team may be an effective way of enabling the community to share responsibility in the training of its novices.

Here again, however, the traditional method has a good deal to commend it; the role of the novice master is of proven value. The need for stability and unity in direction is evident, and the novice should not be in a position to play one spiritual guide off against another, even half-consciously. Moreover, monastic tradition has always realized the significance of a right personal relationship in educating a young man in the ways of God; this insight is in fact older than Christian monasticism and may derive from the tradition of the Old Testament sages. It is good for the novice to face early the difficulties and demands of forming a right relationship with an imperfect human being in authority, and with a single novice master he cannot dodge the issue as he might with a formation team. Just as an 'open' novitiate might enable him to escape the challenge of right relationships with his peers, a formation team might afford a refuge from the challenge of a right relationship with the novice master with whom he has to come to terms. The difficulties that will probably arise sooner or later can be a valuable experience, if the novice encounters a more mature and stable personality.

2. Practical conclusions

However the novitiate is organized, its structures must not stand in the way of the development of a personal relationship between the abbot and a novice even from the beginning. This relationship is a Benedictine characteristic and is indispensable.

Further, it is obvious that in deciding on the best organization (for example, a single novice master or a team) the resources available in the community will be the main criteria. With regard to the choice between an open or a relatively closed novitiate, and between a team and a single novice master, it is usually possible in practice to combine some of the advantages of both methods by taking an intermediate position. With a novitiate that is in principle relatively closed it is usually possible to find some areas of the community's work into which novices can be integrated; this is especially true in the case of the nuns where there need be no great difference between the work of novices and that of the professed. And a single novice master can co-opt other members of the community with special competence to teach certain subjects, and so secure some of the benefits that would have come from a team, while a team almost certainly needs a leader and so may not lose the advantages of the single novice master.

3. The novice master

Perhaps the greatest service that can be rendered by a good novice master is to meet the novice's need for support and encouragement. When a novice is struggling to respond to his vocation and to grapple with his personal problems he needs the steady support of someone who knows him well in all his weaknesses but will go on believing in him when he has for the time being ceased to believe in himself.

The novice master's influence is, however, more general than this. Much theory about monastic life is absorbed during the novitiate, but unless the novice can see it working out in human living it will remain unconvincing or merely notional. It is in the novice master that he will first have the chance to see it, and this means that certain qualities are desirable in a good novice master. First of all he should be unmistakably sane and balanced, and thoroughly human. He needs to be a man of deep faith, humility, and prayer, who has experience of what he teaches and is open to the Spirit. If he is to educate young men to monastic life he must himself be truly monastic; this means that he must be convinced of the spiritual value of his way of life, and must be so steeped in the essentials of monastic tradition that he will not be excessively caught up in details or contingent forms of observance. Hence he should be able to rethink the tradition in terms of the contemporary situation and discern what is authentic in new expressions of ancient ideals. For such discernment he needs a sympathetic understanding of human nature, an openness to the minds and desires of others, especially the young, and an ability to listen. He may learn very much from the novices and think of his role as that of their companion in their search for God. All these qualities would be needed, *mutatis mutandis*, in a formation team.

4. Deepening of the novice's faith

Among the signs that a candidate is ready to start his training[69] is the fact that he has already achieved some initial degree of personal maturity and emotional stability; otherwise his novitiate will be largely spent in sorting out adolescent crises and emotional problems instead of being a genuine trial of his monastic vocation. However, there are many human problems and problems of faith which will inevitably arise in the novitiate; these should be faced and dealt with and should not be taken as a sign that the novice is unsuited to monastic life. It is unwise to presume so much certainty and clarity in a novice's mind that instruction can be limited to specifically monastic spirituality, leaving Christian doctrine and theological training until later. Fundamental questions of faith are likely to arise in the novitiate and can be seen as crises of growth and of prayer from which a novice emerges with a more mature faith.

He can also be helped in this deepening of faith by a well-integrated system of studies covering both novitiate and juniorate, in which 'spiritual' training in prayer, asceticism, the Rule, and similar topics is given from the first in the context of a wide programme of properly monastic studies. Study should not be regarded as simply a preparation for the priesthood. Some kind of co-operation by members of the community other than the novice master is necessary here and offers possibilities for further formation later on, reducing the danger that a newly professed monk may find himself in a vacuum and without support when he leaves the novitiate.

Growth in community

a) Lifelong call and formation

The novitiate is only the beginning of formation. The call is not a once-for-all event but a lifelong reality. The apostles followed Christ in obedience to his initial call, 'Come', but that was only the first step. They had no idea where it would lead them, but they went on following and being formed by him, to the cross and the resurrection and Pentecost and beyond, until their perfect conformation to him in their own death. All this was not foreseen but was accepted implicitly in advance in the obedience of faith. Similarly the Benedictine calling is an ongoing reality; entering the monastery is the first step, but from there a person has to go on in generous acceptance, in a continual 'Yes' to God, a daily choosing anew. We create our life as we go along, by creative free choices, and our formation into Christ continues until we are conformed to him in death. A monk can go on growing all his life, and it is important that he should be growing into monastic life rather than growing out. If God is calling him to the monastery the abbot and the community will be the living, loving environment through which the Spirit will work on him and fashion him in the likeness of Christ.

Maturity is not attained by our deliberately seeking it. Rather it comes with true knowledge of oneself and one's limitations, with humble realistic self-acceptance and with unreserved self-giving. He who loses his life will find it.[70] By living responsibly and giving himself in loving service to God and his brethren the monk finds a personal maturity that he would not have found through anxious preoccupation with his own growth.

b) Community life and growth in love

Hence no one can mature in isolation. Love is the driving force in a monk's life, and the community is there to sustain him in his love for God and to give him the chance to realize it effectively in loving and being loved by his brethren. He has to be involved with others to discover God and himself; he must be able to find both human and divine love in his community. A married man finds in his home and family the certainty of being needed, accepted, and loved. A monk must similarly sense that his community needs him, that he has something unique to give, and that his contribution is appreciated. But he must also be habitually aware that he is accepted, loved, and forgiven for his failings. The security that flows from the certainty of forgiveness is essential to human growth.

Unselfish, non-possessive friendships help to create a climate of deep acceptance.[71] Right friendships can be important even in the novitiate, and guidance in how to give and receive in healthy friendship can be a significant part of novitiate formation,[72] but real monastic friendships become still more vital later. They are not primarily affective or emotional, but they provide the certainty that one can speak one's mind freely and unburden oneself without being judged. Personal maturity and good community relationships imply the ability both to benefit from friendship oneself and to provide it for others. The ground of true monastic friendships is not primarily common commitment to a work project, such as a school, but monastic profession itself, whereby the community totally accepts a person with all his weaknesses.

c) Personal guidance

If a monk is to be helped all his life in his search for God it is clear that there is a need for spiritual guidance. The abbot is at the service of his monks; he above all creates the atmosphere in the community. His role as father and teacher, paramount in the Rule, is still a reality today.[73] If a formation team operates in the service of the novices, it may also be able to share the abbot's responsibility for the lifelong education of the community by organizing lectures and discussions, by providing reading for the refectory, and by any other means available. But personal, individual guidance is also needed, and in this area too the abbot's responsibility can be shared. Ample precedent for co-responsibility in the work of providing competent spiritual direction exists in the ancient monastic tradition of the 'spiritual senior',[74] which is paralleled in the Eastern Orthodox figure of the staretz. This kind of service is the one thing in which monks, precisely as monks, should be professionals; it should be rated high in a community's scale of values and kept in view in the allocation of manpower. The skill and wisdom of the spiritual seniors can help to 'educate', i.e. to 'bring out' the best in each monk, can help him to become Christlike in his own way, and so to grow all his life into the person God means him to be. Lifelong spiritual deepening is the effect of God's grace working through personal response, spiritual help, and the life of the monastery. In a good community life a monk can find everything he needs to help him in the struggle to establish unity in his own being and to respond to love.

9

Commitment to God in the Community

Introduction*

Historical patterns of vowing

Within the Christian tradition religious vows have found various expressions. The monastic practice of making vows of stability, conversion of life, and obedience existed for several centuries before the Church's theologians attempted to articulate the meaning of religious commitment. With scholastic theology the constitutive elements of a vowed Christian religious life came to be designated as poverty, chastity, and obedience. This scholastic theological tradition gave rise to the ecclesiastical norms for religious life that were eventually codified in canon law. Consequently contemporary monastic communities inherit two traditions concerning the form of religious vows. The Rule of St Benedict describes the monastic commitment in terms of stability within a community, conversion of life, and obedience under the Rule and an abbot. The majority of ecclesiastical documents emanating from the Congregation for Religious and Secular Institutes speak of the religious life as one lived in an approved institute in which the members have vowed poverty, chastity, and obedience.

The challenge to the human possibility of vowing

Before one can understand the nature of monastic commitment to God in the context of a community, the question of the viability of religious life in today's evolving society must be confronted. One must first of all have a clear grasp of the intelligibility of a vowed life in the Christian

* This material was originally published in *Benedictines* and appears here with the approval of the author, S. Mary Collins, O.S.B., and of the editor, S. Mary Paul Ege, O.S.B.; it has been edited for purposes of incorporation into this volume. We are very grateful for the permissions given.

tradition before one examines the Benedictine tradition of vowed life.

In the light of the canonical definition of a vow as a deliberate and free promise made to God concerning some good which is possible and better than its opposite,[1] two interrelated problems pertinent to a contemporary understanding of the making of religious vows must be discussed. Is an enduring vow humanly possible? Are religious vows made to God or to the human community? To answer these questions requires an understanding of what it means to be a human person.

a) Contemporary sense of impermanence

Until recently, little attention was paid in Catholic circles to those outside who claimed that religious vows were incomprehensible. Proponents of such a view were usually self-acknowledged critics of religion and religious experience. More recently the charge has been made even by people who claim to be religious that any enduring vow, marital or religious, is humanly impossible and therefore incomprehensible. An understanding of the nature of man and a concomitant world-view are at issue.

Among the powerful ideas bequeathed to the modern world by the nineteenth century is the doctrine of evolution: higher forms are continually developing out of lower. Originally a brilliant and imaginative synthesis of certain observed biological data, the idea of evolution has since the mid-nineteenth century been extrapolated from the field of biology and applied to all aspects of reality, mental and spiritual as well as physical. Although the applications have not always been justified, an evolutionary interpretation of life and experience colours the thinking of most educated people today. Contingency and impermanence characterize the universe and man who is part of it. The fact of continual change has led to the development of process philosophy which describes man as one who is always undergoing creation. In this context the question is urgently raised: Is there anything permanent or fixed in the world?

We live in a throw-away culture, experiencing the accelerated pace of change in human institutions as they are confronted with change in human needs and desires. We experience the transformation of persons as they become increasingly conscious of their human potential. Persons and their relationships, then, are not constant. Even God, recognized in faith to be infinitely reliable, has revealed himself as baffling and elusive. The Israelites learned that their God was in many ways unpredictable.

Though always faithful to his promises, God constantly summoned his people to achieve what was humanly impossible and to attain the unexpected. The new covenant which God made with his people in the Lord Jesus is a call to achieve that which is naturally impossible, namely deliverance from the alienation and isolation that characterize human existence,[2] into the freedom of the sons of God.

Contemporary theology has addressed itself to the religious implications of man's consciousness of his own contingency and impermanence. Awareness of a constantly changing world has challenged the Church itself to acknowledge its provisional status as the servant of God in history and as a community of pilgrim people. Living in this contingent and uncertain situation, many Christians today ask whether man can know himself and his God well enough to risk binding himself to God for a lifetime.

b) Man's openness to God's revelation

In the light of Christian faith man has been described as a creature who is open to God and in need of God. He discovers himself as a creature who is capable of making choices which determine to a great extent the person he is becoming. As a Christian, he believes that God is operative everywhere in human life. God's presence to man establishes an orientation in human life which radically transcends man's natural powers. What makes man truly human is the call to share in the divine. Given this human self-understanding it is certainly true that no man can know either himself or God so completely that his relationship to God can be predicted throughout a lifetime.

A man cannot come to know who he is unless he is informed by another. Since man's destiny is divine, it is ultimately God's word that initiates him into self-knowledge. The Lord Jesus begins even now to reveal to us who we are. But the Word of God who became incarnate in Christ is in some way present to man in human conversation everywhere and always. God is for ever revealing himself to man in and through Christ. The history in which God reveals himself is not simply the history of the Church. Because of his faith in the Lord who sends his Spirit to renew the face of the whole earth, the Christian believes that he can hear God's word and respond to it everywhere and always. Man and God are related in an inevitable dialogue. The radically divine act is to come and to call forth; the radically human act is to reach out and to respond.

For the man of Christian faith who devotes himself to a life of explicit search for God and an acknowledgement of his presence in history, contingency and uncertainty in life are basic to man's reception of God's further revelation of himself in history. Given this understanding, the man of faith is not thwarted by the provisional and unpredictable nature of life's experiences. On the contrary, if there existed the possibility of clear knowledge of God and oneself at any moment of human history, only then would the act of vowing oneself to God *in faith* become unintelligible.

A man is summoned to hear God's word spoken throughout his whole life; and so it makes sense to a man of religious faith to bind himself for a lifetime to attentive listening and response to God's revealing presence. It is this understanding of man which underlies the assumption that man can seek God best by a permanent commitment.

Vowing to God

a) Personal commitment and the changing self

The act of binding oneself to listen and respond to God in faith is thus a humanly intelligible act, in harmony with what we know of the nature of man and the self-revelation of God. But the crux and scandal is the assertion that such a commitment can intelligibly and justifiably take the particular form of binding oneself for life to continue the listening and the response within a definite context, such as marriage to a particular person or the framework of monastic vows. This very specific decision is mysterious; it is grounded in faith and in the individual's conviction that God wants precisely this of him. That such a decision is not necessarily unreasonable or impossible can be shown from our experience of the meaning of free promises.

An essential element in human life, or at least civilized life, is that a person can pledge himself to future action and that his fellows can count on the pledge being kept. In the traditional human code underlying our civilization it is recognized that to keep a promise is honourable, to break it without coercion dishonourable, and to keep it in circumstances of great difficulty a mark of supreme excellence. Every engagement between men, whether of supply and delivery or of labour, service, and remuneration, depends on fidelity to a given word. The value and necessity of this fidelity are most obvious where personal relationships of love are involved, but any 'I and Thou' relationship immediately raises the question of the changing, developing reality of the human person engaged.

Personal development is not chaos, however, nor a process of random change; there is an underlying continuity of the person, and while freedom may be growing there is also the gradual building of a character which is the living and unique centre of the free responses. Growth includes integration, an increasingly rich unification of the understanding, experiences, ideals, and powers of the person round the central core of his identity. This process implies acceptance of oneself and the realities of the world in the light of one's own destiny as so far understood, and the most powerful factor in its furtherance is love. As a person grows to maturity he becomes more – not less – capable of honouring a promise. Serious engagement to fidelity 'for better or for worse' therefore becomes a possibility. Even though there may be a sense of change on both sides,

> . . . love is not love
> which alters when it alteration finds,
> or bends with the remover to remove. . . .[3]

and it can grow towards the constancy described by St Paul in 1 Corinthians 13. To say to another, 'for ever', is to express in quantitative terms a certain quality of loving: that is, the unconditionality of love which cannot be satisfied by the partial and revocable. Among Christians such fidelity in loving, whether in marriage or in religious life, is explicitly recognized as the fruit of grace and is sustained by faith in God who is a partner in any Christian covenant.

A promise made and accepted involves two partners; the 'other' to whom we promise is in some sense committed too. Religious or monastic vows are promises made to the living God, who has been the first to promise and who has shown himself faithful; they are accepted by the Church in his name. The person who vows is not alone, nor does he rely on his own fidelity; he stakes his life on the faithfulness of God.[4] His vocation is God's gift, and therefore the vows are more truly understood as the acceptance of a gift than as the undertaking of obligations.

It has sometimes been pointed out, however, in connection with celibacy, that since celibacy is a charism we have no right to assume that God cannot later withdraw his gift. According to St Paul charisms are relative; love alone abides for ever.[5] To this it may be replied that we should not isolate celibacy or any other particular engagement from monastic life as a whole; there is a charism of monasticity, and this does include the notion of permanent commitment. Yet even this does not eliminate the mystery. The root of meaning in monastic vows is the making over of a human person to God in love. Normally this dedication is lived out in the community of profession, in that form of life which was the direct object of the promise. But there can be rare occasions when a special call from God or a special need may involve separation from the community, or even from monastic life, without breaking the engagement to God.[6] The relationship to God can be estimated by him alone, and one should not too readily assume that there has been a rupture, even when there has been a dispensation from vows.

Profession remains, therefore, a real risk of faith. But it is man's nature to take risks. No human security can ultimately intervene between the person and God.

b) Choice, faith, and structures

No claim is made that a religious community is the only context in which a Christian can pursue a life inspired by the gospel. But the need and power to choose and to stand by one's choice are part of human dignity, and any decision implies (as the word itself suggests: *decidere* = to cut away) the cutting off of other possibilities incompatible with the course chosen. It is a psychological trap to think that by remaining uncommitted one is more free. Each person approaching adulthood must experience his limitations, which reveal that a man cannot orientate his life in all directions at once. Everything beautiful and noble, everything that might be possible in itself, cannot be crammed into one life. Therefore at a certain moment each person must begin to focus his life and its development in a specific direction. Direction is necessary for meaning, and therefore refusal to choose because he wants to remain open to all possibilities will not favour personal growth. If he is a believer this choice has the character of response to the word of God to which he is trying to listen in his life; to the extent that it is truly a faith-commitment it carries in itself the element of risk. To turn to the God who offers himself not only in general human history but in the particularity of everyday life, to choose to be open, and to say 'Yes' with one's life to him does not immunize the believer against risk and anguish.

Here we confront the mystery of incarnational faith. Monastic vows are a lifetime commitment to search for God not in the abstract but in the midst of human history and the concrete realities of daily life. Man cannot live humanly at any level without organizing his approach to existence. He must create structures to support his search for meaning and to preserve what he values: in this case, the Lord's revelation of himself. This is the origin of religious institutions and the reason for their endurance.

However, in maintaining those institutions which originally supported consciousness of God the Christian often loses contact with the primordial experience of persons, things, and events in which God's presence was first and is still to be known. Often the very sacred symbols which ought to reveal God obscure his presence. Religious institutions and a language of symbols grew out of the commitment to God of persons who had gone down in faith to the roots of their being, who embodied their awareness of God and supported their response to him in forms that inevitably were limited and culturally conditioned. The maintenance of these forms may provide subsequent generations with a vehicle for the same awareness of the living God and commitment to him. Unfortunately they may also serve as a tranquillizer or an insulation against the risk of faith.

In his efforts to see that God alone is adored, the Christian must therefore often be soberly iconoclastic with regard to the idols pretending to be God in his life. In the Old Testament absolute reverence for and adoration of anything less than God himself was called idolatry. Contemporary man in his experience of misdirected allegiance is apt to speak of alienation from authentic existence. Religious man today frequently asserts that the very preservation of certain institutions can have the effect of alienating him from his search for God's presence. The same religious conviction which has led persons to vow their lives to God may also prompt disaffection from existing religious institutions.

It is a central tenet of most religious communities from the time of St Benedict down to the present that one of the best supports for a publicly committed religious life is a stable community of similarly committed persons. However, it is only by continual effort that any stable community of religious can remain open to development and able to counteract the pull towards institutionalism which generates alienation among its members. Institutionalism prevails whenever the arrangements made with a view to supporting the vow to seek God become obstacles to genuine religious experience. Perhaps we can understand some of the contemporary questioning by vowed religious themselves of the possibility of lifetime commitment in a single community if we recognize that any institution humanly conceived and maintained, even a religious institution, can at some time become an alienating factor.

The underlying error is the failure to recognize the relative character of everything that structures man's search for God. The Christian must remember that he will never achieve perfect fulfilment in this present life and that the structures which support his search for God will always be inadequate. The stable commitment to vowed life, being made to God, transcends the commitment to a particular set of institutional arrangements. And yet vowed life must find support in a human community with concrete provisions that will assist each person to seek God in historical situations involving persons, places, and things.

The vow of stability taken explicitly by many monastic communities and implicitly by other religious congregations in the Church constitutes the ultimate paradox for the contemporary man or woman who understands the problems of idolatry, religious alienation, and institutionalism. With their awareness of this paradox, some religious have proposed as an alternative a conditional commitment in which the individual religious and the community set forth agreed conditions under which the commitment to stability within the community will be honoured. Certainly such an arrangement would obviate the risks of idolatry and alienation in the process of vowing oneself to a lifetime of seeking God. Unfortunately, however, it would also introduce a constant process of mutual evaluation and the testing of each other's trustworthiness.

The cenobitic tradition of vowing oneself to God through a local community transcends all consideration whether the given community of persons is to be viewed as reliable and worthy of full trust in advance. The writings of a modern philosopher on the possibility of fidelity to one's word suggest that the person vowing himself must not extend unlimited credit to or demand a warranty from the community in which he makes his vow. 'I can usually call into question the reality of the bond linking me to some particular being; in this domain disappointment is always possible. . . . But on the other hand, the more my consciousness is centred on God himself . . . the less conceivable this disappointment will be.'[7] We cannot count on anyone less than God as support in the adventure of finding him.

Near the beginning of this Introduction two questions were raised about the contemporary understanding of religious vows. In the discussion of the first (Is an enduring vow humanly possible?) the answer to the second (Are religious vows made to God or to the human community?) has already emerged. At the present time the Church has authorized religious communities to accept from new members promises to the community rather than direct vows to God. These promises cannot be construed as equivalent to traditional religious vows. The Church maintains its traditional understanding that such vows are a fundamental commitment to God.

Conclusion

In accepting the gift and making his vows a person pledges himself in faith to the God who knows from the outset the whole life of his servant, both what he is and what he will be. Only in the context of faith can the apparent conflict be resolved between the traditionally recognized value of constant fidelity to one's pledged word and the contemporary value of authenticity in one's personal life at every stage of growth and development. Faith in the living God is the absolute precondition for vowed religious life. Where it exists, lifelong commitment in a religious community is a human possibility, even within the world-view of contemporary western culture, dominated as it is by the awareness of impermanence. Its possibility depends, first, on a personal living faith in God as the one who speaks to man in human history; and, second, on a self-understanding which acknowledges that even while experiencing the necessary limitations of human life in time and space, man can be open and receptive to the God who calls him to a fulfilment beyond them.

Stability

Having considered the general question of the intelligibility of a vowed life, we now turn to the explicit and implicit vows taken by monks and nuns in the Benedictine tradition. It is probable that St Benedict thought of stability, conversatio morum, *and obedience not as three separate vows but as three aspects of the single, total commitment to monastic life. But since it has long been customary to mention them separately in the formula of profession, the following chapters treat them as distinct.*

And first, stability, which though not a new concept in St Benedict's time was more stressed by him than by his predecessors, and has come to be regarded as one of his most characteristic contributions.

For men truly seeking God, St Benedict proposed a life in community under a rule and an abbot as the setting in which they would come to know God. He invited them to make a public commitment of their intention to obey God by reaffirming the basic promise of conversion which the Christian makes at baptism. He proposed to give a structure and order to the monk's professed desire for conversion through the discipline of life shared with an abbot and a community. St Benedict stands in the cenobitic tradition which reacted against the abuses associated with wandering monks. He required that those who entered his monastery should commit themselves to persevere in obedience even in times of difficulties and contradictions.[1] In the Rule stability is discussed in terms of the monk's continual search for God, his residence within the monastery and community, and his perseverance in the monastic vocation.[2] The monk 'should say nothing and hold fast to patience in his heart, enduring all without growing weary or giving up. For Scripture says: He who endures to the end will be saved.'[3] Standing firm, or patient perseverance in obedience, is fundamental to what St Benedict means by stability,[4] for stability is the outward expression of perseverance.

In an attempt to understand St Benedict's treatment of stability, we shall discuss first the legal, then the personal, then the communal and geographical aspects of the vow.

a) Legal stability

Although St Benedict was unfamiliar with the legal technicalities that later surrounded monastic profession,[5] he did presume that a monk would remain in the monastery of his profession.[6] However, he did not make geographical stability in a particular community an end in itself. Stability should not be interpreted in such a rigid way that every departure of a monk from the monastery of his profession is looked upon as a kind of apostasy. There is sufficient precedent in the lives of holy monks[7] to indicate that a change of place or a transfer to a different community may sometimes be desirable for a monk.

b) Personal stability

St Benedict was above all concerned with the monk's stability in his search for God. The novice seeking admission to the monastery is to be examined to see if he is truly seeking God; he is to be told the difficulties of the way that leads to God and asked if he will persevere in that way. In Chapter 58 and also in the Prologue St Benedict links perseverance with patience, which he interprets in its original sense of suffering. Stability involves both bearing from day to day the inevitable trials and disappointments which are part of human life and profiting from them. By persevering in obedience even to death the monk responds to the words of Christ, 'If any man would come after me, let him deny himself and take up his cross daily and follow me.'[8] Stability ensures that he will not evade the cross, particularly the cross of obedience.

Stability in faithful response to God's love assures the monk that he will share in the Kingdom.

As we go forward in our monastic life and in faith, we shall find our hearts expanding, and we shall run along the way of God's commandments with a delight of love that cannot be described, so that, never leaving his guidance but persevering in his teaching until death in the monastery, we may by patience share in the sufferings of Christ, and so deserve to share also in his Kingdom.[9]

God's faithful love for men was consummated in the giving of his Son, who is the 'Amen', the 'Yes' by which God ratifies all his promises.[10] This faithfulness was mirrored in the human response of Jesus Christ to the Father, and is shared by all who find in their union with Christ the strength to say 'Yes' to God. The Church responds to God with a created echo of the unconditional stability of his own commitment to men. Although the vows represent a man's offering to God, what he offers has first been created in him by God. So stability of heart is first God's gift to man, and when a monk vows it he does so in response to the abiding faithfulness of God.

c) Communal and geographical stability

There are various texts in the Rule where stability clearly means stability of place. The monk is a member of a particular monastery and a particular community. In Chapter 60 St Benedict stipulates that clerics who may wish to join the monastery must promise to observe the Rule and to remain in the monastery. The same is required of monks who may come from another community.[11] In contrast to the gyrovagues, St Benedict's monks are to be stable in one community.[12] At the end of Chapter 4 he indirectly links stability with community life when he describes the monastery and stability in the community as a workshop where the monks labour with the tools of good works, many of which are concerned with fraternal charity.

Perseverance in the monastic life normally involves permanence in the same community and the same monastery. Because he commits himself to a specific community by public profession of stability, the monk will share the geographic stability of that community. But the emphasis in St Benedict's Rule is not on the material dimension of stability, permanence in a place; it is rather on the spiritual dimension. Obedience to the abbot, and community commitments too, may require a monk's absence from the monastery. Therefore stability is basically a faithful and shared experience of life, of which physical presence is a normal but not indispensable sign. It is with stability of heart that monks must be principally concerned. It is possible for a monk to remain within the confines of the monastery all his life and still be unstable in the Benedictine sense. He may become so preoccupied with his own work that he has time neither for God nor for the community. A monk's heart must be genuinely committed to God and to the community, or else he will seek diversions which will deflect him from his vocation.

At a time when inherited structures are changing, the real ground of stability becomes clearer: it is a 'belonging to the people' who make up one's own community. Genuine belonging demands continual conversion of heart for the sake of trust. The real enemy of stability is not moving about but personal alienation, and especially the alienation which is not a passing pain but a rigid habit. To be fixed in a personal hardness, or to make it difficult for others to escape from such an attitude, is not stability but staticness. The community can discourage growth and conversion in its members by labelling people, by not expecting them to change or by not believing it when they have. If the community were not made up of persons seeking God through conversion of life, there would be no reason why loyalty to a given group of human beings should be made the object of a vow. But if the community is an assembly of believers trying to be open to God in continual conversion of heart, then their shared faith, common prayer, fraternal concern, and mutual trust will constitute invaluable support for each monk publicly committed to a life of conversion. By search for and response to the revelation of God in the midst of the community, both the individual monk and the community as a whole will come to share more deeply in the mystery of Christ.

Incarnate love for one's own community, as for the family into which one is born, is not the same as an unrealistic idealization of it or a sense of superiority with regard to other communities. Stability implies a total acceptance of it with all its shortcomings, and acceptance of an inheritance which has in large measure made the community what it is. A monk loves his own community not as unchangeable or static, not as already perfect, but as the sacrament of the divine mercy in his life. He acknowledges his need for his brothers, a need which is well fulfilled in a stable community. He needs others because of Jesus Christ. If acceptance of one's own poverty is the original conversion, then to be a Christian is to be needy and to recognize that this is a state of blessedness. Only the poor man can grow rich in the gift of another; so only a poor man can be enriched by God and saved in Jesus Christ. But this enrichment, this salvation, comes to the Christian above all through other people. He needs his brothers to express his love for Christ; he needs them if he is to hear the word of God proclaimed; and he needs them in order to communicate and share the word of God which he has himself received.

A monk also acknowledges his need for some geographic stability. The world is not simply something given to man as an object to be examined and put to use. The world is man's home at the present time.

But being at home in the world implies a certain rootedness, 'a grafting on to the local scene'.[13] This human need to be rooted in a particular locality is behind the monastic exercise of stability with reference both to material objects and to people. A tree often transplanted does not bear fruit. A man usually comes to know himself, and in that knowledge to know God, when he dwells for long periods in a stable relationship to places and persons. The sense of belonging which is generated by familiar surroundings tends to create a focus for man's awareness, so that he is able to ask himself, 'Who am I? Where have I come from and where am I going?' This sense of belonging grows even more from stability in relation to persons, from knowledge of the constancy and predictability of persons established over a long period of familiarity, and from the mutual trust, love, respect, and appreciation which come about only with time and struggle. It is part of the essence of man to be in a situation; hence he is able to receive and integrate his surroundings into himself. There is a close link between the questions, 'Who am I?' and 'Where am I?' Through his incarnate situation man discovers his identity and his true relation to God.

A man will be able to share his life adequately with others and receive other men only if he has also begun to know his own identity. This knowledge comes with the capacity to be at home in a particular situation. A man must first create his world before he can welcome someone else. In the same way as man is humanized by his environment, the environment is humanized by man. But various tendencies militate against man's being at home in the world. Rapid developments in communications media have led to man's being surfeited by external stimuli. This results in the sterility of human meetings when not enough time elapses to allow the individual to assimilate and evaluate what has happened to him. Through his vow of stability a monk commits himself to patient growth and development, so that he has a sense of continuity in his life.[14] His self-awareness spans the years and is not confined to a series of interrupted moments of consciousness. He is aware that the Kingdom of God is to be found in our midst. He is stable in his search for that Kingdom though provisional in the structures which he establishes to facilitate the search.

Stability of commitment, thus understood, cannot be static, because life is not static; it is always either growth and development, or disintegration and a sinking into death. If stability is a living commitment of love it must therefore deepen and mature as the person grows. In marriage the partners cannot remain fixated at the level of mutual commitment proper to the honeymoon or even to the first few years of their relationship; as they change and grow they must grow into their marriage and deepen their commitment, integrating into their love all the experience of life, joy and suffering, failure, self-knowledge, maturity, and broadening horizons. This is just as true of monastic stability. It is not merely a precondition for growth in monastic life; if it is really to be an aid to continuous, lifelong growth it must be reaffirmed and chosen anew at times of crises and testing and in the light of unfolding experience of what the original commitment meant. This is true for all the vows, but the nature of the vow of stability brings the need into sharper focus.[15]

d) Witness value of stability

Monastic stability in its personal, communal, and geographical aspects has significant witness value in our contemporary world. A fundamental ministry consists in representing the New Testament ideal of the brotherly community among men that is possible only in Christ.[16] This perspective opened up by the vow of stability shows that community does not exist only for utilitarian purposes, such as team work or division of labour. Community life is an evangelical witness; it is an existential proclamation and a manifestation of a feature proper to the essence of Christianity. The proclamation of the Easter message is possible only when the Church is a community. As long as we do not transcend our differences of origin, social status, training, and tastes in order to unite with one another, we are not truly Christian. The gift of Christ is precisely that he has broken down the dividing walls that isolate men from one another.[17]

Through the vow of stability Benedictines bear witness, in a torn and individualistic world, to Christian unity which knows how to overcome barriers. Unity among the brethren is demanded by Christ in order that the world may believe. Life in community is by its very nature a specialization in the Church's fundamental structure designed to foster belief in those who do not profess faith in Christ. To live in community is to make the approach to Christ more clearly visible. Likewise the vitality and the unity of mind and heart that are proper to a Benedictine community make it a place where new life-experiences may be evaluated in a critical yet unprejudiced way. In an unstable world where life is characterized by mobility and fragmentation, a Benedictine community can be a centre where life is deeply experienced and where others come not only to share in silence and prayer, but also to discuss the social realities of the present time. The question with which many people are immediately concerned is not whether God exists, but whether the power of Jesus Christ can really so transform men that the values of the gospel are expressed in personal and social life-styles. Stable monastic life confronts the fleeting character of human experience, so evident today, and seeks an understanding of the meaning of life itself. It warns man that he must constantly purify his heart. It shows people the actual repercussions of fraternal love and makes clear each man's responsibility to live in peace with his neighbours.

The basic simplicity of the monastic way of life can help people to realize that material progress is the servant of life, not its master. God can be glorified by technology as much as by untamed nature, and monks must accept technological advances, though without accepting uncritically the value-systems that often go with them. The humanizing of the environment by man can be greatly furthered by the discerning application of modern skills, but technology will fulfil this purpose only if used with wisdom and a sense of direction that keep the priorities right and resist the claim of the profit-motive to oust all others. This technology is serving its true purpose when it enables men to dwell in communities which are of a size to allow for genuine concern and collaboration, which provide the leisure necessary for personal development and which give them working conditions that are humane. In so far as monastic communities realize these aims, they can be a stabilizing factor in society itself, their members bearing witness by peace and simplicity of life-style, a shared Christian life of response to God's self-revelation, and a stable commitment to God and to one another in Christ.

Conversion and Asceticism

Man needs roots in order to grow, and the vow of stability, considered in the preceding chapter, consecrates this aspect of his humanity to God. But he is also a pilgrim on earth, having here no abiding city, and he is a sinner on the way home to his forgiving Father, responding to the call of a God who is always out ahead, baffling and mysterious. The second of the vows formulated in the Benedictine tradition is that of conversion, which consecrates a monk or nun to God under this different aspect.

Introduction

The phrase *conversatio morum* or *conversio morum* has an archaic ring and is difficult to translate into modern languages, but the meaning of this second Benedictine vow is as new, and as old, as the gospel itself. It expresses the monk's decision to follow Christ in the spirit of the gospel by faithfully living the monastic life.

Conversatio meant for the ancients a definite 'way of life', the context making clear what particular type of life was envisaged. In monastic contexts the word was therefore used as the practical equivalent of 'monastic life' or 'the profession of a monk'.[1] When the novice makes his promise *de . . . conversatione morum suorum*, he is, in St Benedict's mind, engaging himself to live the whole monastic life according to the Rule. There is an integrity and breadth about the promise to which later analytic notions that seek to define precisely 'the object of the vow' are foreign. He vows to be a monk, and the Rule as a whole, interpreted in the light of monastic experience, makes clear the content of the promise. This obviously includes celibacy and personal poverty, which are thus covered by the vow. But St Benedict interprets it above all in terms of persevering obedience to God.[2]

The richness and complexity of St Benedict's notion of *conversatio* are best illustrated by the vivid ending of his Prologue:

144

So we must establish a school of the Lord's service. . . . If for good reason, for the amending of bad habits or the preservation of charity, there be some strictness of discipline, do not immediately be alarmed and run away from the way of salvation (*viam salutis*), the entrance to which is necessarily narrow (*angusto initio incipienda*). But as we make progress in our monastic life and in faith (*processu . . . conversationis et fidei*) our hearts will be enlarged, and we shall run (*curritur via*) in the way of God's commandments with unspeakable sweetness of love; so that, never abandoning his rule but persevering until death in his teaching in the monastery (*ab ipsius numquam magisterio discedentes, in eius doctrina usque ad mortem in monasterio perseverantes*), we shall share by patience in the passion of Christ, so that we may deserve to be partakers also in his Kingdom.

All the essential ideas are here. The monastery is a school where the monk learns to serve God; this service is concerned with getting rid of vices and growing in charity. The life is a way, a road. It has an entrance, it represents a persevering, lifelong journey and it leads to perfection in love; similarly in Chapter 73.3–5 St Benedict speaks of the *initium conversationis* and the *perfectionem conversationis*. *Conversatio* is very closely linked with faith; they may even be synonymous. It is a way of life in which monks share in Christ's passion and travel towards union with him in glory. Monastic *conversatio* is enduring and dynamic.

The spirituality of the Rule is thus a spirituality of *metanoia*, not simply in the sense that being a monk is the living out of the initial conversion implied in becoming a monk,[3] but rather because monastic life is a continuous conversion: a turning away from sin, a sharing in the passion of Christ and a growth in love. The process is described in RB 7, though the word *conversatio* does not occur there; and in the Prologue the monk is addressed as God's sinful son who has strayed away from his Father by the 'sloth of disobedience' but now seeks to return to him by the 'labour of obedience'.[4] This element of 'turning' or 'returning' by means of a change of direction in one's life is inherent in the monastic vocation. A man's decision to enter the monastery implies that he has opted for a certain set of values and has determined to give a specific orientation to his life. By his basic decision he enters upon a lifelong task of conversion. It is not surprising, therefore, that the phrase *conversio morum* began to occur very early as a substitute for *conversatio morum*, since it was both more readily intelligible than the latter and a just epitome of the spirit of monastic life.[5]

Conversion is a rich biblical theme. In Christian and monastic tradition it is closely associated with asceticism. The content of the Benedictine vow, then, is best explained in a biblical context and in conjunction with asceticism in the monastery.

The biblical doctrine of conversion

a) The Old Testament

The Old Testament is an account of God's repeated attempts to convert his people to himself. In the covenant which he made with his people God invited them to accept the gift of his life-giving word which alone could deliver them from their bondage and isolation. The response he sought was a penitent heart, one open to hear and accept the saving word of God. The Old Testament concept of sin presupposed a personal relationship between Israel and God. It implied a violation of the covenant through which God united himself to his people in an enduring bond of love, and through which the people were united among themselves.

The idea of conversion was worked out principally by the Old Testament prophets. They asserted that man must acknowledge the absolute demands of God, and then proceed to repent and confess his sins and obey God in faith and trust.[6] As time went on, the prophets were struck by the total impossibility of the sinner converting himself. Jeremiah proclaimed a divine intervention which would enable hardened hearts to come to a new knowledge of God.[7] In its final development in the Old Testament conversion meant the return of the sinner to a personal and loving God, a return made possible by God's own grace.

b) The New Testament

As the last of the prophets, John the Baptist appealed for a change of heart. He preached a baptism which symbolized man's conversion and confession of sin.[8] Conversion meant not only a repentance of past sins but a radical change of life. The Baptist also gave conversion an eschatological character, since he linked it with the imminent coming of God's reign and of the Messiah who would inaugurate that reign.

Although only a few sayings of Jesus specifically mention conversion, the synoptics are clear that salvation has come in the person of Jesus

Christ, and that acceptance of salvation demands a profound conversion of heart (*metanoia*). Such a repentance consists essentially in faith in the person and mission of Jesus Christ. This was the substance of Christ's own teaching: 'The kingdom of God is close at hand. Repent and believe the Good News.'[9] When Jesus declares that he has come to call not the just but sinners, he implies that God is ready to pardon the greatest of sinners, and that in the person of Jesus God is himself taking the initiative and offering pardon to all.[10] As the gospels often indicate, Christ's message of conversion naturally came into conflict with human self-sufficiency in its various forms.[11]

In the Acts of the Apostles the invitation to conversion is linked with the resurrection of Jesus. Not only are repentance and conversion regarded as gifts of God,[12] but they are looked upon as effects of the Easter mystery and are associated with the saving work of the risen Christ.[13] In the Pauline and Johannine writings conversion has evolved into faith which implies assent to the new covenant and total dedication of one's life to Christ.[14]

Conversion in the Church

The mystery of redemption that everywhere summons man is proclaimed and celebrated in the Church. The involvement of God in the redemption of man was first fully manifested in Jesus Christ. In our own time it is in the community of believers that both the call to conversion and the power to be converted to Jesus Christ are present.[15] The content of the call is a summons to receive God who communicates himself, liberates man from enslaving idols, and makes it possible for him to hope for full liberation and freedom with the final coming of Jesus Christ.[16]

Conversion is *faith* as a concrete concern about the call, and as obedient reception of Jesus Christ who is the content of the message. It is *hope* as trusting oneself to an uncharted way of life which leads into an incalculable future where God comes to man. It is *love* as a giving of oneself to one's neighbour because this is evidence of a real love of God. Conversion implies a sober realization that one's whole life must be open to the possibility of change, since God is constantly revealing himself to man in the gift of new life.

The need for conversion applies not only to individual Christians but also to the whole Church and to every local community within the

Church. It is celebrated symbolically and effectively in the liturgy of Lent. A community which realizes its need for constant conversion and renewal provides a supportive and challenging context for the individual person to hear the call and accept the power to be converted to Jesus Christ.

Conversion in the monastery

The vow of conversion is in a sense the most explicitly 'evangelical' of the monastic vows. It pledges the monk to the renunciation of all that would make him 'ashamed of the gospel',[17] the gospel of free salvation in Christ for all who know their sin and their need. At the heart of the Good News is the disconcerting reversal of merely human expectations: the mighty are pulled down from their thrones and the lowly exalted; the hungry are filled and the rich sent away empty; the poor man obedient unto the death of the cross is exalted and receives a name above every other name. Worldly value-scales are turned upside down; human self-sufficiencies, whether of power, wealth, grabbing, or moral self-righteousness, are rejected; the Kingdom stands open to the poor and the repentant. The spirit of the Sermon on the Mount and the Beatitudes is the 'logic' of every authentic Christian conversion, and is central to the monastic ideal of conversion of heart.[18] The vision may be blurred by institutionalism, and still more by personal infidelity, but the freshness of the original inspiration is re-created whenever a monk turns back again to the Lord, aware of his own poverty and need of mercy, and heartened to begin anew in the power of the forgiveness he finds. The motive for this continuous willingness to be converted, an experience so deflating to human self-esteem, can only be love.[19]

By his profession of conversion, a monk bears witness to the dynamic character of Christian life. He implicitly rejects a static concept of perfection based solely on rules, and chooses rather a free response to God's summons spoken in the challenges of human persons and events. He attempts to be docile to the Spirit urging both within his own person and in his concrete historical situation. He is convinced that only when Christ returns in glory will the image of Christ in him be finally perfected by the work of the Spirit, but he confesses that his salvation in Christ is already being accomplished here and now.[20]

The monk's conversion takes place within the context of a community of faith which is meant to support, encourage, and build up the brethren.

The monk benefits from the support of good example given by his brethren as they pray, suffer, work, study, and recreate together. But just as the monk's own fidelity to his commitment is influenced by the good example of his brethren, so too he has the responsibility to give support and encouragement to others so that they may continue to be converted to the Lord. The monk's own experience of difficulties and doubts should help him to be sympathetic with the failures and difficulties of others. In this light it is clear why St Benedict stressed the malice of murmuring in the monastery:[21] this vice destroys the very core of community life and tends to weaken the continuing conversion of the brethren.

The vowing of lifelong conversion is not an affirmation of faith in one's own moral character or strength of purpose. It is rather an acknowledgement in faith that one expects that throughout one's lifetime the living God will reveal himself and invite one to live and be reborn in unexpected ways. If the vow of stability within the community is the response to the utter reliability and faithfulness of God to his people, the vow of conversion is a response to the experience of God's unpredictability. The spirit of lifelong conversion entails a willingness not to cling to the signs that have, for a time, been the bearers of God's grace and presence; it entails a constant letting-go, a consent to having one's successive idols successively smashed. The vow of conversion implies growth in readiness for, and openness to, the inbreaking of God's Kingdom. It implements St Paul's words: 'Forgetting what is behind me, and reaching out for that which lies ahead, I press towards the goal to win the prize which is God's call to the life above, in Christ Jesus.'[22] Not only must the individual monk be open to the unpredictability of God, but the monastic community as a whole must learn to live provisionally in order to respond to the new challenges that God gives to his people as history unfolds.

Asceticism in the monastery

a) Asceticism in general

Traditionally Christian asceticism has meant the deliberate and persevering endeavour to respond to the grace of God offered to man in Christ. Since there are many obstacles to such an endeavour, asceticism necessarily implies painful struggle, self-denial, and renunciation. Positively the term implies a turning towards God and one's neighbour in love. It is of value only if it is accompanied by an honest acceptance of, and reverence for, the created order, and a sense of responsibility for the world and its development.

Since monastic life is a concrete living out of one's baptismal commitment, it implies a daily dying to sin and crucifixion with Jesus Christ. It is a life of mortification which means a denial of all that hinders a person's free response to God. Although the monk has been converted to God in Christ, sin still has power over him. Hence he acknowledges the need for asceticism so that he may die totally to sin and come to the fulness of resurrection. Through obedience to God's word and through the use of the tools of good works he progresses towards that perfection which Jesus Christ will accomplish when he returns in glory.

b) Asceticism and faith

The fundamental Christian asceticism is the response of faith to God's gift of himself. God who makes himself known in his revelation must be answered, not once but every day. This acceptance of faith not only brings fulfilment and enlightenment; it also implies a renunciation on man's part. In faith the Christian accepts the mystery of God[23] and gives himself to God in trust without knowing fully what has been promised;[24] he also renounces any isolated attempt of his own to find the meaning of his existence and of the world in general.[25] The believer orientates both the world and himself towards God, and no longer holds fast to the created things which alone would seem to provide fulfilment. He no longer builds his life on himself and his own person, but on God.

In order to transcend himself, the Christian must first accept himself, his painful limitations, weaknesses, and inadequacies, and also the sorrows, disappointments, and frustrations of life. In the end he must accept death itself as the ultimate absurdity of human existence. It is only when a man accepts himself and his own life that he is able to acknowledge and accept God as his saviour in Jesus Christ. Only when such an obedience of faith is practised daily do the various ascetical practices common in Christian and monastic tradition make sense. They must be based on the obedience of faith, integrated with it, and pervaded with its spirit.

As a Christian the monk is mindful of his own sinfulness and his need for repentance. His life is always to have a Lenten character.[26] He associates sin with suffering and death, and accepts them because of his own guilt. Daily experience of the gap between his ideals and his performance, of his weakness and inconstancy, and of his total inability to save himself, means that his relationship with God is one of habitual compunction. As the old monastic fathers understood it, compunction is the opposite of morbid self-absorption and scrupulosity; it is the honesty and trust of the publican, to whom St Benedict likens the monk who has climbed the ladder of humility. In compunction there is joy and hope, with readiness to accept forgiveness and to forgive oneself.

Although the monk's conversion is rooted in his baptismal commitment, it finds regular expression throughout his life in the sacrament of penance. In the theory and practice of Christian reconciliation God must be central, because the heart of the sacrament is the forgiveness and love of God offered to man in Christ. Through the light of Christ's Spirit the monk comes to understand himself as a mysterious combination of strength and weakness. But the great grace of penance is not so much the grace of awareness and self-understanding as the grace of self-acceptance. A person is able to accept himself if he realizes that he is acceptable. In penance one is accepted by God, and this acceptance is sacramentalized by the minister of the sacrament. It is only when a monk accepts himself as he is that he is able honestly to acknowledge his strength as a gift from God and his weakness as a manifestation of his constant need for a Saviour. In its root meaning the term 'confession' implies praise for God's gifts offered and accepted, and repentance for the gifts refused. The monk himself, then, is the real matter of the sacrament. What he articulates in the sacrament is simply an expression of his own identity.

However, if a man has not learned to admit his identity to his fellow-men he will rarely be able to express himself honestly in the celebration of penance. St Benedict was aware of this problem, and consequently provided for fraternal correction and reconciliation among the brethren.[27] Although the traditional chapter of faults has been generally discarded in our communities today because it frequently degenerated into a formalistic practice, it would seem advisable for communities to search for new forms within which the monks can experience the ministry of both corrective healing and communal reconciliation, in the spirit of the Church's renewal of the sacrament of penance.

In order to prepare himself to be available for God who reveals himself in history, the monk has traditionally sought to train and discipline himself by voluntary acts of self-denial. Historically this custom often led to exaggerations and was frequently supported by a defective anthropology which failed to integrate the various forces in the human person. Today, however, contemporary theological developments, the results of the modern behavioural sciences and the patterns of modern life must be taken into account in arriving at an asceticism which is suitable for our time. In the past, ascetical practices regularly took a negative form, such as abstinence from food, sleep, and recreation. Such practices may still be very useful today. However, the demands that modern life makes on people are often so heavy that much asceticism is built into the fabric of life itself. Long hours of physical, intellectual, and administrative work, concern for the disturbed and underprivileged in our society, and the difficulties of daily life all make heavy demands on the modern monk. If he responds generously to the good work he is called to do he will certainly find that his own self-will is often denied. Likewise he will find that a true spirit of joy grows in his life. An exaggerated emphasis on negative ascetical practices often makes people gloomy and irritable, whereas the result of true love is always a spirit of mercy, peace, and joy.

c) Christ as model

Christ himself is the model for the monk's asceticism. Christ not only speaks the word of the Father's forgiving love, but he also took on our human life and lived it out to the end.[28] He exposed himself to the sins of men, to their obtuseness, their ruthlessness, and their hatred. He carried the guilt of mankind to the cross, and in his body he suffered the penalties of our sins.[29] In obedience to the Father he endured the cross and became 'the pioneer and perfecter of our faith'.[30] Not only did he place himself completely in his Father's hands, but through his voluntary suffering and death he 'cancelled every record of the debt that we had to pay; he has done away with it by nailing it to the cross'.[31]

The monk's asceticism must be at its deepest level a sharing in Christ's asceticism. Baptism gives the fundamental grace of participation in Christ's redemptive death and resurrection, but the monk, like all Christians, must constantly take Christ's death upon himself and die with Christ each day: 'If any man wants to be a follower of mine, let him renounce himself and take up his cross and follow me. For anyone who wants to save his life will lose it; but anyone who loses his life for my sake, and for the sake of the gospel, will save it.'[32] Conversion and asceticism are truly Christian when related to the mystery of Christ's passover; they imply a readiness to share his sufferings and a firm hope of sharing his glory.

d) Asceticism and eschatology

The asceticism of faith and of the cross look forward to the promised final glory beyond this world. Although the monk shares here and now in the life of Christ and experiences the love, peace, and joy that come with that life, he is still a pilgrim, part of the pilgrim Church, on his way to the holy city which God has prepared for his people.[33] In this redemptive situation the monk lives in patience, watching and waiting for the coming of the Lord. Enduring hard work and disappointments, he has through prayer and mortification the means to conquer weariness, discouragement, and indifference. Open to the future, he is not obstinate in his opinions or plans, and avoids Pharisaism, legalism, and hardness of heart. Although he hopes to become more conformed to Christ as the years pass, he becomes perfect not only for himself but above all for the honour and glory of God and the service of God's people.

Asceticism is necessary not as a means whereby the Christian or the monk converts himself – he is impotent to do that – but as an expression of his openness to God and his willingness to be converted. The action of God's Spirit changes men from sinners into friends and sons of God, from egoists into integrated human persons in whom the love of God has unified all the resources of the personality. This is the Holy Spirit's transforming action, but it passes through men's desire. Thus asceticism is not so much a question of striving as of receiving, in an act of willing acceptance, the gift which God makes of himself to those whom he loves. The final goal of monastic asceticism is really the same as that of conversion; it is union with God and the community of God's people.

Celibacy

Monks and nuns in the monastic tradition do not mention celibacy explicitly in their vows since it is an invariable characteristic of Christian monasticism and is therefore comprehended under the vow of Conversion of Life.

Chastity is that virtue which helps us to integrate sexuality into our lives as human beings and as Christians. It is for all, but takes different forms according to vocation and state of life. Dedicated celibacy and virginity are particular forms of Christian chastity which entail abstinence from marriage. They have been part of the Church's experience since the apostolic age. In our sex-conscious era they are incomprehensible to many, and have come under fire from philosophers and psychologists whose studies have helped to reveal the meaning and importance of human sexuality and personal relationships. The findings of these disciplines have, however, also thrown a flood of light on the celibate vocation for those who are following it. This chapter therefore suggests the theological setting for celibacy, and also attempts to relate it to the philosophical and psychological preoccupations of our day.

Introduction

a) The contemporary problem

That there has been a crisis about celibacy in the Church, heightened since Vatican II, scarcely needs demonstrating. It is not sufficient to dismiss contemporary questioning of celibacy as merely an instance of the penchant for doubt and radical solutions endemic in the student generation. Nor is it adequate to the facts to see all defections from the priesthood and religious life as examples of simple infidelity, predictable consequences of the influence of a permissive society seeping through the cracks of the Church's loosened discipline. If the causes of present unrest went no deeper than that, it would be impossible to suppose that there could suddenly be a new problem about celibacy that no one had ever thought of before.

Much more significant is 'a crisis of the mind, not of the flesh',[1] brought about by certain philosophical currents which have penetrated the minds of a whole generation of believers and unbelievers alike, and coloured its way of thinking and feeling about human behaviour. Since Freud, the enormous significance of sexuality for personal development has been increasingly recognized, and from this recognition has come the accusation that celibacy is unnatural. This assertion is still heard today, but it has a crude ring, and probably has much less power among celibates and potential celibates than the more subtle and elusive questions which surround the whole mystery of personal commitment, fidelity, and the bearing of legal obligation on human freedom.

A philosophy is at its most influential when it has disappeared by absorption and is no longer acknowledged. The Existentialist movement has caused a widespread change of mood and outlook, afforded a new perception of certain values, and given currency to a specialized, not to say hypnotic, vocabulary. The ubiquity of such words as 'sincerity', 'dynamic', 'commitment', 'relevance', 'authenticity', 'choice', 'freedom', and 'experience' indicates a new scale of values. For those who look at life in this way, the key to human and Christian living is the continuing choice of an 'authentic' way of life.[2] Inauthenticity means sheltering behind the trivialities, the routines, the morally undemanding patterns of everyday life. To be authentic means to acknowledge basic moral challenges, to be open to the ambiguities and the underlying anguish of life, and to respond to them by committing oneself afresh to the values one perceives. But to be authentic in this sense involves risk, since all the factors cannot be known in advance and any fresh commitment made in response to a new insight may entail the abandonment of a position hitherto securely held. To opt for safety is to opt for inauthenticity. Hence any contractual obligation is suspect which, although initially undertaken in authentic freedom, so predetermines the individual's future that a new direction cannot be taken in response to later experience.

From this summary it can be seen that the contractual aspect of a lifelong dedication to celibacy appears to many people irreconcilable with serious human living. To bind oneself by vow for a lifetime is alleged to block the possibility of personal growth and deeper commitment in the future, since the demand for a more real, free, and risky commitment may supervene on existing obligations. This is a problem which lies at the root of the whole question of a lifelong commitment in any form,[3] but it is particularly acute in the area of celibacy because here personal relationships of the deepest and most powerful kind are directly involved, a person's capacity for loving and being loved. We may not accept the often unexamined assumption of Existentialists that contracts necessarily diminish liberty; we could argue that one of the main purposes of any contract is to protect not just one liberty but several, or that it is a psychological truism that a person can deliberately choose to limit his freedom at one level in order to develop it at others. Nevertheless Existentialists have done much to clarify the nature of 'absolute commitment' and 'authentic response'. Ideally, the authentic response made here and now forms part of a continuous pattern with a network of previous responses and is part of a process of commitment that grows deeper and richer as it is constantly renewed. The question about the vow of celibacy is thus rather a question about the meaning of fidelity. If the adherence to a way of life once accepted is grounded in nothing but a fear of breaking a juridical bond, it is not true fidelity and forfeits its claim to moral stature and credibility.

The influence of the Personalist wing of Existentialism has sharpened the problem. Any mode of human life or fidelity not grounded in personal relationships is unintelligible to many people, and a celibate way of life is presumed to exclude them. Writings from the extreme Personalist position therefore question not merely the contractual aspect but the whole meaning of institutionalized celibacy: commitment is achieved in loving and responsible relationships with other persons and in a non-sexist understanding and use of sexuality, not in adherence to institutions, legal obligations, or an establishment.[4]

Modern novices have breathed the same air as modern students. Monks and nuns of today have been influenced and enriched by these philosophical currents which touch so profoundly the meaning of monastic vows and the mystery of self-giving which underlies monastic life. Theoretical considerations may also seem to be endorsed by personal experience of difficulties on the part of those already committed to celibacy; most monks and nuns know at times discouragement, temptation, weakness, and loneliness. They may be vulnerable to suggestions about immaturity and 'missing out', and they are always conscious of the gap between ideal and performance. Moreover they are aware that the Church's theology of sexuality and marriage has for some time been moving away from a rigidly hierarchical view of the 'ends of marriage', and a narrow focus on procreation, towards a more positive appreciation of the goodness of human sexuality, and of marriage as a community of love and a vocation to holiness.[5] Any statement on monastic celibacy today must therefore be situated within a humane and developing Christian theology of sexuality, and must proceed from a sympathetic openness to the contemporary mood, even though it may find many of the current protests and solutions shallow, onesided, or simply wrong.

b) The indications of the Rule

Celibacy has been one of the most constant and invariable characteristics of Christian monasticism since the fourth century, and was a significant feature of those earlier forms of dedicated Christian life which can be regarded as antecedents of monasticism from apostolic times down to the launching of the monastic movement. St Benedict took it for granted as primordial and essential. He does not give the impression that he was self-conscious about celibacy, and he seems to have disregarded or been unaware of those positive values of sexuality in human and Christian life which are recognized as important today.[6] There is therefore very little in the Rule that bears directly on celibacy; a few allusions plus a general climate for understanding the matter are all the help St Benedict gives.

The first allusion is RB 4.80, where one of the tools of good works is 'to love chastity'. Apart from the fact that this is so terse as to be obscure, St Benedict was here in direct literary dependence on Chapter 3 of the Rule of the Master. Underlying the Master's chapter was probably one or several of those lists of the details of the *ars sancta* common in ancient literature and usually concerned with Christian life in general. It is quite possible therefore that the reference is to the general Christian virtue of chastity rather than to its celibate monastic form.[7] Another mention of chastity occurs in RB 72.12: *caritatem fraternitatis caste impendant.* No expansion of the idea underlying 'chastely' is provided, but the climate of community life described in this spendid chapter is one of warmth, simplicity, and humanity, of forbearance and humble hope.

There remain two parallel statements which are sometimes regarded as implicit references to celibacy. RB 33, 'Whether Monks should have Anything as their own', has affinities with various early monastic writers, but the intensity and vehemence with which St Benedict insists on total expropriation seem to be his own. Monks are to possess nothing whatever as their own property, for 'they should not have even their bodies and wills at their own disposal'. Similarly in RB 58 St Benedict echoes Cassian and Basil[8] in insisting that the newly professed monk must despoil himself entirely of all property and all chance of acquiring it, 'knowing that from that day onwards he will not have dominion even over his own body'. The thought in both these passages is concerned with total renunciation of *proprietas*, dependence on the abbot in obedience, and the surrender of the monk's will in union with Christ who delivered himself, body and will, for us. But the language echoes 1 Corinthians 7.4: 'The wife does not have dominion over her own body, but the husband; similarly the husband does not have dominion over his own body, but the wife.' It is possible, therefore, that there is some reference in these passages to the monk's making over of the rights over his own body to the Lord, as expressed in vowed celibacy.

St Benedict seems to have been a very balanced man, and perhaps he was following a sound Christian instinct in refusing to deal with celibacy, or with any sexual problems, in isolation from a human person's whole purpose; it is the autonomy of sex in the modern world that gives rise to much of the trouble. Brief as the Rule's indications are, it is worth noting that St Benedict thought of chastity in connection with community life and warm fraternal relationships, and possibly as an aspect of personal poverty. His doctrine of lifelong conversion in the monastery and above all his references to love provide the context of understanding: the monk is to 'prefer absolutely nothing to the love of Christ',[9] and to trust that faithful following of Christ will bring him to an 'enlargement of heart' and an 'unutterable sweetness of love'.[10] Of equal significance are the Rule's allusions to that 'purity of heart' which was so vital a concept in the spiritual tradition of the ancients, a singlemindedness far wider than sexual purity but including it.[11] A primary means of growth in purity or integrity of heart is prayer. In speaking of loving relationships in a Christian community, and of purity of heart in connection with prayer, St Benedict was dealing with the two Christian realities which are fundamental to monastic celibacy. For further understanding we must look to Christian tradition as a whole.

It is no more possible to prove that a lifelong commitment to celibacy is valid than it is possible for someone in love to prove that his fiancée is the right person for him. For most people the choice of Christian celibacy is not the final stage in a rational argument, but part of an intuitive response involving the whole man, a personal response in faith. Many people make the choice, without analysing the justification for it, because they have encountered celibacy as a brute and beautiful fact in the lives of others, and as something that seems to work. Or again, they may have realized that celibacy is part of the lives of most of the 'peak' human beings in Christian history – Christ, Our Lady, St John the Baptist, St Paul – but in such a way that it is an element of their total dedication rather than something focused on for its own sake. Nevertheless we can try to indicate the theological foundations of Christian celibacy, and to show the compatibility of consecrated celibacy with a fully human life. If it is not possible to supply a proof, it may be possible to suggest a vision: a vision of monastic celibacy as a call to a complex of relationships rooted in freedom and love.

The theological context of Christian celibacy

a) The scriptural data

1. Sexuality, marriage, and the covenant in Scripture

Sexuality in man is akin to animal sexuality but transcends it, because man has received the gift of sex from God as a moral responsibility and a task, and because, rightly developed and used, this gift becomes for human beings a matter of free decision and of personal, spiritual love. Moreover human sexuality has become inextricably involved in the affair between men and God which develops throughout the story of salvation. A Christian understanding of sexuality must therefore take into account the threefold perspective of this story: creation, sin, and redemption. Our theology must include respect for those mysteries of life and love where human persons share in a privileged way in God's creative act, awareness of the disorder in our nature resulting from sin and of the need to struggle for control, and joyful hope in the Lord whose victory was won 'in the flesh'. This victory we already share, but we look forward to its consummation in the glorifying of our bodies.

The Priestly Writer in Genesis[12] describes the creation of a bisexual humanity as the climax of God's work. Man and woman together, in their complementarity, form the human image of God.[13] The stress is on their capacity for fruitfulness.[14] In the Yahwist's account[15] there is at first no mention of procreation; the emphasis here is on love and companionship. The woman is God's idea for overcoming the man's loneliness; she is a 'Thou' for the man in a way that the animals could not be, and their delight is to become two in one flesh, a communion of loving selves. The glory of human sexuality as the mystery of a human person ordained to another is already suggested, and so a sign is given of humanity's likeness to God who eventually reveals himself as a communion of loving Persons. In the fulness of time the highest meaning of human sexuality will be revealed: it is to be a vehicle for the mediation of God's agape.[16]

The story of the Fall which follows is not a statement that humanity's primal revolt against God took the form of sexual sin.[17] But it does give a picture of the effects of sin on sexual equilibrium and on human relationships. The man and the woman quarrel and he blames her; shame, violent desire, the instinct to dominate, and painful childbearing are mentioned as part of the new order of things. However, the account of the Fall ends with the reaffirmation of sexuality and its power to give life through alliance with the creative love of God: Eve gives birth to a child with a primitive yell of triumph.[18] God does not intend to let human life gutter out. Still more significantly, the obscure promise of redemption is linked with the exercise of the sexual faculty, for the future deliverer is to be the 'seed' of the woman.[19] God evidently intends that the marvel which he created and man spoiled is to be rehabilitated and used in the plan of salvation.

As the story moves forward, the repeated articulations of the promise are bound up with carnal generation. Salvation is to come through the seed of Abraham, and later through the seed of David. Carnal descent is an invariable factor in the plan, but never sufficient of itself, for the promise is pure grace from God and looks for answering faith. So Abraham is father in his flesh, but by the power of the promise. The gratuitousness of God's saving will is shown by the frequency with which sterile women are enabled through their faith in his word to bear the promised children of destiny.[20] God chooses the weak things to make it clear that redemption will be sheer grace and not the achievement of human potency; this mystery culminates in the virginal conception of the Redeemer. But always the messianic line, the lifeline of hope, passes through human begetting and childbearing.

Meanwhile the appreciation of love and marriage among God's people was being refined. 'The way of a man with a maiden' was one of the things too wonderful to understand.[21] A picture of the perfect wife emerged, hardly to be surpassed as a picture of dignity, responsibility, and fruitful co-operation in married life.[22] In a far more lyrical vein the Song of Songs celebrated the glories of love and passion between man and woman with a frank delight in the physical that sprang from pure, simple gratitude to God for the gift of sexuality.[23] From Hosea onwards the mystery of tender, faithful, forgiving love, experienced in actual human relationships, was used by God as the most frequent and typical image of his covenant of love with his people. Human experience of marriage at its noblest could thenceforth be a medium for understanding God's saving love, while at the same time the dignity of the human relationship could be raised still further by its function as a sign. This process of mutual illumination between marriage and the covenant continued throughout the Old Testament and the New.[24]

In the fulness of time God sent his Son, born of a woman, like to us in all things save sin. The Word was made flesh, embracing the whole reality of what it is to be man and ennobling every element in the human condition, including sexuality. He was sent 'in the likeness of sinful flesh',[25] that is, in a human bodily nature which without being, like ours, an instrument of sin, was capable of suffering and death because of sin and was to be the instrument of his obedient sacrifice. The same law of solidarity with men that operated in his incarnation held also in Christ's passover; he drew mankind with him, so that just as he had been exposed in our flesh to the effects of sin and death, we might be exposed in him to the effects of God's holiness and life.[26] Thus God 'condemned sin in the flesh';[27] the event of the redemption took place in that dimension of man's personal existence which is simultaneously that in which his guilt becomes most tangible and that in which his guilt is overcome.

The power and holiness of God consumed Christ's offering, lifting his sacrificed humanity into the divine sphere and transfiguring it by the Spirit. He rose gloriously in his flesh: 'Handle and see. . . .' He is not merely a living being through the gift of God's breath like the first Adam.[28] He is a 'vivifying Spirit',[29] for his entire humanity – his human mind and his body including his sexuality and all his affective powers – has totally assimilated the Spirit and become the source of life for us. Our salvation is effected by the engrafting of the body-person of each Christian into the body-person of the risen Christ. In this union is life, truly given now and pledged in fulness for eternity. The final consummation of this life of the Spirit, poured out through Christ's risen manhood, is the glorification of our bodies; the indwelling Spirit is both the pledge that this will be and the principle of our longing for it, just as he somehow voices the longing of the earth itself to which our bodies and all their processes inextricably belong.[30]

Under the new covenant it is therefore possible for marriage to be no longer a mere symbol of the covenant-love of God for his people, but a true sacrament of the redeeming love of Christ for his bride, the

Church.[31] The self-giving, cleansing, forgiving love of Christ who prepares the Church for final union with himself is given a new realization in every act of marital love between Christians living his Easter life. The highest meaning of human sexuality is at last revealed: it is a mediation of God's agape. Our flesh and our sexuality are drawn into the radiance and power of the glorified Christ. This is true of all Christians, whether it is by marriage that they are related to the mystery of the covenant, or by the different grace of celibacy.

2. Celibacy in Scripture

With sexuality as positively implicated as this in the economy of salvation it is hardly surprising that celibacy was not at first seen to have any value. In the Old Testament barrenness, and therefore also the unmarried condition, were considered a disaster and a disgrace. Jephthah's daughter mourned the fact that she would die a virgin rather than her imminent death itself,[32] and the recurrent expression 'virgin daughter of Zion' refers less to Israel's future nuptial relationship with the Lord than to her forlorn and hopeless condition in time of catastrophe. At a stage when there was little positive revelation of a future life, the prolongation of one's own life in that of one's children and grandchildren was the primary way of ensuring survival.[33] It was the coming of Christ and the revelation of eternal life in him that made the difference.[34]

The only clear case in the Old Testament of celibacy undertaken for religious motives is that of Jeremiah, who in a time of impending disaster was forbidden to marry and beget children, with all that such a way of life implied of rootedness in the social order, as a sign to the people of Judah that the social order was doomed.[35] St Paul's recommendation of celibacy in 1 Corinthians 7 is often interpreted in the same light. Certainly his thought is heavy with the presage of the final convulsions; if the created order is soon to be abrogated by the Second Coming there is little point in getting engrossed in its concerns. The fact that St Paul was mistaken in his expectation of an imminent parousia has seemed to many to rob his recommendation of celibacy of its relevance. Others, in an attempt to rescue the teaching on celibacy, have redefined the eschatology in a more general sense: Christian life is essentially eschatological and celibacy is a sign of this.[36] While there is truth in this approach it is probably more satisfactory to recognize that though Paul's belief that the end was imminent lent urgency to his teaching, it did not determine its content. His main concern in the whole of this chapter is with the freedom of Christians to care only for the Lord: 'I want you to be carefree. The celibate's care is how he may please the Lord, but the married man has the worldly care about how he may please his wife, and so he is divided.'[37] In other words, the celibate has greater freedom to care about the new order of things centred on the risen Christ, the 'Lord', while the anxiety of the married bears on the things of 'this age'.[38]

Paul recognized, however, that while freedom for the Lord was in a general sense necessary for all Christians, the particular expression of it by celibacy was a consequence of individual grace.[39] This was Christ's own teaching in what is probably the only formal gospel text on celibacy. The conversation recorded in Matthew 19.10–12 appears to have been originally an independent unit, not directly connected with the preceding exchange between Jesus and the Pharisees about divorce but inserted here by the evangelist. Jesus mentioned two classes of eunuchs: those who were impotent from some accident of birth and those who were the victims of inflicted violence. The harsh character of the saying, added to the fact that this classification of eunuchs was customary among the rabbis, makes it clear that Jesus meant not merely 'unmarried' but strictly 'incapable of marriage'. But he added a third category of persons who are equally 'incapable' in consequence of something that has happened to them, namely 'the Kingdom'. It is vital to remember that in the early preaching of Jesus the Kingdom is not first and foremost a demand for self-sacrifice made on men but an overwhelming gift from God. The twin parables of the treasure and the pearl[40] give the clue: the overwhelming joy of the Kingdom seizes a man and blots out all else. Everything that formerly seemed worth striving for pales beside the glory of what he has discovered, and no price seems too high. He is *unable* to pursue those other things any more. But it is also clear that while Jesus taught people to pray for the coming of the Kingdom as something future, he also summoned them to recognize that this gift was already present and offered in himself. Instead of 'because of the Kingdom of heaven' he could equally well have said, 'because of me'.[41] There are some who have recognized it and have followed him. They cannot involve themselves in the responsibilities and ties of marriage; they have 'made themselves incapable' of marriage, apparently for life, because they have let the sheer joy of the Kingdom possess them and fill their whole horizon. The Kingdom takes some people that way.[42]

b) Motivation for Christian celibacy

The decision to remain unmarried is not, in our society, unambiguously significant. Apart from the fact that many remain unmarried for economic, social, or other reasons without practising sexual abstinence, there are those who from unselfish motives postpone or renounce marriage and sexual involvements as a means to some end which to them is supremely valuable. This type of decision may be 'professional', motivated by a person's desire to devote his time, energies, and money to some career, to art, research, or social service, more totally than a married person could do. Such a commitment sets up a special relationship between him and the professional community whose interests and aims he espouses. Or again celibacy can be chosen for some kind of 'philosophical' reason, as a step towards personal solitude, for the purpose of discovering one's inner truth. In this sense it is akin to the celibacy adopted by many in the higher non-Christian religions as a means to inner liberation and enlightenment. Hence this choice also has a relationship to a wider community, since there is likely to be sympathy and the possibility of communication between persons committed to a similar quest.[43]

Even the Christian choice of non-marriage for the Kingdom is not a single, simple reality. Behind a certain common form of behaviour (namely, not getting married and sealing this decision by vow) lies a diversity of understanding about how the commitment relates a Christian to the covenant between Christ and his Church. Before these particular crystallizations of motive can be considered, however, it is necessary to look at two primordial realities which underlie them. The first is Christian discipleship with its consequences of fellowship with the Lord and with the brethren in charity; the second is purity of heart. These realities are inherent in the Christian mystery and are prior to the choice of marriage or celibacy as a way of life; indeed, they are compatible with a variety of concrete choices. But together they provide us with a context in which the option for celibacy makes sense.

1. The basic Christian motives: discipleship and purity of heart

Jesus called the people who do his Father's will his brothers and sisters and mothers,[44] contrasting human family ties with the bonds between himself and the disciples who abandon all things for the sake of the Kingdom. Discipleship in Jesus's group springs from a personal relationship of love and obedience with Jesus himself, and through him with the Father. He spoke of it also as friendship: 'You are my friends if you do what I command you. No longer do I call you servants . . . ; but I have called you friends.'[45] The agape which is the life of God is the life also of the brotherhood of disciples. The barriers are down between men and God, and therefore the barriers of race, class, sex, and age are down between the disciples: 'There is neither Jew nor Greek, slave nor free, male nor female'[46] for they are all one in Christ. This friendship within the Christian *koinonia* transforms sexual and family relationships but does not depend on them, for the choice of celibacy by some disciples as a faith-response to the Kingdom proclaims the fact that agape can exist without the sexual relationship of marriage. The Kingdom-centred choice of celibacy thus of itself gives the celibate an essential relationship to the *koinonia*, and may have the further consequence of special availability when celibacy is accepted as a necessary, or at least very useful, means to some evangelical end. One must become and remain a disciple of the Lord, related to him and his brethren in love, if one is to undertake a particular service.

To be a created person is to have a capacity for loving in truth. The primordial encounter, that which makes the person to be and gives him consistency and the power to love, is the encounter with God. The condition for this encounter is an 'emptiness' or 'spaciousness' in the innermost heart, a receptivity at the deepest root where created being empties itself in order to receive God. This is possible for fallen human beings only within the self-emptying of Christ; the natural 'innocence' of childhood is not enough, for each of us is born already burdened with the betrayals, avarice, lust, and violence of our ancestors. We must be born anew through the re-creative act of God at the centre of the creature's being.

In this encounter where man is in communion with God he experiences pain and poverty because of the emptying, but also joy and achievement in receiving God for whose friendship he was created. In communion with God lies the human person's integrity and truth. Fidelity to its demands in all things is a recognition of the lordship of God and his absolute claims; it establishes the human person in that fundamental unity which is a consequence of Christ's redemption,[47] and it is the ground of worship. In this sense the relationship is exclusive. This is the 'purity of heart' of which the early monks spoke, and it is described in St Benedict's seventh chapter.

Integrity or purity of heart is an interior value of the person, and cannot be imposed juridically from without. Its outflow from the centre of the person is chastity.[48] This is true for all Christians, whether they are called to celibacy or to marriage, but recognition of this basic Christian value provides a context for understanding the option for celibate chastity. In Christian celibacy the ultimate relationship of receptivity to God and exclusive worship of him is embodied in a person's life-style.

The threat to both discipleship and purity of heart in the lives of Christians is idolatry. An idol is a created reality which should be transparent and relative, should refer beyond itself to God, yet claims to be ultimate. Loving in truth demands a continual exodus, for the fulfilments of love point beyond themselves. Idols are lies, 'mere nothings', pseudo-riches. They promise what they cannot give, and by deceiving us they can enclose us in the merely human. If they usurp the place of God they diminish or destroy the Christian's purity of heart. So the root of chastity can be cut even though there is no sexual sin. It is very significant that both Old and New Testaments constantly link idolatry with impurity as sins against the God of the exodus.

Sexual love in marriage can become an idol if it seems to promise ecstasy and immortality, entrapping the partners in a static relationship. Celibacy chosen for the sake of love should therefore be a reminder to all Christians that sexual fulfilment is subordinate to God and a gift from him. But celibacy itself can become an idol. This may happen in the life of an individual if the person's self-image of purity becomes an ultimate value; celibacy is then distorted into an emotional isolation and invulnerability, a self-sufficiency and self-absorption that are incompatible with Christian discipleship. So the person may become trapped in complacency, perfectionism, and pride. Or again, at an institutional level, celibacy may seem to promise status and security, masking the fact that the only ultimate source of security is the lordship of God. This can be a kind of 'structural idolatry'; a community may need to be recalled from its corporate pride that it may once more make a space for God in poverty of spirit.

Our rebirth in integrity takes time and many repentances. Paul was aware that we bear our treasure in vessels of clay and was constantly troubled by his 'thorn in the flesh', but equally certain where his unassailable security lay: 'I am sure that . . . nothing in all creation will be able to separate us from the love of God in Christ Jesus our Lord.'[49]

Within this Christian context there are psychological differences which can conveniently be summed up under two types: the 'functional' and the 'marital' approach to celibacy.

For some people celibacy is not so much an expression of their vocation as a preparation or condition for following it. Although their relationship with God is the support and focus of their lives, they do not experience their celibacy precisely as intrinsic to that relationship, but rather as a means to an end. The end may be freedom for the apostolate. It may be the detachment and tranquillity that favour contemplation, to which celibacy appears to be an ascetical means. Under present discipline, the end may be the priesthood and a ministry of universal love and availability. For some the end is simply monastic community life. Probably those whose resolution for celibacy is of this type recognize their own vocation in the Lucan teaching on renunciation and in 1 Corinthians 7.

Other people experience their relationship to God in Christ and the coming of the Kingdom in their lives in such a way that earthly marriage appears to be not so much excluded as transcended or absorbed. Because God has so possessed them, and they have consented, they are incapable of engaging themselves in another total relationship of the marital type, as a person in love and happily married is incapable of marrying someone else. This is not a rational conclusion from the matching of means to end, but an existential fact. They may recognize their vocation in the Lord's saying on eunuchs, or in Ephesians 5.25 ff, more readily than in other New Testament texts on celibacy.

These two types are not sharply separate, and some element of both is inherent in many people's vocation.[50]

2. Particular crystallizations of motive

The underlying realities of discipleship and purity of heart, which by relating a Christian in love to the Lord and to the covenant-community provide the foundation for virginity, can be articulated in different ways. The emphasis may be on imitation of and union with Christ in his virginity, on sacrifice and the paschal mystery, on eschatological life, or on the mystery of the Church as Bride of Christ. These can now be considered in turn, though they shade off into each other.

(i) The example of Jesus Jesus's virginity during his mortal life expressed his relationship of intimacy with the Father, and his total dedication to the Father's will. It is parallel to the virginal conception through which the Logos had become man: there was no ontological reason why God's

Son should not have had a human father when he was made flesh, but the virginal conception embodied and made luminous the fact that he was sent from the Father. Salvation is wholly from God, and the humanity of Jesus is a 'new creation'. Similarly, Jesus could have lived a life of absolute dedication if he had been married. But the theme of the gospels is his proclamation of the Kingdom and identification with his Father's will, and the inner face of this mission is that relationship of love and intimacy with the Father which was deepened in his constant prayer. His virginity was the embodiment of this, the most glorious relationship of his life. The relationship between man and wife would not have been incompatible with it but would have been inappropriate, because it would have partially obscured the truth.[51]

He came from God and returned to God. Throughout his life his virginity was already sacrificial, not primarily in the sense that it was painful (though no doubt it was sometimes) but because it was a mode of living towards death. His whole life was commanded by the pull of his passage to the Father, and his virginity expressed his paschal vocation.

It represented, moreover, a radical homelessness and insecurity, set over against marriage which is an affirmation of the reality of life in this world. As such, it made Jesus a 'marginal' person, unacceptable and challenging to the Jewish society of his time; the rabbis, regarding Genesis 1.28 as a formal divine command, insisted on the duty of every Israelite man to procreate.[52] But this marginal way of life gave him pastoral freedom, not only the external freedom and mobility that result from being unattached to wife, children, and home, but an interior freedom for universal friendship. His virginity clearly had nothing to do with misogyny or a melancholy and withdrawn temperament. He was intensely alive, joyful, and passionate, and obviously very attractive to both men and women. He related easily to them, swiftly and spontaneously. The gospels are neither biographies nor psychological studies of Jesus, but his authentic humanity in all its strength, warmth, and sympathy is unmistakable, and one of the most wonderful things the gospels reveal is Jesus's relationship with women. No two anecdotes are alike: he related differently to his mother, to Mary Magdalen, to the woman at the well, to the sinful woman who anointed his feet, to Martha and Mary at Bethany, to the Syrophoenician woman – to each one he encountered. But he was always at ease with women, never afraid of them, respectful but never stiff, loving and accepting to each one. He thus made it possible for each of them to be herself with him. The point was admirably made by Dorothy Sayers:

Perhaps it is no wonder that the women were first at the Cradle and last at the Cross. They had never known a man like this Man – there never has been such another. A prophet and teacher who never nagged at them, never flattered or coaxed or patronized; who never made arch jokes about them . . . who rebuked without querulousness and praised without condescension . . . ; who never mapped out their sphere for them, never urged them to be feminine or jeered at them for being female; who had no axe to grind and no uneasy male dignity to defend; who took them as he found them and was completely unself-conscious. There is no act, no sermon, no parable in the whole Gospel that borrows its pungency from female perversity; nobody could possibly guess from the words and deeds of Jesus that there was anything 'funny' about woman's nature.[53]

Since Jesus was willing to be vulnerable, and unworried about his reputation, he was able to accept the erotic and transform it from within. The stories of the sinful woman who wept on his feet[54] and Mary Magdalen at the tomb[55] suggest something of his power to take an erotic and passionate attachment on their part, without rejecting or destroying it, and deepen it to the level of faith and spiritual love.

One of the most moving stories is that of the adulteress.[56] Jesus never condones adultery or suggests that it is of no importance, but he shows no disgust, disdain, or embarrassment. The Pharisees are tense, but he is calm and relaxed throughout; he accepts the woman openly and lovingly, as an adult and as a person. He has a sureness of touch; he can handle the situation and the relationship with her because he has nothing to be afraid of in himself. Not only had he no sin, but he must have completely accepted and integrated his own sexuality. Only a man who has done so, or at least begun to do so, can relate properly to women.

(ii) Sacrifice and the paschal mystery The sacrificial aspect of virginity is very close to that assimilation to Christ already considered, since all Christian sacrifice is a sharing in his cross and resurrection. To keep this connection clear saves us from that aberration in religious thinking which measures the meritoriousness of a human act not by the degree of charity which prompts it, but by the degree of difficulty and pain its performance causes in the agent. The heart of sacrifice is not destruction but making over to God. For the Christian, sacrifice is his dignity and glory. Created in the image of God, he is being re-created in the image of Christ the priest, and participation in Christ's sacrificial love is a consequence of the royal priesthood of the baptized.

To make any religious vow is a cultic act, but each vow expresses the worship of God in a different way, and vowed virginity is in a special sense the worship of the body.[57] The body of a Christian is the new temple of the Holy Spirit[58] and shares in that 'better cult' of the living God carried out by Christ the priest. All Christians are exhorted: 'Present your bodies as a living sacrifice',[59] and from the second century virginity was associated with martyrdom as an exemplification of self-offering in union with Christ's sacrifice. St Ignatius of Antioch spoke of virginity as undertaken 'to the honour of the flesh of the Lord'.[60] Martyrdom, virginity, and the Eucharist form a very ancient constellation of ideas. All are rooted in Christ's paschal mystery; all are mysteries of self-giving love expressed through the gift of the body.

The pain of renunciation is real enough, however, and in virginity it is not as swift as in martyrdom. The sacrifice involves the physical renunciation of pleasures for which the organism was created and for which it clamours, renunciation of the right to share one's life with another person in an exclusive and unique alliance of companionship and support, and renunciation of parenthood. Whether this complex sacrifice inevitably entails the diminishment of the human person, in the sense that one so vowed must look only to the next life for deep happiness and fulness of humanity, will be discussed later. But it certainly means that we 'carry about in our bodies the death of Jesus . . . that the life of Jesus too may be manifested in our mortal flesh'.[61] In other words, Christian virginity means an experience of both the cross and the resurrection here and now; but the suffering is part of the birthpangs of the new world.

(iii) Celibacy as an eschatological value To the Sadducees' question about the future fate of the woman who had seven husbands Jesus replied, 'You understand neither the Scriptures nor the power of God. When people rise from the dead, they neither marry nor are they given in marriage; they are like angels in heaven.'[62] Attempts to explain this passage have sometimes pointed out that since in the future Kingdom there will be no death, there will be no need to fill up gaps in the ranks by procreation. This, however, is not adequate, since it seems to reduce the significance of sexuality to its procreative function. The saying is obscure to us since we know so little about heaven, but from the little we do know we can glimpse that the relationships of love between the saints are the ultimate in human fellowship and are modelled on the relationships of knowledge and love between the divine Persons. Hence all that sexual communion

has meant on earth (even though in a clouded and ambiguous way) of personal self-giving and acceptance of the other, of tenderness, compassion and healing love, of affirmation of the other and being affirmed oneself, of trust, openness, understanding, celebration, and joy, must be more than found again, but in some mode transcending the limitations that are inherent in it now.

Yet from the earliest days of Christianity there has been a conviction that in some way celibacy has a peculiarly immediate connection with the end-time and the coming of the Kingdom. This is still a Christian motive for embracing it, but the emphasis varies. Christian life is poised between the 'realized eschatology' of eternal life enjoyed even now (which is the 'already' aspect of the Kingdom) and the tension of hope as we wait for the Kingdom to come in fulness (the 'not yet' aspect).

From the former point of view, virginity is eschatological because it is an experience and expression of charity. Personal, reciprocal love between God and his servant is the core of its meaning. The gift of the Spirit is the pledge and first-fruits of the union that will be, and the effects of his indwelling are the joy and peace that belong to God's reign in the hearts of men. The knowledge of God possible through faith and charity is already a beginning of eternal life.[63] To this experience virginity is personal, joyful response.

But the Church is still a pilgrim, walking in faith and hope through the mysterious in-between phase. Watching and waiting for the Second Coming are essential to the Church's task; the Lord frequently enjoined 'Watch!' On the paschal night the Church keeps watch for him. Christians are like servants waiting for their Master to return,[64] or like the ten virgins whose duty was to keep awake and be ready for the Bridegroom's arrival.[65] This aspect of the Church's vocation is embodied in a special way in those who experience virginity as an eschatological vocation in the 'not yet' sense. So the monk is a pilgrim, and his virginity accentuates the fact that he has not yet arrived home. Virginity is the vocation of one who stands in the vanguard, one who accepts the loneliness of not having yet caught up with his heart's desires.

Either of the above views of virginity as eschatological can include, though they are not reducible to, the idea of eschatological witness or sign. To men of faith the celibate's life speaks of God who calls man to life and bestows life in abundance; it reminds the Body of Christ that its Head is risen. The God whose grace has enabled the celibate to live for the Kingdom reveals his own power to fulfil the deepest human longings. The essential message that Christian virgins should communicate is that

God matters supremely and that it is worth staking one's life on his reality and faithfulness. Such a message will be credible only if the celibate life is patently inspired and sustained by love for God and other people.

(iv) *The Church as Bride of Christ* There is a dual perspective in the relationship of the Church (or the Christian) to Christ. Prayer can be a matter of our being taken up into the prayer *of* Christ, yet prayer *to* Christ is equally valid and necessary. Monastic obedience can be understood as a participation in the obedience *of* Christ to the Father's will, yet Christ is also the Lord *to* whom our obedience is given; both perspectives are found in St Benedict's Rule.[66] In other words, there is an identification with Christ, and there is also an 'I-Thou' relationship to him. This duality is at the heart of the ecclesial mystery, for the Church is both the Body of Christ, in him, identified with him, and also the Bride of Christ who stands facing him.

The specific motivations for Christian virginity so far considered have tended to dwell on aspects of our identification with Christ. For one whose motivation is particularly concerned with the mystery of the Church as Christ's Bride the same kind of identification is possible. As Christ's friend, brother, and co-worker a person can be identified with the redemptive love of the Bridegroom who spent himself for the Church and gave himself up for her, who feeds and cherishes her and prepares her for the final union.[67] Priestly celibacy takes on a special significance in this connection, and in the case of a bishop the identification becomes explicit in the ring which is a sign of his wedding to the (local) church.[68]

Nevertheless it is in this mystery of the Bride-Church that Christian virginity finds the clearest of all expressions of its 'I-Thou' relationship to Christ, the identification being now not with Christ himself but with the Church which is the object of his love. Women called to virginity often find in this ecclesial mystery both the heart of their vocation and the deepest meaning of their femininity. A woman is by nature fitted to stand as a sign of the Church under this aspect, and a consecrated virgin can rightly be called 'bride of Christ' in so far as she makes present in her heart and life the Church's life of responsive, faithful love.

For these reasons the Church has from the earliest Christian centuries celebrated with special joy the consecration of a woman to God as a virgin, and the ancient rite of the *Consecratio Virginis* has been, and still is, combined with the solemn monastic profession of many Benedictine nuns. Its use raises certain questions, however. The words 'virgin' and 'virginity' carry a meaning in Christian theology which does not exactly correspond to their meaning in secular parlance. Our secular culture is content to define virginity in physical and negative terms: a virgin is a man or woman who has never had full genital intercourse. Christian theology, while acknowledging the secular meaning, defines virginity in spiritual and positive terms: the fact of not having had genital intercourse is the material of the virtue of virginity, but its formal cause – that which gives it meaning – is the resolve to abstain perpetually for the sake of devoting oneself to the things of God.[69] In those who have preserved their virginity physically in order to consecrate it to God, the state of bodily integrity is a sign of grace, and as such not a matter for pride but a token of God's mercy.

Hence the coverage is not the same; some people who are virgins in the secular sense are not fully so in the theological sense, because the interior purpose is absent. On the other hand, Christian theology, which views the intention of the heart as the primary and essential element, recognizes that the grace of Christian virginity can be present in varying degrees and is capable of growth. It can also be recovered through repentance by one who has earlier lost the material element.[70] But in this case the matter has to be considered at three different levels when there is question of the liturgical consecration of virginity associated with monastic profession.

First, there is the theological and spiritual essence of Christian virginity, which is purity of heart. A person's past record does not matter; the old things have passed away. In Christ Jesus there is neither circumcision or uncircumcision, but a new creature. Conversion of heart is what matters, and the forgiveness of God re-creating the person in grace. The 'bride of Christ' image is not static, for the Church is the Church of sinners washed in Christ's blood and standing in unceasing need of purification and mercy.[71] There is therefore a harmony between the monastic spirituality of conversion and the ideal of Christian virginity. The purity of heart implied in the latter is the radical meaning of monastic solemn profession too.

Second, there is a bodily and psychological level to be considered. Sexuality and a person's attitude to it involve patterns of behaviour, bodiliness, psychological resonances, cultural norms, and (in a Christian context) sacramental realities. The sacramentality of Christian life takes up and consecrates certain natural values; it does not simply nullify them. And there is no doubt that in many cultures natural virginity is held in honour when it is purposely 'kept for' a love-relationship which is to consummate the person's sexuality; non-Christian literature exalts the special magic and joy of sexual love in marriage when both partners have kept their virginity beforehand. Many people in western society have lost this intuition, and take the loss of virginity before marriage for granted. We may well ask ourselves whether we too have been so conditioned by the post-Christian climate that we think of virginity as unimportant in the natural order, and so, taking this as our starting-point, seek to eliminate from the *Consecratio Virginis* elements which assume it. Perhaps Christian tradition should make us more critical of our assumptions, for in the consecration of a person who is a virgin something important is being said about sexuality. To absolutize the human value concerned is to make virginity, falsely understood, into an idol; but the fact of having 'kept oneself' is something real, and in a Christian perspective it can be like an outward sign of the essential inward grace of virginity. The latter is the prime reality, but the former is not to be simply dismissed as meaningless.

Third, there is the common meaning of the words 'virgin' and 'virginity' to be taken into account. It is true that theology can refine, correct, and deepen the meaning attached to words in ordinary usage. But since in this case the theological level of understanding can be so far removed from the common meaning as almost to reverse it, there is a danger that the rite may be misunderstood and appear dishonest.

The Roman instruction accompanying the revised rite of the Consecration of Virgins[72] disqualifies only those who have been married or who have lived *publicly* in a way contrary to chastity. The advantage of this policy is that it puts the accent firmly on the spiritual and Christian meaning of virginity (i.e. on the intention of the heart) and makes the liturgical rite a *public* consecration of something that is real *now*, namely the candidate's intention for the present and future.[73]

The difficulty of using the rite in monastic life has derived especially from its being too closely linked with solemn profession. It is also very questionable whether the rite as generally used expresses an adequate theology of Christian virginity. Any rite or practice is undesirable that puts the accent in the wrong place, obscures the meaning of Christian conversion, places psychological burdens on those aspiring to monastic life, sets up distinctions within the community or threatens to lead people into idolatry and pride. But this does not mean that an ancient rite must be abandoned, a rite which, rooted as it is in psychological truth, celebrates the harmony between nature and grace in the dedication of a woman to God. The surrounding sexual *mores* should not be allowed to dominate the human and theological insights embodied in the rite. It ought to be possible for the Christian community to celebrate the consecration of a virgin, when appropriate, with thankfulness and joy, subordinating the aspect of bodily integrity to the primary theological meaning of both virginity and monastic profession, understanding it as a promise and a hope.[74]

The Church has traditionally placed greater stress on virginity in women than in men because of the aptness of the symbolism, but the ecclesial aspect of virginity is not the prerogative of women. Many male saints have been intensely aware of it and have interpreted their vocation in its light; within monastic tradition St Bernard is an obvious example. The love between Christ and the Church is a mystery that is to be lived out and experienced even here on earth. The union between husband and wife is a sacramental sign of it. In virginity the reality of which marriage is a sign is present in a different way: there is no one to represent Christ but simply an incarnation in the life of a baptized Christian of the Church's union with him. 'Virginity is not a sacrament because Christ in glory is no longer a sacrament.'[75] Christ's continuing self-gift makes possible the answering self-gift of virginity. Where integrity in responsive, sacrificial love exists it is the work of the Holy Spirit and is always fruitful.

An ancient Christian intuition linked virginity to the Eucharist, and in all four of the Christian motives for virginity just considered, the Eucharist is in some way implicated. Jesus's way of life excluded marriage not because marriage was too carnal but because it was too particular and restricted; he was destined to give his body in so total and radical a way that it transcends the 'possible particular sexual union'. The given body offered in sacrifice and glorified in his passover is made totally available to the Church in a union which 'recalls his passion, fills the soul with grace, and gives us a pledge of the glory that one day will be ours';[76] as virginity also looks back to the cross, is a sign of love now, and looks to the future Kingdom. Christ 'nourishes and cherishes'[77] the Church his Bride, with whom he has become one flesh. The central act of Christ, and of his Church, is sacramentally presented as a personal and carnal indwelling. The perfect achievement of Christian virginity is to be able to say with and to Christ: 'This is my body, given for you.'

Personal implications of the celibate vocation
a) 'Marginality'

There are two primary bodily relationships with other human beings into which a person can enter: full sexual relations with a person of the opposite sex, and parental relationship to children. These primary bodily relationships insert a person into the human community in a fundamental way. Since the celibate does not actualize these relationships, his mode of belonging to the human group is different. He is a marginal person. The eunuchs of whom the Lord spoke are those who lack the natural status given by sexuality and marriage, and so are without the source of human significance that most people have; voluntary celibates freely choose not to have this status, and so join the eunuchs in the marginal position.

Marginality is an important phenomenon in any society. The man who lives on the fringe, rejecting the normative way of life and many of its values, is often the object of fear and suspicion, particularly on the part of those whose interests lie in keeping the normative system going. Yet if he is not right outside the group but continues to camp on its borders, caring passionately about the good of the society and reminding it of the insufficiency of those things on which it spends most of its energies, he may serve it as a witness and a prophet. Monasticism had been from the beginning a marginal vocation. Monastic vows are meant to lift a person out of the struggle for money, position, and power, out of the social consequences and inherent limitations of sex, into a freedom for the Kingdom of God, and into a 'freedom to construct on the frontier an alternative society where joy can, amazingly, be found without sex, wealth, or the rat race. . . .'[78]

Unfortunately, though perhaps inevitably, the social non-status of early monastic movements seldom lasts; 'the monk flies to the desert in one generation, but he turns up in the corridors of power, maybe indeed in the House of Lords, in the next.'[79] Through the circumstances of history and their own vocation, EBC houses are generally in touch with, and more or less influenced by, the values and standards of an upper middle class way of life. The problems of conscience this recovery of status raises in the domain of monastic poverty will be discussed later.[80] Celibacy, however, is different; this is a matter in which we can be truly marginal, because no compromise is either necessary or in fact practised where celibacy is concerned, and yet there is in the EBC a broad, humane, and kindly tradition within which the positive values of celibacy have room to grow. Nevertheless there must be an element of real poverty in the celibate life or it will cease to be truly marginal. Not only must it be undertaken in full freedom; it must also manifestly free those who embrace it for the Kingdom of God. If it seems to free them instead for long hours before the television or the indulgence of petty fads it will witness to nothing of importance.

During most of Christian history the Church has exalted celibacy or virginity as an ideal at the expense of marriage. The New Testament gives little warrant for this, but Encratite tendencies appeared very early, and from St Augustine's time onwards the official teaching reflected a distrust of sexuality. Trent declared that it is better and holier to remain in a state of celibacy or virginity than to marry,[81] and the impression remained in the minds of very many Catholics until the twentieth century that from the spiritual point of view marriage was a second-class option. But a growing understanding of the values of marriage and sexual love precisely in view of Christian holiness was sanctioned by Vatican II,[82] and since the Council this understanding has so prevailed that among many committed Christians there is no longer much appreciation of the significance of celibacy. This is a spiritual revolution; we now have a situation where marriage is coming to be exalted among Christians at the expense of celibacy.

Up to a point this development is healthy. For many centuries the Christian system was built around the celibate, making him central. This was unhealthy and abnormal, because it led too easily to the suspicion that the exercise of sexuality was somehow sinful. Now the celibate is being pushed to the fringe, even in Christian thinking, which is right and proper because that is where he belongs. The reaction can, however, go too far. Just as it was unsound to extol celibacy at the expense of marriage, so Christian marriage stands to lose by the devaluation of celibacy. The two vocations are mutually necessary and neither gains by the disparagement of the other. Christian marriage and vowed Christian celibacy are both lifelong commitments to which the concept of fidelity is crucial; both are grounded in self-giving love; both involve painful self-denials when more attractive alternatives seem to promise instant 'fulfilment'. In a post-Christian permissive society where marital fidelity is no longer endorsed by the culture, faithful Christian couples can feel that they too are becoming almost marginal. They can then find inspiration and strength in the corporate witness of celibates, just as celibates in their turn are inspired by the fidelity of the married. Both ways of life require the support of a Christian community if they are to be sustained.

b) Poverty of spirit

Celibacy, looked at in itself, is a human deprivation, for the human person needs other persons if he is to grow and fulfil himself. Since growth in love, through the experience of giving and receiving and self-transcendence, normally comes to the individual above all in sexual love and marriage, the absence of such experience cannot in itself be a good thing. The vowed celibate therefore stands in a position of unalterable poverty, and virginity in the strict sense is a particularly sharp case of the personal poverty implied by celibacy in general. This situation is spiritually ambiguous. The unmarried condition can be, like material poverty and starvation, not merely a physical privation but a moral and spiritual stunting of the person and an occasion for bitterness and resentment. Like material poverty it can, however, be freely assumed in faith and love by the individual who responds to a personal call, and if so assumed it can be a means of self-emptying and openness to God who in the mystery of the redemption has overthrown human self-sufficiencies.

The celibate is taking a risk when he renounces marriage, because he is opting out of many things that would have forced him to grow up. Built into married life are not only the possibilities of happiness and human satisfactions, but also suffering, anxiety, disappointment, and responsibilities. The demands of marriage and parenthood provide the partners with ample opportunity for learning to be unselfish and considerate, flexible, realistic, and forgiving; and unless they learn these attitudes and grow towards maturity it is unlikely that the marriage will work. Celibates have to learn them too, and they can fail to do so. The tragedy of celibate life is to sink below the normal level of adult behaviour into seeking compensations for the emptiness within. If abstention from marriage fosters pettiness, little self-gratifications, hypochondria, crankiness and fussiness, self-pity and rigidity, it is not genuine Christian virginity at all but a means of narrowing and shrivelling the spirit.

This is a caricature, but it may help to indicate where the real risk lies for monastic celibates. It is not the risk of falling foul of the authorities as a troublesome deviant like Jeremiah; nor is it the kind of risk demanded by some Existentialists for authentic living, which might entail the abandonment of securities (such as leaving monastic life in middle age in response to a new experience of sexual love). It is the risk that, by cutting oneself off from certain experiences which are loudly proclaimed to be essential for personal growth, one may fail as a human being. Everything depends on our freely chosen attitude to a given situation. If we assume it with faith and love we have the power to transform a human emptiness into a spacious receptivity to God. This is not easy because there can be in faithful and generous celibate lives a real sense of personal diminishment and loss. What is sacrificed by the vow of celibacy can seem like the widow's mite, one's all. There is a genuine dimension of unfulfilment in the life of every celibate, and there are times when he or she feels celibacy to be sheer negation and can only hold on blindly. This felt tension between the desire for natural fulfilment and fidelity to the celibate vocation demands faith, a lived faith in the power of celibacy to foster charity. This is the real cross. There is a mysteriousness about celibacy which is not eliminated by the vision and the experience of wholeness in love which rightly inspires celibate life.

Mary's virginity at the time of the incarnation embodied the highest hope of the Old Testament. This expectation of Israel had been articulated in a very pure form in the prayer of the 'poor of Yahweh',[83] the people without status who, bereft of human supports and power, looked to God alone for their vindication. Closely related to this current of hope was the theme of sterility made fruitful.[84] When human potency is at zero but there is unconditional faith in the word of God, the redemptive incarnation takes place. Redemption begins with an act of pure grace.[85] Mary's faith, like Abraham's, is given to the God who brings life from death,[86] and 'her childbearing . . . is part of the new beginning of the world'.[87] In the story of the Annunciation and its sequel there are anticipations of Christ's new birth from the dead: the 'lowliness' of the handmaid foreshadows the obedient self-emptying of the Servant.[88] Her virginity already had a paschal character.

For Mary, virginity meant personal self-emptying for the Lord, complete availability for his plans, obedient faith, and identification with the Easter Christ. In her is signed forth the meaning of Christian virginity and celibacy.

c) Personal growth

Since Freud, it has been commonly recognized that human sexuality comprises both genitality and affectivity; that is, it includes not only a genital-physiological but also an affectionate-social side. These two are distinguishable but not entirely separable. Their integration is a human and Christian task. During childhood and adolescence they are out of step; the capacity for affection and friendship develops before the awakening of genitality at puberty, and it is usually only after some years of adolescent turmoil that the person's affections, tender emotions, and loyalties are sufficiently unified with the genital side to make his or her sexuality a spearhead for personal love and self-giving in marriage. Human sexual maturity is thus not an automatic achievement like physical maturity; it is the result of struggle and failure, of learning and many free choices.[89] Its perfection is the work of a lifetime, and it is as necessary in a celibate, who offers his sexuality to God with all it represents of his potential for love, as it is in those called to marriage. Unless celibates discover the meaning of sexuality in their lives, they cannot become fully human or free to love. Since the two sides of our sexuality cannot be entirely separated, it is necessary to accept and feel comfortable with the biological and physical side of maleness or femaleness, even though it will not be directly used, if the affective powers are to be given free play.[90]

Most people emerge from childhood and adolescence with many inner wounds, feelings of insecurity, and some lack of confidence. They may feel unwanted and uncertain of their own worth; they may be secretly unconvinced that they are lovable, and therefore afraid of any close, sustained involvement because others may find nothing acceptable in them. Unless the experience of steady, accepting love reduces these fears, the person will spend much of his or her psychic energy on merely staving off personal disintegration. Mature chastity in the celibate life, as in any other, demands a firm inner conviction that one is a lovable, valuable person, capable of faithful and responsible relationships. The predictability and faithfulness of one's own community which flow from vowed stability have therefore a special supportive part to play in the growth of monastic celibacy, by building up a person's sense of being loved, trusted, and needed, and so freeing him to love others. It may well be true that without the emotional support and inbuilt demands of marriage, without the sense of achievement that rightly results from giving life, it is in some ways harder to mature and to arrive at the fulness of humanity. But it is not impossible. Human fulfilment is not an automatic consequence of sexual arousal and release, or of entry on any particular state of life; it comes only from unselfish loving, whether in marriage or in celibacy. The only ultimately maturing thing in human life is love, and to this every Christian is called in fulness. The celibate is called, and by God's grace enabled, to explore a different dimension of loving, and to give to God a special quality of love. Moreover the great range of relationships which monks and nuns commonly have means that some growth is demanded of them all through their lives.

The gradual process of being freed from inner impediments to perfect love that continues through years of monastic life is therefore also a growth towards mature chastity. Fear, residual repressions, guilt-feelings, and any sort of non-acceptance of self are eroded by the love of God and that of human persons, and a steady unification of the whole personality is achieved around the central commitment expressed by the vows. Temptations may be as frequent and powerful as ever, but they are met on the strongest ground, where the person is in love with God.

In times of difficulty and temptation, and as his insight into his vocation develops, a monk must choose celibacy anew, with deeper understanding and greater freedom. The vow of conversion of life commits him to being open to growth; it has the dynamic quality which any relationship of love between persons must have if their love is not to die. It is also important that the renewed choice of celibacy be realistic. We can talk about the ideal of marriage and the ideal of celibacy. But married people experience the difficulties of marriage, and celibates the difficulties of celibacy. If comparisons are made, it must not be between the ideal of the one and the experienced difficulties of the other. A lonely or discouraged celibate can deceive himself by dreaming about an ideal of marriage, just as he can present a false case for celibacy if he compares the problems and frustrations of marriage with the ideal of his own vocation.

The process of integration implies the incorporation of the positive characteristics of the opposite sex under the unambiguous sign of one's own sexual identity. A man wholly masculine, or a woman unrelievedly feminine, would be intolerable. For a man, sexual maturity implies the integration of such supposedly feminine qualities as gentleness, intuitiveness, imagination, sympathy, patience, warmth, and receptivity. For a woman, it means integrating objectivity, rationality, strength and steadiness, the power to grasp the whole picture without getting lost in the details, clarity, outgoingness, and other qualities usually associated with men. In either case it means not a blurring of the characteristics of one's own sex, but an enrichment and balance.

The task of attaining maturity also involves acceptance of the degree of heterosexuality and homosexuality operative in one's personality. To label a person simply 'homosexual' is coming to be recognized as naïve, because there is a continuum of which only the two extremes – exclusive homosexuality and exclusive heterosexuality – are pathological.[91] All normal mature people are 'bisexual' in the sense of having an ability to relate to persons of either sex. The normal range is a broad plateau, not a knife-edge. It is inhabited by those (the majority) whose predominant orientation is heterosexual but who are capable of warm, deep, tender relationships with members of their own sex; and also by those whose basic preference is for their own sex but who are capable of warm affective relationships with members of the other. Each person has to come to terms with his or her particular sexual make-up, learn to be responsible for it, and discover how to make his or her particular contribution to human and monastic life.

One whose primary orientation is homosexual but who is on the way to achieving this integration should not be automatically excluded if he wants to be a monk. Such a person has the right and need of every human being to love, and to live a fully human life; he needs support, companionship, acceptance, and human warmth like anyone else. He can respond to God's love and is in principle as capable as any predominantly heterosexual person of dedicating his life to God in the monastery and of living out his dedication fruitfully in the service of God and his neighbour. There may, naturally, be special difficulties for such a person. Social disapproval of the homosexually oriented often causes them much suffering; it may therefore be harder for him to accept himself and come to terms with his sexuality than it is for most people. There may well be need for more vigilance and self-discipline on the part of a person living in a community of the sex to which he is naturally attracted. On the other hand, although his love and friendship for members of his own community will be qualitatively different, it need not be any less genuine or less needed in building up the community. He can be helped to see that he has a special contribution to make: his orientation is one of the 'given' elements in his personality and vocation, allowed by God and to be turned to good account.

An immature, non-integrated, and irresponsible person of homo-sexual orientation is not, however, a suitable candidate for monastic life. If he has so far failed to accept himself and his sexuality in lay life, and cannot control his impulses, he should not be encouraged to think that he can escape from his problems by entering a monastery. It is true that a monastic community is a healing environment, but normality and balance are required to sustain the responsibilities of a monastic vocation in celibacy as in any other area.

'Self-control' is one of the fruits of the Holy Spirit, together with love, joy, peace, and kindness.[92] The action of the Spirit begun at baptism purifies and transforms a celibate throughout his life, leading him towards wholeness. At the beginning a person is 'fleshly' even in his mind, according to St Paul, in the sense of being selfish and closed in on himself, impenetrable to the Spirit of God.[93] By the end, he is 'spiritual' even in his body,[94] for the creative action of the Holy Spirit has made the whole man transparent to the new life. Holy people sometimes seem to grow beautiful in old age, as the body becomes a transparent sign of the spirit. Eastern Orthodoxy treasures the memory of saints who while still living were seen to be transfigured by the divine light.[95] This is the consummation of the sacramental life, and more generally it is a sign that the long, slow process of assimilation to Christ is nearing its goal. The body is destined to disintegrate in death, but death is the Christian's final yielding to the Lord. The redemptive process will be complete when the body as well as the spirit of every believer shares in Christ's risen glory.

The Christian Fathers loved to speak of man as the microcosm in whom all the elements of creation are present;[96] he is born to be a mediator, for while bearing material creation within his own being he is also stamped with the divine image. He uses his body for worship, for creativity, for sacramental encounter, and for play. Sacred dance is in many cultures a body-language for the joy of communion with God. The body is far more than a vehicle for sex; it is man's means of communication with other persons and with the entire cosmos. Christian purity is not negation but intensity of life, the wholeness of a person mobilized for love in whom the full range of powers, passions, and emotions are under the sway of the Spirit and become instruments for loving and communicating, according to the person's vocation. In the mature celibate acceptance and peaceful, loving control of the genital side of sexuality, together with socialization of the affective side, releases all the richness and power of the personality for love. Compassion is an almost invariable sign of a sexually mature person. So is joy.[97] In this unity and wholeness of his being he can let himself be guided by his love, because the reflex movements of passion and sensibility no longer dominate but, developed to their full potentiality, enrich and strengthen the spiritual love of charity, as servants of the free spirit. The chaste person is one in whom flesh and spirit, healed and made whole by grace, are a living and loving unity.[98] This is real freedom, the integrity of heart and clarity of vision evoked by the gospel, the blessedness of the clean of heart.[99]

d) Friendship, prayer, and fruitfulness

Three joys at the heart of celibate life are friendship, prayer, and fruitful ministry.

Christian community life is based on friendship, friendship with God and with others who share God's life. A monastic community therefore lives and thrives on homosexual friendships in the positive sense of this expression: that is, on friendships which are non-genital and non-exclusive. The classic expression of the theology of Christian friendship is that of St Aelred, and it was worked out in a fully monastic environment. Aelred approves a tentative translation of the Johannine text: 'God is friendship (*amicitia*), and he that abides in friendship abides in God and God in him.'[100] Man was made in the image of God, and so true human friendship springs from 'the high estate of man and his heart's longing'.[101] It can exist only where Christ is mediator: 'Here we are, just the two of us, and I hope Christ makes the third.'[102] Jesus called us his friends and he has given us the formula of friendship, says Aelred, quoting Ambrose, namely, 'the accomplishment of one's friend's will, and the frank communication of one's deepest feelings and thoughts'.[103] My friend is a guardian of our mutual love and a guardian of my spirit, to preserve all my secrets, to cure or endure my faults, bear my burdens, rejoice in my joys, weep at my sorrows, and feel as his own all that I experience.[104] This friendship tends towards Christ who becomes more and more the bond of union, and in him it is constantly purified. The full flowering of the human person in the friendship of community will be realized only in heaven.[105]

To this community friendship the members rightly look for the main affective support in their lives. Freed from inhibitions, fears, and the desire to dominate, a mature celibate is able to love others in simplicity of heart and without the need for genital expression. Close friendships within the community focus and strengthen the general love, and give a monk the chance to make some return for all he has received.

But if the affection which sustains the community is allowed to veer towards genital expression, a wrongness comes in. The persons involved are privatizing the warm friendship on which the whole community lives, because they are appropriating this general love and trying to express it in a way proper to the private heterosexual relationship of marriage.[106] Such an intense one-to-one involvement inevitably makes them less open and available to the rest of the community, and is therefore destructive of the *koinonia* which is one of the bases of monastic celibacy. Even a relationship which stops short of genital expression is destructive if it becomes a psychological appropriation of the other person, exclusive, possessive, and devouring. This is fundamentally selfish in that it fails to respect the other's freedom and is inimical to the general friendship of the community. This is the real evil of 'particular friendships' in the pejorative sense of that famous phrase.

Heterosexual friendships are of such great significance that it is difficult to believe that mature celibacy is often achieved without them. Partnership, collaboration, exchange of ideas, and friendship between the sexes are part of the Creator's plan and should not be excluded by celibacy. It is a common experience that while a celibate may enjoy close and warm friendships with members of his or her own sex, contacts and friendships with members of the opposite sex are enriching and enjoyable in a different way. It is normal for men and women to enjoy each other's company, to stimulate and inspire each other, and to rejoice in their complementarity. Celibates are perfectly aware that this experience is in a broad sense sexual;[107] affection naturally develops and genital feelings may be aroused. This should not give rise to alarm; a mature celibate can recognize and control these feelings and understand that their activation is an aspect of the activation of his whole personality. Indeed, in the measure in which he is really chaste they are bound to be aroused; St Thomas remarks that insensitivity is a vice,[108] and if someone has been living monastic life generously for years his or her capacity to love, appreciate, and respond should be intensified, not atrophied. This is not to deny the need for prudence. There is no area in which self-deception is easier. Exposure may not always be the best for everyone, and a person who feels the need for some shielding should not be goaded into rash behaviour by fear that he will be thought immature if he acts otherwise. To accept a certain apparent lack of human fulfilment is part of a celibate's essential poverty of spirit, and readiness to acknowledge one's limitations a mark of maturity. Nevertheless, mature chastity brings equilibrium as well as sensitivity, and a person can be conscious of attraction without feeling that he is slipping over the edge. Healthy heterosexual friendships can therefore bring confidence, together with joy, freedom of heart, and gratitude to God for the gift of friendship. It is like meeting a fellow-pilgrim along the way. The celibate's dedication is thereby strengthened.

The matter is not radically different when a celibate thoroughly committed to his vocation and not necessarily lonely realizes that a friendship with someone of the opposite sex has grown to a point where the relationship is like no other. He may find that this friend calls out things in him that no other person calls out, and touches places in his mind and personality that no one else touches; that he can find understanding and response in her as in no other, and relate to her precisely as a man to a woman.[109] This realization should not arouse panic or guilt-feelings, nor should it be denied. The person concerned should admit the truth of the situation to himself and to God, and pray for wisdom to handle it according to God's will. He should be honest in watching for any signs that the friendship may be going wrong; these signs could be a tendency to give up prayer, erosion of one's commitment to the community or to obedience, resentment about sharing the friend's love with others, possessiveness, or a gravitation towards genital exchange in the expression of love. But being aware of these possibilities does not mean that the friendship becomes a matter of nervous watching for boundaries that must not be overstepped. He should act as a happily married man passionately in love with his wife would act towards a friend of the opposite sex. With the help of grace the experience can then be a lifting of the heart and sheer gift from God. He can discover in it his capacity for an open, trusting, faithful relationship of a deeply loving kind, and this *within* the abiding commitment to the Lord in virginity. The result is an inner release and a new sense of freedom, of personal worth, and of confidence in his uniqueness and sexual identity, which then becomes the basis for a freer, deeper, and more joyful renewal of the dedication to God by vow. In peace with this love-commitment to God and enriched by the experience of human love he can love the brethren and all men better, with more insight, humility, and compassion. The understanding support of a superior is invaluable to anyone going through this. We should be aware of the successes as well as the failures.

The effect of warm community relations and of close friendships rightly handled is not to diminish the solitude of heart inherent in a monastic vocation, but to provide the climate of love in which a monk can find the meaning of his solitude and so of his celibacy. This inner solitude is a condition for self-knowledge and deep prayer, an experience in which a person grows in purity of heart and comes to grips with his vocation. Personal prayer of an intimate, frequent, and demanding character is a necessity for the attainment of mature chastity by a celibate who chooses to be vulnerable and open in the human sphere, if he is to have a sufficiently strong interior focus.[110]

But solitude is felt, and it may feel like loneliness. This experience may not have anything to do with celibacy as such; it may be simply a problem of living, the kind of problem that anyone who lives life deeply must face. But it is important that those preparing for vows should be warned of it, and not deceived with any glib talk about 'finding compensation' in community life. Community relationships are not meant to be a substitute for married love, since they lack the physical expression, the one-to-one exclusiveness and (usually) the emotional reinforcement proper to marriage. If this is not made clear to potential celibates in the time of training, a person who later feels the bite of solitude may conclude either that he has no vocation to celibacy, or that he is failing God, or that the community is failing him, when in fact he is undergoing a desert experience and the kind of 'death' from which comes rebirth and spiritual fruitfulness.

Work is a vital element in a monk's availability for others and so in his celibacy. The wrong kind of busyness is an enemy of chastity because it is an evasion of the desert experience and can become a state of habitual commotion which diminishes real personal availability to God in prayer and to the community in love; it can also be a seeking to enlarge the self in a way that conflicts with the spirit of poverty. But there is a right way of being hard worked that stretches the person, gets the best out of him and calls him to a self-transcendence and a fruitfulness he would not have thought possible. Part of the celibate's sacrifice is renunciation of biological fruitfulness; it is a great achievement to extend one's life into the life of another. But there are other ways of living fruitfully. Priestly ministry and teaching are special forms of self-giving, life-giving love. Artistic work, scholarship, and such domestic arts as cooking and gardening are creative activities that foster life. Supporting the sick, the weak or the troubled, or any form of community-building is an act of creative love, and prayer is always fruitful whether we see the results or not. Christ has told us that the Father is glorified by the fruitfulness of our lives, and that the condition for bearing abundant fruit is to abide in Jesus Christ by loving obedience.[111]

Eucharistic union with Christ and one another is at once a means of our fruitful 'abiding' and the promise that human loneliness will eventually be overcome. Human sexuality at its mature fulness desires interpersonal union at the highest and deepest levels of which human persons are capable. The desire and dream of lovers is the two-in-one-flesh of mutual indwelling. Christians are promised a fulfilment of their desire for personal communion in the fellowship of the saints, but even now we are closer to one another in the Body of Christ than we can be in any purely natural union, although our senses do not help us to realize it. The daily Eucharist in monastic communities is an act of consent to life in the Body, to the many-in-one-flesh union with Christ and one another, to the bearing of the burdens and sins and wounds of the Body, and to the responsibility of receiving love from Christ through the others that we may give it again.

Obedience

'Hearing the word' and 'the obedience of faith' are among the earliest descriptions of the Christian response to God's saving act in Christ. Obedience is a paschal, baptismal calling; it is the vocation of all Christians and is inseparable from hearing the Good News of salvation, inseparable from faith, from the following of Christ, from sonship to God, and from brotherhood in God's people. Monastic obedience finds its full meaning only in this total Christian context. It is not an ascetical extra, but is Christian obedience articulated in a special way. To reduce it to a mere execution of a superior's orders is therefore to denature it.

The monastic vows and the monastic way of life together form an integral unity. This fact has been noticed already in connection with Stability and Conversion but becomes still clearer in the chapter which follows, where obedience is seen as intertwined with the personal and social responsibilities flowing from the other vows.

This chapter therefore considers monastic obedience within the broad picture of Christian salvation and monastic life, and relates it to personal growth, freedom, and love.

Introduction:
the historical tradition

In his doctrine of obedience St Benedict was heir to a complex tradition. On the one hand he was strongly influenced by the teaching of Cassian and the Master, which itself viewed monastic obedience in two different perspectives.[1] On the other hand St Benedict enriched this double tradition derived from Cassian and the Master with insights more closely related to the cenobitic tradition of Pachomius and Basil. There are thus at least three perspectives, and it may be helpful to distinguish them historically before considering their bearing on monasticism today.

a) Obedience to Christ

The abbot (or in Cassian's writings the 'ancient') was understood to be Christ's representative and as such the spokesman of Christ.[2] By standing as heir to a succession of teachers stretching back to the apostles he is in a position to mediate to the disciple the 'divine law' or will of God in particular circumstances. Cassian justifies this assumption in terms of his customary myth according to which cenobitic monastic life originated in apostolic times;[3] the Master attempts to establish it more rigorously by presenting the abbot as endowed with the 'teacher's' charism. But in either case the typical obedience situation is the same: the disciple, as an ignorant and sinful man, is assumed to be unable to hear the word or know the will of the Lord unaided. He therefore has recourse to Christ's representative and opens his mind freely to him, revealing his thoughts, desires, and actions. The superior's duty is to discern, on the basis of what he is told, the will of Christ for the disciple and to mediate it to him. The typical text used to ground this kind of obedience is Luke 10.16, 'He who hears you, hears me': in listening to and obeying his superior, who is Christ's representative, the monk listens to and obeys Christ.[4] It should be noted that in this perspective the main stress is on discovering the objective content of God's will. Further, the quality of the one who commands in Christ's name is vital: the abbot in this teaching capacity must be 'learned in the divine law' and himself be Christlike.

b) Monastic obedience as an imitation of Christ's obedience

For Cassian and the Master Christ is not only the Lord to whom the disciple's obedience is due, he is also the Son who obeys the Father and by his sacrificial obedience redeems the world. Hence he is the exemplar of the monk who is by adoption God's son. The typical texts they use when obedience is seen in this light are John 6.38, 'I came to do not my own will but the will of him who sent me'; Philippians 2.8, 'He was made obedient even unto death'; and Matthew 26.39, 'Not my will but thine be done.'[5] Christ obeyed his Father by submitting to Mary and Joseph, to the civil authorities, and even to his executioners, all of whom in their several ways were his Father's instruments. It follows that the monk who imitates and participates in Christ's sacrifice can find opportunities for obedience not only in submitting to the will of the abbot but also in obeying the brethren and regarding all the circumstances of his life as occasions for abandoning himself to the

Father's will. The stress is now not on the objective content of God's will as something to be discovered, but on the subjective dispositions of the disciple, for whom obedience is the means of renouncing his self-will, practising humility, and aligning his will with the redemptive will of Christ. Obedience is an act of going forth from himself to embrace the will of the Other; it is the means of his 'martyrdom' and as such his *bonum*. Cassian considers that in view of the importance of this type of obedience the superior has the duty to 'mortify' the disciple's self-will by imposing hard, stupid, unreasonable tasks on him.[6] It is interesting to see how St Benedict departed from this doctrine in his sixty-eighth chapter, inspired probably by St Basil.

c) Obedience and community life

The more thoroughly cenobitic tradition represented by Pachomius and Basil contributed another perspective to the understanding of monastic obedience. The *koinonia* of the monastic brotherhood is for them the means of making present the apostolic life of the first disciples, and the monks imitate Christ's *kenosis* precisely by their mutual love and service, for Christ became the servant of all.[7] This insight is clearly present in St Benedict's Chapters 71 and 72. Further, the cenobitic tradition of the abbot as the unitive centre of the brotherhood, with responsibility for the good of all its members, points to an understanding of obedience which situates it in the whole context of community life, shared responsibility, and the monk's commitment to the community by his vows of stability and conversion.

If monastic obedience is understood in sense (a), it must be seen as something that a monk can to some extent grow out of. Cassian recognized that a monk, at first ignorant and sinful, could mature in conscience to the point when he was able to discern God's will for himself.[8] Then he could depart to the solitary life, where although he could have recourse to the advice of desert veterans in particular difficult cases, obedience as a regular practice was no longer necessary to him. The end had been achieved, and the means could be discarded.

However, obedience in sense (b) could not be left behind; on the contrary, the need and desire for this conformity with Christ might be expected to grow stronger as the monk grew in charity. So Cassian tells a story of the hermit John who after twenty years of solitary contemplation returned to the *cenobium*, partly because he wished to be freed from solicitude about his temporal needs, but partly also because he wanted to be obedient unto death like Christ.[9] It is also clear in the light of the Augustinian-Pachomian-Basilian tradition of community life that obedience in sense (c) cannot become obsolete either.

It may be suggested, therefore, that in the modern context where the general standard of education is higher, where wide reading is normal in monastic communities and most monks are priests, the educative function of obedience (type a) is less important. In obedience, as in prayer, education is necessary and prominent in the early years; later the need for it diminishes, though it can never be wholly superseded for any monks. The highly educated may stand in great need of the abbot's help in discerning the will of God for them, and an earlier chapter has discussed the abbot's function as teacher in monasticism today.[10] But this perspective is probably less significant for most monks where obedience is concerned than perspectives (b) and (c). It is with these, therefore, that the following pages will be mainly concerned.

Personal aspects of obedience

a) Obedience as a personal relationship with God in union with Christ

St John's Gospel presents the life, death, and resurrection of Jesus as a revelation of the glory of God. The will of the Father is Jesus's 'food';[11] he came down from heaven to do not his own will but the will of him who sent him.[12] When the 'hour' to which Jesus several times alludes has come, it is the hour of both his passion and his glory,[13] but not in the sense that there is a simple chronological sequence: first suffering, degradation, and death in obedience to the Father's will, and afterwards the glory. In some way difficult for us to grasp clearly, the fourth evangelist sees the passion-resurrection of Jesus as the final, single, and undivided 'sign' of the glory of God revealed in his obedient Son; the 'hour' of the passion is the time for the 'exaltation' of Jesus, which implies simultaneously his lifting up on the cross and his ascension to the Father. In this hour the Son of Man is glorified, and the Father is glorified in him.

Pauline Christology suggests a similar insight in the 'Christ-hymn' of Philippians 2.5–11. Its opening lines are usually understood in a concessive sense: '*Although* he was in the form of God, Jesus did not consider equality with God something to be grasped, but emptied himself . . . and became obedient unto death. . . .' But it is also grammatically and theologically possible to translate them, as is done by a respectable minority of scholars,[14] '*Because* he was in the form of God. . . .' The statement would then be not concessive but causative: self-giving love, an obedient love that empties itself and holds nothing back, is a Godlike quality.

Both this interpretation of the Pauline hymn and the Johannine theology of glory suggest that Godlikeness and divine sonship, when translated into terms of human living and dying, find their only possible expression in total obedience. Of course there is a *prima facie* contradiction, for a man hanging on a cross is not in any obvious way a revelation of the glory of God. But this is because Christ's act of loving obedience is consummated in a sinful world and in the conditions of our flesh. Deeper than the physical suffering and the spiritual 'Godforsakenness' of Jesus is the Godlike will to give. Jesus 'sought not his own glory'[15] but the One who sent him sought it and glorified him, for the very refusal to seek his own aggrandizement was already an expression of the nature of God. He came into the world to 'bear witness to the truth',[16] and the manner of his life and death bore witness to what God is like. He saw his vocation to live out Godlike manhood not (as we might) in terms of self-will or domination, but as a call to self-emptying and self-giving, and his resurrection revealed the glory that had been the 'within' of the act but had been concealed by the conditions of his sacrifice. This paradox of humbling and exaltation is found in Jesus's own teaching,[17] and may be thought to underlie St Benedict's description of the monk's *kenosis* as he climbs the ladder of humility.

Recent scholarship has shown that underlying the Prologue to the Rule of the Master, and therefore indirectly the Prologue to St Benedict's Rule also, there may well be a post-baptismal catechetical sermon treating of conversion and designed, in its adapted form, to teach the monk the way of Christian life.[18] It thus links monastic obedience very closely to paschal, baptismal obedience. The monk or would-be monk is the sinful son who is to find in the 'labour of obedience' the way back to his Father, from whom he has wandered by the 'laziness of disobedience'. Later, in Chapter 7, St Benedict explicitly associates the monk's obedience with the redemptive obedience of Christ,[19] and in Chapter 2 speaks of the call to adoptive sonship through the gift of the Spirit. For a monk, therefore, obedience is his calling in the Spirit; it is the Spirit who conforms him to the obedient will of Jesus, enabling him to take the gospel seriously and to know and love the will of the Father.

This does not mean that he finds the Father's will primarily in the material content of the command; rather it is to be found in the *form* of monastic obedience, in the willingness to hear, in the attitude of heart that enables a man to hear, in humility. St Benedict's obedience is not in the first place 'executive' obedience, a means of getting something done. The value and the Godlikeness in it derive not from the end-product but from the manner in which the human spirit becomes free and is conformed to Christ. That St Benedict understood it in this way is evident from his statement that if a monk carries out the command but murmurs, even in his heart, his obedience is worthless.[20] This could not be the case if God's will were to be sought simply in the content of the order.

Thus the heart of monastic obedience is the monk's personal, free, humble, and love-impelled surrender to the will of God. He is invited to *listen* and incline the ear of his heart;[21] through obedience he offers himself to God without reservation.[22] He sees this attitude as 'suitable' or 'becoming' for one who holds nothing dearer than Christ,[23] and knows obedience to be his 'good' because it is his road to God.[24] This will to obey is possible only because 'the Spirit that we have in common' enables us to 'have this mind among ourselves which was in Christ Jesus';[25] monastic obedience is not merely an imitation of the obedience of Christ but a participation in it through the gift of the Spirit of sonship.

In practice, therefore, obedience becomes for the monk an effective expression of love, and a means of gaining freedom to follow the will of God by directing his own will towards God and away from self-deception. As St Benedict points out, obedience is also closely related to prayer.[26] The heart of prayer is the loving act of wanting God's will, and since monks are dedicated to the single-minded love of God in purity of prayer[27] the connection between their prayer and the simplicity of heart fostered by obedience is inescapable.

All this is clear enough. The difficulties begin when the theory is applied to the concrete business of living, and particularly to the relationship between the 'reasonable' obedience that any sane human being practises all his life and the 'supernatural' obedience that leads a monk into the area of faith and mystery. Obedience in situations where the one in the subordinate position can see the good which the command intends to achieve is a human and intelligent act, and may be a mature act of great dignity: to co-operate in some team effort (as in scientific research, or in a surgical operation, or in sport) by sinking one's own opinion and preferences in the interests of the good to be achieved is a human and adult act. Civic obedience can be a larger instance of the same thing. Similarly, men naturally follow a leader who is seen to be stronger, wiser, and more trustworthy than most others. And we have no difficulty in appreciating that it is reasonable to study the maker's instructions or follow the doctor's orders.

All these and other forms of rational obedience can be seen in the wider context of God's government of his universe through secondary causes, and in healthy monastic life they should be normal. It follows that the monk's spirit of obedience need be in no way eroded by the fact that he can appreciate the reason for a course of action required of him, or for an arrangement made or an order given by his superior. On his side the abbot or the holder of delegated authority should be willing to give reasons when he can; the maximizing of information generally promotes charitable community life and adult obedience.

The same harmony between faith and reason still holds in the case where the monk cannot in a particular instance see the reason for an order (perhaps because the superior is obliged to withhold some information out of respect for another person) but knows that his abbot is accustomed to govern justly and wisely. This is not to say that obedience is always easy, even in these cases when the command is seen or assumed to be reasonable. A person can experience resistance within himself because his will is seeking an alternative good, namely the assertion of individual identity. But this is a hardship, not a problem; the duty of 'reasonable' obedience, though not easy, is simple and clear.

The sweet reasonableness of God's universe has been disrupted, however, especially in the domain of human affairs, by the unreasonableness of sin. In the rare case where a monk finds that an order given him conflicts with what he understands to be his duty of obedience to God as a Christian the matter is clear. But the unreasonableness of sin touches our experience of obedience in more subtle ways than this. Monastic obedience is a personal relationship, and the sin-situation in which all men are involved sometimes spoils personal relationships, even when there is no question of sinful abuse of authority. Sooner or later the monk will collide with the effects of sin and sinfulness not only in himself but also in his abbot or other superiors. These effects may take the form of prejudice, fear, suspicion, or lack of trust; they may manifest themselves in misunderstanding, narrowmindedness, or blind spots. They may not be crystallized in a particular episode but simply leave the impression that things could be a good deal better and that more vision is needed. What then? The monk is not asked to practise 'blind obedience' or unreasonable obedience. But he is asked to step for a time with Christ on to the plane of obedience in faith, into the mystery of the redemptive, loving obedience of Jesus who faced and accepted as part of the Father's will the whole unsatisfactoriness of things in a sin-spoiled world, and by his attitude transformed all the circumstances of his death into the stuff of sacrifice. This is the folly of the cross, the foolishness of God that is wiser than men,[28] and in some mysterious way it was necessary for Jesus himself, in order that he might become 'perfect' at the level of his human understanding of his sonship and his human response to it. Son though he was, he 'learned obedience through the things he suffered'.[29]

St Benedict anticipated that heroic obedience of this calibre would sometimes be called for, as is clear from his description of it at the fourth rung of the ladder of humility: 'Meeting in this obedience with difficulties and contradictions and even injustice, he should hold on to patience with a quiet mind, and enduring neither tire nor run away. . . . In all these things we are more than conquerors, through him who has loved us.'[30] But he surely did not expect that this would be the *normal* experience of monastic life, and he did distinguish this paschal spirit of obedience from *contristatio*, which he regarded as a major obstacle to monastic fulfilment. Among the most frequent causes of *contristatio* are a defective respect for obedience on the part of the monk, and faults in the exercise of authority on the part of superiors or officials.[31]

b) The vow of obedience

By virtue of the vow of obedience the value of our activities is reinforced by the overall intention to follow God's will in each particular situation. Hence while Scripture acknowledges the excellence of sacrifice, it also declares that obedience is better than sacrifice.[32] The constant teaching of the prophets was that the heart of true sacrifice is an obedient and humble will. Obedience is a safeguard against the danger of Pharisaical pride in religion.

A monk pronounces his vow of obedience in the presence of God and his brethren, in order to give outward expression to his inward dedication, and to give public witness to his determination to follow God's call in the monastic life. This outward corporeal action is a sign of his union with Christ who said, 'You have prepared a body for me. I come to do your will, O God.'[33] By that will 'we have been sanctified through the offering of the body of Jesus Christ once for all'.[34] Christ's human body was the means of communication with men on earth, and when glorified it became the source from which the Spirit could be given to all men.[35]

The redemptive mystery revealed in Christ includes both personal and communal realities. The monk as an individual returns to God in Christ, and by allowing the Spirit to lead and transform him responds to his vocation as God's son. But this return and the perfecting of the human person in adoptive sonship are achieved through communion with other human persons in the Body of Christ, within a network of relationships transformed by the power of the Spirit. It follows that monastic obedience implies both a highly personal asceticism of surrender to God in love and humility, and also the experience of transfigured human relationships – relationships of love, trust, and commitment between monk and abbot, monk and community, and abbot and community.

Obedience and community life

a) The total context

A monk's obedience is due to his Creator, from whom he accepts his being and his particular gifts of nature and grace. His obedience is to the gospel, as the Spirit through the lifelong process of conversion likens him to Christ and perfects him in his calling as God's son. His obedience is to his monastic vocation, and so not only must he walk in the Spirit but he may also expect from the abbot and community the help he needs to discern and obey his vocation. His obedience is to the abbot and the brethren, for this is the sign of his wholehearted concern for the will of the Father, the sign of that radical obedience to God which is the meaning of his vocation. His obedience is to the Rule and Constitutions, but as in Scripture all law must be understood in the service of covenant; it defines the conditions of the covenant-relationship with God and with the covenant-community.

It is important not to isolate any of these elements. In St Benedict's system the role of the abbot and the place of obedience are paramount, but they are set within monastic life. If obedience to a superior's order is isolated from, or set over against, the Rule or monastic tradition or community life, anything can be deemed 'monastic' simply because it is ordered, and monastic obedience can lose its true character. Obviously among sinful human beings conflicts are to be expected at times. At one extreme, the abbot has the right and duty to insist on obedience, even over a minor issue, if he considers that by his behaviour a monk is preferring self-will to the will of God. At the other extreme, cases may arise where a monk has a duty to follow his own conscience, even if this leads to conflict with the abbot or the community. But the very occurrence of these limit situations points to a failure on the part of the abbot, or the community, or the individual monk.

Conflict between the different elements in obedience can be minimized by the maintenance of a good tradition, not only in the exercise of authority and personal response to it, but in the whole monastic life which is the setting for obedience. The vow of obedience is intertwined with the other monastic vows. In promising stability a monk binds himself to the community, in which the abbot plays a key role, and to every member of it. His obedience is thereby invested with a special quality of responsibility for others and situated fully in the context of community life. Stability implies an acceptance of the structured character of the community in which each has his part to play, and an acceptance of belonging to the community together with all that flows from belonging. If this is kept in mind, obedience on the one hand and initiative or responsibility on the other cannot be competing values but are correlative. The social dimension of obedience entails the duty to speak the truth in love, a duty for which the monk is answerable because of his stability. If obedience is divorced from this community responsibility, both true tolerance and mature obedience are lost. Either flabbiness and irresponsibility can be rationalized as obedient submissiveness, or an irresponsible whim to speak or act without regard to the structured character of the community can be mistaken for genuine obedience to one's vocation and the gospel. Similarly monastic obedience is intertwined with conversion, because the dynamic conversion going on all through a monk's life under the action of the Spirit deepens the mystery of obedience, transforming the person and enabling him to know the will of the Father.

The vow of obedience reinforces a monk's responsibility for his life and actions in the individual domain as well. A militaristic conception of obedience might favour the tendency to abdicate conscientious decision on the grounds that a man must do what he is told. The monk on the contrary should have a heightened sense of his personal responsibility for forming and following his conscience, not only at the time of his profession but in his continuing free choice to devote himself to God in the monastery.[36] Even when asking permissions of his superior he in no way abdicates his personal responsibility. He shoulders the responsibility himself in deciding to ask for a permission, and remains answerable to God for all his deliberate actions, whether they are done with the superior's consent or without it. Through multiplied individual fidelities of this kind a strong tradition of mature obedience is formed in a community.

b) Obedience to Rule and abbot

The word of God calls us to the obedience of faith,[37] and this obedience can be rendered to God by listening to the teaching of superiors authorized by the community of faith. In the case of the Benedictine monk, this obedience is directed particularly to the Rule and the abbot.[38]

Obedience to the Rule of St Benedict ensures that the monk enjoys the support of the living tradition from which the Rule itself arose, and to which it contributed. The local 'Rule'[39] and the example of the elders enshrine the particular traditions of the house and provide the monk with the immediate framework within which he can best exercise his monastic ministry of service to the brethren, the Church and the world, and respond to his baptismal vocation. Just as the gospel is a source of spiritual life and not a mere revision of the Mosaic law,[40] so for the monk the Rule is a positive stimulus to monastic living rather than a rigid code.[41]

Acceptance of the gospel is above all acceptance of the person of Christ, and in the Benedictine response to the call of God a certain primacy is given to the person of the abbot: the monk's obedience is not addressed in the first place to an abstract tradition or even to a concrete institution as such. It is fitting that one person be designated as the sign of the unity that flows from true charity,[42] and the abbot 'is believed to hold Christ's place in the monastery'.[43] The abbot cannot replace Christ in the life of the monk, but the Rule is pervaded by the idea of sacramental encounter with Christ in persons, things, and circumstances, and the abbot's role is particularly significant in this respect, as St Benedict explains when mentioning his title, *Abbas*. This title 'Father' indicates that he loves his monks and serves them in such a way as to promote their growth to maturity in monastic life. St Benedict insists on the abbot's duty to study the needs, gifts, and grace of each monk, in order to help him to obey his Christian vocation to the full.

c) Obedience to the brethren

The abbot acts within the life and tradition of the community, and his task is not to stifle new thinking but to foster the community's growth in accordance with its own tradition. The abbot's own obedience to God is set in the context of the community's search for God, and his duty to listen to the community is dictated not merely by human prudence but by the fact that the living spirit of the community is incarnate in the individuals who compose it. It is not as a private individual, however charismatically gifted, that the abbot receives the monk's vows. He is authorized to do so by being chosen from the community, normally by election and normally from among the monks of the house, and his appointment must be ratified by the authority of the wider ecclesial community.[44] And since the monks promise stability in the community until death, they undertake a loyalty to the community involving acceptance of whatever persons may be legitimately chosen to hold the office of abbot.

Obedience to the community is fundamentally a matter of charity; it both gives expression to the monks' love of God and promotes growth in that love.[45] Again this involves love of persons rather than a love of some abstract idea or ideal of what the community is or should be. The community's true identity is grounded in right relations between its members and in their common desire to be monks together under one Rule and one abbot. Even where the law of love prevails, legislation is still needed to help in understanding 'the kind of act in which love is or is not likely to be present'.

A monk's obedience to his brethren shares certain qualities with his obedience to the abbot, but there is an element of abbatial authority that cannot be delegated and must not be usurped. St Benedict treats this theme explicitly in terms of the unity, peace and charity of the community, which would be threatened or destroyed if the officials of the monastery, and particularly the prior, were to claim an obedience equal to that owed to the abbot.[46]

In those areas where the abbot can and must delegate authority he should, however, show confidence in his officials and allow scope for their personal competence and initiative.[47] This is especially true of monks assigned to pastoral and educational work, which involves immediate responsibility to other people. In their turn the monks who work under officials should remember that their general commitment to obey the abbot and all the brethren will apply in particular to the monks under whose immediate authority they have been set. The quality of obedience owed to officials will vary according to the kind of delegated authority they hold. Officials such as the bursar have an executive role to which the 'educative' element of the abbot's authority and the disciple's obedience is irrelevant; but other officials who are placed over their brethren for the latter's good, such as the novice master, junior master, or superior of a dependent priory, genuinely hold some delegated element of the abbot's authority to teach and discern, and the obedience of their subordinates should therefore be similar in kind, though not in degree, to that owed to the abbot.

The delegation of real autonomy to a monk in a position of pastoral or executive responsibility requires of him the effort to find a just balance between his official duties and his obedience to the common life of the Rule, with regard, for instance, to attendance in choir. Another delicate balance has to be struck between, on the one hand, a monk's duty to shoulder the burden within his own sphere of competence, giving of his best to the work and bearing the responsibilities of judgement and decision, and, on the other, his duty to keep the abbot informed. This is a question of adequate and trustful communication; it will clearly vary according to circumstances, but it is essential to monastic obedience.

Some consequences

a) Obedience and dialogue

The overall attitude of obedience necessarily finds expression in following the particular precepts of legitimate authorities without hesitation, reluctance, or complaint.[48] This does not, however, imply that the monk always can or always should conform his interior judgement to that of his superior, and he is encouraged to communicate his considered convictions humbly but openly to the abbot, whether in private or in council with the brethren.[49] Where there is a real and deep relationship of trust between monk and abbot, and a genuine spirit of obedience in both of them, the dialogue that precedes a decision about a course of action can be honest, open, and a real act of giving on both sides. The monk feels free to open his mind and state the whole truth as he sees it, because he knows that his superior trusts him and knows that he will obey; the abbot on his side feels no need to assert his authority by deciding prematurely or arbitrarily.

The discussion then becomes a genuine search *together* for the will of

God. But it is perhaps illusory to think that only one of the possible options can be 'the will of God'. The outcome may be that the abbot leaves the monk free to choose between alternative possibilities, and if so there is obviously no incompatibility between obedience and the exercise of choice. One could go further and say that the shared effort to discern the will of God in the situation has led to the conclusion that God's will is precisely that we should sometimes grow by accepting the uncomfortable responsibility of making a choice without any secure feeling that we have certainly chosen rightly.

b) Perspectives of growth and maturity in obedience

Just as the mechanical conformity which reduces obedience to mere disciplined behaviour can be less demanding, so a conception of the will of God as something that can be neatly discovered, understood, and performed is something less than the mystery into which obedience invites us. The Christian and monastic model for discerning God's will in a given situation is not that of finding the solution to a crossword puzzle, where the answer must be exactly right, fitted to some preconceived plan. A better model is that we are given building blocks and have to see what can be done with them, using in the task all our intelligence, sensitivity, and love. The vocation to obedience is therefore an invitation to growth and self-transcendence. St Benedict suggests this in Chapter 68 of the Rule, where after provision has been made for the monk's right to make suitable representations to his superior when given a command that seems impossible, the situation is envisaged in which he may simply have to try. In such a case he must 'obey out of love, trusting in God's help'. Even if this does not refer to any miraculous intervention by the Lord, it clearly does present obedience as a stretching experience, drawing out of the obedient man abilities he did not know he had: 'The arrow endures the string, to become, in the gathering out-leap, something more than itself.'[50]

It is not in accord with Benedictine tradition to interpret obedience primarily in terms of scrupulous attention to minor precepts, and with the rise in standards of education and personal responsibility the Benedictine tradition has on the whole developed away from concentration on minor regulations towards a better appreciation of the broad principles of obedience. The EBC has perhaps been aided in its consciousness of the distinction between sound obedience and detailed supervision by the large degree of independence that was necessary for monks working on the English Mission. Nevertheless the Congregation was not immune to the influences of the Counter-Reform during which it was re-founded, when a concept of obedience fundamentally different from that of St Benedict became widespread in the Church. It is of great importance that in the rapidly developing open society of the present day we appreciate and practise an obedience that is intelligent, responsible, and grounded in love.

Even within a sound monastic tradition, however, and in communities where the greatest goodwill is present, tensions are bound to arise sometimes. Obedience rendered to God by persons indwelt by the Spirit ought to be joyful, even, in the strict sense of the word, ecstatic. In practice, because both superiors and subjects are still to some extent living 'according to the flesh', obedience may often be experienced rather as the slow heave of the will and the painful acceptance of discipline. But human maturity in any area includes the ability to live with certain tensions, and the peaceful acceptance of tensions in a life of obedience may be an indication that the obedience is mature.

c) Freedom and love in obedience

The New Testament never opposes genuine freedom to obedient service of God; rather in God's service a man finds perfect freedom. St Paul plays on the paradox: the man who was free in secular society becomes the Lord's slave at his conversion, whereas the former slave becomes the Lord's freedman.[51] A man becomes truly free when he finds and accepts his true identity as a son of God, and expresses this relationship in obedience. Just as a child's freedom must be exercised within the context of his family and home, so our freedom is created freedom, given to us to make possible a relationship of love; it is not something absolute and independent that could grow and reach its perfection apart from God. When we yield our freedom to God who created it, we find it.

By free co-operation with the divine will[52] the human will of Christ realized the highest degree of freedom possible to human nature. The monk in conforming his intention with the will of God similarly attains a quality of freedom not otherwise available to him.[53] The support of the Rule, the abbot, and the brethren gives him a greater impetus to the free use of his initiative. He is set free from anxiety and the limitations of self-will; secure in the fundamental stability of his commitment he is enabled to give 'as he has made up his mind, not reluctantly or under compulsion, for God loves a cheerful giver'.[54] Obedience is one of the great forms of giving in monastic life.

The outpouring of the Spirit means the creation of a 'new heart' in man,[55] a transforming, re-creative action of God at the deepest springs of man's freedom. Only God, the author of finite freedom, can touch us at these depths without bruising or constricting us, and one of the effects of his indwelling Spirit is the interiorization of law.[56] Hence obedience is from the 'heart'[57] and becomes the expression of what the human person most deeply and truly desires. This is the promise held out by St Benedict in two of the most profound passages of the Rule. At the end of Chapter 7, after the laborious climb of humble obedience has been described, he sketches the picture of a monk whose obedience is no longer motivated by any fear or achieved by painful effort; it has become a matter of 'delight' because perfect love has cast out fear. Even more significant, perhaps, are the closing lines of St Benedict's Prologue. The hardness of the road and the narrowness of the gate that leads to life are not concealed, but we are promised that perseverance and faithfulness will lead us into a way where we can run 'with hearts enlarged', in unspeakable sweetness of love.

Poverty and Sharing of Goods

Non-ownership and the sharing of all things among the brethren are for St Benedict an indispensable part of community life, being the outward sign of the unity in love that makes community. Renunciation of personal ownership is therefore essential to the monk's vocation and is implied in the monastic vow of Conversion. St Benedict does not use the word 'poverty' in this sense at all, but in the development of religious life during the medieval and modern periods it has been usual to mention 'poverty' explicitly as one of the vows. The word is probably too hallowed by tradition to be replaced, but it is in some ways unfortunate because it can lead to confusion in a world where for millions involuntary poverty is rampant and crushing.

The problem of world poverty is enormous, but in Christ we can begin to discover ways of transforming it from within. We need simultaneously to be aware of the situation as a whole, and to accept in faith our own very limited job within the manifold Christian response to it. In the conviction that monasticism has its own service to render, this chapter attempts to consider the ideal of monastic poverty, some of the questions it raises today, and how monks can, by fidelity to the ideal in both personal and community living, help to counteract the forces of materialism, blindness, and greed which lie at the roots of world poverty.

Poverty and the contemporary scene

Poverty is a sign of our times. As never before in history, we are conscious that the majority of the people in the world live in destitution, but at the same time the Christian Church finds itself aligned both culturally and structurally with western society, which is preoccupied with economic growth and characterized by a consumer style of life. We are increasingly conscious that destitute countries and destitute peoples within prosperous countries are prevented from attaining human dignity not as an inevitable fact of human society but as a result of the same social and economic processes that ensure affluence for the rich. Worse than material poverty is the powerlessness of the poor, their inarticulateness and apathy, their inability to make themselves heard or shape their own destiny, their fatalism and loss of hope. There is no scapegoat on to which we can load these things, for western society itself is part of the problem. There is an intrinsic violence in the modern way of life in the West which may be more dangerous, because less recognized, than the overt violence with which many people are concerned.[1] Violence has also characterized our exploitation of natural resources until, confronted with a severe ecological crisis, we are coming to realize that the created goods around us are not simply there for the asking, always in unlimited quantities; they must be used with caution and handled with concern lest we soon exhaust the supply.

It is becoming increasingly clear that mankind has paid a frightful price for the present affluence of western technological society. Part of the price has been exacted from the poor nations of the world whose people have been exploited so that their fields and forests may produce food and other raw materials for the rich. Part of the price has been paid by the poor who live and labour within the rich countries without sharing in the plenty. But a great part of the price has been paid by affluent western people themselves. While gaining the whole world, they have often lost their own souls. They have purchased prosperity at the cost of a staggering impoverishment of their own humanity.

The change must therefore begin in the hearts and in the life-style of the consumers. Not only must the destitute be delivered from their destitution; modern man, and especially Christian man, must allow himself to be liberated by God from the oppression that comes from an acquisitive mentality. The social and economic conditions of millions constitute a call from God to the wealthy of the world to be freed from the economic and political assumptions about affluence and power which shackle their own freedom as well as that of the destitute. Indeed, for the latter there is no ultimate liberation from destitution except through the deliverance of the affluent from blindness and greed.

The Christian response to the situation must be threefold: a response of service, a response of just decision-making and a response of witness through life-style. Every Christian is called to make this threefold response according to his ability and grace.

The response of Christian service to the destitute is the caring love and perception that are outlined in the twenty-fifth chapter of St Matthew's

Gospel. It is a deep desire, not so much to give to others, as to share with them; it is gratitude to God who is the Father of all men, and it is recognition that things are to be owned personally only if they are held in trust for the service of those in need.

The response of just decision-making goes more deeply to the roots of destitution and recognizes that if charity is to be efficacious it must first be concerned for justice. Justice is concerned with the objective relationships between men. The enemy of justice is often not so much malice or lack of goodwill, as blindness and lack of vision. Poverty as a sign of our times urges the Christian to reflect, to contemplate his actual position within his social milieu and the position of his community within the social structures of the world. Contemplation liberates by revealing truth and urging radical decisions.

The response of witness through life-style, following the simplicity and detachment demanded by Christ of his disciples, has always been the Church's clearest proclamation of the nature of ownership and of its essentially communal character. It has also revealed the reverence that men must have for things, which are basically God's gifts rather than achievements of men. Above all its shows forth the personal and immediate dependence of man upon his Creator and Father. It is only in a style of life which makes real this personal simplicity and communal sharing that the word of God can first be heard and then proclaimed to others. Such a style of life is the immediate choice of one who belongs to the 'anawim, the poor of Yahweh.[2]

These three responses have become central to the Church's role in contemporary society. The monk, by his Christian faith and monastic vocation, is called with a special urgency to make them. His task is to live out in community the values which the theologian teaches and the preacher proclaims. At a time when many people seem insensitive to and uninterested in traditional Christian truth, the world is nonetheless keenly alert to detect what difference Christianity makes in the lives of those who profess it. Furthermore, many people yearn to be liberated from the sophisticated, domineering, and alienated consumer mentality which characterizes technological society. To this yearning for liberation the monastic life itself can be a significant reply, for only through contemplation can man become fully aware of his personal and social condition and thus find the inner courage to transcend what seem to be the inevitable processes of development in the modern world. Within a community of life based on simplicity and integrity a person can discover the freedom that belongs to the Kingdom of God.

Poverty in the Bible and Christian theology

In the Bible the full meaning of poverty is presented as inescapable distress which opens a person to God, and also as the humble, loving abandonment of one's own rights. Hence it is not only an economic and social condition but also an interior disposition.

a) Old Testament attitudes to poverty

Initially the Old Testament writers were accustomed to represent wealth as a blessing. Poverty was therefore a misfortune to be borne, or a manifestation of divine retribution.[3] The sapiential writers acknowledged that there were virtuous poor people,[4] but experience taught them that wretchedness was often the result of laziness or disorder.[5]

Many of the poor were victims of the injustice of their fellow-men.[6] They were defended by the prophets who denounced violence and robbery, fraud in trading, abuse of power, and enslavement of the lowly.[7] In their attitude towards the poor the prophets echoed the Mosaic law which prescribed charitable attitudes and social measures to mitigate the sufferings of the needy. Yahweh was a God who identified himself with the unfortunate people on the margins, and his compassion was given as the motive in one of the oldest legislative texts providing for the protection of the poor man: 'If he cries to me, I will hear, for I am compassionate.'[8] Prophetic preaching also proclaimed a Messiah who would defend the rights of the wretched and the poor.[9]

Even before the exile the prophets had helped Israel to realize that the rich man is apt to harden his heart to the distress of others, to enclose himself in self-righteousness and to exploit the underprivileged. But in the light of the humiliating experience of servitude in Babylon and the disappointments of the return from exile, prophets and other inspired writers helped the Israelites to understand poverty as a religious value, more or less synonymous with humility and piety. They came to appreciate it as a virtue which enabled man to find refuge in God and to await his coming with trust.

b) The incarnation: divine sharing

The religious significance of poverty was clarified with the coming of Christ, whose own life of self-sacrifice and self-denial revealed the glory

of the Father.[10] The incarnation is both the sacrament of God's love for us
and an example for us to follow. At the same time it is the revelation of
God's own life which is characterized by complete sharing among the
Persons of the Trinity. The self-emptying of the Son in the incarnation is
a sign of his total receptivity to the Father and his full response of love to
the Father's own love. In his incarnation Christ reveals the trinitarian
basis for all comunity life and sharing.[11]

It took the incarnation of the eternal Son to reveal the boundless
depths of God's love for us. But the divine wisdom often seems to man an
act of folly, beyond all due measure, almost beyond all belief. God trusts
in man and hopes in man far more than man hopes in God. Time and
again he speaks his saving word, he sends his prophets, and time and
again men reject and betray him. So at last God sends his beloved Son
whom men put to death. Yet in that only Son, in his very passion and
death, we are redeemed and sanctified. Christ lays down his whole life
for his friends, in spite of their folly and sinfulness and fear. He gives his
Spirit to us to pray and hope and love in us, to open our hearts to grace
and life and salvation. Hence the incarnation is the revelation of the
depths of God's saving love, of love that risks everything, even the only
Son.

At the Last Supper Jesus asked his disciples, 'Do you understand what I
have done? I have given you an example so that you may do what I have
done for you.'[12] It was not just the loving gesture of foot-washing to
which Jesus referred, but the whole pattern of his life. If God trusts us –
and he trusted himself completely to men in the incarnation – then we
must trust him and one another. And trust, as God himself has shown us,
cannot be half-hearted and cautious; it implies total commitment.

c) The example and teaching of Jesus

In his inaugural discourse Christ taught that the poor were the privileged
heirs of the Kingdom he proclaimed.[13] As the Messiah of the poor he
lived a life of poverty[14] and invited the weary and burdened to come to
him as their meek and humble saviour.[15] He criticized the idolatries of
power, pleasure, and possessions not by violently attacking them but by
identifying himself with the materially or morally indigent, by sharing
his love and his life, by non-violence and by inviting men to trust the
Father in heaven who knows their need. He promised salvation to all
those who trusted him in time of hunger, but the food he promised was
the Kingdom of his Father.[16] He proclaimed that with him and in him

the Kingdom of God had arrived, and that by the coming of the Kingdom men are placed in a situation where they must make an absolute and radical decision.[17] According to Jesus the advent of the Kingdom of God means that human riches have become a danger and an obstacle to the acceptance of God's reign in man's heart, to such an extent that it is easier for a camel to pass through the eye of a needle than for a rich man to enter the Kingdom of God.[18]

This is not to say that possessions are immoral in themselves, or that the absence of possessions in itself constitutes a moral value. Jesus's attitude to the rich is not one that is sociologically opposed to them as a class. What he does say is that riches, the accumulation of possessions, is a grave danger for men in that, once they have become preoccupied with the cares of the present world, they become blind to the presence of the Kingdom, deaf and unresponsive to the radical summons of God. The man attached to riches does not have at his command that freedom of spirit which is necessary for a whole-hearted acceptance of the Kingdom. Hence Jesus requires of his disciples that in order to receive the Kingdom of God they must share their possessions with the poor and be prepared to become poor themselves. He did not commend poverty out of contempt for wealth or for purely ascetical reasons,[19] but because it helps man to acknowledge his ultimate dependence and enables him to be open to the needs of others.[20]

In the teaching of Jesus poverty is a condition for a man's response of faith. The poor are apt to be better recipients of the Good News of salvation. Why riches should constitute an obstacle to Christian faith is not fully developed by Jesus. He does maintain that the man who is rich is likely to be full of cares,[21] to want yet more riches, and to give himself up to pleasure. He is likewise apt to delight in the power and security his possessions bring him.[22] His treasure is on earth rather than in heaven.[23]

Jesus's remarks about poverty were inspired by the concrete realities of everyday life as he encountered them; his words must not be interpreted in a doctrinaire manner. Jesus himself did not live in a state of destitution nor was he usually threatened by hunger. He did have money,[24] and he had the opportunity to obtain support from his wealthy friends when he needed it.[25] His lavish generosity at Cana,[26] and his sharing in the joyful feast in Matthew's house,[27] suggest a spirit of magnanimity far removed from any puritanical condemnation of the enjoyment of good things. Yet he could also say that the Son of Man had nowhere to lay his head.[28] He was radically free and detached in his use of goods because of his dedication to his mission.

In his teaching on discipleship Jesus requires the man who voluntarily decides to become poor for the Kingdom of heaven's sake to give his riches to the poor who are his brothers in the Kingdom of God.[29] The Kingdom unites men who have fallen into disunity through the presence of sin in the world. When faith in the coming of the Kingdom is lived out in the form of voluntary poverty, this faith must be further expressed by the unity in love of all those who are united in God's Son. The man of Christian faith does not defend the sphere of his life occupied by material goods as though it were the bastion of his own self-defence against others, but rather he gives others a share in these goods because he can look upon them in a spirit of trust and can love them as fellow-citizens of God's Kingdom. Hence the acknowledgement that all men have a right to the wealth of God's creation is an intrinsic element in Christian poverty. Holding property in common is a gesture which expresses the brotherhood of all men in Christ.[30]

The primitive Christian community had a clear grasp of the spirit of Jesus's teaching concerning poverty. They realized that a literal application of his teaching was neither essential nor always possible. Paul had a budget for his missionary and charitable work,[31] but he often preached the gospel without any recompense, and he lived in want and distress.[32] The early Christians shared what they had with one another and with those in need.[33] Service rendered to the poor was an expression of their love for Christ who being rich became poor for our sake, so that he might enrich us by his poverty.[34]

Poverty and monastic tradition

In the *Dialogues* St Gregory says that St Benedict 'had left all his possessions with the desire of pleasing God alone'.[35] In the Rule St Benedict directs that his disciples should have no other goal than to seek God.[36] They are to give away all they possess.[37] To assure his lifelong conversion to God the monk must be protected from all personal attachment. After his profession he is unable to possess anything as his own; he shares everything with the community.[38] Although moderation is characteristic of the Rule, St Benedict is uncompromising with regard to the renunciation of possessions. The monastery may possess goods, but the abbot is counselled not to be over-solicitous for material possessions.[39] The produce of the monastery is to be sold 'a little cheaper than it is sold by people of the world, that in all things God may be glorified'.[40]

St Benedict was conscious of the community's responsibility to share its goods with the poor, the sick, and the stranger.[41] He feared avarice in his monks and reminded them of the fate that overtook Ananias and Sapphira.[42] However, he prescribed that monks should receive what they needed from the resources of the monastery. Without entirely excluding certain amenities in daily life, he forbade his monks to have luxuries.[43]

Throughout history the basic Benedictine attitude towards material goods has been that of stewardship.[44] Unlike mendicant communities in the Church, Benedictine communities have rooted themselves deeply in the local scene. As an implication of their stability they have attempted to establish a creative, harmonious relationship with the natural world which surrounds them. St Benedict was conscious of the dangers of physical idleness; hence he made it a rule that all his monks should work with their hands in the fields and in workshops. As a result, Benedictine monks have achieved an intimate and creative relationship with the world around them. Although St Benedict did not intend his monks to become scholars, a tradition of learning and of artistic skills developed progressively in the Benedictine abbeys, along with the continuation of manual work. A way of life was thus created in which practical and theoretical skills could be embodied in the same person. This development proved to be of great importance in the furthering of European technology and science. Benedictine abbeys did not always immediately launch into scientific investigations, but by encouraging the combination of physical and intellectual work they destroyed the artificial barrier between the empirical and the speculative, the manual and the liberal arts. This created a climate favourable to the development of knowledge based on experimentation.[45]

Whereas the first chapter of Genesis speaks of man's dominion over nature, the Benedictine Rule seems inspired rather by the second chapter, in which the Lord placed man in the garden of Eden not as a master but as a steward. Throughout the history of Benedictine monasticism monks have actively intervened in nature as farmers, builders, and scholars. They have brought about profound transformations in nature, but in such a manner that their management of it has enhanced the environment. In this matter Benedictine tradition has something to say to human life in the modern world and to the human condition in general. By establishing the right order of relationships between man and nature, between man and his fellow-men and between man and God, St Benedict established the primacy of persons over things, but at the same time he saw the importance of a respect for material things and an ordered and humane environment in helping his monks to develop as persons whose whole life is directed to glorifying God. Monastic life is an interpretation of life in its totality as saying 'Yes' to the Kingdom, and this response is made here on earth through people and things. St Benedict saw that without frugality in their lives monks would lose this wholeness and be distracted from their true goal.

There remains the problem that poverty, celibacy, and obedience, when allied with hard work, can in the course of time make for corporate wealth simply because monks have limited wants and no families to consume the fruit of their labours. Furthermore, the large scale of the enterprises attached to a Benedictine monastery as well as the nature of the life itself require a spaciousness, both mental and physical, denied to the great majority of men. This is a situation which, even if it cannot be changed, needs to be constantly reassessed if the spiritual sensitivity of both the monk and his community is not to be dulled.

The theme of poverty and riches, then, is rooted in the whole of Christian revelation and tradition. The actually poor man is a sign of what every man is before God: he is needy and damaged. Hence a theology of monastic poverty which loses contact with the life and experience of those who are poor in fact also loses a sound basis for its language and practice.

Monastic poverty today

a) Dissatisfaction

Christian tradition from the Bible to the Rule and down to the most recent papal and conciliar documents on religious life maintains that an interior attitude of poverty is an absolutely necessary quality of Christian life.[46] But some impact on one's way of living must result from this interior attitude. A purely spiritual poverty is illusory since a person lives out in each moment's choices his true sense of values. 'Wherever your treasure is, there will be your heart also.'[47]

Recent years have seen a growing restlessness among many monks with regard to poverty in their lives. There is an increasing embarrassment before lay Christians who sometimes find the comfort and security of monks scandalous. Furthermore, many monks have had a training in poverty that has been not scriptural and theological but extremely legalistic and individualistic. Such a materialistic approach to poverty had led to a casuistry of permissions, a common life that is more often conformism than fraternal sharing, and a tendency to justify accumulated possessions in the name of apostolic works.

Acquiescence in such an inadequate understanding and practice of monastic poverty is no longer a Christian possibility. Scriptural studies, the insights provided by Personalist philosophies, and the development in the Church's teaching on social justice in the years before and since Vatican II have contributed to the pressing need for creative reflection and action concerning the poverty of our monasteries. Moreover information about the subhuman living conditions of millions of human beings is widely publicized; knowledge of the exhaustion of natural resources and the depreciation of the earth is available to all. An entirely new situation has thus arisen in the matter of social justice, putting world poverty and human responsibility for the earth's resources among the most crucial moral issues of our time. On our response to these issues we shall all as Christians be judged. Monastic communities cannot therefore be credible as embodiments of the Christian way of life unless they are in some way related to these facts, and in their own way facing the issues.

b) Monastic response to the challenge

1. Personal poverty

One of the worst things Christians can do when the magnitude of the problem comes home to them is to despair. It looks too big to solve, and the individual feels helpless and guilty. But guilt-feelings are not creative. To absorb the economic facts through the mass-media without seeing any positive Christian way in which one can, compatibly with one's vocation, respond to them is to acquiesce in the very materialistic outlook which has produced the problem. A society naïvely and wholly bent on material well-being cannot find within itself either the vision or the spiritual power to change, but Christians have a vision of faith and hope which assures them that the human spirit can by God's grace transcend structures and enslaving systems. With the knowledge of Christ's redemptive power and his lordship of history they can begin to transform the world by responding to the call given to them, individually and in groups, to do the work each is able to do in his own place within it.

The monastic response will therefore be different from that proper to the social reformer or to religious traditions of non-monastic inspiration. The essential discernment for monks is to see how monastic tradition speaks to and is spoken to by those human factors, especially blindness and greed, which lie at the roots of the problem of poverty and of those structures which maintain it.

At the heart of the contemplative monastic tradition are values which directly oppose blindness, materialism and greed, and the structures which dehumanize the individual. These values are above all poverty of spirit, simplicity, sharing and giving, self-denial prompted by love, freedom of heart, gratitude, care for persons, and the kind of soundness of judgement with regard to created things that proceeds from exposure to the Creator in prayer. To develop and give practical expression to these values is the most vital contribution that monasticism can make, and unless the perspectives of faith are kept when a community tries to assess its practice of poverty, the wrong criteria will be applied. Material privation is not an end in itself, and it is in no way part of monastic poverty to assess everything economically by materialistic standards or to override aesthetic or other values for the sake of cheapness or squalor. Such a mentality narrows the spirit and even creates those very evils accompanying destitution which all Christians have the duty to banish from the earth.

Monastic poverty can be understood only with the reality of Christ and his mission in mind. It is rooted in faith, and must be, like Christ's own poverty, the outward expression of trustful dependence on the Father. Life is the Father's gift; all within it is gift, and gifts are for sharing. Joy and gratitude are better motives for sharing than are feelings of guilt. Sharing gifts in joy promotes the increase of life all round; things and time, the resources of the human person, the power to make friends and to serve – all are gifts to be shared for the increase of that life which men desire even more than the food, clothing, and shelter which support it. 'The whole point of living free, of sharing, of not building barns for tomorrow, is a direct response to the sovereignty and fatherhood of God. If God is God then things are for sharing. If you cling to them, gather them in around you, possess them, then your heart will be in them.'[48]

Of all creatures man is the neediest, precisely because he has such potential for development. But for his development he requires both material resources and the help of other people. One of the sure signs of maturity is the honest acceptance of one's need for other persons. A mature man is poor psychologically because he realizes his dependence on others. He willingly accepts the services and ideas of others, the gifts of life and its continuance, and the gifts of community and shared existence. In order to grow, the human person must live in the rhythm of alternation between receiving and giving, taking in the gifts of God and of others, and sharing generously as others have shared with him. This pattern of sharing, of giving and receiving, is basic to the life of a cenobitic community.

Furthermore, the mature person views material things with reverence, sensing that they are signs of God's love for his creatures. Instead of being possessive and manipulative, the truly poor man grows in detachment, which manifests itself in the constructive and creative use of things. His attitude towards his own life and talents is one of stewardship. Attachment to oneself and one's talents or goods brings anxiety, a bondage which ties the human spirit down to the earth and allows no enlargement of heart. Riches of any kind – material, intellectual, or spiritual – tend to close a person, for they give him a sense of independence of other men and even of God. Human and Christian detachment is not a disparagement of good things, nor a fear of their power; it is a just appreciation of them as gifts of God. A man who grows in poverty of spirit is likely therefore to find his powers of appreciation growing sharper with regard to natural beauty, human goodness, and the achievements of mankind. Correspondingly, he grows in gratitude to God who gives these things.

Perhaps the greatest service monks and nuns can render to a world at grips with the problems of poverty is prayer. Monastic communities do have an important part to play in the spheres of education, social justice, and the works of mercy and assistance, but this is best exercised if based on that awareness of the roots of social problems which derives from contemplation. Direct effort to eliminate destitution by welfare work and hand-outs is certainly necessary, but this is not a monk's primary mission, nor does he usually have the training or the resources to deal with the problem at this level. Unless monks can in some way stand clear of the system they cannot help, for their minds are formed by the same cultural forces that have created the problem of poverty and perpetuate it. By a truly contemplative life a monk can help to counteract materialism and deepen his own conversion of heart; by the continual effort to walk in the light of truth which contemplative prayer demands he is doing what is within his power to overcome his own blindness, and so also the blindness of those with whom he is in contact. Through prayer he learns his dependence on God and his constant need of mercy and grace. He thus lives in poverty of spirit, learns to rejoice in his neediness, and grows compassionate and open-hearted towards others.

From this experience of prayer and sharing a genuine sense of identification with the poor is born. This is given substance by frugality of life-style and the continuing effort to overcome blindness and greed, whether individual or communal. The thrust of affluent societies is towards a constant increase of what is considered necessary for the efficiency of their work. Living in the midst of such societies and working with people who take this increase for granted, monastic communities are apt to raise their standard of living without being sensitive to the demands of the gospel. An honest attempt must be made by the monks to live out their poverty in their intellectual and manual work. Communities need periodically to reassess their 'necessities'. This reassessment should be a normal process in monastic life; the monks have a duty to educate one another, for this is part of the way in which a community overcomes blindness. It could be a function of the chapter of faults or whatever takes its place. Monks need to be very clear-headed about this, because maintaining their security in an inflationary world can lead to a very aggressive attitude about their privileges, an attitude of (collective, even if not personal) greed and dimness of vision which aligns them with the very forces against which they are called to work. The acquisition of superfluous material goods can easily obscure the spiritual values on which monastic life is based. The community as a whole and its individual members must set themselves a frugal standard of personal living, especially in such things as food, travel, entertainment, comfort, and dependence on personal and domestic services. The standard needs to be honestly reviewed from time to time, since it is very easy to assume that what is commonly accepted or commonly done must be right. A realistic attempt to live frugally is a way of seeking to use all things in accordance with a loving and non-violent relationship to nature and to all men, and a freeing of minds and hearts to respond to God's Kingdom in daily reality.

One sign of poverty of spirit which is of particular importance in monasteries today is willingness to change and to grow, especially to change one's attitudes and way of living when good reason warrants it.[49] Attachment to material possessions produces people who are in turn possessed by their goods. Such people usually oppose change and lack imagination; their lives are often characterized by smugness and complacency. Their attitudes are reminiscent of those of the Laodiceans: 'You say to yourself, "I am rich, I have made a fortune, and have everything I want", never realizing that you are wretchedly and pitiably poor, and blind and naked too.'[50] The detached man can be free and independent of those with wealth and power. Throughout history monasteries have often been closely associated with rich and rigidly conservative benefactors who maintained reactionary views of social reality. In order not to lose favour with their patrons, the monks themselves have often assumed the same attitudes and have become unduly attached to a particular style of life.[51] Genuine poverty of spirit means freedom to be concerned with pleasing God rather than patrons and benefactors,[52] and hence it implies freedom to change when God calls an individual or a community to do so. A monk therefore finds poverty of spirit to be inseparably connected with the conversion of heart which he promises in his second vow.

2. Corporate poverty

At the level of community sharing, self-denial, giving, personal poverty of spirit, contemplation, and simplicity of life, monks can themselves be changed and converted, and so help to touch the problem of world poverty at its roots. But at the level of the community's corporate existence more intractable problems arise. The structures of community life have an objective existence independent of the personal virtues of the monks, and these structures have their inevitable impact on the members of the community. Objectively, for example, monastic communities are landowners. One consequence of the difference between having property and not having it is a difference in the stratum of society with which one is identified or related. A stable monastic community may therefore be related to a rather narrow band of society considered as a class, even though it may have plenty of personal bonds with *individuals* from other classes. This state of affairs may tend to produce the blindness endemic in international or national élites. It may also happen that some inherited work, with the particular range of personal contacts and the material setting it entails, becomes a barrier to awareness; in this case the community needs to consider whether its work should be in some way changed. But against this possibility has to be weighed the influence exerted by a monastic community whose members are personally poor in spirit upon that stratum of society which they serve. The rich too need liberation.

The fact of material security creates a problem for most monks and nuns in any consideration of the outward forms that poverty should take today. For the generality of men, wealth has a double significance: it enhances one's being in the present and provides a security against the future. One of the sharpest features of world poverty today is therefore the agonizing insecurity felt by millions of people about their own future and that of their children. This kind of insecurity is something that monks do not know in their own lives. St Benedict wanted his monks to have their basic needs met,[53] and without degenerating into anything resembling luxury monks today can find in their monastery the equivalent of a welfare state which precludes every worry about food, education, medical services, care in old age, housing, and clothes. A 'poverty' which is reducible to mere dependence on superiors for permissions and the supplying of needed goods may have some ascetical value and may liberate the monks so that they have time for prayer, but it may also tend to produce irresponsibility. Unaware of contemporary inflation, they can be insensitive to the rising cost of clothing, education, heating, food, and machinery.[54] But even when this is not the case, even in a community where all work hard, live frugally, and keep in touch with contemporary conditions, the problem remains: most monks are not witnessing to their day-to-day dependence on God's providence by any real need to exercise heroic trust where the availability of material things is concerned. It is useless to say that this is a sign of low standards in monastic poverty that should be remedied; there is little possibility of altering the situation while remaining within ordinary Benedictine life.

The best solution is probably to recognize that while every Christian, and therefore every monk and nun, is called to respond to the challenge of world poverty by service, just decision-making, and witness of life-style, there is a legitimate pluralism within the monastic response with regard to the way in which this is done. To over-simplify: a rough distinction can be drawn between being poor with the poor and being 'rich' for the poor. Both are dependent from day to day on God's providence, but the external expression of dependence is different.

(a) Being poor with the poor was part of the mendicant ideal in the Middle Ages, and is a special glory of some contemporary religious such as the disciples of Charles de Foucauld. There is room for this expression of poverty within the monastic tradition too; it is exemplified by some small breakaway monastic communities whose conditions of life and labour assimilate them closely to the poor of the area in which they live. They can establish true brotherhood with the involuntarily marginal members of society and live a poverty that is clearly evangelical. Unfortunately monastic communities of this kind often lack stability, but if this problem can be overcome, their witness is of great value.

(b) Being 'rich' for the poor, rich not in material terms but intellectually, culturally, spiritually, humanly, is a different grace. This is the kind of life more particularly envisaged in the preceding pages. Its practice, and therefore incidentally its witness, is concerned with stability, genuine community sharing, willingness to share with guests and others who come in whatever way they need it, respect for things, hard work, a sense of stewardship, and the cultivation of certain human and civilized values. This type has on the whole tended to be more characteristic of EBC monasteries, and it is not easily compatible with type (a). A monk called to this way of life can hear constantly the word of the Lord: 'Freely you have received, now freely give.'[55] He has received freely from his family and education, from the rich monastic tradition, from the abundant life of his own community, and from the manifold mercies of God. He is therefore a rich man compared with many who ask his help; they may be financially and materially comfortable, yet in all other respects much poorer than he. So his life becomes a matter of constant giving, of honestly trying to respond with love and intelligence to every demand made on him, of abandoning every attempt to fence off areas of time for himself.[56] And since he is able to give like this only because he is an 'enriched' man, he has to forgo the spiritual security that might be his if he were materially more insecure. Yet he would be arrogant if he thought of himself as always giving. In fact he may be enriched spiritually, culturally, and humanly by many who come to him for help. Moreover his giving must be the expression of deep personal poverty of spirit and proceed from a frugal, undemanding life-style.

Conclusion

The monk gives up completely his right to possess things as part of his response to God's Kingdom. He places his material security in the hands of his abbot and community, entrusting himself to God his Father. By covenant, he expects to receive from the abbot and community all he needs for his life, but he must be conscious of his responsibility to contribute to the support of the community by using his gifts of nature and grace. He must share what he has, above all the resources of his own person, with those who are less fortunate. His life should be marked by frugality, simplicity, and gratitude for the gifts of God, and he must be aware of his duty to witness in a materialistic world to the dependence of men upon their heavenly Father, and to their need and destiny for a happiness beyond material fulfilment.

Word of God

Introduction

The next five chapters of this book deal with certain privileged occasions for the transmission of God's word in monastic life. In the Eucharist a community whose hearts have been prepared by repentance opens itself to the Good News proclaimed through Scripture and preaching, before Christ, who has been present in his word, becomes present in his powerful passover. In the *opus Dei* the community listens to the word in scriptural readings and responds in the God-given words of the psalms. In *Lectio divina* the monk or nun enters into dialogue with the Word of God through the medium of written words. In personal and shared prayer that communion of love which is implicit throughout monastic life becomes explicit as the individual listens and responds, alone or with the brethren, in words or in silence.

Before dealing with these separate aspects of monastic life in relation to the word of God it is necessary to examine in some detail the special significance given to the term 'word' in all that follows.

a) God speaks creatively, evoking a response

God sends his call to what has no being, giving life where there is no life.[1] His word came to Abraham as a promise; it would create a people to be his own. He spoke again to Moses, and through Moses to the whole people, revealing himself, his saving plans, and his demands for their loyalty to the covenant; here too his word and his mighty works interlocked, for he revealed himself as the God who acts. So *dabar*, the 'word' of Yahweh, came to mean for the Israelites both message and event. The word of the Lord seized upon the prophets, made new men of them, and was efficacious in their mouths for victory or defeat. Sometimes it came as promise, sometimes as judgement, but always as a meeting between God and men within the events of history: 'Prepare, Israel, to meet your God.'[2]

Through Isaiah the Lord called his people to silent, trusting stillness rather than dubious foreign alliances and feverish preparations that drowned his word. To 'hear' for the Hebrews meant to obey, and in obedient listening to the word was Israel's salvation: 'O that you had hearkened to my commandments! Then your peace would have been like a river, and your righteousness like the waves of the sea.'[3] The Lord spoke continually; there was always a new 'today' when they must listen to his voice and not harden their hearts. The response of faith meant not only obedience but also prayer. The prayers of the Old Testament and especially the psalms are made of human words in which a great range of human experiences finds expression, but they are also part of God's word to man, for the Scriptures are the deposit from that river of life which was Israel's history guided by the Spirit. Whether in faith, in obedience, or in prayer, God's word was creative, evoking men's response.

The creative power of Yahweh's word through Moses and the prophets led the minds of believers to a further realization. God's creative act in the beginning had been like a word: 'Let there be light . . . let the dry land appear . . . let the earth bring forth living creatures.' He had spoken, and all things had come to be. By his word the heavens had been made, by the breath of his mouth all the stars. Israel knew Yahweh first as the saving Lord of the exodus; faith in him as Creator was perhaps the result of later synthesis. But creation was never isolated from salvation.[4] In Second Isaiah the imagery of creation and exodus are used to evoke a still greater saving act to come. This further salvation was to be a new covenant, a new creation at the centre of man's being, a new gift of life through the breath of Yahweh's mouth where there was only death and hopelessness.[5]

In some poetic texts the word was almost personified: it was the efficacious messenger of the Lord who would not return to him 'void', a healer, a warrior who leapt from God's royal throne to work his will.[6] In these passages the Word is very like the figure of divine Wisdom personified elsewhere. Drawing on the whole Israelite tradition the writer to the Hebrews described the incarnation of the Son as the final speaking: God who spoke to us in the prophets so often and so variously has now at the end of time spoken in his Son. St Luke is in the true line of Old Testament understanding when he refers to the event of Christ's birth as a 'word'; the shepherds say, 'Let us go over to Bethlehem and see this word which has happened.'⁷ St John took the final step, calling Jesus the Word of Life.

b) Jesus Christ, God's Word to men

Anointed with God's Spirit, Christ came to preach the Good News to the poor, sight to the blind, release for prisoners. The word of the Lord was still message, still saving event, but now also a Person, man among men. So Christ was himself the content of the Good News he preached. All that he was and did gave utterance to the reality of God and God's love for men. Revelation and divine presence were totally identified in Jesus. He is the manifestation of the Father, the sacrament of the Father's presence. The miracles that accompanied his preaching were signs of his victory and his powerful, saving love. He spoke efficacious words: 'I will, be clean. . . . Lazarus, come forth. . . . Your sins are forgiven. . . . Get up and walk. . . . Go in peace.' His words had cleansing power in human hearts.⁸ They gave joy.⁹ They challenged the hearers to faith and led people to the light.¹⁰ But if rejected, the words of Christ would judge those who refused to hear.¹¹

The healing of the sick, the deliverance of the possessed, the conversion of sinners, and the drawing of many to obedient faith were signs of salvation. But these were partial words and restricted acts. Only by the supreme self-giving of his death could Jesus fully reveal himself and his Father. The Father's act of delivering up the beloved Son to the cross, the Son's acceptance, and the Father's act of raising and glorifying him are the ultimate word of God's self-giving love to men. Rising from the dead, Jesus spoke the word of the new creation: 'Receive the Holy Spirit. Whose sins you shall forgive, they are forgiven.' The new creation is promised and effected by the Word of the Lord and by the breath of his mouth.

c) Jesus Christ, mankind's word of perfect response to God

The self-communication of a person cannot take place unless there is someone to hear and respond; there must be a receptivity or the word of self-revelation cannot be uttered. Persons become fully present to one another when each is open to the other's self-communication. Israel had existed through the word and for the word, but the Lord had mourned the deafness of his people: 'The ox knows its owner, and the ass its master's crib; but Israel does not know, my people does not understand. . . . Who is blind but my servant, or deaf as my messenger whom I send?'[12] But once, at last, God's word of self-disclosure was heard perfectly – in the human consciousness of Jesus. He was open to the Father's self-giving. Revelation is meeting and covenant; it is perfected only in the Lord Jesus, who is both God bestowing and man receiving. As incarnate Logos he is the Father's gracious, saving Word, but by his prayerful communion with the Father and his whole obedient response he reveals what it means for a man to live as God's son. 'Sacrifice and sin-offering you did not desire, but you have given me an open ear.'[13] The incarnate Word was silent for his first nine months on earth. He lived the longest part of his human life in the silence of Nazareth. He later spent nights in silent prayer to his Father, listening. Interrogated and accused in many words during his passion, he was silent. The obedience consummated in his death was mankind's supreme hearkening to the word, receptive participation and response at their highest.

d) The Church both speaks and listens to the word

In breaking through death Jesus beheld in his human consciousness the glory that was his. The resurrection is the glorifying of the total humanity of Jesus, not only of his body but also of his mind. The New Testament symbolically presents the 'forty days' as a time when the glorified Lord shared with his disciples the meaning of his cross and resurrection and of the words and actions of his public life.[14] He lives in this glory for ever, and therefore continues to be the centre of the revelatory communion of love between God and man.

Through his abiding presence with the Church Jesus is God's irrevocable word of love, but this word must be unfolded and spoken in every culture and every generation. The Gentiles had never been wholly excluded from the revelation which came in a privileged way to Israel; as the Jews had received the law, so the Greeks had sought God through philosophy.[15] In some way every other great civilization and achievement of the human spirit had been a possible meeting-place for God with man; and beyond the limits of the great civilizations too he had never left himself without a witness.[16] The Word is the true light that enlightens every man,[17] and thus the Christ who is preached to those whom the Judeo-Christian tradition has previously never touched does not come to them as a total stranger. The Church is the sacrament of his presence in the world, and must in obedience to his command bring to fruition the seed of the word sown among all nations. The work of the

Spirit is to 'receive' from what is Christ's and 'show it' to men;[18] and to open the hearts and minds of the hearers so that the word can strike home. At Pentecost the Spirit's action 'pierced' the hearts of the crowd at the apostles' preaching,[19] and he continues through the gift of compunction to prepare human hearts to receive the life-giving word.

The Church in the persons of the apostles listened before speaking, and the Church in every age must continue to listen to the word. Our Lady listened in silence and faith, conceived the incarnate Word in faith through the overshadowing Spirit, nurtured the Word and gave him life within her life, pondered his mystery in her heart, and gave him to the world. The Church must do likewise. As Israel was the people called into being and assembled[20] to hear the word of Yahweh, so the people of the new covenant are called out to be the Church[21] by the incarnate Word, Jesus Christ: called to listen, to respond in prayer and obedience, to say in Christ their 'Yes' to God's word,[22] and to speak his word to others.

e) A monastic community listens to the word and preaches

Like the Church, a monastic community is a community of faith. It has been gathered together only because each of its members has already heard the creative, summoning, grace-filled word of the Lord in his or her own vocation; and it holds together, lives, and grows because the members continue to be called and to respond. The community must therefore listen constantly to the Lord, individually and collectively. In the Prologue to the Rule the scriptural word of God addressing the monk is shown in action in the same way as when it addressed the prophets: a powerful word able to call to man and to effect what it says, a word of summons and promise. The monk's whole life is to be a dialogue with the word that converts and shapes him. In listening to the Lord and acting upon his words, the community is building its house on a rock.

Monks fully hear the word only if they are open to the Spirit with repentant and obedient hearts, and are silent. The silence which enables us really to listen is much more than a physical state; it is abandonment to God, the stilling of the inner storms of passion and self-will, a readiness to hear and a climate of awareness. As Pieper described it,

> Leisure is a form of silence, of that silence which is the prerequisite of the apprehension of reality: only the silent hear. . . . Silence, as it is understood in this context, does not mean 'dumbness' or 'noiselessness'; it means more nearly that the soul's power to 'answer' to the reality of the world is left undisturbed. For leisure is a receptive

attitude of mind, a contemplative attitude, and it is not only the occasion but also the capacity for steeping oneself in the whole of creation.[23]

The enemy of this kind of leisure is not hard work but *acedia*, which is a deep-seated lack of calm. *Acedia*, says St Thomas, is an offence against the third commandment by which we are called to have 'peace of mind in God'.[24] *Acedia* means

> that a man does not, in the last resort, give the consent of his will to his own being; that behind or beneath the dynamic activity of his existence, he is still not at one with himself, or, as the medieval writers would have said, face to face with the divine good within him; he is a prey to sadness.[25]

'Be still and know that I am God', says the Lord through the psalmist; and indeed this inner silence and expectancy are his gift, his creation.[26] Within it we both hear and respond in prayer.

The word we hear often judges us, exposing the falsehood and unfaith that lurk in our lives. It pierces like a two-edged sword to the division of soul and spirit, joints and marrow, discerning the thoughts and intentions of our hearts. But it is out to create, not to destroy. Amid the many words, we constantly hear the word of love that calls us into greater fulness of life, forgives, feeds, and confirms. 'Fear not, for I have redeemed you; I have called you by name, you are mine.'[27] The word shows us to ourselves as we are,[28] but also shows us to ourselves as we will be, as we already are in the eyes of the One who calls us by our new name. This is true not only for the individual but also for the community as it listens to the proclaimed word in Scripture and liturgy and tries to discern the Lord's will in the events of its life. And as Israel needed prophets to interpret historical events as Yahweh's word, so there are prophets in every monastic community who through their openness to the Spirit can help others to hear and respond.

Since God has willed to reveal himself and to make use of human words, there has been a great variety of expression for the divine Word, inscripturate and incarnate. The prophets were seized by a power not their own, yet the message came through the idiom of each spokesman: through the country speech of Amos, the nobility of Isaiah's mind, the sensitivity of Jeremiah, and the lyrical imagination of Second Isaiah. The Word made flesh whom Mary bore must have strongly resembled her. God still speaks through Christians, in preaching, sacraments, counselling, and example, and his word is always a new expression of the mystery of Christ in whom all is said and given. The human variety in a monastic community, the creative fidelity of its members to their own call, and the community's corporate response to its vocation are new occasions for the utterance of the word. A monastic community should preach by its whole life, proclaiming the word of hope and salvation. God's word to men is message, event, and encounter in a Person. In faith a monastic community hears the message, participates in the events through life and liturgy, and allows the Person of the Word made flesh to be its response, its prayer, its obedience, and its life.

10
Eucharist

The very life of the community of faith mediates the word to the believer, making present Christ who is the Word of God to man and man's Word of response to God. This is eminently true when a faith-community gathers to celebrate Christ's passover, when it allows the Christ of Calvary and Easter to gather it into his movement of sacrificial obedience to the Father, to give it his life and make it his Body — when, that is, it allows Christ to form it into a eucharistic community.

In one sense there is no specific 'monastic Eucharist', since it is not precisely by the Eucharist that a monastic community is called into being; when it meets for this celebration it does so simply as a Christian family. But in another sense it is true to say that in its common celebration of the Eucharist a monastic family finds the means to celebrate and deepen those aspects of its Christian life which are implied by monastic profession: listening to the word, mutual forgiveness, shared joy and praise, self-sacrifice, self-transcendence and obedience, communion with Christ and with one another in love.

The high proportion of priests in many monastic communities adds a special value and dignity to the celebration of the monastic Eucharist, but also raises certain questions. The individual has a double identity: as a monk he is a member of the monastic community and united in brotherhood to all its members; as a priest he is distinguished from his non-clerical brethren, within the eucharistic celebration, by his power and function. It is possible for tension between these two identities to be felt, and to be reflected in a similar tension within the community itself when its primary identity and unity as a monastic family are taken up into the identity and unity of a eucharistic family.

This chapter indicates the positive meaning of the Eucharist in monastic community life, and also the tensions. It may be salutary that in the sacramental mystery which most powerfully symbolizes and promotes our unity, there our differences can be most acutely felt. The chapter suggests how these difficulties, in giving occasion for charity and unselfishness, can be taken up into the sacrificial action.

The aim of this chapter is not to present a complete tractate on the theology of the Eucharist, but rather to strengthen the eucharistic faith and practice of the monks and nuns who read it. This will involve dealing with controversial issues, the solution to which lies (1) partly in accepting that the unity of faith is quite consistent with a plurality of theological models; and (2) partly in the lived-out, continuing experience and faith of the contemporary and future Church. In certain areas of its life and doctrine the Church is bound to be on the pioneering edge of its development, and patient waiting for the future may be needed before its inspired voice can be heard clearly.

Some lessons from the history
of the Eucharist

In any study of the relation between history and theology, we should remind ourselves of the axiom, simple yet with wide implications, that all truth is not given to any one generation; that the mysteries of God, given once for all in Jesus Christ, are unfolded slowly but surely, under the Holy Spirit's guidance, over many different historical epochs, and in many varied historical forms. Each age thus stresses different aspects of what, after all, is an infinite *mysterium*, and human time can never be sufficiently extended to allow us to claim that we have exhausted the mystery of Christ. Until sacraments cease and the reality they signify is revealed in its fulness, the Church will continue to discover new depths in their meaning, as the Holy Spirit continues through human history his work of leading us into all truth.

This is eminently true of the doctrine of the Holy Eucharist, where we have the supreme sacramental concentration of the divine love. The history of eucharistic doctrine and practice shows constant changes of theological emphasis, sometimes revolutionary changes, from one generation to another; but, throughout, the same mystery is being believed and loved and witnessed to in the Church; throughout, the whole Church as well as the individual believer is growing into the fulness of the eucharistic mystery.

How is the Church able to distinguish between genuine developments of eucharistic doctrine and practice, and movements which claim to be such, but which, if accepted, would prove to be declensions from the way of truth, or even abuses and corruptions?[1] No simple answer can be given, nor one which will grant us a kind of mathematical certainty. On the other hand, we have more than the provisional certainty associated, for instance, with the pursuit of scientific historical studies. The criterion which the Catholic possesses is twofold. First, he has the living voice of the contemporary Church; this is not only the ordinary teaching of the Pope and bishops, but also the *consensus fidelium*, the practice and faith of the total Catholic community. Second, he has the appeal to apostolic tradition: *quod semper, quod ubique, quod ab omnibus*. This includes not only the written word of the divine Scriptures, but also the orthodox line of interpretation and teaching, stretching through the early Church Fathers and medieval doctors into the Church of modern times. These two criteria are of no help if they are polarized; they must support, complement, and guarantee each other. The eucharistic faith of the true believer will be nourished by the united witness of the Church's past and present.

Furthermore, it is to be expected that the Church's certainty, and therefore acceptance, of a particular eucharistic practice, doctrinal formulation, or theological approach will take several generations of patient reflection and experience before it matures. Living through such periods demands the generous exercise of humility and loving obedience, as well as a prudent boldness and courage in following the leadings of the Holy Spirit of truth.

Looking more closely now at our actual situation, we may ask what we have inherited from our recent eucharistic tradition. What values and what shortcomings has the last millennium of Catholic life passed on to our generation?

a) Positive values in the tradition

First, we have inherited a deep appreciation of the Real Eucharistic Presence of Christ, the most intense self-gift of God to us in this life. Not only is this documented in the solemn Magisterium of the Church, especially in the teaching of the Council of Trent, but, over many centuries, devotion to the Mass and the Real Presence has been the outstanding feature of Catholic life at every level in the Church.

Second, the Church accepts from its past a firm belief in the sacrificial nature of the Holy Eucharist, that is to say, in the sacramental identification of the Mass with the events of Calvary. The Mass has been seen as the great prayer of the pleading of Christ's merits in propitiation, being offered for both the living and the dead.

Further, and linked with the preceding points, our inherited tradition has stressed the high role of the ordained priest as consecrator and offerer of the eucharistic Victim. The traditional Catholic respect and reverence for the priesthood have their roots in this sacral function, even though this has often been overstressed at the expense of other priestly functions such as those of teacher and shepherd, steward and servant.

Another value from the past eucharistic millennium is our understanding of the Mass as the great sign of unity between Christians. The Church's oneness, holiness, catholicity, and apostolicity develop only in, through, and with the sacrament of the Eucharist. Even though this unity has often been envisaged in much too canonical and external a sense, usually contenting itself with concern for universal uniformity and obedience to a defined set of rubrics, nevertheless a real notion of unity in the divine Son of God has been the object of Catholic faith, hope, and love.

A final positive feature, inherited from the recent past, has been the fact that the Latin Mass of the Roman rite, in its manner of celebration, has produced an atmosphere of prayer and contemplative stillness. From this has grown a deep personal devotion and commitment to the Mass and the Real Presence, and many are reluctant to abandon it.

b) Some shortcomings in the tradition

The same tradition which has been responsible for this spiritual inheritance has, however, brought with it certain drawbacks.

(1) The deep personal love for and commitment to the Mass has often taken too individualistic a form. It has lacked much understanding of the Church (i.e. the real, locally assembled community) and the Eucharist as two realities which are mutually formative. So lacking in 'community dimension' have been this devotion and eucharistic understanding that the reception of Holy Communion, and the devotions surrounding it, have been conceived of in an almost completely private way, leaving the common worship of the Church as an impersonal, official ritual. One of the great needs of our time is to bring together the two realities of 'personal piety' and 'community'.

Such practices as private thanksgiving after Communion are to be highly commended, especially when they are part of an overall communal piety. Certain other inherited practices, however, such as the 'meditation Mass', common in some of our monasteries until recent years, and the practice of celebrating individual Masses for the sole motive of private devotion, seem to lack the signs of a community-centred eucharistic life.[2] To that extent they fall short of the norm upheld by Vatican II and recent papal teaching.

(2) Neither the individualist nor the sacrificial stress in Catholic piety has generally been integrated with the paschal element of the Eucharist, the joyful thanksgiving and praise for the fact that Christ 'dying . . . has destroyed our death, and rising has restored our life'. It is while we are proclaiming our joyful thanks and praise in the eucharistic prayer that the heavenly Father lavishes upon us his most abundant gifts, the Body and Blood of his Son, through the action of the Holy Spirit. Indeed, a truly paschal understanding of this sacrament necessarily involves an appreciation of the role of the Holy Spirit in our eucharistic life. Not only does the Church call upon him for the consecration of its gifts; it also calls upon him as the effective agent in the growth of ecclesial unity and love.[3] The centrality of this paschal aspect can hardly be over-stressed.

Catholic spirituality – clerical, monastic, and lay – has not been alone in suffering from an over-emphasis upon the *memoria passionis* at the expense of the *mysterium paschale*; the spirituality of our Anglican and Protestant brethren has also suffered from the same Calvary-centredness. Nearly all the recently revised Catholic and Anglican eucharistic texts put this imbalance to rights as far as formulae are concerned.[4] It still remains for subjective spirituality, including that of monks, to assimilate this renewal.

(3) As already indicated, our inherited eucharistic tradition has suffered somewhat from a certain clericalization, or overstress on the function of the priest, with a consequent neglect of the function of the community he is leading. This has resulted in an exclusion of practically everyone else from any active liturgical role in the Mass since at least the High Middle Ages. The recent liturgical revival has been responsible for a renewed emphasis on the priesthood of the baptized and their real and active participation in the Mass, but it will take a considerable time for such a great change, even though it is a return to the Catholic norm, to be felt and experienced in the minds and hearts of Catholics at large. The practical effects of this upon our clerically-dominated monasteries of men will be discussed later.

(4) Since the Real Presence of Christ in the Host has often been conceived of in a quasi-static way, and rather in isolation from the sacrificial action, secondary eucharistic devotions have until recently tended to overshadow the central idea of the Mass as a common proclamation of Christ in his passover and self-giving sacrifice, and a sharing in him as food. Thus while practices such as Benediction of the Blessed Sacrament, Exposition, Visits, and other devotions to the reserved Sacrament have a place in Catholic practice and piety, they are kept in their proper perspective only when viewed as flowing from, and subordinate to, the theology of the Mass as a sacramental and sacrificial meal.

Some principles of eucharistic theology

Since fairly comprehensive guidelines for eucharistic theology and practice have been given by the Second Vatican Council, especially in the Constitution on the Sacred Liturgy, and in subsequent Roman and local documentation, no attempt at a full exposition of eucharistic doctrine will be made here. Nevertheless it would seem useful to highlight briefly certain aspects of eucharistic life which appear to bear most significance for contemporary monastic practice.

a) Sacrament

Eucharistic piety is primarily 'sacramental' rather than 'cultic'; that is, the sacrament of the Eucharist functions as a sign bringing about the effect it signifies, and not as a separate 'object' or sacred 'thing' in its own right. The Mass is the effective sign of God's love for us in the supreme gift of himself in redemptive offering, taking us through Christ's passover to the glory of his resurrection and the ever-further releasing of his Holy Spirit within us. It is also, however, a sign from us to God. Since God's self-giving is at the same time an invitation to participation and involvement in the trinitarian movement of reciprocal self-giving, offering us an opportunity to grow into Christ and demanding human responsibility, the Mass is also our human sign of response to him in loving self-sacrifice. The Eucharist thus constitutes a dialogue between the divine Father and ourselves, which is more than a dialogue of speech; it is a dialogue of the movement of love between two hearts. Thus any use of the Blessed Sacrament outside the specific liturgical action of the Mass, even the worship given to the reserved Real Presence, must always be regarded as an extension of this movement, or dynamism, of the self-offering of God and men, and not in terms of any static 'cult-object'.

b) Community

Since the Eucharist is a sacrament of human response, the human context of liturgy is of great importance. Man finds his human integrity through relationships with others in the love and the joy, the strains and the stresses of community living, and therefore his eucharistic wholeness or holiness will grow only in so far as it becomes the reflection of the communion (*koinonia*) between himself and his fellow-men. Thus it is specially important for monks to think of their eucharistic piety in the context of, and as dependent upon, their aspiration towards communal unity through their vows of Stability and Conversion of Life.

In this context it would seem necessary to think in terms of the availability of different presences of Christ. A true appreciation of the Eucharist will be possible only when this sacrament is seen as the central focus of many modes of sacramental availability of Christ's presence: in our fellow-men, especially the poor; in the word of God in Scripture, read privately or liturgically; when two or three are gathered for prayer; in the other sacraments. Of all these the Eucharist is the crown and climax, as being the most intense or concentrated of the forms of Christ's presence. Since the same divine Person is common to all, the more we grow in our appreciation of the other areas of divine activity, the more we will appreciate the Eucharist itself. Eucharistic maturity is thus intimately related to the attainment of Christian maturity in our human relations.

c) Memorial

The Eucharist is the celebration of the mystery of Christ made present here and now in the symbols of the rite. This memorial (*anamnesis*) brings us into contact with God on the level of salvation history, involving the participating community in the original archetypal events of the Christian revelation. The memorial concept, chosen by Christ himself, far from implying a mere act of human remembrance, involves the belief that through our human performance of that *anamnesis* the person of the resurrected Christ and the abundance of his power and grace actually become present and available to us in the here and now of human history.[5] So, if the Eucharist is to become a true 'memorial' for each single person sharing in the communal celebration, he must realize that this *objective memorial* is now, in this symbolic event, becoming part of his experiential contact with the mystery of Christ. In fact, it is primarily through, in and because of the Eucharist that each person actually comes to know the Christ of revelation and redemption. All other modes of knowing about him are here brought to their vital fulfilment in a direct, intimate, person-to-person communion with him in the celebration of the Eucharist.

d) Eschatology

The Kingdom of God, both in the individual person and in the world at large, develops as an organism, increasing in the here-and-now that power and glory which essentially belong to our destined future. The Eucharist is the spearhead of the coming of the Kingdom, since the object of our hope, eternal life, is here most effectively guaranteed and given in 'the Bread of Life and the Cup of eternal salvation'. The eucharistic sacrament should therefore be seen in terms of an ever-deepening participation in the eschatological Kingdom through the growing lordship of Christ over our hearts, which is the object both of our present enjoyment and of our future hope, the yet-to-be-achieved.

Monastic life and the Eucharist

The monks and nuns of St Benedict, as envisaged by his rule, are men and women who deliberately arrange their lives, in the framework of their vows in community, to ensure a sacred 'leisure' (*otium sacrum*) for growing in knowledge of God. This growth comes about primarily through communal and private prayer and *lectio divina*.

As a praying community, a monastery is centred on its daily office, that round of praise and intercession to which the monastic legislator devotes twelve chapters of his Rule. This constitutes the monastic *opus Dei* to which nothing is to be preferred, since the office is itself sacramental, being a verbal memorial of the *magnalia Dei*. But in so far as these monastic families are also Christian families, their communal worship finds its consummation in the regular celebration of the eucharistic mystery.

There is, however, no specific monastic liturgy, either in the sense of a rite different from that of the local Christians, or in the sense that a monastic family necessarily forms a completely structured eucharistic community in the same way as a diocese round its bishop and presbyterium, or a parish round its priest. This is most obviously true of non-clerical monastic houses, such as communities of nuns. Monastic communities share in the eucharistic life and attitudes of the Church of their era. Thus early monastic life partook of the contemporary emphasis on, and practice of, the weekly celebration of the Eucharist, the monks probably worshipping with the local Christian community in many places. In the High Middle Ages the theological emphases and liturgical practices of the 'secular' Church – the emphasis on the transubstantiated species themselves, the private-Mass system, the lack of lay participation – were fully shared by the monastic houses. Similarly today in the post-Vatican II period our monasteries are called to the same eucharistic renewal as other Christians, and so to share in the same tensions of the liturgical change of gear experienced by the whole Church.

Nevertheless, monastic life has an orientation which gives a specific nuance or tone to its eucharistic spirituality, namely its cenobitic or communal orientation. While it is true that all Christians have certain elements of community-living in their lives – after all, relation to others in some form is vital for any human maturity – yet monastic living as envisaged by the Rule of St Benedict assumes a daily involvement with others which is more pervasive, more intense, and therefore more demanding than most other forms of Christian living. This is because the monastic community is primarily a community of faith; that is, it finds its *raison d'être* and ultimate purpose as a community in faith alone, and not necessarily in any natural bonds of association. Such a cenobitic life is all the more subject to the possibilities of breakdown and tensions, and the temptation to opting out and self-seeking. In such a way of life the Eucharist, the sacrament of unity, has obviously a heightened role to play.

Monastic communities have therefore not merely an obligation but a deep essential need to celebrate the sacrament of unity together, and this for two purposes. First, they need to express, to symbolize, and to celebrate that unity which God has already vouchsafed to this community, or of which it is already conscious; a present unity which is rooted in the community's incorporation into the paschal mystery, the historical passing over from death to life of Jesus Christ. Second, there is the need to increase that unity and bring it to a fulness which is both human and divine: the 'peace and unity of his kingdom' which the Eucharist is constantly bringing into the world. The common monastic

Eucharist thus celebrates and proclaims the unity already achieved in the death of Christ, and effectively brings about the fulness of that unity, our true future, the object of our hope.

No matter how unified the monastic community, however, tensions between the present situation and the future ideal will be felt and experienced by individual members in different ways. There is thus often a practical lack of unity within a community concerning the methods and forms of eucharistic celebration, and concerning how best that community should move into the liturgical future. However, unity should not be confused with uniformity. There may be a healthy pluralism of forms in eucharistic celebration, accepted by the community as an expression of its diverse elements and as a means of discovering appropriate forms of worship. But variety should be balanced by a regular, though not necessarily daily, celebration of a single Eucharist in order to manifest and build up the unity of the whole Body.

Situations of disunity and division of opinion within a monastic house must be recognized as calls and opportunities to practise generosity and mortification of one's own will, to show patience with what one cannot see, or tolerance of what one cannot accept. Such an attitude should be regarded not simply as making the best of a bad job, but as a means of furthering charity, and therefore unity, among the brethren by exercising the virtue of obedience to one another recommended by St Benedict.[6] If the situation is not approached and turned to good account in this way, it will act like a cancer eating away at the love and unity already existing in the community.

On the other hand if each member participates in the Eucharist with the intention of giving support to the others, he will be co-operating with the whole purpose of the Eucharist – to build up the Body of Christ – and become more truly assimilated to what he eats. As each individual has something to bring to the Eucharist in service of his brethren, so all should lay themselves open to be fashioned by the action of Christ in a mystery which goes far beyond any human contribution; for unity and charity are gifts of the Spirit granted to those who are ready to accept them in humble gratitude.

Monastic practice and the Eucharist

a) The question of frequency

Our western monastic tradition has inherited two tendencies with regard to the frequency of eucharistic celebration. The first is the weekly rhythm of the solemn Sunday celebration, honouring the perpetual *memoria* of the paschal mystery of Christ's resurrection. The second, of less ancient provenance in the Church, is the rhythm of a daily Mass, a practice endorsed by the official exhortations to daily Communion by the popes of the twentieth century. Each of these tendencies embodies a set of religious values which should not be dismissed lightly. The weekly rhythm, for instance, clearly witnesses to the celebration of resurrection joy and encourages a well-prepared reception of Communion, being less liable to the temptations of routine. On the other hand, daily Mass is based on a natural rhythm, encourages daily dedication to self-sacrifice, and can constitute a more demanding spiritual standard.

What seems necessary in our present situation is a structure which enables us to combine the values of both, since the two tendencies seem to suit different forms of spiritual maturity. Thus the Sunday celebration should stand out as the supreme liturgical event of the week, when Mass is celebrated with a joy, solemnity, and dignity not matched on any other day. The celebration on weekdays should be much simpler and less formal in its manner of performance, with fewer readings, less solemn musical settings, and less ceremonial. In all circumstances, the individual's freedom to celebrate and receive Communion daily, or to refrain therefrom, should be carefully respected.

b) Monk-priests

Special circumstances arise, with their own problems, where monk-priests form a large proportion of a monastic community. Experience has shown that the spirituality of a monk can be considerably enriched through his exercise of a pastoral ministry, inside or outside his enclosure. At the community Mass itself, however, the priesthood of a monk must be exercised in such a way that it effectively promotes the unity it is intended to serve. Care must be taken that the priestly prerogative of some members of the community does not become a divisive symbol, and that the unity all are concerned to build is not undermined by the pointed abstention of individual members. In this respect certain points may be made.

(1) In such priestly communities all, both priests and non-priests, should consciously grow into the typical monastic eucharistic attitudes of mutual forgiveness, shared joy and praise, common sacrifice, and communion in love. Such characteristics are formative of Christian community life, and are the indispensable roots from which any monastic priesthood thrives. Thus at the Eucharist what the monk-priest has in common with his non-clerical brethren is of far greater significance than whatever might differentiate their functions.

(2) The recently inherited pattern of clerical-lay relationships and assumptions is considerably different from that laid down by St Benedict. For the latter, the priestly function and expression are to be firmly under the control of the abbot, and subordinated to the good of the monastic family; whereas in more recent centuries, partly as a result of the over-clericalization of the liturgy in the Church at large, respect for the priesthood *in se* has overshadowed the communal characteristics of eucharistic celebration. The change needed, therefore, is not so much a down-grading of the priesthood as a rediscovery by communities of themselves as eucharistic families, in which that priesthood finds its fulfilment.

(3) How then should priests celebrate in monasteries? Here again, two traditions have been inherited and find expression today in our houses. The first, accepting as the established norm a daily rhythm of celebration and believing that each priest should symbolize his priestly character fully at every liturgy, tends towards the practice of private celebration of Mass. Around this type of celebration, in which the priest performs in abbreviated style the roles of all the participants in a eucharistic assembly, a deep spirituality or mystique can develop, centred in the priest's individual offering of the sacred elements. The other tendency is that which, believing strongly that the chief *raison d'être* of the monastic Eucharist is the unity of the monastic family, holds that each priest should integrate himself into the common eucharistic celebration, not necessarily outwardly symbolizing his priestly role, unless called upon to preside.

The revival by the Church of the ancient practice of priestly concelebration, which has been adopted in most monasteries, has offered a compromise solution in which the priests of the monastery, without separating to celebrate privately, yet retain some of the role, gestures, and dress of an individually celebrating priest.

Without purporting to offer a solution to this question, the following points should be considered:

(i) The rite of concelebration is intended to signify the unity of the priestly body, as a presbyterium or ministerial college, under the bishop. It therefore belongs primarily to a diocesan context. The result of its adoption in monasteries can be beneficial in so far as the priestly body are brought together to the community Mass, and at appropriate times are enabled fittingly to express their priestly solidarity. But concelebration can also result in an even sharper division between the clerical and non-clerical sections of the community than was previously the case, with a reinforced feeling of clerical domination over the rite.

(ii) The present form of concelebration, while offering the possibility of the exercise of a communal priestly ministry, seems to many an unsatisfactory compromise. There seems to be no strong theological reason, however, why on weekdays a much simpler rite of concelebration should not be used, in which, while care is taken to ensure that the priest's internal consent of mind and heart to the words and actions of the sacrifice is given adequate expression, minimal outward distinctions would be made between cleric and non-cleric.[7]

(iii) Neither the stipend system nor any other pressure ought to be allowed to limit the freedom of a priest to choose his own frequency of celebration. In making this choice he should weigh up the nature of the freedom to which he is called – namely, self-transcendence in the priesthood of Christ – and he should take full account of the needs of his community situation and the responsibility of mutual support.

(iv) The conventual Mass ought to be celebrated with such care and preparation, and concern for actual personnel, as will ensure a celebration in which as many as possible may be able to find communally that opportunity for a personal and prayerful piety which the private Mass affords in an individual context.

c) The Eucharist and lectio divina

The monastic commitment to sacred reading should ensure that a considerable portion of a monk's day will be occupied with growing in the knowledge of God through meditating upon the sacred Scriptures and other spiritual writings, as well as through the study of exegetical and theological works. Therefore it would seem that a monk is in an especially privileged position with regard to the eucharistic Liturgy of the Word. He, above all, should be able to discover the manifold depths of God's presence available in the Service of the Word, and to communicate something of its riches to others.

d) The Eucharist and the vows

As men and women vowed to the love of God through Obedience, Stability, and Conversion of life, the members of monastic families have a special obligation to internalize and make their own the eucharistic spirituality outlined above, as the sacramental focus of their daily living. Thus the monastic Eucharist should be:

(1) *A celebration of mutual forgiveness:* the community, with faith in the ever-forgiving nature of the divine Father, here renew their forgiveness of each other, pardoning each other the unkindness, the criticisms, the thoughtless actions, and the unthinking attitudes of daily life.

(2) *A celebration of shared joy and praise:* here the monastery celebrates the supreme act of praise which is the culmination of its divine office. Here, as a locally assembled church, the *conventus* offers praise and thanks to God for the salvation and spiritual gifts which he is conferring on the community, though ever conscious that its love is not confined within the monastic community. The practice of monastic hospitality, and all other forms of monastic outreach involving concern for persons and their work, also find their highest expression in the eucharistic action.

(3) *A celebration of common sacrifice:* the Mass brings together, in union with Christ's self-sacrifice, all the actions of a selfless and loving kind which the individuals of the community perform towards each other in the process of their daily growth in conversion of life and obedience. The eucharistic sacrifice which they offer as a family thus constitutes the most effective regular method of renewal of vows.

(4) *A celebration of communion in love:* the Eucharist offers the supreme sacramental expression, as well as the best critical criterion, of our human relationships within the community, since our communion with God in this sacrament is intimately and directly related to our growth in unity and love for each other.[8]

II

Opus Dei

*While the monastic Eucharist organically relates the community which
celebrates it to the local bishop, the office is a domestic form of prayer,
specifically monastic and non-clerical in origin. This chapter points out the
historical difference between them. Nevertheless, Mass and office have for
many centuries been intertwined to form the liturgical worship of monastic
communities. In both, monks and nuns listen to the word of God which
found its final utterance in the Word made flesh; in both they say their
'Amen' of faith, praise, and love through Christ to the Father. This
dialogue is particularly evident in the psalms which are part of God's word
to Israel, but which were used as prayer by Christ himself and received in
him a transposition of meaning.*

*The present chapter discusses the place of the opus Dei in monastic life,
and some of the questions that arise when a community is trying to make its
choral prayer a true expression of its corporate life today, while remaining
in living contact with the liturgical tradition which has been the bearer of
God's word in the past.*

Introduction

Since Christ is the one Mediator through whom we have access to God,
the prayer of the whole human race has a profound and necessary
relationship with the prayer of Christ.[1] The whole of his earthly life
among men was animated by continual prayer to his Father; now raised
from the dead, he is living for ever to intercede for us all.[2] As the Head of
renewed humanity he prays to the Father in the name and for the good of
all mankind. All true prayer to God is made through him, even by those
who do not yet know him, for he is before all things[3] and it is through his
grace that they are moved to seek God;[4] but there is a special bond
between Christ and those whom he has made his members in baptism.
They receive all the life of the divine sonship, flowing from him as Head

into the whole Body of the Church, and since through adoption they share Christ's sonship they are enabled to share in his priesthood[5] and take part in the worship of the new covenant.[6]

From the beginning the Christian Church has been a praying community; its first description in Acts is that of a community gathered in prayer 'with the women and Mary, the mother of Jesus, and with his brethren'.[7] Those who had been baptized 'remained faithful to the teaching of the apostles, to the brotherhood, to the breaking of bread and to the prayers'.[8] Celebrating the breaking of bread in their own homes, they also continued to attend the temple services, for their awareness of being the messianic community made it inevitable and natural that they should take over the psalms and readings of Jewish worship. After the dispersal of the Christian community the faithful continued to devote themselves to prayer at certain hours. For them, nothing in time or space was profane[9] because all came from God, and now in Christ they had been called to a worship in spirit and truth that transcended all boundaries, pervading their whole being. Nevertheless there remained a human need to mark in time and space certain moments and places where the prayer which pervaded the whole of their lives found its focus. Such moments of privileged awareness would neither be divorced from the rest of life nor imply that other dimensions of man's life were not holy; rather they would be moments for beginning afresh, moments which would help to penetrate the rhythms of work and rest with the dynamism of Christ and provide an approach to that spirit of prayer without ceasing enjoined by the Lord.[10]

Historical perspectives[11]

a) The office in early monastic tradition

1. The desert tradition

For the monks of the desert tradition the whole of life was an endeavour to arrive at uninterrupted prayer. Nevertheless, formal prayer at certain hours of the day and night constituted a fixed framework which was a help towards achieving this end. The recurring hours of common prayer marked the times for renewed endeavour and for mutual encouragement and stimulus, but they were only one of the ways of sustaining a life of continual personal prayer, and did not take on the aspect of being a monk's primary service, as they did for later generations. In its oldest form the office consisted of psalms and silent prayers, and was organically related to the rest of they day with its simple manual labour accompanied by 'meditation' – which meant the spoken repetition of scriptural passages – interspersed with prayer. The essence of the office was the periodic realization in a communal form of the spontaneous, unceasing dialogue with God which a monk enjoyed during his work. During the whole of the day the word of God sounded in the ears of the monks, arousing frequent prayers in response; but at certain moments all other business ceased, listening to the word became more attentive, and the prayers in response were more concentrated.

2. Communities attached to local churches

The Egyptian hermits and the Pachomians did not give great scope to liturgy in their life; for them asceticism was more important, and the prayer of the psalms more personal and interior than the celebrations of the whole Christian community could be. However, side by side with the desert type of monastic life there existed also another form, equally ancient and venerable, which did not entail such a radical break with the world. This type of monasticism was lived within the framework of the sacramental and liturgical institutions of the existing Christian community. When the community came together for prayer Christ was in their midst, and in praying together they were the Church. 'Where there is a psalm, a prayer, a choir of prophets, a faithful band of singers, one would not be wrong in saying that there is the Church.'[12] The hours of the office were considered as the work of the whole People of God, but those who were not involved in the responsibilities of family or property multiplied these assemblies, lengthening them, and giving them a more stable form. Such were the ascetics and virgins of Jerusalem in the time of Egeria and the monastic communities serving the Roman basilicas. This type of monk made liturgical prayer the basis of his devotion. It was these monks who transformed the occasional night vigil into a regular office; under their influence the little hours became public instead of private, and the offices of Prime and Compline were introduced.

These groups were non-clerical; the clergy were bound only to Lauds and Vespers. Only the monks celebrated the fuller cursus of the hours daily, and in particular it was the monks attached to the Roman basilicas who drew up the framework of the hours and the cursus of the psalms. This does not mean, however, that there was a single arrangement of the office everywhere; on the contrary, each monastery, each basilica, had its own cursus and canon of prayer, and uniformity was arrived at only little by little.

3. The office in the Rule of St Benedict

Benedictine monasticism in the West was a later evolution combining the two earlier tendencies, though it received a liturgical orientation from the important place given to the office in the Rule. For St Benedict monks were not servants of the basilicas, the communities of which had by now become clericalized, and the Benedictine office had a purely domestic character without explicit reference to ecclesial responsibility. Nevertheless his concept tended to make a certain separation between the *opus Dei* and the other activities of the monastery. Whereas, for example, in the Egyptian tradition the monks worked with their hands during the scriptural readings of the night office,[13] St Benedict expressly enjoins that the oratory should be what its name implies, and that nothing else should be done or kept there.[14] Instead of the hours of the office marking points of intensification in an unceasing effort of continuous prayer, the *opus Dei* was rather the prayer performed in common at the proper times with the purpose of sanctifying the hours and divisions of the day and night.

b) The character of psalmody

At some period between the time of the desert fathers and St Benedict the character of psalmody seems to have changed: instead of being primarily the word of God addressed to man it now appeared more as the homage of man to God. The former view was given expression in the practice of solo recitation of the psalms while all listened in silence; it invited the response of silent prayer by all the brethren and a common collect. In its latter aspect the psalmody itself had become prayer rather than the prelude to it, for the psalter contained not only the inspired word of God to men but also the prayers of men to God. For St Benedict the service of the monks in the office is to render praise to their Creator 'for the judgements of his justice'.[15]

It would obviously be far too categorical to make a sharp historical distinction between prayer and *meditatio*, since the two have always interpenetrated. Nevertheless a shift of emphasis does seem to have taken place. There were probably several reasons for this development, corresponding to legitimate needs and influences. It had, however, far-reaching effects. Once antiphonal chanting had been established there was nothing to suggest that the psalms were originally listened to. Since they themselves were prayer, the need for the response of silent prayer after each of them was no longer felt; hence the gradual disappearance of this element, although it is possible that St Benedict's requirement that prayer in common be very short[16] refers to silent prayer within the office, either after the psalms or at the conclusion under the general heading of *supplicatio litaniae*.[17]

The idea of psalmody as worship grew stronger from the sixth century onwards, and with it an increasing splendour in the liturgy, elaboration of melodies and ceremonial, and the proliferation of additional offices and prayers. God was worthily praised by the offering of as solemn and extended a liturgy as possible. At a later stage when Latin was no longer the common language, intelligibility was not considered indispensable, since the office was above all a sacrifice of praise which the Church offered to God. Accretions to the office, the clericalization of monks (which led to the insertion into the horarium not only of the daily conventual Mass but also of a large number of private Masses), the growth of feudalism, and the introduction of lay brothers (which relieved monks of manual labour) all contributed to the vision of the *opus Dei* as a form of *laus perennis* continually rising up to God from the monastery choir. But if the interests and spiritual needs of men were sometimes lost sight of, it was not thought that the magnificence of sung psalmody and solemn ritual was necessarily incompatible with sincere and deep devotion.

c) Juridical developments

The influence which the monastic and clerical offices exerted upon each other throughout the course of history is very complex. Undoubtedly the monastic cursus had a formative effect upon that of the clergy, who adopted the same hours, although until the eighth century these were shared out between the different clerical communities of each city. At the time of the Carolingian reform, when daily solemnization of the whole office in each church was made obligatory for all clerics attached to its service, the model followed was the splendid liturgy carried out by the large communities serving the Roman basilicas. Imposed by Charlemagne throughout the empire, the Roman office from that time became obligatory for the clergy of the whole Latin church; the same period saw the imposition of the Rule of St Benedict on all monasteries. At this time monks were clearly differentiated from the clergy serving the local churches. The former separated themselves more and more from the ecclesial communities to form cloistered communities of their own, while the clerics or canons continued to live a common life centred on the church, becoming what later came to be known as 'secular clergy'.

The Gregorian reform initiated the medieval development of a more juridical idea of the Church, which also affected the monastic office. Another factor was the invention of printing which in practice meant the suppression of many elements of choice in the breviary. Uniformity was, moreover, introduced into the office by the religious orders founded during this period, as an aspect of the common observance they wished to ensure. When in 1568, on the instructions of the Council of Trent, Pope Pius V imposed his reformed Roman Breviary upon the whole Latin church, those breviaries which could claim to be 200 years old were allowed to remain in use, but they too became subject to the centralized legislation of the Congregation of Rites. From Trent to Vatican II the liturgy was in a static condition.[18] For the liturgical renewal of the late nineteenth century it was 'a sacred heritage, not to be meddled with . . . a holy thing coming from somewhere far off in the early Christian ages, inviolate and unchangeable as the Word of God itself'.[19] Worship expressed itself in a loving care to recite the ancient melodies with as much beauty and ceremonial dignity as was possible. It nourished itself on the age-long endowment of prayer, meditation, and interpretation (often accommodated) with which these texts were saturated. This spiritual treasury, enshrined in the melodies themselves, acted as a vehicle of communication between generations.

Although the liturgy in this phase of its history ran the risk of becoming an aesthetic show-piece, a veneration of ancient cultures for the sake of antiquity, it also represented a true recognition that while man is caught up in continual change, God abides for ever. Prayer and worship are a constant flowing back and homecoming of restless, wavering men to the peace of God. Thus the very forms through which God had been glorified in the past seemed to take on a kind of sanctity, consecrated as they were to God like a votive offering which must not be taken away from the sanctuary once it is given.[20] Nevertheless, the Church's renewal has firmly distinguished between the transcendent and enduring elements in the liturgy and their expression in changing periods and cultures.[21] 'The Liturgy of the Hours should not be looked upon as a beautiful monument of a past age, to be preserved almost unchanged in order to excite our admiration. On the contrary, it should come to life again with new meaning and grow, to become once more the sign of a living community.'[22]

By the nineteenth century the ancient idea of the purpose of the office as the sanctification of the principal hours of the day and night had long been lost. Even in the Rule of St Benedict the office is beginning to be spoken of as a *pensum* or 'due measure of a monk's service' which he is to say by himself as well as he can if he is unable to be present in choir at the proper time.[23] In the centuries which followed there developed an increasing distinction between the *opus Dei* and other monastic occupations, and thus it came about that the hours of the office were no longer organically related in men's minds to the natural divisions of the day. For the 'age of rubrics' which followed the Council of Trent it had become an obligation *sub gravi* to recite a fixed quantity of texts with legal exactitude, a performance to which was attributed a kind of efficaciousness almost *ex opere operato*. This concept was bound up with an ecclesiology which was juridical in character and which was shared by monks as well as by everyone else. Since they were also priests, monks were in fact deputed by the Church to praise God officially in its name, but this mandate was not clearly distinguished from the commitment to the office which was theirs in virtue of their monastic profession. Thus a confused situation arose.

However, to make formal praise in the name of the Church the essential element in monastic life is to confuse the role of the monk with that of the canon. The monastic office must not be thought of first and foremost as the official public homage rendered in the name of the Church by virtue of deputation from the Holy See and in the form determined by it. The official character of the clerical office derives from the mandate given to sacred ministers to recite the *Liturgy of the Hours*[24] in union with their bishop, in order that through them the duty of the whole local church community may be fulfilled.[25] Although the monastic office too is certainly the prayer of the Church,[26] this is not principally because of a deputation received from a higher authority, but because it is the expression of a community's response to the call to seek God in the monastic life and to worship him in common prayer according to its rule. It is an integral part of a way of life oriented to prayer which the Church authorizes and recommends as a contribution to the fulness of her mission.[27]

The concept of the office as a 'thing to be done', whether in choir or out, lies behind many of the difficulties associated with the individual's obligation of making up in private the hours he has been unable to recite in common with the brethren. On the one hand there are some who interpret this obligation as meaning that the hours in question must be recited to the letter, with all those repetitions and responses which are meaningful only in a choral context; on the other there are those who have found such a practice so unprayerful that they have abandoned any attempt to fulfil the obligation out of choir. A key to understanding the obligation is to remember the ancient relationship between the communal office and the Christian and monastic duty to pray without ceasing.[28] Thus a solid basis for responsibility in this matter can be found in acknowledging a real obligation to *pray*, and to remain linked with one's community by praying in a way which is related to the community's common prayer. The manner in which an individual may do this is a personal one which can vary from one monk to another or according to circumstances, provided that it is accepted by the abbot and community. Seen in this light, what has often in the past been experienced as a problem area will prove to be a help in strengthening the bond with the community.

The character of the monastic office

a) Stability and change

A stable but flexible structure is needed for common prayer. On the one hand liturgy of its nature requires routine and repetition; it is an on-going process of prayer which sustains and moulds the community, forming a common mind in the brethren as they take their part in it. On the other hand when liturgy becomes over-rigid it runs the risk of becoming irrelevant and alienating; like every living organism it must be capable of some degree of adaptation to contemporary conditions if it is not to become fossilized. Liturgical forms are for man, not man for liturgical forms.[29] Thus the liturgical cursus in the Rule of St Benedict is an instance of liturgy composed by a layman for laymen vowed to the search for God, a liturgy taking its inspiration freely from among those already in existence in the Church, and presented to monks with the reservation that they should arrange it otherwise if this seemed good to them. Monastic liturgy needs to achieve an equilibrium between fidelity to liturgical tradition, the needs of the local group, and its creative impulses.

The hours of the office are meant to sanctify the daily life of the monk and to make of it an offering to his Creator, and this life which is to be sanctified and offered must be his own authentic life, shaped and influenced by the social conditions of his time. The daily life of sixth-century monks with its simple agricultural work, its lack of a daily

Eucharist, and its dependence on the hours of daylight was offered to God in the balanced service laid down in the Rule, for which the literal interpretation of the biblical idea of perfection and fulness in the text, 'Seven times a day have I given praise to thee', was well suited. Subsequent generations whose life had become less simple or was based on a different daily rhythm tended to retain the literal interpretation but to lose the balanced proportions of prayer, *lectio*, and work which were an integral part of St Benedict's idea. It has been a common fact of monastic experience that when a community or an individual is under pressure the area of life which is the first to suffer encroachment is that of *lectio divina*; this is the element which contemporary changes seek to safeguard. In the twentieth century the movement both for adaptation to present conditions of life and for a recovery of evangelical simplicity and poverty, shown by a real sharing in the lot of modern working men, has led monks to concern themselves with the restoration of the Rule's original balance, a restoration to be achieved more by fidelity to its spirit than by adherence to the details of the letter. No longer dependent upon daylight for their activities, and working in the midst of a society which demands far greater skills of those who would earn their living, they have less leisure than their forbears. It is still their own daily lives that are sanctified and offered to God in the community office, but the hours of this office now follow the rhythm of a twentieth-century working day.

Conditions for the nuns have undergone similar changes since the days when it was normal for monastic communities to be maintained by dowries. The Church has in recent times clearly and repeatedly pointed out to contemplatives their duty of earning their living.[30] In England the additional economic burden of heavy taxation for the nuns means that, like the monks though for different reasons, they have experienced the need to re-establish the balanced proportions of the Rule in the rhythm of their daily life.

In most EBC houses the solution to this question has been the adoption of an office in the early morning when all can be present before the day's work begins, an office in which God's word is listened to in humble receptivity and responded to in psalms and hymns, so that the whole of the day at its outset is dedicated to God. In common with their neighbours they make a break in their work at midday, and at this time come together again in common prayer. At the end of the day's work there is an evening office of praise and thanksgiving, of confidence and trust in the God whom they have served throughout the day. Given the rhythms of a twentieth-century day this is generally satisfying. It may still be asked, however, whether monks should not rather be creatively criticizing these rhythms as the impositions of an artificial environment. Each community has the task of realistically integrating its work with its corporate praise. The two extremes to be avoided are (1) the mentality of the rat-race, which allows the work to impose its own pressures on the office to such a point that the primacy of the latter is completely lost; and (2) the 'monument' idea, which regards the office as untouchable and endeavours to fit the work in round it, to the detriment of apostolic commitments and the due proportion of the elements of monastic life. It is not easy to find the right balance, but a major criterion must be the need to rediscover that wholeness of living for which St Benedict provided in his own way.

The Church in its renewed liturgy has recognized the need for some element of spontaneity and choice. On the other hand, an over-flexible office could contain counter-risks of arbitrariness, narrowness, loss of touch with the main tradition of the Church's worship, subjectivism, or domination by one or a few individuals. In renewing its forms of worship a community needs to remain in living contact with the rich liturgical tradition of the monastic past, of which the old breviary contained a kind of distillation. In the breviary the Christian use of the psalms and other scriptural texts was handed down from one generation to another, providing a formation in liturgical prayer for all who used it. The writings of the Fathers commenting on these sacred texts bear witness to the constant reflection on the word of God which the Church has continued down the centuries.[31] In spite of an exegesis and an allegorical manner of interpretation which are often unacceptable today, the work of the Fathers communicates a broad vision of the whole of salvation history as summed up in Christ which is of enduring value. Our forbears understood too the need for the lyrical element in the liturgy to balance the rational, the value of judicious repetition and of the musical phrase in helping to fix the inspired texts in the minds of the hearers. A real continuity with this tradition must be kept: too drastic a simplification or modification of the contents of the office could deprive future generations of these proven values, although a great enrichment is also to be gained from the fruits of modern biblical and patristic studies and from contemporary insights. It is possible too that an effect of reduced ceremonial could be the creation of a purely textual liturgy, lacking in the appeal to the whole man which was provided by the medieval use of drama, gesture, and symbol. The Middle Ages had an understanding of the power of such media which could be valuable for modern man, who learns as much through visual and dramatic aids as through words.

b) The distinctive mark of the monastic opus Dei

Now that the revision of the Roman office has provided a form of liturgical prayer which, while remaining fully traditional, is also suited to modern needs, it may be asked why the monastic office should continue to be differentiated. The theological principles of Vatican II and the *General Instruction on the Liturgy of the Hours* stress the bond between the prayer of Christ as Head and that of the members of his Body, and the consecration of time by the relation of the hours to the time of day at which they are said. These principles are valid for both Roman and monastic offices. It remains to discover what constitutes the characteristic difference of the monastic orders in their common prayer.

It would seem that we cannot look for this difference in any quality of the monastic office as prayer in common, or as performed with special solemnity, or as having an eschatological or paschal character, or as demanding in the brethren a contemplative attitude of receptivity and listening, since all these qualities could belong to the use of *The Liturgy of the Hours*. Is it to be found, then, in the protracted nature of the monastic office? Here it must be pointed out that the length of a community office need not necessarily depend upon the quantity of verbal formulae which it contains; the restoration of that element of silent personal prayer which was so important to the early monks, a more leisurely and meditative pace for the psalmody, and the relaxation of pressure caused by the obligation to get through a quantitatively burdensome amount of office and a heavy work-load have had the effect of making the monastic office qualitatively more fruitful without reducing its length to that of the Roman office. The idea of quantity and solemnity as the measure of a community's generosity and fervour has had a long life, but in our own day one of the simple insights of the early monks has been regained, namely that while the office is indeed a service of praise and worship in which we sing and make music to the Lord with all our skill,[32] at the same time a quiet and humble spirit, conscious of its poverty and receptive to the word of God, gives glory to him as truly as does the splendour of elaborate ceremonial.[33] On the other hand, it would be possible to make the mistake of reducing quantity so drastically that the office no longer took a really important place in a community's scale of values. In a life consecrated to God there must always be a place for the symbol of the precious ointment poured over the Lord's feet:[34] this is the act of faith we make in spending a considerable portion of the day in a work which is non-lucrative and seemingly unproductive.

The distinctive mark of the monastic *opus Dei* is to be found in the fact that the office is the corporate prayer of a particular community having its own legitimate interpretation of monasticism within the wide pluralism of Benedictine observance. St Benedict makes it clear that it is the business of the abbot to regulate the cursus, choose the readings, and make such modifications as seem to him expedient within the general stable framework.[35] Since each monastery has its own charism no two communities will find exactly the same office suitable for them, although they will freely take elements from one another. Yet the broad outlines of a basic pattern have emerged within the EBC, so that monks from one monastery can easily take part in the office of another when they visit it. In a period of evolution there may be much in the monastic office that is untidy, unpolished, tentative. Visitors who come to take part in it may not always find the dignity and solemnity of the past, but neither will they find a popular liturgy laid on to attract them. They should find a community striving to express its own authentic life in the language of its common prayer, rediscovering as it does so the spiritual significance of the *opus Dei* within the Benedictine calling.

The meaning of the *opus Dei* in Benedictine life

a) The value of the psalms

Attitudes to the psalms have varied throughout monastic history. Cassian speaks of the monk's coming to an understanding of his profession and the psalms[36] as though the two were, if not synonymous, at least closely linked. Although in the desert tradition the psalms were *meditatio*, they also expressed personal prayer; this was true even of the 'historical' psalms, for to recount the mighty exploits of the Lord is to praise him. Occasional verses provided spontaneous expression for the monk's interior prayer; he would use and apply to his own needs some favourite verse, especially 'O God, come to my assistance'.[37] Sometimes, said Abbot Isaac, 'a verse of any one of the psalms gives us an occasion of ardent prayer while we are singing'.[38] St Benedict's extremely free use of Scripture in the text of the Rule and his injunction that 'our mind and voice should be in harmony'[39] suggest that a similar habit of adapting the psalms to the needs of personal prayer prevailed among his monks. In

St Augustine's view the important thing is that the whole Christ, Head and members, is praying in every psalm; this approach is more consciously ecclesial but by no means rules out contemporary applications to the situation and needs of those who pray the psalms.

It is probable that great numbers of monks and nuns have prayed in choir throughout the ages in an attitude of general awareness of God's presence, making little attempt to concentrate on the meaning of the words. In times and places where the psalms have been sung in Latin by those without sufficient education to understand them no other approach may have been possible, and, apart from the language difficulty, the Latin versions were in many places too obscure to be a vehicle of the true meaning. The introduction of the vernacular and of good translations makes a great difference, but does not mean that the attitude of 'general attention' has lost its validity. In the past, in spite of the obstacles to understanding, very many people did find in the psalms an instrument of prayer. Moreover it is a matter of common experience that, however familiar the liturgical language, however clear the translation, and however complete the theological formation of those who regularly pray the psalms, there will always be times when weariness and other causes make it impossible or unprayerful to concentrate on the meaning of the words. But the prayer goes on, and then it may be more obvious than usual that Christ is subsuming our prayer into his, rather than leaving us to unite ours with his as best we can. We are then borne along on a current of prayer.

More fundamental than any difficulty of language or inability to penetrate the meaning is the whole problem of why the psalms, which were the songs of a people on the march towards Christ and are penetrated with the faith, outlook, and sentiments of a pre-Christian stage of salvation, should continue to form the staple prayer of the Christian people. The problem is raised in its most acute form when the sentiments of the psalmist are not merely crude and primitive but in plain contradiction to the gospel ethic of love and humility: 'O God, break the teeth in their mouths . . . the just shall rejoice at the sight of vengeance; they shall bathe their feet in the blood of the wicked. . . .'[40] 'O Babylon, he is happy who shall seize and dash your children on the rock!'[41] Our scruples can be soothed up to a point by considerations about barbarous practices taken for granted by the ancients, about the need that justice be seen to be done in the present life when hope of a future life was so undeveloped, about the simplistic identification of Israel's cause with Yahweh's cause, and about the progressive character of Old Testament revelation especially in moral matters. But since so much apologetic is needed to make these psalms viable as Christian prayer, it has been asked whether there is not a good case for discarding them or even a considerable part of the psalter, and substituting fully Christian prayers.

Certainly, one of the many happy results of the revision of both Roman and monastic liturgy has been the discovery or rediscovery of the suitability of the New Testament canticles for choral prayer. The Pauline letters and the Book of Revelation provide a number of lyrical prayers which, while biblical and traditional in flavour, praise God in a specifically Christian key. Some gospel passages which are poetic in form, such as the Beatitudes and the Last Discourse in St John, can also be used in this way. But it is doubtful whether they could entirely supplant the psalter; apart from the fact that the quantity of suitable New Testament material is limited, a wholesale jettisoning of the psalms as outdated would mean a great impoverishment of liturgical prayer.

However, the problem of the imprecatory psalms is more acute than ever when they are recited in the vernacular. The Roman *Liturgy of the Hours* has omitted certain verses expressing violence or cursing, and dropped entirely three whole psalms where violence was judged to be the dominant theme: 58(57), 83(82) and 109(108). This decision was made in full recognition of the problems it raises. There is a liturgical problem in departing from the traditional use of the integral psalter, a literary problem in excising verses from a poem which forms a whole, and a problem of biblical theology since the whole of Scripture is inspired and since the psalmists may have been seized by 'holy anger' against the enemies of God rather than by personal hatred. When due weight has been given to these considerations it may still be judged that those psalms which are offensive to the Christian conscience should be dropped from monastic liturgy as they have been from the Roman office. The whole purpose of liturgical change is to adapt traditional forms to current needs in order to make liturgical prayer intelligible and meaningful to modern men. Psalmody today is not a mere meditation on sacred history in God's presence; it is prayer. To make bloodthirsty petitions directly to God in community prayer seems insuperably difficult. Theoretical justifications for such psalms cannot weigh against the real obstacle they present to authentic prayer. And to visitors unfamiliar with biblical thought and language who may be participating, some parts of the psalms can sound repugnant when prayed by a monastic community.

On the other hand there are many people who have reservations about emasculating the psalter, on the grounds that 'all Scripture is inspired by God and profitable for teaching . . . and for training in righteousness'.[42] Prayer can be thought of as a whole process of facing reality in God's presence, and this includes facing the evil in ourselves rather than papering it over; centuries of Christianity and civilization have refined us but the basic tendencies of sinful men are unchanged. It is possible also that we may become too refined, and then the crude Old Testament notion of the 'wrath of God' may be a valuable safeguard against domesticating him and fashioning him according to our own tastes. The love that is as strong as death[43] is not a mild and accommodating benevolence. No doubt the psalmists were prone to a facile identification of the sin that God hates with their own personal or tribal enemies, but the 'holy war' sung in the psalms is nevertheless a primitive stage in the struggle between good and evil, between God and sin, that reached not a truce but a climax with Christ's combat and victory: 'Now shall the prince of this world be cast out.'[44] Moreover, once bowdlerizing of the psalter begins it is not easy to know where to stop; the smug self-righteousness of some passages is as sub-Christian as the violence.

The psalter, like the Old Testament of which it is the distillation, proclaims on every page that it is not a fulfilment but the record of man's need and God's promise. Given a strong sense of historical development and of the provisional but dynamic character of the old dispensation, many people find it possible to pray unworriedly those passages which are less than Christian, aware that the cry of suffering men and women in every age and place is articulated by the often crude and vindictive expressions of the psalmist, but taken up into the prayer of the suffering Christ to reach the God who inspired the psalms.

There is clearly no consensus, and the best solution is that each community should decide to retain or omit the problematical passages in accordance with its own needs and those of its guests.

The most fundamental justification for the Church's adoption of the prayers and songs of Israel is an awareness not only of the continuity of God's people but also of that continuity in the saving action of God which links type to antitype as stages in the unfolding of God's redeeming plan. In the earlier part of its history God's people, taught by the prophets, responded in faith and worship to the mighty deeds of God in words he had himself inspired. But the mighty deeds were preparations and rehearsals for the saving intervention of God in his incarnate Son, and the God-given words were capable of a new fulness of meaning when prayed by Christ himself. The psalms are transposable, and they can be used for the response to God of a worshipping community at later stages in the story as they celebrate the exodus of Christ and of Christians, the desert march of God's people towards the promised land of eternity, or their longing to see the face of the living God in the new Jerusalem. To pray the psalms while moving freely from one plane to another, or to remain aware of different but compenetrating mysteries evoked by them, demands some degree of biblical formation but is becoming possible for increasing numbers today with the development of biblical theology.

b) Readings

The office is a dialogue with God in which our response to him is evoked by his creative and self-revelatory word to us. The readings in particular recall and interpret his loving activity on his people's behalf in the past, culminating in the passover of Christ. But they also make the power of the living word present and active in those who listen in faith. In a Benedictine community where the life of all the members is organized for the following of Christ 'according to the gospel',[45] the personal and communal effort towards continual conversion of heart finds its inspiration in the word of God. 'These things were written for our instruction.'[46] There is a two-way process: the story of God's dealings with his people and the personal experience of each monk in his life with God illuminate each other. It is his own story that the monk is listening to and reliving in the images and symbols of Scripture and liturgy, and only in listening does he find that his own journey towards God makes sense. He knows the rhythms of call and response, of sin and repentance, of exodus, detachment and freedom, of promise, covenant, preliminary fulfilment, and dynamic hope. He knows them not as the story of something remote but as the drama of God's continuing and constant dealings with his people and with each person; he knows it from the inside. And so the monk's personal exodus to freedom and his painful experience of the desert waste of his own being become the basis of a participation in liturgical prayer which in turn enriches his 'private' prayer. The Holy Spirit who acts in salvation history, who inspires its scriptural record, who makes the written word to be the living and life-giving word here and now, is the same Spirit who is at work in the monk, his workman,[47] freeing him for a union with God in prayer which the Spirit himself will direct and control.

This actuality of the scriptural and other readings emphasizes the need for flexibility in the choosing of them and in particular the possibility of the abbot's using his right to select readings as an opportunity to teach. The introduction of a homily could be important for the same reason. St Benedict prescribed, over and above Scripture, 'the commentaries of well-known and orthodox Catholic Fathers'.[48] There is no need to suppose that this limits us to writers conventionally styled 'patristic'; a reasonable interpretation in this matter is to select passages from writers of any age who have proved themselves to be fully in the mainstream of the Church's tradition, men who, like 'the Fathers', have been fed from the true sources and speak the word anew in terms relevant to their own generation and to ours.

c) The spirit of worship

Deeply rooted in the Old Testament record of man's relationship with God is the concept of the 'fear of Yahweh'. It is a mingling of awe, reverence, obedience, and love, and it implies a habitual 'preparation of heart':

> Those who fear the Lord do not disdain his words,
> and those who love him keep his ways. . . .
> Those who fear the Lord keep their hearts prepared
> and humble themselves in his presence.[49]

This teaching clearly impressed St Benedict and pervades his spirituality. The monk is bidden to 'remember' God and his commandments, and to live habitually in a climate of awareness of the reality and holiness of God.[50] He is to 'know for certain that God sees him everywhere'.[51] The attitudes of deep inner humility and outward restraint that result from this habitual 'remembering' are described throughout Chapter 7 of the Rule. The same concept of the 'fear of God' pervades St Benedict's teaching on swift obedience,[52] on gentleness and charity,[53] and especially on prayer.[54] Because this 'fear' is the authentic attitude of men who are both sinful creatures and sons of God, their reverence, compunction, and humility are compounded with joy, confidence, love, and longing for eternal life.[55] St Benedict thinks of this awareness of God as influencing them at all times, but especially when they stand before God in the office.[56]

One of the principles of Vatican II's reform of the liturgy was that spontaneity and joy should find a place in the worship of God. But however much flexibility and freedom are allowed, it is unlikely that everyone in a monastic community will find that the office exactly corresponds at all times to his personal needs. Unselfish give-and-take is as much needed in an era of flexibility as before. St Benedict calls his nineteenth chapter *De disciplina psallendi* for good reason. Anyone who has prayed in choir for a few years knows from painful experience how much 'discipline' is needed to make a success of it. Choral prayer provides endless opportunity for the humble use of talents, self-forgetfulness, and obedience that are expected of monks in all areas of life.

It also calls us to go beyond our narrow horizons, since we are sharing in a prayer that is not only a community undertaking but also an ecclesial and universal prayer made through Christ to the God whose 'thoughts are above our thoughts'.[57] Instead of focusing on the ephemeral and petty affairs of the moment, we are called to celebrate the passing of God himself through the affairs of men; instead of letting our own needs or sentiments fill the picture, we have to listen to God whose word is often disconcerting and disturbing to our scale of values. We are saved from the danger of trying to fit God into our theological or devotional system, and we are kept in an atmosphere of praise.

The element of praise in the office is vital. Monasticism is a lifelong act of faith in and witness to the holiness of God, but this faith is sacramentally expressed in liturgy. Time, energy, talent, the resources of poetry and music, communal effort, and personal devotion are expended in faith-filled worship of the invisible God. In a society where many are living without faith, and many of those who do believe concentrate exclusively on the service of mankind, the single-minded praise of God for his own sake in monastic liturgy, free from self-conscious striving to 'witness', may in fact be the most effective witness of all.

d) The opus Dei *as the sacrament of monastic life*

Monastic liturgy is a sacrament of what monastic life as a whole is trying to be. This is the conclusion that emerges whether we are thinking of St Benedict's teaching on the fear of God, or of the personal dedication, self-forgetfulness, and shared effort required in the office. In monastic liturgy a community, united in charity and striving for authentic personal prayer, is carried into the prayer of Christ. The office is not the *raison d'être* of Benedictine life; most monks are not professional liturgists nor did they enter the monastery in order that the solemn performance of the liturgy might be assured. But it does sacramentally express the movement of a monastic community through Christ and with him and in him to the Father, and the paschal mystery of Christ which is central to the Church's prayer is central to the monk's lifelong conformation to Christ. 'Let them hold fast in their lives to what they have grasped by their faith', says the Liturgy Constitution, quoting an Easter prayer;[58] the reference is to all Christians but has a particular relevance for monks.

Human life has its rhythms – its times of work and rest, of communication and solitude, of maturations and new beginnings. Monastic life involves a continual effort to integrate all these things, and liturgy is the consecration of these living rhythms. In the Rule the term *opus Dei* seems to be reserved to liturgy as such, but there is some evidence to suggest that before St Benedict it was sometimes used to connote the whole 'work' of the monastic undertaking: the labour of ascesis, growth in likeness to Christ, and return to God.[59] If this is true the evolution of the term *opus Dei* to a specialized sense is suggestive, since it has come to be applied to the sacramental expression of the whole work of the monk.

Growth in likeness to Christ is not, however, the result of the monk's own ascetical endeavour but the work of the Holy Spirit in him. In this sense the term *opus Dei* could be thought of as containing a subjective genitive, referring to God's work in the world, in our communities, and in our own hearts. Conformation to Christ and identification with him are a dynamic process; 'the plans of his heart are from age to age'.[60] The more we are identified with him and ruled by his Spirit, the more we shall be in a position to seek today's answers to today's problems with the mind of Christ. Monks can and should play a prophetic role in society; how far they are actually able to do so will depend on how far 'God's work' is effective in them.

12

Lectio Divina

The monk's daily service of God as described in the Rule was poised on the rhythmic succession of three elements: prayer, manual labour, and reading. On these the equilibrium and health of Benedictine life continued to depend for many centuries. In monasticism today prayer and work, though not always free from problems, are usually pursued with zeal and accorded a generous measure of time. But with regard to lectio divina *modern monks and nuns often feel uneasy: not only has this duty become a Cinderella in the allocation of time, but our approach to it may also seem profoundly different from that of the ancients because of the intellectual and cultural changes that have intervened.* Lectio *was often regarded as the most typically monastic and contemplative element in the life, the occupation which really 'made the monk'. Yet monastic prophets of doom speak today of 'the death of* lectio divina'.

Contemporary monasticism can neither reverse the historical trends that have produced our problem nor dispense with so vital and formative a part of our heritage as lectio. *We need first to discover it in that earlier setting where it was so powerful and full of meaning, and then to search for ways of incarnating its values anew in the conditions of modern monastic life. The present chapter addresses itself to both these tasks.*

Introduction

Sacred writings have been venerated in many religions as a privileged form of divine communication. In them God, using chosen men as his instruments, can reveal himself in human language to generations of mankind, while men can both communicate to others their own experience of God and express to God their response to his goodness in the form of a public confession that will endure. It was because it had this time-defying quality that writing itself became an awesome thing (apart from the fact that in an age of illiteracy it required the services of specially qualified men, the scribes). By putting pen to paper an author could not only speak directly to distant generations with little fear of distortion, but also made an act of faith that subsequent history would bear out the truth of the claims to which he had committed himself so irrevocably. For this reason prophecies and commands which at first sight might have seemed to possess neither likelihood nor wisdom gained an added force when God ordered them to be written down. Events in the future would prove them true.[1]

Christianity is not only one of the 'religions of the book', requiring that its adherents 'live according to the Scriptures'.[2] It also claims to offer an especial God-given enlightenment for understanding the Bible, which gives a new conviction of the unity of the Scriptures and of their transformative power. The Church received this enlightenment as one of the first-fruits of our Lord's resurrection.[3] The presence of the Holy Spirit in the Church enables all who accept its guidance and live in its communion to read the inspired Scriptures by the light of the same Spirit by whom they were written.[4] The revelation of God in Christ, it is true, took place not through books, nor primarily through teaching, but in a life which unfolded in a series of historical events and was continued in the spiritual fellowship of a human society. But the written words of the New Testament are an inspired record of and witness to those events, the self-expression of that life and that society. They are a place where Christ can still be encountered[5] and where he has promised that his words will transform those who receive them.[6]

But just as the Divine Wisdom is directly offered to men in the inspired literature of the Old and New Testaments, so other books by Christian authors, while not having the same status or origin as the Bible, can communicate a wisdom and truth about the things of God[7] which have been widely recognized at all levels in the Church and borne out by Christian experience. Among these the Fathers of the Church have an outstanding value inasmuch as they were the teachers who instructed the Church in the message of the apostles during its infancy and first growth, and are for us a collective witness to the Church's tradition and communion in truth and holiness. The reading of the Scriptures, the Fathers, and the Christian spiritual masters can be for us a means of experiencing the communion of saints which transcends time and space, a communion which is realized by the work of the Holy Spirit.

Among the problems peculiar to our own post-literate age is the possibility of our becoming strangers to this literary communion of the faith. Recent technical discoveries have made widely available media and combinations of media which are far more potent and vivid than books, especially in transmitting to distant audiences impressions of events, of a person or of a fellowship.[8] Experience of these media has shown, by contrast, how much the limitations of the book-form, the way of life it presupposed and helped to create, and the human relationships it set up between author and reader, have influenced the content as well as the expression of the message itself. It is no accident that the age of printing rapidly adopted as its ideals individualism, specialization, literary private property, and detachedness in making judgements, while the attitude fostered by the new audio-visual techniques has been summed up as the 'total and simultaneous involvement of everybody in everything'.[9] At first sight this new state of affairs may seem to have relegated to the past or to the preserves of academic scholars all the forms and equipment which we have traditionally associated with spiritual reading, as instruments now too abstract and feeble to communicate to the generality of men all the dimensions of spiritual experience. But the chief prophet of this era, Marshall McLuhan, has seized upon the ancient monastic practice of *lectio divina* as one of the best historical illustrations of these new conditions, anticipating them in the remote past.[10]

Lectio divina in early monasticism

In our present vocabulary the phrase *lectio divina* has been supplanted by 'spiritual reading',[11] but a brief comparison between certain features of ancient and modern monastic practice will show that something more than a change of name has occured.

a) *Its place in the time-table*

In a modern monk's horarium a relatively minor place is allotted to spiritual reading. It is only one duty among many; the time assigned to it is comparatively short; on many days dispensations from this exercise are officially granted.[12] It is a practice which often has to fight a losing battle against the encroachments of work.

But the tendency which reached its climax in the Rule of St Benedict and was given lasting expression by him was one in which *lectio divina* was acquiring a mounting importance. In the Rule of the Master it is a duty of the first order, and the time allowed to the practice is far longer than in any previous monastic document.[13] St Benedict carries the process still further. He not only prolongs the time to be devoted to *lectio* so that it occupies more or less four hours daily according to the season of the year (almost as much time as he allots to manual labour); he also is far more discerning than any of his predecessors in allocating the time for reading to those periods of the day, especially in the morning, which are physically most congenial for that exercise.[14] The lengthy hours he assigns to reading embody an aspiration he has in common with all his monastic predecessors: that the monk should be incessant in his attention to God's word.[15]

b) Its subject-matter

Today 'spiritual reading' is very widely interpreted, and generally according to a subjective criterion: the books which each monk finds personally helpful, edifying, and inspiring. Also, when reading a book for the first time he would prefer to judge it in its own right, to let it speak for itself rather than see it as deriving from or subordinate to Scripture, even if only remotely, unconsciously, and anonymously.

But, as the adjective *divina* indicates, the content of ancient monastic *lectio* was almost exclusively the Bible and patristic works of biblical interpretation. Many of the early Fathers described their conversion, whether to Christianity or to monasticism, in terms of a turning away from secular literature to embrace the Scriptures and the overcoming of their initial repugnance to the Bible.[16] St Jerome also commends *lectio divina* as a means of self-purification, asserting that the love of the Scriptures should become the sole passion of the monk, chasing away all others.[17] Even those who, like Augustine and Cassiodorus, welcomed and stimulated the study of secular sciences deprived them of their autonomy and harnessed them immediately to the deeper knowledge of the contents of the Bible.[18] This literary puritanism in early monastic ideology was a negative consequence of their conception that *lectio divina* was not just one department of a monk's life, but an aspect of that life as a whole, and one whose realization required a certain single-mindedness.

We may recoil from the apparent narrowness of this programme of reading, or see it as a by-product of the shortage of books. But it did ensure that the monks related to the Scriptures as understood through tradition everything they read and did, that they made their own the language and mentality of the Bible, and that they lived in vital contact with the sources of revelation.

c) The part played by the Church and the community in lectio divina

Because personal needs and tastes in spiritual reading are so very different, we rightly expect today that a monk's liberty of spirit in this matter will be scrupulously respected. But the negative consequence of this liberal attitude is that the full weight of a very difficult exercise is thrown upon the individual as a personal obligation, while the abbot and the community count for very little in it.

The phrase *lectio divina* began its career as an equivalent to *sacra pagina* when that name was used to describe the objective text of the lessons in liturgical worship, and although it gradually came to centre on the individual reader and on the personal frame of mind he brought to his reading, or the benefit he derived from it, it never altogether lost the liturgical and corporate associations of its original context.[19] It was never a private activity without any relation to the life of the Church, to which the Bible was in the first place committed as to the society where the Scriptures find their natural context.[20] The parallel between the Eucharist, which is the supreme self-expression of the Church, and the reading of the Scriptures was frequently drawn. Also the practice of reading Scripture in conjunction with the Fathers reflected a consciousness that the Bible should be understood in the light of the living tradition of the Church. Above all, the Church is the fellowship of men and women drawn together by the same Holy Spirit by whom the Scriptures were written, and in whose light they should be read.

In his *lectio* the monk was given the help of his community also. To solve the more difficult passages of Scripture there were frequent colloquies with the more experienced brothers and with the abbot,[21] whose chief duty indeed was to expound the law of God.[22] In the Rule of the Master the brothers were grouped into their deaneries to hear the reading.[23] Pachomius laid it as a task on the community to train or even force the illiterate to read,[24] and this reading was often intended to prepare the monks to understand better the psalms and lessons of the Mass and office. Moreover, only a community had the considerable economic resources necessary to provide the codices or the leisure for the reading.

In these circumstances St Benedict was making no small innovation when in several of his prescriptions he catered for reading in private.[25] This concession shows great and unprecedented sensitivity to the special needs of individuals, besides an awareness that a degree of silence and solitude is often necessary for a finer understanding of God's word, if the whole man and not just the collective man is to be engaged. But all St Benedict's other provisions on the subject of *lectio divina* show that, though it was not always to be a community exercise, he did intend it to be an activity in which the monk had the fullest support and guidance from his abbot and community.

d) The psychological dispositions of the monk in lectio divina

One of the aims of modern education is to train people to read with discrimination and in a spirit of critical analysis. This attitude is also fostered by the physical conditions required by reading since the invention of printing – privacy and the specialized use of certain of one's senses and faculties to the exclusion of others. It is demanded also by the nature of so much modern 'spiritual reading' which is the work of human authors discussing spiritual topics in abstract terms, and so needs a reader's cool appraisal. Very often too the language in which their works were written is, for various reasons, one which is no longer our own, and which therefore demands an effort of translation on our part. Generally, and often necessarily, our aim is to master rather than to surrender to what is read.

The early monks were buoyed by the certainty that in reading the Scriptures they were not operating on some alien material, but were having a real encounter with Christ analogous to sacramental communion with him.[26] They envisaged the Bible as a letter from God to men revealing something of God's own secrets, giving a foretaste of the vision of divine glory.[27] St Benedict's own practice in the Prologue is to personify the Scriptures.[28] When the monk embarks on *lectio divina* he is therefore engaging in a conversation with God like the one we hear conducted with St Benedict's new recruit in the Prologue, using the words of the psalter.[29] In this way reading and prayer became a continuum, not two complementary exercises but two stages of one and the same thing: 'We speak to him when we pray; we listen to him when we read the divine sayings.'[30] This kind of prayer as a response to the dialogue initiated by *lectio divina*, a reading and a reacting, became the distinctive characteristic of monastic spirituality, so that *lectio divina* became the monastic spiritual exercise *par excellence*.[31] It was especially through his meditative reading of holy Scripture that the monk was caught up into the loving dialogue between the heavenly Bridegroom and his bride, the Church.

Since the Bible was thus pictured as having personal rather than bookish attributes, it had to be approached in an attitude of eagerness and of whole-hearted surrender.[32] Every faculty, physical as well as intellectual, social as well as personal, was enlisted in an effort to render God's word fully articulate and incarnate, and also to prolong its effects.[33] Hence the normal practice of reading aloud,[34] of frequent muttered repetition of the words (*meditatio*), of savouring and lingering over them (*ruminatio*),[35] and of requiring monks to commit whole books of the Bible to memory.[36] The result intended by these efforts was to make reading a full and intense as well as a social experience, not one which remained on the conceptual level, but a really 'Catholic' one, in the sense that it affected the whole man.

The lively promptitude of these early monks for *lectio* should not lead us to suppose that they were moved by a naïve undiscerning enthusiasm which we have lost. The most eloquent advocates of the practice, those too who were already well versed in secular literature, almost all confess to an initial strong revulsion from the Scriptures because of the barbarity of their style and content.[37] But after persevering they concur with Taius of Saragossa that 'holy Scripture somehow grows in stature with those who read it'.[38]

e) The purpose of lectio divina

Lectio divina may be defined as 'slow meditative reading in search of a personal contact with God rather than mastery of an area of knowledge'. But spiritual reading today is often regarded as an activity whose chief value lies outside itself, in its usefulness to some other monastic occupation; it might, for example, provide material or an intelligent direction for prayer or for the apostolate.

For the early monks, however, *lectio* was an all-absorbing activity to be practised for its own sake, in the sense that they read not simply for any information they might receive, but because of what the act of reading made them become.[39] We approach Scripture wanting to know what we can do with it; the Fathers were more concerned with what the Scriptures could do with them. They had that keen sense of the dynamism of words which is to be found throughout the Bible. The act of reading was itself transformative.[40] Self-assimilation not only to the

267

mind and spirit of the Bible but also to its author was the ideal which is achieved *quando lector fit auctor*;[41] hence the predilection for applying to their reading words derived from food and eating. *Lectio divina* was not subordinated to some other monastic practice but led immediately to the final objective of the monastic life which, according to Cassian, is 'purity of heart which consists in charity'.[42] And since it occupies this penultimate place in the hierarchy of monastic values, *lectio divina* was often considered to be the integrating activity which gave unity and point to all other monastic observances and became the rationale of all ascetical practices.[43] *Lectio divina* in the widest sense, the uninterrupted communion of prayer and listening to God, became coextensive with the entire life of the monk, and this general attitude would be brought to its focus and point of expression at the time of *lectio* in the stricter meaning of the word. Bibliolatry was excluded, however, as Scripture was considered a means, not an end, and therefore as requiring discretion lest it be abused.[44] This is why St Benedict in both Chapter 4 and Chapter 73 described reading as a 'tool'.

What monastic theology sought in *lectio divina* was not knowledge of a forever lost past, nor satisfaction of an avid curiosity for knowledge. It was rather nourishment for a faith which, taking the sacred texts and the facts they recounted as its starting-point, desired to experience the mystery of Christ and his Church, in order to grow in Christian living and contemplate in advance the eternity to which it was directed.[45]

Lectio divina was also regarded as the chief means of a monk's discovery[46] both of himself and of his monastic inheritance. It did not just put him in contact with documents but enabled him to enter the biblical world, a world in which the monk felt very much at home.[47] As we can see in monastic hagiography the monks saw themselves in Elijah, John the Baptist and all the prophets, apostles, wisdom-teachers, and martyrs who people the Scriptures.[48] They claimed, with more spiritual than historical validity, to have originated in the community life of the early Church of Jerusalem as delineated in the Acts of the Apostles[49] and to be kinsfolk of the desert-dwellers described in Hebrews 11.37–8. The words of Scripture became *the* incentive for monks. They sought to justify every monastic practice by biblical texts, sometimes carrying this process to extremes by applying it to the details of monastic dress and to the number and distribution of the canonical hours.[50] It was the Bible too which provided the chief weapons in all monastic controversies. Thus the monks inserted themselves into the biblical history of salvation, and felt that it was still continuing in them. This unity between the Bible and their own actual existence made it easier for them to take for granted the unity between Old and New Testaments[51] and the consequent legitimacy of reading the Old Testament according to the Christian spiritual sense.

Limitations of the early monastic conception of *lectio divina*

We should not be led by this rather exalted historical description of *lectio divina* to nostalgia for a golden age which we must try to reproduce in our own idiom. St Benedict himself, as we have seen, made some small but significant adjustments to accommodate this practice to the weaknesses of human nature. For us, the transposition to be effected is not just in that direction; the growing powers and rights of the human mind of the reader as well as the human contribution to the writing of the sacred text must also be taken into account.

(*a*) The lengthy periods assigned to reading in ancient rules were due very often to the need to fill up the monks' time somehow so that idleness would not drive them to sin when the weather did not permit manual work.[52] At first sight this does seem to be the mentality shared by St Benedict who in Chapter 48 introduces his regulations on reading and manual labour alike with the same dry aside, 'Idleness is the enemy of the soul'; but in Chapter 73 he does proffer very attractive and readily intelligible incentives for reading which contrast strikingly with the poor motives for the practice adduced by his contemporaries.[53]

(*b*) The deep consciousness the early monks had of the divine origin of the Scriptures ('sermo *divinae* auctoritatis' . . . 'legatur coram hospite *lex divina*'[54]) often resulted in a failure to do justice to the human authors, traditions, and other agencies that were also responsible for their composition. Thus they would miss a great deal of the very message of the Bible for which they were so eagerly searching. And this neglect of the literal sense of the Bible, that sense intended by its human authors, persisted throughout the centuries in monastic theology, long after its claims had been vindicated elsewhere.

(*c*) The rejection of all literature other than books bearing directly on the Bible not only led to a certain indifference to human values[55] but must also often have closed their minds to the possibility that God's word for them might be found in books and events other than holy Scripture.

Our problem and some suggestions

Practical necessity has driven us to curtail drastically the time St Benedict allocated to reading, and might therefore seem to have upset in a serious manner the equilibrium of the life he sought to establish with its three more or less equal components of prayer, reading, and manual labour. But it is not therefore necessary for us to correct this imbalance by making efforts to restore to *lectio divina* something like St Benedict's quantitative allowance of time. We no longer have to master the schoolroom rudiments of reading which made it a very laborious process for St Benedict's monks. For many of us preparations for the academic and pastoral work which has taken the place of manual labour in our lives cannot often be easily distinguished from what we call spiritual reading. But it does not follow that we should acquiesce in the present state of affairs as though it were inevitable.

(*a*) One way of aligning ourselves better with the way of life pictured in the Rule is to find intelligent means of giving higher relief to reading in the short space of time that is available for it, of making a little go a long way. It may be that to place the first or even the entire accent upon the personal obligation of the monk to give half an hour a day to spiritual reading, though sometimes useful for bringing disorganized or even recalcitrant human nature to grips with a problem that might otherwise remain in the ideal world, can defeat a more resourceful approach.[56] Just as it is the pressure of community tasks which has largely forced *lectio divina* to the periphery of monastic life, so it is the community's duty to play a larger role in the activity of spiritual reading than has hitherto been the case. It could give more positive assistance in replenishing the spiritual and intellectual capital of its members by inviting visiting lecturers, or by offering courses to explain the biblical readings at Mass or the office, or by organizing free discussion groups to master the message of the gospels, while respecting the wishes of those who find they can do their best privately. The teaching of ascetical theology and of the history of spirituality might be restored to the programme of ecclesiastical studies. In the 'school of the Lord's service' we never stop learning, and with due adaptations many of the practices of modern universities might be put to use in the monasteries, while the possibilities opened up by new technical inventions can be exploited without violating stability or enclosure. A modern equivalent, though certainly one more positive in character, is needed for St Benedict's provision that the abbot should depute some seniors to invigilate the brethren during the times when they should be reading. The abbot and the community should, now as then, provide some motivation for *lectio divina*, even if it is only to take a personal interest in what individual monks are reading.[57]

St Benedict required that when guests arrived at the monastery 'the law of God be read before them for their edification';[58] the aspiration behind this provision seems to be that visitors should to some degree share in the *lectio divina* as in other elements of the monastic life. Their share might well be one of giving as well as receiving.[59] But all these proposals should be regarded as aids to *lectio divina* rather than as substitutes for it; and solitude, quiet, and a simple, uncluttered life are aids that are still more valuable.

(b) It might also help if the two modern descendants of *lectio divina* – studies and spiritual reading – could be brought into closer relation with one another so that ecclesiastical education could become more spiritual and spiritual reading more theological. In the Middle Ages there was a distinctive monastic theology which aimed at wisdom rather than science[60] and which preferred to dwell upon the central Christian truths rather than to pursue all their logical consequences.[61] Such a total integration of dogmatic theology and spirituality may no longer be possible or desirable, and may even threaten the rightful autonomy of intellectual disciplines. But some treatment of the consequences of each theological topic for the life of the Church and the life of the soul might have the result that monks would regard such a theology as a continuous study throughout their lifetime and not only as a professional preparation for the priesthood.

(c) A certain self-discipline in one's general reading may well be necessary in these days of over-production by the printing presses if the thoughts acquired through *lectio* are not to be crowded out by more sensational items harvested elsewhere. While it is especially necessary for those engaged in pastoral or educational work to keep abreast of the events and opinions of the times, a certain moderation in reading newspapers and magazines may well be advisable if the news-value of the gospel itself is to have its full impact on a monk's life.

But this does not require a merely negative disposition towards secular literature. There are many books with no overtly religious pretensions which are nevertheless 'attending seriously to the distinction between good and evil, compassionate about our human predicament . . . deeply conscious of the impenetrable mystery in which human life is lived, and liable to leave that disturbance in the mind out of which thoughts about the meaning of existence naturally arise'.[62] This does not mean that one should either try to force out of a book a religious meaning which its author never intended, or dispense oneself altogether from explicitly 'spiritual reading' on the ground that a really vital portrayal of all the questions at stake can be better found in secular guise. But it does mean that fidelity to spiritual reading does not excuse a merely shallow awareness of human realities, a facility with the answer rather than exploring the question, or a toleration of low standards in one's general culture, since this should form a continuum with one's spiritual reading.

But there is also an asceticism, a care for mental stability and hygiene, to be exercised even within the field of spiritual reading if it is to lead to conversion of heart and not to mere knowledgeableness. This St Benedict recognized when he classed reading of a certain resolute kind (*per ordinem ex integro*[63]) among the monk's Lenten exercises, and required that the monk be 'intent on the reading'. The proliferation of books, the desire to be well informed and the habit of rapid reading can all be impediments to the slow tempo, prayerful approach, consciousness of God's presence, frequent interruptions for raising the heart to him, and constant return to the relatively few books which suit one's own case which are the traditional accompaniments of *lectio divina*,[64] where each new thing learnt about God is a new reason for loving him.

(*d*) Many monks would have strong reserves about restoring the dominance which the Bible exercised over *lectio divina* in early monasticism. Today the priority we rightly give to the literal sense forbids us to impose prematurely a spiritual meaning on those passages of the Scriptures that strike us as savage, smug, or just boring. Because we are more aware today that the sacred writings are in their totality the work of human authors as well as of God, their great variety and many limitations come to the fore. But if God chooses to humble and reveal himself in human language, then limitations there must be in the nature of the case, even if he had chosen for his purposes the most excellent human instruments. No more than the incarnation or the sacraments does the Bible yet offer the full vision; like them it points, often obscurely, to what is to come, and demands faith from its readers if it is to be of real service to them, especially a faith in the unity of the divine plan revealed by the Scriptures.

But the scandal of the Bible, though it cannot be removed, must nevertheless be confronted, and false scandals removed so that the lines of the true scandal may emerge. This is all the more necessary now when there is so much Bible reading in the office and the Mass, when the texts of the Canons and Prefaces contain so many biblical formulae and images that an unprepared audience might easily be surfeited by them and dismiss too summarily their own prospects of access to God through the Bible. One should be as patient with the problems of Scripture as with those of philosophy. More attention might well therefore be paid to preparing communities in advance with explanations of the readings they are to hear in the liturgy. In this way they might attain better the reflective pondering on the word of God which aims at giving the monks an awareness of God's presence, a consciousness of the immersion of their personal lives in the mystery of God's activity as revealed in sacred history. They might also be drawn to identify with all those persons introduced to us by the Scriptures who reveal the right dispositions in their meeting with Christ.[65] 'Anyone who does not know the Scriptures does not know the power and wisdom of God either; ignorance of the Scriptures is ignorance of Christ.'[66]

13
Personal Prayer

Fed by the Eucharist, by the Scriptures that form the staple of the opus Dei, *and by individual* lectio divina, *personal communion with God is at the heart of monastic life. For this vital but hidden encounter between the monk and the Word of God we have no satisfactory name. To call it 'mental prayer' makes it sound like an intellectual feat; to call it 'private prayer' is inaccurate because a Christian always prays as a member of the Body of Christ and of the Communion of Saints whether he adverts to the fact or not; to call it 'meditation' would seem to identify the whole enterprise with what is in fact only a part: namely, the active use of reason and imagination. In this chapter the term 'personal prayer' has been preferred because it emphasizes (1) that the basis of all prayer is an intimate personal relationship between God and man, and (2) that the strength of liturgical and any other form of community prayer depends upon the personal contribution of each individual present; which is to say, upon his personal prayer, springing from his personal relationship with God.*

Two different approaches are possible. We may start from human experience, and lead on to prayer; or we may begin by considering God's initiative, which calls forth the human response of prayer. This chapter attempts to cover both perspectives. The first part deals with the natural need for prayer; the second and subsequent sections discuss prayer within a specifically Christian framework, beginning with the divine initiative and the human response in faith.

The human need for God

a) Experience of self

As we turn our thoughts to the depths of our nature our hopes and fears come to mind, our likes and dislikes crowd in, we feel the sense of sin and shame, desire seeks its unworthy objects, there is confusion and conflict, and the very meaning of life becomes distorted. But beyond all this we feel something that is unique. At the personal level, I discover a small world that is made up not only of mind, but of heart and soul. And holding its disturbing elements together and supporting them is myself – my selfhood. I am myself, and there is no other being exactly like me. Where do I come from? It seems that no power of nature can account for my uniqueness; only one who is supreme, who is above nature, who is Uniqueness itself, can give me the life and being of which I am conscious.

I am aware too of a great void in the depths of my being. It is this void that God alone can fill, and it is here that I meet him. He has created me and sustains me in being. His voice comes to me out of the silence and, as I turn to listen, he fills my being with faith so that I can be enlightened and understand him more, and from this knowledge unite myself with him in the supreme act of love. Here is 'personal prayer', union with God in the silence of my own being.

This turning to God in ourselves is the constant theme of spiritual writers as well as the experience of great men who have struggled with the mysteries of our existence. St Augustine in his *Confessions* cries out: 'Behold, thou wert within me, and I out of myself, when I made search for thee.'[1] Pascal, looking into his troubled mind, says: 'In every man there is the infinite abyss that can only be filled by an infinite and immutable object, that is to say, only by God himself.'[2] Newman turns to his inner conscience for belief in a personal God.[3] Some existentialists today look into the depths of man's nothingness and, having discovered the contradictions in his nature and his lack of genuineness, face the problem of life and death and find only the void. This line of thought leads easily to despair. But there is another solution: to discover the transcendent in our lives, and to look into ourselves to find God.[4]

The natural human instinct to pray will not be actualized without a personal conviction of the need for God in our lives, of our utter dependence on God as our Creator. We have to recognize that God is all in all, and that no effort of ours has any spiritual value without our being united to him. The psalmist tells us to listen to the voice of God calling to us from the mountains and the seas, in the thunder and the storm, from the sun, moon, and stars in the heavens. They fill us with wonder and speak of the greatness and the majesty of God, but this experience alone may not convince us of our absolute need of God. For this we have to look for, and find, God in ourselves. We must dig into our inmost being and uncover the hidden depths of the soul. It is from the great silence of the universe that the intimate voice of God comes, and there is no greater silence than in the very heart of our being.

b) Instinct and intuition

This meeting with God can be approached in another way. In the animal world the various species are guided in their lives by instinct. Without previous experience they know what is for their good, how to achieve it, and how to order their lives so that they will develop according to their type.

In the human sphere instinct becomes a conscious power, so that we can see with the inward eye,[5] and conscious instinct becomes intuition or insight. An older philosophy spoke of the idea of God as innate in man, as an insight given along with man's existence and self-understanding. Jeremiah spoke of man's knowledge of the Lord as something comparable to the instinct that prompts the migrant birds to seek their homes at the proper seasons;[6] the comparison suggests that man's search for God and response to him are not some optional activity but built into human nature. Contemporary existentialist theologians prefer to think of 'anxiety' as the feeling, inseparable from truly human experience, which discloses man to himself in his creatureliness and directs him to search for the ground of being; directs him, that is, to the question of God.[7]

At the same time men have the powers of reflection and choice. Insight should tell them what is for their good and perfection: that God's will is the law of their being. But their power of choice may lead them away from the right path. Men can disobey – the tragedy of human existence – but God remains with them, calling them to himself and offering reconciliation. When a man obeys, choosing to follow his insight and seek true perfection, he acknowledges his dependence on God, and disposes himself for further enlightenment as to his destiny and the way to achieve it, and for growth in the love which unites him to God.

In the gospel, when Nathanael doubted Philip's word about finding the Messiah, Philip replied, 'Come and see.'[8] He did not attempt persuasion but asked him to see for himself. Commenting on this, Tillich says: 'Where we see, we unite with what we see. Seeing is a kind of union. . . . Our language has a word for it: "intuition". This means seeing *into*. It is an immediate seeing, a grasping and being grasped.'[9] To us also God is continually calling, 'Come and see.' This is the call to prayer, the call to union.[10]

c) Surrender of self

The experience of imperfection and alienation, and the need for fulfilment, are inseparable from the human condition and provoke in us a divine discontent.[11] The activity that leads to true fulfilment is the search for union with God in prayer. In this union we find the freedom to offer our selfhood to the Creator. This giving of ourselves, this act of detachment, is of its nature contemplative; there can be no true contemplation without first the surrender to God. In the silence of the heart love and adoration are born. Prayer is an offering, not a formality; a movement, not a formula; an emptying of self in a surrender to God.

Christian prayer

a) God's initiative

Christian life is a response, not an initiative; not our pursuing God, but God pursuing us. Prayer and love are gratuitous gifts of the Spirit creating our response. 'God works in us both to will and to accomplish.'[12] The initiative is all God's: faith has been given to guide us, the Spirit of God has made his abode in our hearts, our very natures have become Christlike.

Since the Spirit breathes where he wills[13] we should expect God's gifts of prayer to take a unique form with each individual, a form which will be best for him but not necessarily best for another. Similarly, one person's prayer is not 'better' than another's merely because it represents a different activity of the same Spirit. For this reason great freedom should be allowed in the practice of personal prayer; a legalistic attitude breeds resentment and a sense of burden. But this is not to deny the need for a freely chosen discipline to act as a breakwater against our weakness. Prayer is a privilege, giving that access to the Father in the Spirit which is granted to the adopted children of God. We cannot afford to neglect this opportunity made available to us in prayer.

Prayer gives a practical expression to our faith, and is inspired by faith. Dealing with the whole man, his material as well as his spiritual side, prayer acknowledges that we are sons of God, and as sons heirs to his Kingdom. As prayer develops it becomes the grand gesture of love, and since it is the nature of love to create, the emphasis must be on what we can give in prayer, rather than on what we can get from it.

We pray as we can, and God himself transforms our prayer. The half-hour on our knees, spent in vacant dreaming, with scarcely an inspired thought to disturb it, may be – certainly *can* be – a loving gesture to God. The good intention is there, but our better self seems to have come to a standstill. There is no need to be disheartened; as Thomas Merton says, 'The activity of the Spirit within us becomes more and more important as we progress in the life of interior prayer. It is true that our own efforts remain necessary, at least as long as they are not entirely superseded by the action of God "in us and without us". But more and more, our efforts attain a new orientation.'[14] We do not have to be aware of the secret growth of the seed within us.[15] Growth in prayer is a hidden process, hidden not only from others but from ourselves.[16] Our business is to trust God whose life is growing in us, and to live out faithfully our response to him.

Prayer, then, implies a gradual purification which allows the Spirit to work in us. This is a twofold process: first, an emptying of self, and secondly, union with God. But the two processes are simultaneous and progressive. Both are directed by the indwelling Spirit, whose action may become more apparent as we yield to him. At first, prayer is a communication or dialogue on the 'I-Thou' level, but later a union of love, of silence. Therefore in our prayer the important petition must be for the gift of the Spirit who achieves this union.[17]

b) Prayer and the mystery of redemption

1. Prayer, a death-resurrection event

Prayer has been called a 'death-resurrection event' because our participation in the paschal mystery is impossible without prayer. Jesus Christ offered himself as a victim for the redemption of the whole of mankind. From his death he rose triumphant; his victory is both the guarantee that we are sons of God and an invitation to live out our sonship. From death to life, from darkness to light, from sin to purity of heart,[18] these are the terms in which the Christian message is given to the world. As we become identified with Christ, we die to ourselves so as to live with him and to be more fully incorporated into his Body as members of his Church. This incorporation is realized and expressed in prayer. Prayer brought Christ face to face with his own reality as Son.[19] Our prayer is in Christ the Son.[20] We pray with Christ, and with him renew our certitude of the Father's presence.

This belonging to Christ makes our relationship with God easier and more personal. If we accept Our Lord's invitation to join him in prayer, we are freed from the temptation and the danger of looking for him 'out there'. 'In thy light we shall see light.'[21] Through Christ, the Holy Spirit takes possession of us and so the three Persons of the Trinity enter our lives, and in truth we become partakers of the divine nature.[22]

The paschal mystery embraces the whole Christian message; there is no Christianity without the cross of suffering, death to self, and rebirth in the Spirit. 'Christ did not die for himself' summarizes the message that should inspire us as we become identified with him and share his life and death.[23] Rising from the dead, Christ is constituted Head of the Body, the Church.[24] Through baptism and faith the Christian shares in the death.[23] Rising from the dead, Christ is constituted Head of his Body, living with his Spirit.[25] 'So we, though many, are one body in Christ, and individually members one of another.'[26] In all his actions, and especially in his suffering, the Christian builds up the Body of Christ.[27] 'I rejoice in my sufferings for your sake, and in my flesh I fill up what is lacking in the sufferings of Christ, for the sake of his body, which is the Church.'[28] 'I endure it all for the sake of God's chosen ones . . . that they too may attain the glorious and eternal salvation which is in Christ Jesus.'[29]

Suffering for the sake of the world cannot be separated from prayer. It is through prayer that we discover the truth about suffering, that love really is the 'unfamiliar name' behind the torment. In prayer our sufferings are taken up into the sufferings of Christ, so that in him our prayer becomes completely God-centred, and thus the driving power of the apostolate. This is the real meaning of Christ's sacrifice in which all Christians share: by glorifying the Father Christ gives eternal life to all men.[30] The words 'sacrifice' and 'suffering' do not necessarily mean any specially sought-after ascetical practice,[31] but rather the ready acceptance of the pains and trials of our ordinary human existence, which are seen for what they really are: prunings that we may bear more fruit.[32]

2. Intercessory prayer

Prayer of intercession and petition is not an attempt to change the course of nature or the mind of God. It is best understood in the context of the Christian's membership of the Body of Christ. As the saving power of God flowed through the humanity of Jesus Christ, through his words and his touch, so it still flows through the members of his Body; God wills to use human channels for his healing work. The Spirit forms the mind of Christ in us, creating in us the will and desire to be used in this way. So when the Christian prays for another, his loving concern brings to conscious realization the union established between them by the Spirit of the risen Christ. 'Whatever you ask in my name, I will do it.'[33] Here is the guarantee that Christian intercession always has an effect, even if this takes place at a more profound level than we expect, for it is based on the power of Christ's sacrifice. When prayer is answered, God is giving the prayer as well as the answer to it.

3. Our Lady, model of faith and prayer

Christian tradition has always stressed the essential place of Mary in our salvation and in our prayer. In the gospels her maternal bond with Jesus is closely associated with her profound relationship to him in faith and love.[34] In fulfilling her role she appears as a woman of great faith and prayer, who was subject to the same difficulties as other believers, and so is the perfect model for our personal relationship with God. From the moment of the Annunciation Jesus was the object of Mary's faith, a faith which was enlightened and supported by the prophecies of the Old Testament. The revelations that were made to her at the Annunciation and Presentation asserted the mysterious origin and destiny of her Son. St Luke recounts Mary's reactions to these disclosures: her consternation, her difficulties, her amazement, and her lack of understanding.[35] Faced with mysteries that go beyond her understanding, she prays, meditating on the message and pondering its meaning in her heart.[36] She is a woman who is completely attentive to God's word, one who welcomes it with a 'Yes' to God even when it disrupts her plans and disturbs her life.[37]

Mary's response to the word of God is beautifully summarized and communicated in the Magnificat, which remains a model prayer for Christians. Her humble acceptance of God's will opened her heart to receive the greatest of God's gifts, his only Son. Everything that God permitted to happen in her life served to deepen her dependence on him and to enrich the surrender contained in her 'Fiat'. Time and again she had to wait on God, certain of his will and power to help, but quite uncertain when and where his help would appear. It was this faith and utter poverty of spirit that Jesus declared to be blessed.[38]

Mary's God-centredness and her total willingness to conform in all things to the designs of God are the central points made about her both in Scripture and in the liturgy, central because they show us the basis for our personal relationship with God. Our Lady's immaculate conception, her virginity, her divine maternity, and her assumption are prerogatives that the Church celebrates because they reveal the power of God and the intimacy of the personal relationship that is possible when a Christian responds to God with generosity and love.

In her commitment to God's will, Mary was also committed to God's people. Immediately after narrating her God-centred 'Fiat', Luke adds that she rose in haste and went into the hill country to be of service to her cousin Elizabeth.[39] At the foot of the cross, where she united her will most perfectly with the will of the Father, she was commissioned by Christ to become the mother of all men.[40] Our personal relationship with God must, therefore, be fully integrated with a special relationship with Mary who loves us as a mother. It is because of her closeness to God that she is in some way involved in all prayer.

c) Prayer in St Benedict's Rule

The habitual attitudes of God-centredness and willingness to conform to the designs of God that are so perfectly seen in the example of Mary are the very points emphasized by St Benedict in his treatment of faith and prayer in the life of the monk. He gives a working model for the development within monastic life of a close personal relationship with God through faith in his divine presence and providence, and through personal and community prayer.

1. The primacy of faith

The faith required of a monk is essentially the belief that he lives in the presence of God, and that God is always near him. Monastic life is, above all, a life of prayer, and faith gives assurance that an intimate relationship with God is possible. The monk is required 'faithfully to fulfil the admonition . . .', to have 'his loins girded with faith', and to 'go forward . . . in faith', so that God's ears will be open to his prayers.[41]

By faith the monk is to know for certain 'that God sees him everywhere',[42] that he 'is always beheld from heaven by God'[43] and that he must 'believe that God is always present'.[44] This is summed up: 'We believe that the divine presence is everywhere, but especially . . . at the work of God.'[45] From this belief it follows that everything is done 'with the fear of God'. So important is this that it must be shown by the example of all the officials of the monastery from the abbot downwards: all are to be 'God-fearing men'. The awareness of God's presence awakens a sensitivity to the Spirit and gives a spiritual value to all the monk's activities. 'Prayer must penetrate and enliven every department of our life, including that which is most temporal and transient. Prayer does not despise even the seemingly lowliest aspects of man's temporal existence. It spiritualizes all of them, and gives them a divine orientation.'[46]

2. Spontaneous and occasional prayer

The Rule requires informal prayer, spontaneous in nature, prompted by any and every occasion in daily life: 'Whatever good work you are beginning to do, beg him with most earnest prayer to perfect it', so that 'God will supply by the help of his grace what is not possible to us by nature'.[47] This type of prayer should be 'short and pure',[48] but 'frequent'.[49] Its occasion should be every self-denial, bearing of wrong, provocation in speech, instance of flattery, evil thought, reminder of one's enemies, demand of God's will, act of obedience, trial of patience, temptation to murmur or be grieved, and humiliation, so that God may be glorified in all things, and the monk advance more and more in godliness.[50]

As examples of short prayers prompted by the occasions of daily life, the Rule prescribes some formal instances: the weekly servers are to ask for prayers,[51] the reader is to ask all to pray for him,[52] all are to pray for the newly professed monk[53] and for the excommunicated.[54] Younger brothers when meeting their elders are to ask a blessing,[55] and the porter is to answer, 'Thanks be to God.'[56] Those going on a journey are to commend themselves to the prayers of all, and to beg further prayers on their return.[57]

Besides inculcating spontaneous prayer these instances witness to belief in the value of prayer for others, which is explicitly stated by St Benedict: 'Let (the abbot) add what is still more powerful, his own prayers and those of the brethren',[58] and a commemoration of the absent is to be made at the last prayer of the work of God. This mediation of the grace of God to the brethren also occurs on another level. Monks affect one another by their personal prayer, and by the way they perform their public duties. This is evident from such expressions as 'singers should edify', 'mind and voice should accord', brethren should 'encourage each other', 'hasten with all speed, preferring nothing to the work of God', and from the importance of the brethren being all together for meals.[59] A life of prayer is a life of listening to God's word and responding to it, and this word addresses a monk not only in the liturgy and in his reading, but also through the life of the community. In the bearing and example of the brethren, in their understanding of their vocation, and in the living tradition which all share he can hear God's word of invitation, judgement, love, and encouragement. It is difficult to decide how to express our spontaneous prayers in words, or to know whether words are needed at all. Our own thoughts and feelings may be conveyed through the inspired prayers of the Church, striking sayings that come from spiritual reading, or formulas from a meditation book. All may help to direct the mind to God. But in the end it is awareness of the presence of God and sensitivity to the Spirit that lift the heart to him. God does the rest. We gradually realize that prayer does not matter, but God does. We develop a simplicity in formulating our intentions and self-offering as we reach out in prayer to ever-widening horizons.[60] Life becomes prayer in action, and so it is that faith in the presence of God and spontaneous personal prayer characterize the Benedictine spirit.

3. Personal prayer

Formal private prayer does not seem to have been legislated for until much later than St Benedict's day, but a powerful custom of prolonged private prayer existed long before explicit legislation.[61]

Personal prayer is the moment of focus when we say 'Yes' to God, face to face. Habitual assent to the will of God is expressed throughout monastic life; obedience is all-pervasive. But prayer is this 'Yes', concentrated and neat, the explicit surrender of love to the will (that is, to the reality and love) of God. There are many occasions for saying 'Yes' to God when climbing the rungs of the ladder of humility, and so it is a very personal prayer that St Benedict is implying when he says that 'supplication should be made to the Lord God of all the universe with *utter humility* and the purest devotion. . . . We are heard with favour not for the length of our prayers but for the purity of our heart and the smarting tears of compunction. Prayer ought to be short and pure.'[62] There is no more short and pure, simple and direct prayer than saying 'Yes' to God. Again, with regard to private prayer: 'If anyone wants to pray privately by himself, let him just go in simply and pray, not with loud cries but with tears and earnestness of heart.'[63] This link between prayer and compunction is very significant; anyone who has ever made a sustained effort to pray knows that while deliberate refusal to yield to God's will in any area blocks prayer until it is repented of, the experience of frailty and of our need for God's mercy is helpful. The poverty of spirit born of this experience puts us into the position of forgiven sinners, the only position before God from which our prayer can be authentic.[64]

Silence, recollection, meditation, and a detachment from worldly interests are necessary to achieve genuineness in the interior life. Each monk should set aside some convenient period of the day when he can keep a rendezvous with God for silent personal prayer, free from interruption and distraction, apart from the times appointed for the divine office. The two activities will assist each other, for 'liturgy, by its very nature, tends to prolong itself in individual contemplative prayer, and mental prayer in its turn disposes us for, and seeks fulfilment in, liturgical worship'.[65]

Difficulties in prayer

a) Human weakness

However diligent our preparation for prayer may be, there is always the experience of what seems to us unsuccessful prayer. There is the struggle to keep the mind fixed on things spiritual; the imagination gets out of control and runs riot; a host of distractions crowd in, bringing with them the burden of our human concerns; there is a loss of the power of concentration, and we make abortive efforts to free ourselves from a feeling of lethargy. To all these may at times be added indisposition of body due to sickness or weariness, and even a complete blank with its sense of frustration and impending despair. 'Is this prayer?' we ask ourselves.

Here we must distinguish clearly between prayer and ourselves as the human instruments of prayer. The instrument may be faulty, but God is the listener, and by his help the discordant notes will be set in tune. St Paul says, 'The Spirit helps us in our weakness, for we do not know how to pray as we ought; but the Spirit himself intercedes for us with sighs too deep for words.'[66] Commenting on this passage, Tillich says:

This is why prayer is humanly impossible. It is God himself who prays through us, when we pray to him. The 'Spirit' is another word for 'God present', with shaking, inspiring, transforming power. Something in us, which is not we ourselves, intercedes before God for us. We cannot bridge the gap between God and ourselves even through the most intensive and frequent prayers; the gap between God and ourselves can be bridged only by God himself.[67]

The difficulties that seem to arise from human weakness are a constant reminder to us of our utter dependence on God, and are part of the complexities of life with which we must be patient. No activity is entirely simple, no motive single. Much depends on the intention of the will; if the will is turned to God, all the powers of our being, however disorderly, will obey, and nothing will obstruct the action of the Spirit.

b) Unanswered prayer

One might think that many of our Lord's prayers were unanswered: the cup did not pass him by; the Church is not as united as he wished; his choice of disciples included a traitor. Yet the Letter to the Hebrews says: 'During his life on earth, he offered up prayer and entreaty . . . and he submitted so humbly that *his prayer was heard*.'[68] The next verse goes on to explain this: 'Although he was Son, he learnt to obey through suffering.' If prayer really unites us with Christ, we also will learn to obey through suffering, for as co-heirs with Christ we must share his sufferings so as to share his glory.[69] This is the criterion of prayer 'working'. We learn to 'obey through suffering' if we live with Christ's own Spirit as true sons of God. Then we will be mediators of salvation[70] as ministers of the new covenant in the Spirit,[71] and exercise our share in Christ's high priesthood. So, again, we should pray more earnestly for the gift of the Spirit.

c) Sense of unreality

Various factors contribute to a feeling of unreality in prayer: failure to experience that intimate contact which is necessary for any union of love; a feeling that God is so far removed from our world that it is hard, almost impossible, to get in touch with him; and a crowding out of the transcendent because of the cultural lag between the presentation of the truths of the faith and the impressive and promising wonders of the scientific world. God's presence in the ordinary affairs of human life is obscured, because the truths of the faith and the discipline of the Christian life are sometimes presented today in a language and traditional mould that hardly take note of the results of modern research in the scientific, philosophical, psychological, or sociological fields.

In this confused situation it must be expected that growth in prayer will involve a weaning from reliance on feelings as criteria of successful prayer. Devotion and piety differ from person to person, and from time to time. Because prayer is such an intimate personal matter it will have a uniqueness for each individual, analogous to the exchanges and approaches between lovers, which cannot be expressed adequately in words, let alone in generalizations.

It is a false solution to the problem of unreality to resort merely to external works of charity on the grounds that we can find God more surely in our neighbour, the poor, the distressed, and the outcasts of the world. A total response to the presence of Christ and to the gospel demands both prayer and fraternal love; Christ is present in the prayer of the Church and in the love among the brethren, an outgoing love which is at the service of the world. Both elements are based on faith. A genuine prayer springing from faith expresses itself in love, and a genuine love based on faith demands prayer. The integration of prayer and love is achieved in the presence of the one Christ, received in faith. Prayer and fraternal love are the gifts of the Spirit by which the Christian community responds to God's communication of himself in Christ. Both, if they are expressions of faith, are modes of Christ's presence in the Church and in the world.

The initial sense of unreality in prayer may well develop into a more profound recognition of the divine transcendence, and therefore our feeling of unreality may even be expected to grow. God is mystery, and if we are really getting closer to him it is not surprising that our prayer is bafflement and escapes our control. There is real danger that we may create idols for ourselves and reverence them in all sincerity, but as the Spirit takes control of our prayer, our progressively more sophisticated idols are progressively smashed. This is disconcerting, but perseverance under these conditions can lead to a deepening of faith and a closer union with God in love. Then our vision of him in others, and in our work, is a real one. St Benedict lays great stress on humility: we stay in touch with reality when we find God and love him within our hearts by humble effort and the assurance of faith.

Mission of monks to the world

In bringing the message from his Father, Jesus turns the thoughts of his disciples to the Father in heaven and bids them pray, pray always.[72] It is, he seems to say, by prayer that you will fulfil your purpose in life, that you will give to God that honour which is his due, that you will realize the true intimacy of love and be guided in all your ways. In other words, you will have the life in abundance that I have come on earth to give you.[73] As a living example of his teaching, our Lord himself prays to his Father in heaven. He prays in public before his miracles,[74] he retires apart and spends the night in private prayer,[75] when in agony in the garden he prays the more intensely,[76] and his last words on the cross are a prayer. In all these acts of prayer he shows us that for him as man, prayer was the way to achieve union of love with his heavenly Father.

One of the most emphatic themes, then, in the gospels is that prayer is of fundamental importance. St Paul summarizes the message by saying, 'Give yourselves wholly to prayer and entreaty; pray on every occasion in the power of the Spirit.'[77]

A true Christian is not an isolated individual, he is one with all mankind. He shares the illusions, the hopes, the yearning for liberty, and the sense of frustration that seem inevitable in an unbalanced society. But he has Christian hope, which is the direct result of Christ's saving sacrifice and resurrection victory, and it is prayer that makes his hope a power in the world. In prayer he has a remedy for his worst fears, and for cynicism and despair. The man of prayer looks in hope to his Creator for the fulfilment of himself and his fellow-men, and finds this fulfilment already begun as the Spirit of God is given to him. By the power of the Spirit working through him, God's grace spreads abroad to re-establish all things in Christ and regenerate the People of God. In the measure that we are ourselves Christlike, we will give witness to this process of regeneration through prayer.

The commitment of each monk in intense personal prayer, and his personal encounter with the risen Lord, are necessary for the monastic ideal to work in practice, and the fact that it does so is itself a powerful witness to sharing the experience of the Spirit. The primary witness that a monk can give is to 'knowing God', that is, to eternal life already possessed.[78] This witness requires growth towards spiritual maturity,[79] growth from knowing about God to knowing God.[80] But giving witness is incidental to, and the inevitable consequence of, sharing the experience of the Spirit, and is not itself the 'mission' of monks. Their mission is to share in the mission of the Spirit himself, to renew the face of the earth. The monk's chief service in this work lies in the personal contribution he can make to community prayer, through which, especially, his experience of the Spirit is communicated to his brethren and to the People of God.

By his profession the monk is committed to a life in which he continually meets the challenge that underlies separation from the world, but he has to go back into the world in some way and offer it a new outlook. If he is a truly prayerful man, his life and work will communicate to those in urgent need of it the spirit of peace he has drawn from his prayer.

14
Shared Prayer

The Eucharist and the opus Dei, *considered in earlier chapters, are forms of 'shared prayer'. But the latter phrase has come to be used in connection with another mode of prayer, distinct from liturgy, carried on informally in a group. This kind of prayer is increasingly popular in monastic communities and can have a profound effect on their life.*

The present chapter clearly has a special status, since shared prayer in this sense is not one of the time-honoured elements of monasticism, to be considered on the same level as the Eucharist, the office, lectio, or individual prayer. The decision to include it is based on the fact that shared prayer can be a potent instrument for growth and renewal in community life, and one that is harmonious with other elements of traditional monastic spirituality.

This chapter is written from 'within'; that is, from a sympathetic viewpoint, and freely includes value-judgements. It seeks to show the New Testament origins of shared prayer, its power to meet the contemporary need for sharing, and its place in monastic life. Since shared prayer cannot be discussed without reference to the charismatic renewal which has become a significant force in the Church, the chapter also suggests the relationship between the charismatic movement and monastic renewal.

Shared prayer implies a community gathered together to share their response to God's presence in their lives, their response to Father, Son, and Holy Spirit. The manner of their sharing in group prayer is a distinctive blend of extempore prayer, expressions of praise, shared silence, Scripture readings and teaching, spiritual songs, shared faith-experience, and informal petitions.[1] These are the elements of shared prayer, but since it is of its nature flexible and minimally structured, the list is not exhaustive nor are all these elements always present.

Background

It is possible to find in the contemporary human situation certain factors which explain why people today turn readily to this form of prayer; to indicate them does not imply that prayer should first satisfy man's needs. The growth of the human behavioural sciences is a sign of man's interest in breaking down barriers. His awareness of divisions between nations has extended to the divisions of fear, suspicion, and aloofness that exist between individuals. People are communicating more freely today than in the recent past, and shared prayer meets the desire and ability to communicate more deeply.

This process of communication is revealing untapped resources of support between men. In monasteries many are sharing at a deeper level their knowledge, insights and convictions, their faith-experiences and even those weaknesses that have been locked up because of reticence, shyness, and fear. It is one of the most curious features of monastic communities that one notable area of sharing in which monks and nuns fall short is communication about the very reason for their being together. They find it difficult to talk about the Father, about Jesus, and the Holy Spirit. In shared prayer people are led to accept one another at an ever deeper level of conviction and compassion.

The informality of shared prayer meets a need in contemporary man who is, to some extent, in revolt against the technological and impersonal efficiency of modern life. Liturgical prayer, even in today's mode, can tend to the impersonal; shared prayer is one way of emphasizing the personal in prayer. Moreover, with its warmth and intimacy shared prayer may fill a gap left in some people's lives by the passing of certain traditional forms of devotion. This prayer-form provides a different way of worship to complement the more traditional ways; it gives an opportunity for greater spontaneity in community prayer and for deeper faith-sharing in community. It frankly recognizes the experiential in our union with God and acknowledges that worship ought more often to be an attractive human experience. It has the potential to intensify Christian living, to speak to contemporary aspirations, to build deeper unity, and to draw people to prayer. It does, then, seem to fill a void in the prayer-forms of the Church today. Its authenticity must now be established.

Authenticity

a) Scriptural basis

In the Acts of the Apostles and the Pauline Letters shared prayer appears as an accepted practice and is recommended to the faithful. What is here clear and definite must have grown out of something the apostles had learned from Jesus; and indeed there are instances of informal shared prayer from the beginning of the gospel story.

A powerful example was given by Our Lady who listened to the word and pondered it in her heart, and together with Elizabeth uttered praise to God.[2] In his public life Jesus not only taught his disciples to pray; he also deeply shared his life with them. 'He appointed twelve', and the first reason given for this in Mark is 'that they might be with him'.[3] Sometimes he withdrew to be alone with them, and sometimes to pray.[4] There can be no doubt that he shared with them the things of his Father.

After his ascension the group of disciples 'with one accord devoted themselves to prayer, together with . . . Mary, the mother of Jesus',[5] as they waited for the coming of the Spirit. One of the Spirit's gifts to the young Church was joy; the Christians 'went as a body to the Temple every day but met in their houses for the breaking of bread; they shared their food gladly and generously; they praised God and were looked up to by everyone.'[6] Whether or not the presumption of informality is justified, there is certainly an emphasis on praise and glory in common prayer.

What is described in the following account of the petition made by the Jerusalem community is not formal prayer but prayer immediately directed to the actual situation, and this is the earliest prayer of the Church recorded in the Acts: 'Now, Lord, take note of their threats and help your servants to proclaim your message with all boldness by stretching out your hand to heal and to work miracles and marvels through the name of your holy servant Jesus.'[7] When Peter was imprisoned again later, 'earnest prayer for him was made to God by the Church', and on being released by the angel, Peter 'went to the house of Mary, the mother of John whose other name was Mark, where many were gathered together and were praying'.[8]

There is clear witness to God's presence and two men's response to it in the prison at Philippi: 'Late that night Paul and Silas were praying and singing God's praises, while the other prisoners listened.'[9] Again, informal prayer was the instinctive response of the Christians at Ephesus when Paul was to depart: 'When he had finished speaking, he knelt down with them all and prayed. By now they were all in tears; they put their arms round Paul's neck and kissed him; what saddened them most was his saying that they would never see his face again.'[10]

One example of shared faith-experience is clear: 'They listened to Barnabas and Paul describing all the signs and wonders God had worked through them among the pagans.'[11] Again, when Peter returned to Jerusalem after giving orders for the pagans to be baptized, he was criticized by the Jews. He gave an account of what had happened to guide his course of action. In faith he realized that 'if then God gave the same gift to them as he gave to us when we believed in the Lord Jesus Christ, who was I that I could withstand God?' This account satisfied them and they gave glory to God.[12]

In the First Letter to the Corinthians there is a clear picture of each man's preparation for the prayer meeting: 'At all your meetings let everyone be ready with a psalm or a sermon or a revelation or ready to use his gift of tongues or to give an interpretation; but it must always be for the common good.'[13] To the Colossians Paul suggests some patterns of worship: 'Let the message of Christ, in all its richness, find a home with you. Teach each other, and advise each other, in all wisdom. With gratitude in your hearts, sing psalms and hymns and inspired songs to God; and never say or do anything except in the name of the Lord Jesus, giving thanks to God the Father through him.'[14]

To the Ephesians, Paul suggests that their community prayer, whether it be formal or informal, should lead to and support a deepening of their personal prayer: 'Sing the words and tunes of the psalms and hymns when you are together and go on singing and chanting to the Lord in your hearts, so that always and everywhere you are giving thanks to God who is our Father, in the name of the Lord Jesus Christ.'[15] The First Letter to the Thessalonians, with its reference to prophecy and all that this implies of sharing and a non-structured prayer-style, makes a link between happiness and prayerfulness: 'Be happy at all times; pray constantly; and for all things give thanks to God because this is what God expects you to do in Christ Jesus. Never try to suppress the Spirit or treat the gift of prophecy with contempt.'[16]

b) Prayer renewal in the Church

The authenticity of shared prayer is further confirmed by the way it realizes, perhaps more easily, some of the aims of liturgical reform for which the Church is struggling in the liturgy and which monks and nuns are seeking in the divine office. It responds to the call of Vatican II 'to intensify the daily growth of Catholics in Christian living; to make more responsive to the requirements of our times those Church observances which are open to adaptation; to nurture whatever can contribute to the unity of all who believe in Christ and to strengthen those aspects of the Church which can help to summon all mankind into her embrace'.[17] Pope John's 'new Pentecost' is awakening in the Church a new awareness of the Holy Spirit, a true charismatic renewal.

c) Prayer in monasteries

The monastic life itself is increasingly being recognized as a charism of the Holy Spirit drawing men together into community for prayer and witness. If monks have a sound liturgical and theological training, they have a chance, when they move towards shared prayer, to blend the two familiar forms of liturgical and personal prayer. Certainly shared prayer is no substitute for either form. Like all prayer, it is found to be alive and vigorous when the prayer community is genuinely seeking the Lord and acknowledges in expectant faith the presence of the Holy Spirit in its midst, yielding to the Spirit who inspires its prayer. An atmosphere of praise and thankfulness lays the group open to the gifts of the Spirit; and conversely praise will predominate in the prayer only if the members allow the gifts of the Spirit a place in their hearts. These charisms will bring life and perseverance to a community's shared prayer.

Form and content: the prayer meeting

Since shared prayer is unstructured, no description of it can be precise. But typical situations can be mentioned. The larger the group the more need there may be for structure; if the group numbers more than twelve or so, a leader may exercise gentle control and direction, but the more compatible and experienced the group, the less need there is for dominant control.

The prayer may start with a song, a spoken prayer, or a period of silence. Shared silence is characteristic of monastic groups and deeply rooted in their tradition. Awareness that the silence is shared and the wish to share it give it an added dimension. However the prayer starts, the important thing is to deepen the group's awareness of God's presence. 'We believe that the divine presence is everywhere, and that the eyes of the Lord are watching the good and the bad in every place.'[18]

The greater the awareness in faith of God's presence, the greater the need to respond in praise. Praise is central to this prayer form – again in the tradition of monastic prayer. It may take many forms: silent praise, an extempore prayer, a praising psalm read by one of the group, a song of praise, the recitation of the *Gloria*. The number of such prayers, their variety, the time they take, and the type of response elicited are unpredictable. The members of the group always need to be sensitive to the Spirit of Christ and to one another. In a very real sense it is the prayer of Christ, and those who pray expect him to reveal his presence in their prayer.

In some groups the prayer is chiefly based on Scripture. A passage is read and through the sharing of God's word a theme may develop; one passage may stand alone, to elicit a response of gratitude or wonder, or to express our need for God. Silent reflection is one obvious response to God's word. One of the group may express praise and thanksgiving for what has been read of God's way with men. As in the liturgy, response to God's word may be made in song. The Spirit of Christ is present in a group that listens to God's word and responds in expectant faith and prayer. 'For where two or three meet in my name, I shall be there with them.'[19]

In certain monastic groups, formed of people eager for this prayer, an hour of the divine office can provide a structure and a springboard for shared prayer. There can be periods of silence between the psalms or an opportunity for spontaneous prayer in response to the psalms. The reading from Scripture or other writings may lead some to express their reflections, and others to ponder in silence. Biblical canticles may be sung together and intercessions may be prolonged.

At some time during the prayer, petitions can be made. On particular occasions the prayer may well focus on special needs, and petitions will then be prominent. Since, however, such prayers can distract a group from the major prayer of praise, from listening to God's word, and from gratitude for his gifts, they are more usually made towards the end of the session. However, as long as they are related to the main direction of shared prayer, it is entirely appropriate to express the needs of the community, to share them with one another, and to place them before the Father.

Theoretical explanation is no substitute for the experience of shared prayer. To experience it is not the same thing as to have a sure call to it.

Yet it is only by opening himself to such experience that an inquirer can know if this is for him, and only by openness on the part of the brethren can a monastic community know whether this is a useful means and an expression of authentic renewal in its life.

Relation between shared prayer and Pentecostalism

While it is not the object of this chapter to discuss Catholic Pentecostalism as such, it is necessary to attempt to outline its meaning in order to help communities and individuals in their consideration of shared prayer. The term 'Catholic Pentecostalism' or 'charismatic renewal' is understood in two different ways, and it may be useful to clear up this confusion first.

(1) For those not directly involved, or involved in an unbalanced way, or in contact with an unbalanced group, the name 'charismatic movement' may connote an emphasis on particular (or even spectacular) charisms and a particular style of praising God.

(2) For those who have experienced God's grace through this channel the movement represents a deepening of the essential Christian response to the Good News, a revivifying of the faith of the New Testament, and a heightened awareness of the role of the Spirit who makes the risen Christ the centre of Christian life. In this sense there is nothing 'special' about it; it is entirely unimportant as a 'movement' and the name 'charismatic renewal' is unsatisfactory. It is simply that God has used this means to redirect the attention of Christians to what properly belongs to the fulness of their heritage as God's sons.

It is with this latter perspective that we are concerned, and a few quotations may help to make it clear.

This movement is to be regarded fundamentally not as an original interpretation of Christianity or a new school of spirituality, but as a re-emergence of certain authentic aspects of Christian life which have fallen somewhat into neglect. Fundamentally, there is only one way to be a Christian, and only one form of Christian spirituality; this consists in being conformed to the image of Jesus Christ by his Spirit dwelling within us. This has always been the first principle of Christian existence, and it did not take the Pentecostal movement to reveal it.[20]

It would seem that when a greater awareness of the Spirit pervades the

Church, the charismatic renewal will no longer have the appearance of a special movement at all:

Rather than a movement, Charismatic Renewal is a moving of the Holy Spirit which can reach all Christians, lay or cleric. . . . Every Christian is a charismatic by definition; the difference lies in our degree of faith, our awareness of this fundamental and necessary common reality. . . . One American journalist entitled his article 'A Movement that Wishes to Die'. That is exact: the ambition of the Charismatic Renewal is to eliminate itself as soon as possible, much as, on another level, the biblical or liturgical movements have ceased to be identifiable groups and disappeared into the life of the Church. The ecumenical movement, it is to be hoped, will do the same. The purpose is to disappear when the goal is reached, even as a river loses itself when it merges into the sea.[21]

When a Christian is incorporated into the Body of Christ through baptism, confirmation, and the Eucharist he receives the Spirit of God, and as each Christian is filled with the Spirit the Church too receives the Spirit with his gifts and fruits. Any distinction between 'charismatic' and 'non-charismatic' Christians is to be repudiated and lacks foundation in the New Testament. Chapters 12–14 of the First Letter to the Corinthians must be read as a whole; the various (and often unspectacular) charisms have their part to play in building up the Body, but the essential gift of the Spirit is charity. The charismatic renewal simply seeks to bring to conscious realization what the Christian people have received already, so that by prayer and trust in God they may respond to his word of promise. It is in this sense that the following description, by an author already quoted, must be understood: 'The new Pentecostal fire . . . everywhere . . . has largely the same characteristic effects: the charisms, a spontaneous desire to praise God, a powerful attraction towards the reading of Scripture, and a warm spirit of fraternal affection for others, all of which find expression in informal prayer meetings.'[22]

These effects are not confined to any particular movement or to any one style of shared prayer; the Quakers too have their tradition of shared prayer, as do several of the older Christian churches. Nevertheless it was in the context of the charismatic renewal that shared prayer gained prominence among Catholics, and the development is rapid. Many bishops are involved or sympathetic, and Pope Paul VI welcomed the movement as the work of the Holy Spirit.[23] Love for and obedience to the Church, love for holy Scripture, vigorous sacramental life, prayer and praise, and love for one another are widely recognized as authenticating signs.

The style or 'cultural baggage' that tends to go with the movement may be unattractive to many, but it is not important. The charismatic renewal has something to teach the Church. The Spirit breaks down barriers because he is the Spirit of love. He has always led men of expectant faith to a way of prayer that has transformed their lives – sometimes quietly, sometimes dramatically. In the charismatic renewal people have a powerful means of conversion and response to God's love. There is no bypassing of the faith struggle as a person yields to the Spirit. Rather the struggle intensifies; for it demands more faith, not less, to allow the Spirit to be the leader in prayer and to walk in the Spirit in daily life.

In the Catholic Church the charismatic movement has from its beginnings been predominantly lay and popular in character, and as such it has had an enormous influence for good. Monastic groups who have come into this experience sometimes sense that its implications for the monastic and contemplative life still need to be explored, but at the same time they are aware of the deep affinity between it and their own vocation. Christian monasticism too is a life of response to the self-gift of God in Christ and in his Spirit. 'The primary duty of a Benedictine . . . is to achieve and maintain a constant sensitivity to the working of the Holy Spirit within him and a readiness to respond to it in all things.'[24] More and more it is recognized that the monk is called to be a man of the Spirit, witnessing to the Spirit at work in the Church and calling men to listen to the Spirit speaking. More specifically, the experience of prayer and praise, of the power of God's word in Scripture and of the healing love of community, which is characteristic of the charismatic renewal, touches the springs of the monastic vocation. Monks and nuns in contact with the movement have experienced an intensified hunger for prayer, both contemplative and liturgical, a revitalization of sacramental life, an awareness of the power of the Lord Jesus over every area in their lives, and a new discovery of community and fraternal support. 'To each one the manifestation of the Spirit is given *for the common good*', for the building up of the Body of Christ.[25]

Before the significance of shared prayer and the charismatic renewal for community life can be considered further, some questions must be raised.

Some questions

a) Religious experience?

Experience, especially in the context of religion, is a concept that is being rehabilitated. Religious experience has not infrequently been looked upon with suspicion. Experience could be described as the totality of man's reaction to the other, religious experience as all that is contained in a person's knowledge and love of God and the effect this has upon him. It would clearly be wrong to seek religious experience for its own sake; but in the present context what is sought is the Person of the Beloved and a deepening relationship with him. A man's conviction of God's love for him may be without feeling; it would nevertheless be his experience of God, a faith-experience. In a sense, thirst is an experience of water. But a change may occur in a man's life so that he now gives real assent to the truth that Jesus is Lord of his life, whereas before the assent was notional. This is a conviction that leads to action. This is religious experience.

No claim is made that shared prayer alone brings religious experience. There are grounds for believing, however, that a greater willingness among brothers to share their experience of personal relationship with God our Father, with the Lord Jesus, and with the Holy Spirit helps to open them more to the influence of the same Spirit.

b) Self-centred?

It is sometimes objected that shared prayer is more for mutual support among the selfish, weak, or neurotic than for paying homage to God, that people are praying to themselves and to one another rather than to God. The danger of this abuse is ever present. Shared prayer, however, is a time for shared expression of our love and devotion to God and to one another as brothers and sisters in Jesus Christ. It is not a time for public confession, for complaints about difficulties, or for self-criticism, let alone criticism of others. Petition and a simple request for help, however, as already outlined, may be entirely appropriate. These are supported by the Lord's promises: 'Ask and it will be given to you . . .';[26] 'Come to me, all you who labour and are over-burdened. . . .'[27]

c) Élitism?

Where a shared prayer community emerges within a monastic community it may easily appear as a threat to unity. There is always the possibility of élitism, and of this a monastic community must be wary. It is insufficient not to be an élite; the group must not appear to be an élite. Perhaps the threat arises from the evident sharing of a deep experience of God in group prayer that may be lacking in the monastic divine office and in everyday community living. Discontent with the traditional ways may seem to be implied by evident enthusiasm for a new way. The Spirit, however, is in both old and new. It seems incongruous that a way to God for some should be resented by others; the Spirit does not work against himself.

Undoubtedly there are those for whom shared prayer has no appeal, who believe that God does not call them to it. This gives an opportunity for a tolerance in the community greater than that demanded in a more rigid way of life, a tolerance that is bound up with wisdom, understanding, and compassion. 'Bear with one another charitably, in complete selflessness, gentleness, and patience. Do all you can to preserve the unity of the Spirit by the peace that binds you together.'[28] The monastic community expresses its unity in the Spirit in many ways, but it is its accepted common prayer – the liturgy – that speaks most effectively of that unity. As the principle of pluralism becomes more accepted, there may be legitimate variety in forms of prayer. Our Lord has given us a criterion: 'By their fruits you will know them.'[29] It is the love manifest in charismatic prayer communities which most effectively breaks down the fear, suspicion, and prejudice that observers often bring to them. If they pray rather than observing, they may be caught up in the Spirit and rejoice to experience a new openness.

The function of shared prayer in community

However cautious a monk may be in the face of religious experience, it is part of his life. Monks offer to share with men their own experience of God. By their lives, monks can show people that this experience rises out of and satisfies a deep, essential human need. They can help people to become conscious of their need to discover and make real their ultimate vocation – a true union with the Father in Jesus Christ through the Holy Spirit. Shared prayer is a means of realizing the presence of God to man and of man to God, an approach to the radical renewal of our prayer. It also provides a means of learning prayer, through sharing the knowledge and practice of it. This can be true both within the monastic community and in sharing with guests.

Further, shared prayer offers a means of building and strengthening the common life of the monastery through the deep personal relationship of each monk with his Lord. It is another effective human response to God's love for us, calling us at the level of experience to deeper communion with him and with another. At the same time, it is an instrument in building up man's effective faith in God's promises, in narrowing the gap between his word and man's puny expectations. The breaking down of barriers in man's relationship with man helps to open him to God.

Shared prayer has proved an effective instrument of reconciliation and forgiveness. The true purpose St Benedict had in mind when he provided for the *Our Father* at Lauds and Vespers can be lost by familiarity: 'So that warned by the agreement made in that prayer when they say, "Forgive us as we forgive", the brethren may clear themselves of this kind of fault.'[30] It is more evident, when there is no formality to mask it, how incongruous it is for men to pray together unreconciled.

The climate of reconciliation, forgiveness, mutual acceptance, and trust fostered in this way is also the climate in which ancient wounds can be healed by the power of the Lord: the hidden wounds of the individual and also the subhuman, sub-Christian relationships, wounded by fear and suspicion, which are so often their result. The saving power of Christ to heal us and create a space for freedom is available through the members of his Body, and he expects his followers to use it.[31] In a community where monks have learned to trust one another enough to pray together spontaneously and informally, the relationships thus built up are not confined to prayer meetings but become a whole way of life in which inner healing, joy, mutual support, and the bearing of one another's burdens are matters of daily experience.

Whenever Christians engage in a common task, shared prayer can have its place. It is a monastic custom to acknowledge by introductory prayer the presence and lordship of Jesus in every situation. Shared prayer helps to extend and deepen that acknowledgement by penetrating work, discussion, decision-making, relaxation, and all community or group activities. It can be characteristic of Christian friendship. It may be one of the ways in which the Spirit is leading monastic communities. Time and trial, patience, and a sense of humour are necessary if this is to be put fully to the test. As with so much that seems strange or threatening, the words of Gamaliel apply: 'If this enterprise, this movement of theirs, is of human origin it will break up of its own accord: but if it does in fact come from God you will not only be unable to destroy them, but you might find yourself fighting against God.'[32]

It is traditional to recognize the connection between a deep life of prayer and effective ministry, and in a monk's pastoral work shared prayer offers possibilities of deepening his effectiveness. It has been found to be valuable in the confessional, in counselling, in hospital or home visiting. Priests share prayer and reflection upon the readings in preparation for the Liturgy of the Word. It has long been recognized as effective in ecumenism. The priest finds himself given a deeper, more expectant faith as he becomes increasingly open to the Spirit and more aware of God's gifts of power, insight, compassion, and love. He walks in that faith, and so his ministry becomes more truly the ministry of Jesus to the glory of the Father.

15
Work

Work is one of those elemental facts of the human bodily condition – like eating, sex, and verbal communication – which has been lit up by revelation and endowed with new dignity, without losing its earthiness. God is the tireless worker whose creative action never ceases; Christ is the worker who laboured at the task of our redemption and in whom the new creation is already achieved. The Christian, as a man made in God's image, is a co-creator for whom work is a privilege in which he knows something of his glory as God's son, but it is also a part of his life where he experiences in himself, in his collaborators, and in the earth for which he is responsible, the poignancy of a redemption not yet completed.

St Benedict, aware both of the ascetical value of work and of its positive significance as a loving service rendered to God and the community, assigned a considerable portion of time to it but did not specifically determine its nature. The present chapter, after indicating the foundations for a Christian and monastic theology of work, considers some of the practical questions it raises, the types of work prominent in the English Benedictine Congregation, the relation of work to poverty, charity, and personal growth, and the prospects for future development.

Introduction

a) The theological context[1]

God's own nature is known to us through his works in creation. We know who he is by seeing what he does. This is true also of created things: we come to know what they are by observing their actions and responses. In fact they realize their own natures through processes of change and development. Human beings in particular achieve the fulfilment of their personal lives in active relation to their material environment, to each other, and to God. They are themselves works of

God, and they express this fact in their own activities. 'For we are his workmanship, created in Christ Jesus for good works, which God prepared beforehand, that we should walk in them.'[2] The main activity to which a man devotes a substantial part of his time, and by which he normally earns his living, is a means of expressing himself, and therefore it can be made a further means of expressing the nature of God.[3] To the extent that we follow God's call, our work is a participation in the divine self-giving of creation and redemption;[4] our leisure partakes of the divine Sabbath of rest that follows on work completed and seen to be good.[5]

We cannot co-operate in the work of creation as though we shared the divine power by which God holds all things in being; but we have the responsibility of co-operating in the evolution of this created world:[6] 'The expectation of a new earth must not weaken but rather stimulate our concern for cultivating this one.'[7] Similarly it is as a privileged share in the holiness of God that the Sabbath rest is given to us.[8]

Recent advances in psychology have shown to what extent religion is linked with men's desire for self-fulfilment. Our instinctive drives towards power and social position can be opposed to, or can be consciously conformed with, God's command that we should multiply and possess the earth, and become masters of all that is in it.[9] As God's act of creation is a gratuitous gift of himself, so our use of the world need not be selfish exploitation; it can be a means of communicating and freely sharing our capacities. This in turn allows a fuller realization of our powers.[10] 'Grateful to his Benefactor for these creatures, using and enjoying them in detachment and liberty of spirit, man is led forward into a true possession of the world, as having nothing, yet possessing all things. "For all things are yours, and you are Christ's, and Christ is God's." '[11]

In practice, however, the creative and fulfilling functions of work are often spoiled by our wrong attitudes. We do not always see our work in relation to God, and we can even use it as an alternative to reliance on him, seeking to fulfil ourselves purely by our own efforts. Then work becomes a frustrating, painful activity, which increases the gap between human aspirations and their only perfect fulfilment in God.

Even apart from the possibility of wrong attitudes in the person who works, the painful and laborious element in work is for most of us a fact of life in a fallen world. Millions of people in poorer countries experience their work not as creative and fulfilling but as a grim struggle and an almost crushing burden. This hardship is the effect of sin, but not primarily of their own personal sins; they are trapped within the sinful structures of exploitation and injustice. The pain of work, its disappointments and failures, our own weakness, and the recalcitrance of things are inherent in our whole experience of the human condition as dislocated by sin.[12] Into this human situation Christ entered to share fully our experience of work as both a creative joy and a painful, sometimes even crushing, task. In his shouldering of the work of redemption we see the supreme case where the painfulness of work was accepted for completely right motives. Because Jesus did the work his Father had called him to do,[13] he was made perfect through suffering[14] and so became the source of eternal salvation to all who obey him.[15]

Work is therefore an integral part of monastic asceticism.[16] The *dura et aspera* of monastic life and work lead monks to God only to the extent that they accept God's vocation to his service: the fulfilment of their human needs is a consequence of their fidelity to God's call and their awareness of the objective needs of contemporary society.

In the Rule of St Benedict prayer, reading, and work divide the hours of the day.[17] All three are to be centred on God, and the balance of the three is particularly commended to the abbot's discretion.[18] The prominence of work in the horarium of the Rule contrasts with the ideal of leisure cultivated generally in the sixth century. The work envisaged is primarily manual work, 'for then are they truly monks when they live by the labour of their hands, like our fathers and the apostles'.[19] Manual labour has proved its value not only for obtaining the necessities of life and avoiding idleness,[20] but also as providing a relaxation from, and a complement to, the more directly mental activities of prayer and reading.[21] So there is a special significance in directly manual work for those monks and nuns whose lives are predominantly contemplative.[22] But intellectual work is also prominent in the Benedictine life. For example, counselling, teaching, preaching, and writing enable us to share with the brethren and others what we have derived from our prayer, our attention to the word of God, and our secular training. *Contemplata aliis tradere* is one way of participating in the work of the creative Word.

St Benedict's maxim about service in the kitchen holds good for all forms of work: 'Let the brethren serve one another . . . for this service brings increase of reward and of charity.'[23]

b) Integration

The work of monks is an integral part of their monastic life, not something superadded to it and still less something opposed to it. But for this to be realized in practice as well as in theory, there must be a conscious effort to integrate:

(1) the community's works and life-style with its mission in the Church and in the local area,
(2) work with monastic observance,
(3) each monk's work with the life of the community,
(4) each monk's work with his personal development,
(5) the monastery's resources with the needs of its dependent parishes.

Obviously mistakes can be made in each of these areas: the task of integration is difficult and delicate, but essential both for the good of the work and for the good of the monastic life itself.

c) Pluralism

Within the existing structure of the EBC a great variety of work and activity is to be found: education, pastoral work, and scholarship, as well as artistic, manual, and other forms of work. This pluralism is recognized and welcomed. No rigid model of monastic life should be imposed which too readily rules out a particular work as 'unmonastic'. Flexibility is especially important at a time in the Congregation's history when experimentation in new types of work is a part of monastic renewal. Furthermore, the different degree to which each community is involved in external work should be respected, and room should be allowed for both the more enclosed and the more active types of monastic life.

Work in relation to monastic life

a) The duty to work

The duty of working applies to monks as it does to Christians in general.[24] Normally a monastic community should be economically self-supporting and not be a burden on other monasteries or other Christians. Naturally, exceptional circumstances may arise when a community is in need of support and assistance, but the responsibility of earning a livelihood normally lies with each community. This means that the work undertaken should be genuinely useful and efficiently performed. It does not mean, however, that each of the brethren is expected to earn his own living directly, or that his value to the community can be assessed in terms of his financial productivity. It is for the community to employ the talents of the brethren in such a way that the monastery can best serve the needs of the Church without imposing undue financial burdens on others.

b) Unity and co-operation

A common work can be a valuable unifying factor in a community. The effectiveness of the work and the benefit to the individual depend on real co-operation between those engaged in the particular task. This co-operation, though often hard to achieve in practice, builds up the unity of the community and prevents excessive ambition or the identification of personal security with achievement; it also contributes to the success of the work itself.

Nevertheless the ultimate basis of unity in a monastic *conventus* lies not in its work but rather in the monastic ideal, the prayer and Christian brotherhood to which it is committed. This truth requires more explicit and conscious emphasis as the work of a community becomes more varied and diverse. A sense of mutual concern and an interest on the part of every monk in the work of all his brethren are necessary elements in a monastic community.[25]

While a common work involving many of the monks of the community can be a powerful source of unity, it can also create a false impression of a unity that is not in fact there. Sometimes a misguided zeal for success and an exclusive concentration on efficiency impede charitable relations among the brethren. The demands made upon monks can be all the more ruthless for being made in good conscience. In an institution with demanding and longstanding commitments there is a danger of the individual's becoming a cog in the machine, where his work is merely filling a vacancy in the system. The whole community, especially the abbot and those in authority, have a responsibility to watch for and prevent undue exploitation of any individual monk in this way. If fraternal charity rather than mere efficiency is the overriding concern in the organization of the monastery's works, it is possible to respect the varying capacities and even the diverse temperaments of the brethren.

c) Work and the individual monk

The good of the individual, however, is not to be seen in opposition to
the needs of the whole community. A monk is committed to service of
the community, and his basic willingness to take part in the particular
work of the community is a part of his monastic commitment. The
individual should want to further the good of the whole, even when this
means subordinating his particular desires and views to the judgement of
his superior. In this question the right balance requires a profound
freedom of spirit on the part of the individual, and critical reflection on
the part of the community, especially in the matter of a demanding
common task, so that a measure of agreement about the value of a
particular work is achieved. A high degree of honesty and openness
between the individual and the abbot is of great importance, in order
that the monk may freely express his own views about his capacities,
needs, and desires, without implying any refusal on his part to co-operate
in the work, and without prejudice to the abbot's freedom in making a
final decision.[26] There is nothing wrong in an abbot's asking a monk or
even a postulant what work he would like to do, or how he thinks he and
his brethren can best serve the needs of the Church and the world.

In committing himself whole-heartedly to his work, each monk can
fulfil St Paul's demand: 'Each one must do as he has made up his mind,
not reluctantly or under compulsion, for God loves a cheerful giver.'[27]
In most societies there are uncongenial jobs to be done, and the drudgery
of domestic, manual, or administrative work occupies a high proportion
of the time of our monks and nuns. At the community level too, there
may have to be great patience and humility in the monastery's form of
work: being socially acceptable is not the first criterion by which the
work should be judged. Such work need not be an occasion for
grumbling if it is seen as part of the universal human condition, and
therefore as capable of contributing to the world's redemption through
the sufferings of Christ.[28] It is above all in accepting the ordinary trials
and necessities of daily life and work that we take up our cross and
follow him,[29] and fill up what is lacking in the sufferings of Christ.[30]

It would be wrong, however, to set the penitential value of work in
opposition to the monk's legitimate desire for personal fulfilment.
Although work is an integral part of monastic observance, and although
the monk's duty of obedience retains its primacy, it remains true that
work which is humanly satisfying and rewarding develops our personal
maturity and capacities.[31] As Christians we should be free of the

Manichean attitude that there must be something wrong with work if it is actually enjoyed. Nevertheless the abbot may have to impose uncongenial tasks, either for the good of the community or for the good of the individual monk.[32] Cheerful acceptance of work under these conditions can make possible the fuller exercise of the monk's creative powers; it can build up and give expression to his fundamental freedom of spirit.[33]

d) Freedom of spirit

Traditional monastic writers stress the need for 'detachment' from all that might hinder the single-minded search for God. The phrase 'freedom of spirit' is used here to signify the positive and dynamic character of that virtue.

An absorbing task requiring whole-hearted attention and professional involvement contributes to the human and monastic maturity of an individual in so far as he possesses or is searching to acquire a profound freedom of spirit. If this is lacking, the monk is liable to become attached in a possessive way to his work or particular area of responsibility, and jealous of his prerogatives. He is likely to use his work as an escape from his commitments to prayer or to his brethren, and become ambitious in his aims, consequently lessening the value of his service to the community as well as stunting his personal development. On the other hand, freedom of spirit cannot be invoked to justify the kind of aimless dilettantism or mere filling-in of time that has sometimes been associated with monastic work in the past. Laziness can be a real temptation for some monks, and it is a matter for the individual conscience to be aware of, as well as one to be considered by the abbot and the community.

Freedom of spirit renders a monk more sensitive to the needs and problems of those working with him on a particular task, and creates a genuine interest in, and respect for, other activities not immediately related to his own work. Freedom of spirit with regard to work should obtain also at the community level. With new needs and new opportunities arising in the contemporary world and Church, our communities should be ready to abandon cherished and traditional enterprises in order to respond to the inspiration of the Spirit, however difficult and painful this may be. Whole-hearted involvement in a particular work does not exclude being willing to give it up or modify it, if this is what the signs of the times demand; but the signs of the times may also give a strong confirmation of the worthwhileness of existing forms of work. In any case there should be conscious attention to the priorities of works undertaken; the responsibility for this attention lies not only with the abbot, but also with the community and the individual monks.

e) Leisure

It is possible to make a cult of work or activity with a consequent underestimation of the value and importance of leisure. Work for work's sake, the search for self-justification through work, or a sense of guilt when one is not engaged on some job, are neither Christian nor monastic, and can greatly hinder a person's human and spiritual development and create a tense and competitive spirit in a community. In the western world, as opposed to the Christian and non-Christian East, there is a certain preoccupation with work, so that leisure is regarded rather negatively, or at best regarded as relaxation for the sake of more efficient work. Some reassessment of the practice of leisure in our monasteries seems desirable.

Monastic holidays, whether in the monastery or outside it, are a regular and important feature of the monastic life in many EBC houses. In joining a monastery a monk does not relinquish all his responsibilities to his own family, and holiday periods provide an opportunity to spend some time in the company of his relatives, to their common benefit. First-hand experience of the difficulties of everyday family life in the contemporary world can be a means of ensuring that monks do not lose touch with reality in the sometimes isolated situation of their usual work. More important, it can help them to preserve the relevance of their monastic life-style to present-day conditions, for instance in their observance of poverty and their freedom to criticize constructively the standards of contemporary society.

Monks engaged in teaching or other pastoral work need some periodical relaxation from the strains imposed by their work. But it is important that the style of their holidays should not be drastically out of keeping with monastic values, and holidays also provide opportunities for deepening the monks' awareness of the presence of God in their lives.

A certain amount of leisure is required daily for a mature life of prayer, and it is desirable that more extended periods of time be kept free for prayer and reflection during the year and at different stages in a monk's life. This would be specially appropriate when a change of work is envisaged, or after a long and unbroken involvement in one of the works of the monastery. Some form of sabbatical period would be particularly appropriate for those involved in teaching, to enable them to study and reflect further on their subjects. Regular provision for some days of silence and solitude for the whole community, in addition to the annual retreat, would help to strengthen the community's attachment to prayer.[34]

For effective work, but, much more important, for the effective growth of fraternal charity, individuals and communities need to stand back from the rush of active involvement. Far from being a form of escapism or 'dropping out', this would allow a sane and positive assessment of the activities of ourselves and others; and provide the opportunity to share pursuits conducive to health of mind and body, and to relax in the company of the brethren.

f) Work and poverty

At a time when the majority of our fellow-men are deprived even of the necessities of life, monks need more than ever to express their spiritual poverty not only by sharing their goods with the poor, but also by sharing the work which is the poor man's only way of improving his condition. The significance of work as a means of asceticism is a theme continually emphasized by monastic writers, and in the EBC hard work has always been understood as an important expression of our monastic poverty, especially as the standard of living in our communities has been relatively high and other physical austerities relatively few.

Still, there is a danger that the requirements of professionally exacting work may appear to justify unnecessary expense, for instance in travel or equipment, or to be an excuse for excessive periods away from the monastery. Monastic frugality and simplicity can also be eroded by misguided or extravagant use of plant or equipment, whether in the course of work or for personal recreation. Irresponsibility in these matters is the more likely in institutions where individuals can get out of touch with the day-to-day economic realities of the outside world. This deprives them both of responsible judgement in the use of goods, and of the ability to form a proper evaluation of the questions of social justice.

This is a complex and delicate area where good judgement rather than scrupulosity should guide decisions and behaviour. The romantic yearning for a simpler age is as much out of place as an uncritical acceptance of the standards and values of an affluent society. But it must be admitted that there are problems and questions in this area affecting the life-styles of our houses and the impression we make on other people, and these require considerable thought and attention.[35]

Benedictine work is also affected in a distinctive way by St Benedict's understanding of humility. The individual or collective works of monks are not on the whole of a spectacular kind, or in the forefront of public attention, even within the Church. They should never be prominent as a result of deliberate ambition to impress or to occupy positions of influence or power. This does not commit us to a false humility that would deprive the Church of the talents of the monastic communities. There have been occasions when monks have been called by God to exercise prominent functions for the good of the wider community. A monk may justifiably be appointed by his abbot to a work involving considerable publicity, and a whole community may be required to do so by the Church. But any good work would lose its monastic character if a monk were to become self-satisfied by his competence.[36]

Work in relation to those outside the monastery

a) Historical background

The EBC has been characterized since its restoration in the seventeenth century by a strong pastoral orientation. This tradition has greatly influenced the work of many houses within the Congregation. Their work in education, and their apostolic activity first in the missions in England and later in established parishes, must be seen against this historical background. A third element, that of scholarship, has also been of considerable importance. This heritage is clearly a major factor in the present structure of the communities of the Congregation and affords a basis for future developments. It should not, however, become an obstacle to an openness of spirit and a flexibility of approach to the new opportunities arising in the changing world and the changing Church.

b) The monastic apostolate

The primary monastic apostolate, the basic monastic service, consists in the very existence and values of a community of Christians dedicated to the monastic life.[37] All other functions and work undertaken by a monastery rest upon this fundamental reality and are an expression of it.

The renewal of monastic work must always take this truth as its first premise and guiding principle, even when it questions traditional behaviour or types of work. The *raison d'être* of a monastery does not lie in its work, nor is monastic life in itself oriented to any specific work, as the variety of activities undertaken by monks in the course of history makes abundantly clear. This radical freedom provides us with a flexibility and adaptability to change in the matter of work. On the other hand, monastic communities may make a long-term commitment to particular forms of work, and this involvement will inevitably condition and characterize the way of life of a particular community or Congregation.

c) The work to be done

A monastic community is not entirely free or independent in the choice of its work. Not only do history and tradition give a particular generation in a monastery duties and responsibilities, but also the call of God, manifested in the needs of the Church and the world in which the monastery exists, and in the talents of the brethren, requires a response on the part of the monastic community. Our work must have real value in terms of the contemporary situation if it is to be an objective participation in the creative and redemptive work of God. Monasteries have a duty to use the talents of their monks as effectively as possible. They are in the privileged position of being able to direct group efforts to this end, and the involvement of a united group can be more productive than the sum of many individual efforts. Waste or misdirection of manpower is no less reprehensible in a monastery than wasteful use of material goods. It would be irresponsible not to review constantly the actual effects of our work, and compare them with the real requirements of the Church and the world. Whatever works we undertake, we have an obligation to maintain high professional standards in the services we provide, while avoiding the temptation to accumulate material gain.[38]

Involvement in professional work inevitably brings with it a considerable degree of commitment to other groups and communities outside the monastery. For instance, in parochial work there must be co-operation with the secular clergy and the lay community of the parish; in schools monks must work in harmony with lay masters; university work entails participation in the life of the academic community. In these and other areas there are personal and community responsibilities that can make the monk's task of integrating his monastic and professional obligations complex and difficult. Avoiding the extremes of neglecting either his monastic or his professional responsibilities, a monk can overcome these difficulties by his awareness that his own person is the point where the two forms of life must be integrated. He has the support of his abbot and his brethren in his professional commitments; and if his monastic life is truly centred on God, this most certain source and goal of unity will be manifested in his life and work.

d) Present forms of work in the English Benedictine Congregation

1. Education

Education is an activity that eminently shares in the creative work of God. All truth and understanding are of God,[39] and the handing on (*paradosis, traditio*) of divine and human wisdom is the work of the Word of God, communicating the divine life to us.[40] The task of research and exploration is prompted by the Spirit who 'searches everything, even the depths of God'.[41] Such a programme gives dignity to the teaching profession as a whole.

A monastic community, however, has a quite distinctive role to play in education. It will influence the lives of the young to the extent that the monks really give an individual and corporate witness by their Christian and monastic commitment and by their example as true seekers of wisdom. From the point of view of the monastic community, bringing young people to the monastery to receive what the community can give has the advantage that such work can be done within the monastery itself. The work will be pre-eminently community work.

There has been considerable diversity in the course of EBC history in the form and scope of the schools run by the monasteries of the Congregation. In the twentieth century a justifiable response to the needs of the time brought about a transformation, in several cases, of small Catholic schools run by EBC houses into larger national public schools. Such independent Christian schools have contributed greatly to the cause of education and to the general good of the Church. As in other areas of work, the present structure of Benedictine schools is largely determined by past historical circumstances and decisions, and gives to present-day monasteries responsibilities and commitments which have to be met.

Two problems particularly exercise the mind of many at present:
(i) First, there is the question of the independent schools. Many different views are held as to the value of independent schools in the educational systems of the countries where the monasteries are located. Whenever the type of school we are running comes under review, one criterion must overrule all others in deciding what to do, namely, the good of Catholics in our countries. A monastic community cannot plan its future in isolation from the whole society in which it finds itself, and so must be sensitive to the different opinions and attitudes among those for whom the monastery and its school are important.

The situation is the more complex in that the general structure of education, and of Catholic education in particular, is in a state of considerable flux, and in education external pressures and norms are just as decisive for future planning as are the values or ideals of a particular monastic community. In an era of inflation, for instance, there is a danger that the independent schools may become the preserve of the very wealthy. A greater measure of involvement with various levels of society is a desirable way forward for our independent schools, along the lines suggested by a Joint Working Party of the Governing Bodies' Association and the Headmasters' Conference: 'All public schools would benefit if they could draw their pupils from a wider cross-section of society in terms of parental occupation, income, and residence.'[42] Yet it is important that in any process of change we should not sacrifice the value of a monastic presence in our schools.

Furthermore, the close link between work and monastic life in general means that the character of an EBC house is affected by the type of school it runs. Both the entry of candidates into the monastery and the impression made by a monastery on the outside world are greatly influenced by the type of school attached to it.

(ii) The second problem concerns the relation of the school to the monastery. School work is demanding, not only for the individual but also for the community, and inevitably some tension will exist between the demands of the school and those of the monastery. No one would deny the primacy of prayer, but it is possible to depreciate the value of work. A realization of the responsibility involved in participating in God's creativity will be in proportion to the monk's prayerfulness, his awareness of who and what God is.

Tensions between school work and monastic life will to some extent always exist, in that schoolmastering is a highly professional task: justice towards the pupils requires a specialist training, skill, and considerable application in terms of energy and time; the monastic life too makes its special demands on the monk-schoolmaster. It is a grave error to set the two roles in antithesis to each other, since work in the school is an integral part of the monastic life of those monks so engaged. Theirs is a particularly difficult way of life, but to some extent the tension will be minimized by each monk for himself, by his understanding that when engaged in school work he must exercise high professional standards, and that as a monk he must be a man of prayer, aware of the fact that his work flows from and is inspired by his life with God in the community.

Community life makes demands that can at times conflict not only with academic work but also with social and especially pastoral involvement in the various sub-communities of the school. A monk's effectiveness in his school ministry is in direct proportion to his degree of participation in the life of the monastic community. He needs frequently to use his right to be present in choir, at community conferences, at meals and at community recreation. Then through his presence in the school the values of the monastic community can be made available to the wider *familia* that surrounds the monastery.

The abbot, helped by the community, has an obligation to enable the brethren to reconcile any conflicts that arise from the claims of school and monastery. The abbot will be aware of the problems of the headmaster in his task of running the school efficiently; the headmaster in his turn will recognize the abbot's overall responsibility for the welfare of both the monastery and the school. It is the abbot's task, working with the headmaster, to ensure the integration of school work into the monastic life of the community in general and of individual monks in particular.

2. The parochial apostolate

The second main area of work in the EBC, the parochial apostolate, is also largely determined by past historical circumstances and the missionary orientation of the Congregation. This mission has been very largely a priestly one, and it seems likely that we will continue to serve the Church by providing pastoral priests in considerable numbers. Such ministry within the hierarchical structure of the Church derives its power from the mission given by the Lord to the apostles, the 'fellow-workers with God'.[43] Apostolic work thus eminently partakes in the divine action of building up the Body of Christ.[44]

Throughout the long history of monastic pastoral work, there has been a constant awareness on the part of the monks and of the faithful that this ministry is monastic as well as priestly. All that is said about monks in this book applies to monks engaged in parish work, though circumstances may prevent the full expression of the monastic way of life outside the monastery. In particular, the vow of stability gives the missioner real and lasting roots in his own monastic community, and there is a mutual dependence in prayer and in charity between the resident community and those who are sent out to serve the Church in parishes or in other work. In those pastoral works where a group of monks is working together, there is a genuinely monastic character about their community, which is reflected in their pastoral apostolate.

The present pastoral situation in the Church is complex and fluid, and no easy solutions are available for the renewal of this area of our work. However, for those houses which are engaged in this type of work the basic requirement is to develop a form of parochial or other apostolate which is pastorally more effective and in closer harmony with the fundamental values and structure of the monastic life. A greater measure of common life and prayer is a way forward; and clearly a variety of experiments is needed, account being taken both of the historical responsibilities of the Congregation and of the changing conditions and needs of the present time. Problems of manpower, the particular situation of each community, and the decision of each house about its future development mean that the question of renewal in this area lies primarily with the individual community. However, if it is to provide an authentic witness to monastic values in the contemporary world, this renewal must be both pastoral and monastic in character. The two naturally go together, since there is a great need of men and groups who can communicate to others, both Christians and non-Christians, a real experience of God and Christian brotherhood.

3. Other areas of work

Communities and individual monks are active in many other areas, including scholarship, practical crafts, ecumenical work, retreats, and university chaplaincies. A number of basic points seem relevant to these diverse activities.

Monks who are given special forms of work to do, either alone or in very small groups, often render significant service to the Church in their specialized activity. Their work is of benefit not only to themselves but also to their communities. In many cases they can share fully in the monastic and community life of their houses, which enables them both to give a specifically monastic character to their work, and to enrich the community by the experience and human contact their work provides.

A greater range of works will meet the requirements of individual personalities and capacities, though the value of a common work should be recognized. It would obviously be undesirable to spread the monastery's resources over too wide a field, or to divide the monks between two major forms of work more or less equal in importance. But a greater diversity of work will help to broaden the range of entry into the monastery, which is certainly to be encouraged. One area that could be developed is that of monastic hospitality, so that people of every age, background, and belief may be able to experience for a long or short period a living contact with a monastic community.

An important work is performed in our monasteries by the sick and the aged, including those who have retired from long years of active apostolic labours. Their prayer, their wisdom and counsel, and their example of detachment are a powerful reminder that much monastic work cannot be measured in terms of tangible products. Their stability in the monastic family plays an important part in the continual process of building up the community. Their contribution is particularly vital in a time of renewal, when to their experience is added the opportunity to stand back and reflect prayerfully on the activities of the past and the present.

Similarly, monks who are not able to participate fully in the works of the community, because of their studies, through ill-health or for other reasons, can nevertheless provide powerful assistance and support to those who are directly engaged. Through their interest, their prayer, and their fraternal concern they contribute to the integration of all the community's works with the full life of the conventus.

It is not necessary that all the work of our monasteries should be linked to the priesthood: monks who do not become priests should be able to take a full part in the work of the community. The priesthood should not be made the basis of distinctions in performing practical chores, domestic work, and similar tasks in the monastery: this type of service should be shared by all the brethren. But for monks who are priests, and especially for those involved in directly pastoral work, their priesthood commits them to the building up of Christian communities, which in turn serve to consolidate the consciousness of one world community.

The horizons of EBC activity should not be limited to the needs of any one area or country. The urgent duty to meet the challenge of the underprivileged, especially in the Third World, is a real and practical one, which demands genuine involvement. In their educational and pastoral work monks have a notable opportunity of extending our society's awareness of these problems. The task of changing social structures for the better realization of peace and justice, both in our own countries and in the Third World, requires a long-term effort that stable communities are particularly well equipped to undertake. Each community has the responsibility to consider how it can best respond to these most pressing needs of the world, and to take concrete action accordingly. What is said to every Christian is said also to every monastic community: 'As each one of you has received a charism, use it in the service of others as good stewards of the manifold grace of God.'[45]

16
Monasticism and the Priesthood

The purpose of this chapter is to discuss the interaction of priesthood and monasticism, not to present a complete treatise on Christian priesthood; many things are therefore left unsaid.

Though foreshadowed in the Old Testament, Christ's priesthood broke through the bounds of a professional caste and a particular ritual associated with the Aaronic order. Christ the priest proclaimed the mighty deeds of God consummated in his own redeeming work, and through his self-offering reconciled mankind to the Father so that we should become a kingdom of priests to our God. Through their baptism all Christians share in his priesthood: all are called to dedicate themselves and their whole lives in union with his royal sacrifice, and all share in the evangelical mission of the Church. The ordination of certain Christians to the ministerial priesthood focuses and serves the priestly vocation of all.

This chapter suggests how monastic spirituality fosters priestly attitudes of worship, sacrifice, peace, and reconciliation. At the same time it suggests how a renewed ministerial priesthood in the modern Church, conscious of its role in the service of the word and the building of Christian communities, is moving closer to values by which monasticism has traditionally been inspired and sustained. Priesthood and monasticism are thus mutually enriching, and it is in this context that the vocation of monks ordained to the ministerial priesthood is considered. The double vocation of the monk-priest, noticed already in Chapter 10 in connection with the Eucharist, is here confronted directly and in a wider perspective. The problems it raises are mentioned, but an effort is made to lift the whole question out of the sphere of individual anxieties into that of corporate responsibility.

The theme of this chapter has a particular interest for the English Benedictine Congregation, which from its re-establishment in the seventeenth century was dedicated to the English mission. This missionary orientation was believed to be in continuity with a tradition stretching back for a thousand years. It remains essential to the Congregation's life today, but many factors in the modern Church and the modern world prompt us to a reappraisal of the idea of monastic mission.

Contemporary difficulties about priesthood

a) The ampler meaning of Christian priesthood

The Second Vatican Council resuscitated the neglected Catholic truth that Christ's priesthood resides in every one of the baptized.[1] But this rediscovery often seems to have been more conspicuous in its negative effects than in its positive appreciation and appropriation. This universal priesthood has received, it is true, copious recognition in the revised liturgy, that sphere of life where the exercise of priesthood is formally and most clearly manifested. But if it never attains expression, or even awareness, outside the field of church worship, then it will be in danger of becoming an exclusively cultic reality just at the time when it is being rediscovered that Christian priesthood has a far ampler meaning. Of all the problems on the subject of the priesthood which Vatican II has bequeathed to us, the most intractable one of all is likely to be that of persuading the universal body of Christians to view their lives and their work in the world in its entirety as a priestly existence and activity. To this task takes second place that of allaying the confusion in clerical ranks over their identity and the Council's restatement of their marching orders.

The subject of this chapter is, therefore, not just the sectional concern of those who belong to the order of ministerial priests, but is of vital interest to everyone. Monks and nuns, whether they are ordained or not, are Christians with the special monastic engagement of reaffirming, reflecting upon, and living to the full that reality which is the very source and title of their participation in Christ's priesthood, their baptismal commitment. It may well be part of the contemporary vocation of Benedictines to diffuse in the Church that integrated and reverent attitude to oneself as dedicated to God and to everything else as ready to be offered to him in praise, thanksgiving, or repentance, which follows from God's act in setting us all apart for priestly service.[2] And the Rule of St Benedict has many features (later to be enumerated) which, if reflected upon, can help to generate this priestly disposition.

But we can only communicate to others this realization of sharing in Christ's priesthood if their vision of Christ is that of the Priest. The affirmation, 'No priest but Christ!', can all too easily be reduced to meaning, for all real purposes in a man's daily life, no priesthood at all.[3] Seldom is Christ's priesthood an object of contemplation or a programme for action. But it is there for us to dwell upon, whether we consider it manifested in his final sacrifice, or in his present and eternal office of intercessor for men, or in every phase of his earthly existence, both in what he did − reconciling, interceding, reopening communication[4] − and in what he was, a mediator because of the very nature of the hypostatic union.

b) The shifting horizons of the ministerial priesthood

Through the activities of the presbyteral order the priesthood of Christ is brought to bear upon the world not only in a different degree, but also in a different fashion from the way in which it is exercised by every baptized Christian.[5] The specific services of these presbyters are those of Christ the Head ministering to his Body, whether this be considered in the sacramental or in the ecclesial sense.[6] What is signified by the sacrament of orders is the dependence of the Church on the headship of Christ, the primacy of his grace and action.[7]

Nevertheless the democratic and scientific world in which we live and whose attitudes and values we all unconsciously imbibe regards with instinctive suspicion the right to existence of such a hierarchy, though it may concede at least the plausibility of the notion of a universal priesthood of humanity as a whole over the rest of creation. But to exalt a certain class of persons as especially consecrated could seem to give a foothold to that habit of classifying everything as either sacred or profane which, in the ages of myth and ritual, often led to the degradation of most earthly realities. This conception which governed most pre-Christian religion was transformed by the incarnation.

Furthermore, the Council's reappraisal of the theology of the Church, and consequently of the sacramental ministry, as well as its high evaluation of the layman's work of transforming and humanizing the modern world by direct action, has left priests with the lengthy and often painful task of rediscovering their role, both in the sources of our faith and in our new Christian era. Previously a priest's function was both clearly defined and socially accepted as one primarily concerned with the administration of the sacraments. The firm consciousness of what he had to do, the assurance of what people expected of him, was the great strength of the Catholic priest, impelling him to a mission that was always business-like, dedicated and even heroic. The mystification which besets many priests today arises not so much, as is often alleged, from a devaluation of the ministerial priesthood by the conciliar pronouncements and the subsequent whittling away of so many of his traditional functions of leadership, but rather from the Council's reminders that the frontiers of the priesthood are far wider than was often previously supposed.

Now the primary mission of the priest, as the Council has made explicit, is not to say Mass and instruct the Catholic people, but to preach the gospel universally.[8] This activity should result in the emergence of Christian communities who will demand the continued presence and leadership of the priest in order that they may remain specifically Christian. And the specifically Christian character of these communities would be only half-complete if it did not find both its source and its expression in the Eucharist. In many ways, it is true, there is no clear-cut division between these three stages of priestly activity; they overlap and intermingle. For example, the celebration of the liturgy can itself be a proclamation of the gospel and the crystallization of a local church, while preaching, no less than the sacraments, can be a means of sanctification. But as a scale of logical priorities this triple aspect of priestly ministry is not only grounded in the New Testament;[9] it is also the one best adapted to the sociological and psychological realities of a world which is no longer Christian.

In reasserting these evangelical tasks the Council was clearly extending rather than narrowing the field of action committed by the Church to its ministerial priesthood. At the same time its stress on the priest's collegiality with his bishop and on his fraternal relations with the other members of the presbyterate demands of him a more positive, definite and responsible relationship with the bishop and with his fellow-priests than was previously the case, and requires him to share in far wider responsibilities than those directly committed to him personally.

When so many horizons are opened up to them all at once, it is not surprising that many priests should feel disoriented. And an individual priest may well feel intimidated at the sudden imposition of many challenging tasks for which he has not been adequately prepared and for which he perhaps feels himself to lack the requisite personal qualities. But one should not overlook certain encouraging signs which are also evident in this daunting situation. The brotherhood of priests seems to be becoming more of a reality. Co-operation between all ages and all talents is replacing the lonely pioneer as the priestly model, giving reality to the truth that there are no isolated priests, but an *ordo presbyterorum*, cooperators of the episcopate.[10] There is among the clergy too a more widespread consciousness of their need for prayer, a readiness to make strenuous efforts to advance in it, and a desire for a deeper knowledge of the Scriptures. Fruitful exchange between Catholic priests and the clergy of other Christian bodies is now well established. Nearly all these recovered perspectives of the Catholic priesthood have long been central to the life of Benedictines, and it is no accident that recent years have witnessed the forging of much closer links between many monasteries and their dioceses than had ever previously been the case.[11] This can be of benefit to both, since both priests and monks now find their chief correlative realities in the Word and community life as well as in the sacraments.[12]

c) *The special position of Benedictine priests*

In document after document the Second Vatican Council inculcated that the overriding purpose of the ministerial priesthood is to discharge a pastoral mission in the Church. An amendment proposing the Council's recognition of the fact that 'there are religious houses of which many members are priests without exercising pastoral responsibilities or apostolic work' was rejected.[13] This does not mean at all that the Council wished to settle this question definitely, but its abstention from so doing has laid upon priest-contemplatives the onus of justifying theologically that compatibility of their two vocations which the facts of their experience support.[14]

In the case of the English Benedictines the issue is nothing like as clear-cut and inexorable as it is for many other kinds of monks. Throughout the three centuries of its existence our Congregation has never been without a pastoral orientation. Even its more 'monastic' tendencies have not repudiated its preoccupation with the conversion of England, but have had different views on the best way of setting about it. This apostolic dimension has not been a mighty accident, imposed on a body of monks by historical circumstances. If on this point we ask the classical question, 'What would our Fathers say?' the reply that history gives is that at the very beginning our founders made a deliberate choice to be apostolic monks, a novelty hard to justify in their time and in their immediate surroundings.[15] If they had merely wanted to become missionaries, they could have joined the secular priesthood or the many active orders then flourishing. And if they had simply wanted a re-establishment of English conventual life, this could have been done on the Continent without their getting involved in all the political complications and costliness of the English mission. But they experienced, quite independently of one another's influence, a common calling to be monk-priests. In spite of many tensions and imbalances, time seems to have borne out their belief that this combination of monk and priest can be a single viable vocation. The tensions themselves have often been a source of strength and creativity.

But within this framework of understanding different problems do arise. First, there are those felt by men for whom certain elements of monastic existence seem to curtail the full exercise of their priesthood: for them the monk gets in the way of being a priest. The offending item may be the ideal of withdrawal and the distance a monastery sets between itself and the world; it may be the ceremoniousness of monastic observances; it may be the house's social exclusiveness. Factors such as these may seem to incapacitate the monks for those easy relations with other people which are one of the prerequisites of pastoral effectiveness. Others, who likewise put the accent on the priesthood, feel frustrated because in the monastery the major portion of their working lives is consumed by labours which, materially considered, could just as well be done by a layman and where their priesthood is rarely brought to fruition. It is true that, sooner or later, some occasions for pastoral activity do occur. And it is also a great advantage for the Church to have a considerable number of priests in reserve to meet sudden emergencies and fulfil special missions. But, all the same, when one's ministry is only occasional or long-delayed, it requires a very deep Christian maturity to maintain the spirit of apostolic dedication, especially when one is not surrounded by visible reminders of definite people for whom one is sacerdotally responsible.

Second, there are other Benedictines who see the problem the other way round: for them the true development of a monk's vocation is hampered by that close association with the priesthood which has become traditional in our Congregation. Some of them are quite happy with the present state of affairs because they regard their priesthood as a latent potential. It is there to be used when called upon; if it is not called upon, then monasticism takes its place as the primary consideration. But others are more radical. Monasticism, they say, is not true to its nature and to its sources,[16] and it sacrifices that freedom which is necessary if it is to fulfil its role in the Church, whenever it becomes clerical. The monastic vocation is primarily a gift of the Spirit, internally present in the candidate, a vocation which is not given by the monastery even though the monastery discerns and tests it. The priestly vocation, on the other hand, is, in the final analysis, an outside calling of a suitable ordinand by the Church, a vocation therefore which is not fully received until the time of the ordination ceremony itself. So the two vocations are addressed to the monk-priest from altogether different angles, and should not be treated as if they were one. Yet the intellectual formation of monk-priests is harnessed to training for pastoral duties rather than to the pursuit of a distinctive monastic theology. And the climax of a monk's early development is generally considered to be ordination rather than solemn vows. Nor is it easy to reconcile the organic relationship between every priest and the local bishop,[17] reaffirmed so strongly by Vatican II, with a monk's total commitment to his monastic community, not to speak of the fact that this community may well have inherited traditions of the fullest possible independence of the local ecclesiastical system. Furthermore, the role of the priest which is most clearly recognized today is to be the President of a local eucharistic community, and that is a role which usually cannot be exercised in a regular way by the priests of a monastery.

All this does not mean to say that the advocates of a non-clerical monasticism want to be any less missionary. It is true that most of the arguments outlined above are used also in other Congregations by those who feel that contemplative monasticism should be a value in itself without being overlaid by the priesthood. But a strong case can also be made that monasticism functions more effectively as a missionary organism too when it is true to its own nature as a primarily lay phenomenon.

These specifically monastic and even missionary challenges to the fusion of monasticism with the priesthood are now charged with all the more force because they are being delivered at a time when generally, throughout the Church, the hierarchical priesthood is being called upon to give both an intellectual and a practical justification of itself. But it is also difficult to predict yet whether the lay monasticism which is being both advocated and practised in many quarters, and which is already permitted by our Constitutions, will, in fact, be an element in the ranks of the Congregation that has come to stay or even perhaps become the standard practice. It brings in its train certain practical difficulties which need to be faced before any community presents this alternative to men who offer themselves for the monastic life. It would require a very mighty and conscious effort on the part of the monastic authorities to ensure that theological studies retained their importance in the formation of those who do not have as an incitement the goal of the priesthood and its demands for professional expertise. It would be hard to make clear that the option whether a monk would be ordained belongs primarily to the ecclesiastical authorities and is not the personal choice of the candidate. It would have to be manifestly evident to all that the work foreseen for non-sacerdotal choir monks would have a place among the common tasks of the house and not be a self-chosen apostolate.

In any event the ministerial priesthood has hitherto played a major role in informing the life and activities of most of our monks, and will probably continue to do so even if it is no longer, for those who come to join us, the inevitable vocation that it has been. A positive evaluation must therefore be made of its compatibility with monastic existence.

The New Testament's metamorphosis of priesthood

a) Christ: the only true priest

The only person who serves God and man as a priest in his own right is Christ.[18] He alone has the true and fully adequate priesthood – 'true'[19] not in the sense that all other priests are false or ineffectual, but because their priesthood has lost its autonomy and is either a shadow or an image (i.e. expression) of his: a shadow if it precedes, as was the case with the Aaronic priesthood; an expression if it continues and signifies Christ's priesthood, as in the Christian Church.[20] Since Christian ministry is essentially apostolic, it is only an instrumentality, a sacramentalization, of the one effective Priest.

The word 'priest' (*hiereus*) underwent a transformation once it had been applied to Christ. The author of the Epistle to the Hebrews seems to have breached a self-denying ordinance which all the other New Testament writers imposed on themselves against the explicit use of sacerdotal titles.[21] It is frequently asserted today that the word 'priest' is never directly applied to Christian ministers until the time of the Apostolic Fathers. But it is also the case that very rarely in the New Testament is this terminology applied even to Christ. Because he was not a priest in any sense recognizable to them, it required an inspired leap before the Christians could bring themselves to think of even Christ as a priest. The sacerdotalization of the ministry of Christ and those he commissioned is a typical instance of the creativity of the Christian community going beyond the letter of Scripture without, however, intending to betray the spirit of Christ. His great sacrificial action was not cultic in form; it took place 'outside the camp'. One can almost feel this self-restraint from the language of priesthood at work in the New Testament writers, because in spite of their inhibitions they so often find in kindred concepts of the sacrificial and cultic order the aptest expression they can give to Christ's mediatorial work for men and the fitting praise he offered to God.[22] Moreover, once the Christian use of the title 'priest' was permitted, it spread with a rapidity only possible for something that fitted the requirements very naturally. But until then the early Church was rather guarded about presenting Christ in sacerdotal lineaments, in order both to avoid confusion with the Jewish priesthood as long as it was still functioning or a recent and possibly nostalgic memory, and to allow Christians themselves time to apprehend correctly the uniqueness of Christ's priesthood and its communicability to others. It was Christ's person and action that would in future define the meaning of 'priest', not the other way round.

One of the most important of the mutations which priesthood underwent in Christ's work of redemption was its abolition as a system where the clergy sacrificed as expiatory victims certain specified external gifts. Christ's oblation is in a class on its own because he offers his own body: in Hebrew psychology 'body' means his whole self. There is no longer any distinction between the offerer and his gift; the sacrifice is not made by any form of proxy.[23] 'The cultic element is, in fact, quite secondary in Christ's priesthood, as can be seen from the fact that his "sacrifice" was the existential self-sacrifice of Calvary; what happened there can scarcely be considered a cultic act.'[24] In this our Lord was continuing and transcending the line of the Old Testament prophets who proclaimed that it was not other things but the life of man as it unfolds in the world which is the material of worship.

Another adjustment which Christians thought necessary before they could use sacerdotal language for their own purposes was to reinstate the ministry of the word as a constituent element of the priestly office. Even the Old Testament priesthood in its earlier stages had given the primacy among its activities to the promulgation and transmission of the law and of Israel's sacred history.[25] But more and more exclusively it came to devote itself to the sacrificial cult, leaving the task of preaching to others. Jesus reversed this tendency. He united in himself both the sacrificial and the prophetic traditions of his people when he described himself in terms of Isaiah's Suffering Servant: not only did he freely offer to God the death which was unjustly imposed on him, and thereby transform it into a sacrifice which would avail for others,[26] but he added to that sacrifice the two chief characteristics of Israelite prophetism, namely the proclamation of God's righteousness and intercession for sinners. This is underlined in the sacerdotal prayer in John 17, where Jesus, like a priest, consecrates himself as a victim, in the first place for his apostles,[27] but adds to this priestly consecration his prophetic intercession for the whole Church so that through the word of the apostles 'the world may believe'.[28] Similarly in the Synoptic accounts of the Last Supper there is an organic nexus between the sacrifice and the proclamation of the word to men. This is indicated by the phrase, 'the blood of the new covenant', because a covenant which does not include the proclamation of God's word to men is inconceivable.[29] Therefore in his command to the apostles, 'Do this in memory of me', Christ implicitly included 'proclaiming the Lord's death till he come'. This conjunction of sacrifice and word is also well to the fore in the classical full-length exposition of Christ's priesthood, the Letter to the Hebrews. The themes of Christ's priesthood and of his announcing of the word of God are inextricably intermingled, especially in the beginning of the Epistle, but also throughout.

Jesus received a threefold unction, gathering into one all the anointed characters of the Old Testament[30] when he was anointed with God's power, first at his incarnation and then at his baptism and ascension: on these occasions he was marked out to be the Messiah, the Lord's Anointed, not only as priest and prophet but also as a king.[31] He fulfils this last character in so far as he is head of the new people of God, one day to hand them over to his Father as a Kingdom ready for him. As the source of all charisms to his Body, the Church, Christ is the priestly mediator of God's salvation, as in primitive times the king was the priest of the people he governed and united in his person. Through the king all God's benefits were distributed to his people. The function of a king is to constitute, unify, and guide a community, to be responsible for it before God, and to take all the initiatives in that people's history, as 'Jesus has gone as a forerunner on our behalf, having become a high priest for ever after the order of Melchizedek'.[32]

Thus Christian priesthood at its very source has a meaning that is both deeper and wider than the usual acceptance of the term: deeper because it demands that the priest submerge himself in the victim, wider because it subsumes the prophetic and kingly vocations within God's people. It therefore transcends the circumscribed professionalism with which the term is generally associated and impels those who are called to it to a wide range of tasks. It was because he broke out of the boundaries of conventional priesthood that the Letter to the Hebrews locates Christ's priestly ancestry in Melchizedek rather than in Aaron.[33]

Nor was Christ's priesthood a merely external role that he fulfilled by certain events in his history and which only came into operation then. It emanated from the very centre of his being, because of the perfect mediatorship and bridge-building between God and man that was created by the hypostatic union,[34] as well as because in his case alone priest and victim are one. The essence of priesthood lies in the union of the will with that of the Father, and this union is expressed by faithfulness. And since priesthood language had been found appropriate in speaking of Christ's own work, it was inevitable that it would likewise be found appropriate in speaking of the continued actualization of his work in the Church.

b) Christ shares his priesthood with all his people

The corporate priesthood of the Christian people has the same new fulness of content which we have noted already in the case of Christ. Like his, their priesthood has taken over the prophetic and kingly strains in the traditions of the former Israel. This is clear in the context of the oft-quoted passage in 1 Peter 2.9. Christians too have become a priesthood primarily to 'declare the wonderful deeds of him who has called [them] out of darkness into his marvellous light', therefore to be a priesthood with prophetic undertones. They too are a 'royal priesthood', royal in so far as they have allowed themselves to be constituted by God into a free community with their own measure of responsibility for it,[35] monitoring the rest of humanity towards him. Another sense in which Christians are a 'royal priesthood' is that grace will help them to recover by their labours and ascetical efforts that dominion over the material creation and over their own passions which is God's intention for them and which is necessary if they are to offer the world and their bodies to him freely.

Their sacrifices are called 'spiritual' in the same sense as Christ's sacrifice was called 'living': that is, they bring not a dead external offering which can avail little, but one that is animated through and through by their own interior self-dedication and which, because it is joined to the self-offering of Christ, has in the Holy Spirit that effectiveness in heaven which his Pasch merited for him. In this New Testament sense 'spiritual' does not mean 'non-material', and the matter of this sacrifice of the universal priesthood must be the whole Christian life in all its effect upon the world through day-to-day activities performed in faith and love,[36] and brought to its complete and God-offered expression in the Eucharist. 'The real implication of the doctrine of the priesthood of the People of God is that, collectively and as individuals, we are called to bring the spirit of Christ to bear on the things of this world, and to dedicate all human activity by and in our self-dedication to God.'[37]

The Church has succeeded to the prerogatives of the former 'kingdom of priests' which was Israel,[38] but in neither case does this truth of a universal priesthood exclude the right to existence of an order of priests within the people, an order which is consecrated for functions reserved strictly to its members. Indeed, the presence of such an order could be a powerful visible reminder to the whole people of the priestly dedication to which they are all called, of the sacred character of every work they undertake and of the impulse to offer which should become second nature to them. It is a fallacy to think that because some reality is general and omnipresent, it cannot also be verified in a special sense in some particular manifestation of that reality. (Benedictines especially should be immune to this misconception since there are several analogies in their life and Rule to these two poles of a synthesis. St Benedict, for example, maintains at the same time the monk's duty to practise incessant prayer and the focusing of that prayer at the particular hours of the divine office; again, everything in his monastery is a sacrament of Christ, but he would not deny that this was specially and uniquely true of the Eucharist.)

c) Christ gives some men special priestly powers

The new, unique, and much fuller meaning won for the term 'priest' by Christ and communicated to his Body, the Church, was in especial danger of being forgotten through a reversion to Jewish and pagan sacerdotal conceptions when the time came for transmitting Christ's priestly task on earth to a rank of officers within the Church.[39] Labouring under this difficulty, the early history of the Christian ministry, if we consider it in isolation from the course of subsequent development, is complex and obscure, with a blankness open to all the diverse interpretations that have been given to it, until about A.D. 200, when priestly language, as applied to church officers, is in possession of the field.[40]

But Christian priesthood was safeguarded from any irrevocable regression to its pre-Christian types by its close and permanent association with Christ's final sending of the Holy Spirit and of the apostles in close conjunction with each other. This ensured that the Church's presbyters would not come to be considered as further links in an ever-lengthening chain of mediation between God and man, milestones that spelt out a distance, but rather that they would remain living signs of the invisible presence and permanent saving and mediatorial action of Christ the High Priest. They would also be signs and guarantees of the direct access which the Church now has to God because of Christ's work and because of the continuity between the Church and its incarnate Lord. In sum, the role of the presbyters would be representative of Christ rather than vicarious.[41]

The earliest ordination prayers, especially that of Hippolytus, asked that the future ministers be given a communion of that Holy Spirit who anointed Jesus's human nature for the priesthood[42] and whom he bestowed upon the apostles. The basic Hebrew notion lying behind the apostolic office is to represent, to carry not merely the sender's authority but even his presence to other men (*shaliah*).[43] The apostle, when preaching, is a sign of Christ addressing his people and assembling them in the obedience of faith. This function is possible only through the Spirit who constantly keeps Christ present to the Church. Furthermore, for the apostles mission and priesthood were closely connected: 'Consecrate them in the truth. . . . As you sent me into the world, I have sent them into the world.'[44] They share both in Christ's consecration and in his apostolate,[45] in contrast again to the Old Testament priests who were never the messengers of Yahweh as were the prophets. This missionary character of the Christian priesthood was, before the pronouncements of the Second Vatican Council, in danger of being relegated in the popular mind to specialized agencies like 'missionary orders'.

If it is to be a fair representation of the priesthood of the whole Christ, head and members,[46] the ministerial priesthood must reflect the amplitude of meaning in its prototype: it must transcend the conventional categories of priesthood and reach out to include Christ's royal and prophetic features as well. Very early in the history of Christianity, the presbyteral order did in fact bring together into one under the title of 'priest' many different roles which had been present in the Church as pictured in the New Testament.[47] We can distinguish the functions of the disciple, the apostle, the presbyter-bishop, and the president of the eucharistic assembly.[48] (This does not mean that these different roles even in New Testament times were not often combined in the same person, nor that they were not often covered by other names – steward of the mysteries of God, witness, herald, father, shepherd, servant, ambassador, elder, overseer.) In post-apostolic times the differing requirements of these offices were far more than an individual person could satisfy; they became a collective responsibility inherited by the whole local presbyterate. Because of the great variety of services which it had to render, we can safely assume that this college did not demand a uniform pattern of life and ministry from all its members, but tolerated a considerable degree of diversity.

To those who would be his *disciples* Christ held out the daunting ideals of undivided dedication and lifelong commitment with no turning back, of patterning one's life on that of the Master and of listening attentively to his word.[49] The same is required of those who would represent him to others and make further disciples in their turn. The demands of this discipleship within the Church did not cease with Christ's resurrection. This assumption of the disciple relationship has been yet another force which has given Christian priesthood a quality different from that of other sacerdotal castes. No other religion makes such radical demands on its priests. From this disciple-tradition too it has inherited the requirement that neither birth nor professional expertise nor a ceremonial initiation, but a deep, life-changing vocation and response to an Absolute should be the condition of entry.

The keynote of the *apostleship* is strenuous service.[50] Paul's habitual formula for introducing himself is 'a servant of Jesus Christ'; his profession is one which necessarily includes service to others.[51] Many forms of service can be rendered, not all of a vigorous and outgoing kind: prayer and suffering are frequently cited by Paul, the apostle *par excellence*, as foremost among the credentials of his apostolic relationship to the churches he founded. But the primary service for which the apostles were sent was the inspired spoken witness to the gospel,[52] although very often among Christians who had already been converted both the occasion and even the form of this preaching might well be the Eucharist.[53] This may well explain Paul's ready resort to sacrificial terms to describe his ministry of the word. This language is not just metaphor, but derives a new and deeper meaning from the death of Christ, which in Paul's eyes would have outshone every other sacrifice and priesthood.[54]

331

His recourse to this terminology was only natural because of its affinity with the final goal of the apostolic preaching, the 'ministry of reconciliation', a ministry which is both Christ's and the apostle's own.[55] And reconciliation is the final goal of all priesthood too. The *resident presbyter* was deputed to see to the continued care and consolidation of churches founded by the ever-itinerant apostles.[56] Maintaining the purity of the apostolic doctrinal tradition, he was the safeguard of stability, continuity and orthodoxy. He also moderated and co-ordinated all the various charisms given to different members of his flock for the upbuilding of the Church of God.[57] The Pastoral Epistles therefore attach great importance to his having the right qualities of character and judgement.[58] His title, like those of all the early church officers, was borrowed from the usage of civil administration and was interchangeable with that of 'bishop' (*episkopos*). This nomenclature is enough by itself to indicate that his foremost function was to rule.[59] Examination too of the early ordination rites has established that the first purpose of that sacrament was to entrust its recipient with a permanent responsibility for governing the community, since the prayers ask that he be equipped with 'a princely spirit' (*hēgemonikon pneuma*).[60] He is thus the centre of unity of the local church, and his government (when it is a case of a single man rather than a college) has been described as 'monarchical'. In his case the kingly aspects of priesthood take on a very high relief, and he contributes to the handing over of the Kingdom by the Son to the Father at the end of history.[61] But because his position makes him the centre of local unity, he can also preach as effectively as any prophet, because it is through the unity of those who believe that there is brought to men the knowledge that Jesus has been sent by the Father.

The question which the New Testament data leave in the greatest obscurity of all is the relationship between all these aforesaid ministries and that of the *president of the eucharistic assembly*. It was this office which led to the Christian ministry's being understood formally and precisely as a priesthood, once the conclusion was drawn that the Eucharist was the representation of Christ's sacrifice.[62] If historically Jesus had been the priest of the sacrifice, then in the *Memorial*, where his gestures and their profound significance were rehearsed, it was natural to introduce a reference to his priesthood, best rendered by the minister presiding. So far as the question of the connection between this office and the others is concerned, the two terminal points of the course of development during this period of scanty evidence are plain enough: it was the apostles present at the Last Supper who were commanded to continue to celebrate the Eucharist,[63] while the first clear subsequent evidence on the matter in the earliest post-apostolic writings shows presbyter-bishops presiding over the Christian sacrifice. The silence on the issue during the intervening period does not entitle anyone to argue that things were done differently meanwhile. The presbyter-bishops were thus the first officers of the Church to whom were applied the priestly titles *hiereus*, *archiereus*. Other presbyters assisted these bishops and held the office of priesthood collegially with them until the time came when they acquired it in their own right, apart from the special episcopal powers, on their being given the sole charge of outposts of the local church.[64]

Christian priesthood thus gathers together a variety of models of Christian ministry outlined in the New Testament whose common element is a closeness to Jesus Christ. The fusion of these functions was a process which was completed before the beginning of the third century; not one of them was narrowly specialized and purist, but each comprised features more central to the meaning of one of the others, and often more than one of these functions was exercised by a single man.[65]

To recall this broad and diversified background should reassure those who fear that a priest's significance in the modern Church is being relentlessly diminished. But it can also be intimidating to those who cannot help but view the priest in individualistic terms, as one single man with special powers and a wide range of responsibilities. These can be borne only by the presbyterate collectively. For the sake of his priestly equilibrium every priest today needs all the help he can get from those who are his brothers in the same order. But it is unlikely that this support will be the same now as it has been in the last three centuries, that which comes from knowing that one belongs to a very uniform body of men. The intricate pedigree-table which the New Testament unfolds for the Christian priesthood entitles us to expect a rich variety in its development. And it is perhaps when other priests are very different that they can help us most. The grave problem of maintaining unity in this diversity can be borne only by the most direct union of all priests with the episcopate and by deep fraternal comprehension.

The assumption which was axiomatic from the time of the Scholastics until Vatican II, that priesthood can be defined almost exclusively by its twofold power of consecrating the Eucharist and forgiving sins, has a long history behind it. This overshadowing of the ministry of the word by the sacramental ritual led to an evolution of the

Catholic ministry which was broadly similar to that of the Jewish priesthood in the Old Law. This happened partly because the Church, serving a Christian society, no longer had the missionary thrust of earlier days, while the prevalence of infant baptism led to the disappearance of catechumenical instruction. But it was also partly due to the growing influence in the theology of priesthood of the notion of 'character'[66] understood with a particular colouring. 'Character' came to be understood as a permanent consecration of the persons who confer the sacraments similar to that given to church buildings and vessels, objects set apart exclusively for the worship of God. And since the medieval conception of liturgical celebration was predominantly one of ritual and symbol, it followed that the ministry of the word was no longer thought to be intrinsic to the priesthood, but an accessory function which was sometimes better done by laymen like the early friars than by the clergy.

The Council of Trent remained in this line of emphasis when it defined orders as 'the power to offer sacrifice and remit sins'.[67] The visible sacrifice (the Eucharist) demands a visible priesthood. Although this council laid great and urgent stress on the priest's duty to give pastoral instruction, it did not declare that preaching was in any way theologically constitutive of the priesthood. Perhaps it was trying to avoid the Protestant error that preaching alone justified the existence of ministers within the priesthood of all believers. At Trent there also receded into the background the 'royal' aspect of Christian priesthood: its collegiality with the bishops in governing the Church and in planting and building up the Christian community. For when they defined the hierarchy of Church government the council fathers invoked as a model the serried ranks of an army (*ut castrorum acies ordinata*),[68] in which the different degrees of holy orders were stratified and altogether separate from one another, in order to emphasize the superiority of bishops to priests, the point which was then being challenged. But the communion of the bishop with his presbyterate and its participation in the authority by which Christ himself through men builds up, sanctifies, and governs his Body[69] were not mentioned, and this omission of any reference to communion and co-responsibility with their bishops would inevitably entail a weakening too in the sense of fraternity that members of the presbyteral order have with one another.[70]

But although one can fault the Tridentine formula for the essence of priesthood with many sins of omission, no one can deny that during the centuries when it held the field it provided the recipe for many lives of heroic sanctity and great pastoral effectiveness. This is strikingly evident in the case of those who held the fulness of the priesthood, the bishops of the Counter-Reformation. Moreover the establishment of diocesan seminaries in obedience to the Council gave a great impetus to priestly self-awareness as well as fostering an *esprit de corps* among the clergy of each diocese that anticipated the attempts of Vatican II to promote the sense of belonging to the presbyterate. Very often the living realities made good the imperfections of the era's theology of the priesthood, which was unilateral chiefly because it was not situated in any ecclesiology.[71] The majestic influence of Bérulle[72] and the so-called French school of spirituality stressed the links between the eucharistic sacrifice and the sacrifice which Christ offers perpetually in heaven to the worship of his Father; thus the Godward direction of a priest's service received the emphasis which is its right, even though this was sometimes understood to require a turning-away from men and from the world for whose sake Christ had instituted the priesthood.

During the post-Tridentine centuries each priest, having a neat and clear definition of what the Church expected of him, could function confidently, self-effacingly and as if he were a precision instrument. But a priesthood that was understood almost exclusively in terms of administering the sacraments would be less successful in our post-Christian world which needs in the first place to hear 'the mighty works of God' announced and to see Christian communities come into being as at the first Pentecost. The power of the Holy Spirit to meet both these needs lies, as we have seen, at the source of the Christian priestly office and tradition. But monasticism too has a deep vein of experience, especially in those perspectives of the priesthood which have been recovered by Vatican II.

Priesthood and Benedictinism

a) *The general priestliness of Benedictine life*

A Benedictine community should have a special aptitude for acquiring and communicating that priestly consciousness which every Christian should possess if he is to think of himself as he really is. The Rule, like the New Testament, seldom has recourse to explicitly sacerdotal language, but it does portray a life which is shaped and patterned by priestly purposes, priestly dispositions, and priestly gestures.

Peace has always been recognized as the overriding objective of Benedictine life, and it is for the sake of peace – with God, with our fellow-men and with ourselves, a peace that is the fruit of the Holy Spirit received at conversion, a peace that is the restoration of a shattered whole – that all priesthood is exercised.[73] Among the brethren St Benedict sets out to promote union and, where necessary, reconciliation. But the presence of such a union, according to St Augustine who is regarded as St Benedict's source for these passages in the Rule, is the hallmark of Christian sacrifice and priesthood.[74] The purpose too behind every priestly action is to augment or recover a fuller form of life, and this also is the overall purpose of St Benedict's scheme, made explicit in his citations from the psalms in the Prologue. Christian worship does not mean in the first place that we offer something to God, but that we receive in faith the gift God has made to us in Jesus Christ; so Benedictines too, in the words of the Prologue, 'magnify the Lord's work in them'. The monastic world is also, in the largest sense, a sacramental world, that very world in which the priest should be at home: every element in the monk's life is a sign of God's presence. Moreover mediation is the normal manner in which the monk encounters Christ: primarily through 'the ancients' but also through all other persons, at every level of his activities. St Benedict sets out to foster in his monks an attitude towards all the components of daily life – people, times, work, material things – which is that of a priest towards the wherewithal of his sacrifice: all these things are matter that has to be consecrated and offered to the Father in a spirit of thanksgiving and repentance. The chief quality required in a priest is faithfulness,[75] and it is through perseverance and patience that a monk shares in the passion of Christ.[76] His sacrifice is merged with that of Christ, and this union is expressed at profession when a monk's whole life is offered on the altar along with the Eucharist while his written vows are lying on the corporal with the Host.

b) Priests in the monastic community

Both by the terms of its refoundation and by the tradition it invokes our Congregation is corporately committed to the mission, though under its present Constitutions the immediate responsibility for this has devolved upon its component monasteries. Individual members of the monasteries too, whatever their rank or sex, are all pledged to the mission, in more general terms, because of their baptism and confirmation. The existence in our ranks of a strong body of ordained priests does a great service towards keeping alive the consciousness of everybody's responsibility for the apostolate, just as it helps to make manifest the basically priestly character of Christian, and particularly of Benedictine, life. But positive means need to be devised whereby the very explicit and special priesthood of those who have been ordained may not seem to divide them from the rest, but rather bring home to others their own priestly and apostolic calling. For it could be argued that the priestly status of a section of the monastic community is, or at least could be, inimical to that spirit of Christian brotherhood which St Benedict wished to prevail; hence the wariness of the welcome he gave to priests coming to join his monastery.

The Second Vatican Council's restoration of certain neglected aspects of the priestly office – the priority to be given to the service of the word and the duty of priests to create and give leadership to Christian communities – has given renewed emphasis within the Church generally to activities which have always been highly developed in monasteries. At the same time the great variety of tasks which the Council has now attached to the priesthood is more than a single man can competently perform, and priestly collaboration of a very sensitive, hard-wearing, and sophisticated kind between men of all ages, temperaments, and talents is what the future calls for. The developed instincts for community life which should be found in a monastery could make a great contribution here. What is required is something far more than teamwork between equals, contemporaries or kindred spirits. Monks are especially fortunate: their monastic communities provide them with an almost ready-made form of close priestly association which can make good their individual deficiencies and enable them to specialize in certain lines of priestly apostolate which would perhaps be dangerous for the balance and general effectiveness of a diocesan priest (examples of this could be academic pursuits and work among people who for different reasons are on the margins of society). Moreover almost every single requisite of those church offices which primitive Christianity blended into the priesthood has some place in the monastic tradition.

This more corporate approach to priestly ministry might go some way towards allaying the anxieties of certain monk-priests that the monastery gives them individually only very restricted and occasional scope for exercising their priesthood. It is true that a great deal of a monk's work, if it is considered in isolation, has only a very remote bearing on the purpose for which Christ instituted the priesthood, not much more perhaps than Paul's tent-making. But if that work is closely harnessed to the overriding missionary purpose of the monastery, which can be considered as a single priestly organism, if it is animated by a sense of pastoral responsibility and of sacrificial offering, and if it is a genuine contribution towards the building up of the community, then it will shine forth as the work of a priest 'presenting [his] body as a living sacrifice, holy and acceptable to God'[77] and 'filling up what is lacking in Christ's sufferings for the sake of his body that is the Church'.[78]

For most of our monks the full-time exercise of their priesthood is required only if they are assigned to work on the monastery's parishes. These commitments should not be esteemed only as demands on the community's manpower, something which is taken away from the monastery; the monks who undertake them make an indispensable contribution to the life of the house by keeping it in touch with the world of ordinary people and by being perhaps the chief agents responsible for that note of realism which has been a distinctive feature of the English Benedictine Congregation.

From a distant and superficial viewpoint the life and work of Benedictine parishes may not seem to have any distinctive contribution to make that would justify retaining them if there were sufficient diocesan clergy to take them over. Closer acquaintance, however, very often reveals a specifically Benedictine character, hard to describe exactly but nevertheless very palpable and much valued by those who know it. If the monks who serve the parishes are faithful to monastic principles, certain things do follow. It may be that the parish priest unconsciously displays in his pastoral care of his people that combination of qualities − firmness, gentleness, and constant solicitude − which St Benedict required the abbot to show to his flock. It may be a greater care for the quality of the worshipping life of the parish. It may be that the parishioners themselves cherish the links between their parish and its monastery as if they were family connections. The monks who work in these parishes also contribute many special services to the life of their dioceses and to their brother-clergy, services which are expected of them precisely because they are Benedictines. They are in great demand locally to serve as confessors, as directors of nuns and on the diocesan commissions for liturgy, ecumenism, and education.

The fine traditions which are embodied in so many Benedictine parishes should not, if we are to be faithful to them, become a matter of living on the past; they demand to be furthered in a vital way in our own time. If these parishes are not to be mediocre, there should be among them, especially among those which occupy a central and commanding position in the Catholic life of a wide district, some points of growth and creativity. They should not just be a maintenance job, but should embody that greater flexibility and freedom which are truly Benedictine. At the same time monastic humility requires that we be receptive to the many things we have to learn from the diocesan clergy. The style of the monastic parish mission is, however, always shaped by that of the primary Benedictine mission, and new developments in the monastery will be reflected by new ways in which Benedictine parishes are distinctive.

Many of the activities which have hitherto been confined to priests, such as preaching, retreat-giving, counselling, and much pastoral organization, are not necessarily tied to holy orders. Today they are often the work of teams which can include nuns, laymen, and monks who have not been ordained, and there are many situations, especially in what might be called 'pre-evangelization', where such persons can be more effective than a cleric would be. But these possibilities do not render the contribution of a priest redundant; he has his own title to preach the gospel authoritatively. The ultimate goal of the apostolate is to bring man to Christ and Christ to man in as total a way as possible; no halfway house will do. This can be perfectly effected only in the sacrament of perfect union, the Eucharist, source and culminating-point of all Christian activity. Just as Christ put the seal on his preaching by his sacrifice on the cross and completed our redemption in his death and resurrection, so too the celebration of the Eucharist remains the centre of all Christian ministry. True, it may not be the task of a monastic community to complete the mission by bringing those converted to the sacraments. In many cases the contribution of a monastery to someone's conversion may have been made at some point long before he has come to the stage of receiving the sacraments. And in all cases it is important that, once converted, the new Christians should find their rightful place in a local eucharistic assembly. Nevertheless the presence of priests in a monastic community helps to give the necessary eucharistic direction and sacramental responsibility to all the apostolic efforts of the house.

c) Priesthood and the missionary nature of English Benedictinism

The two goals of the seventeenth-century monks who refounded the English Benedictine Congregation were, first, the establishment of

English communities following the Benedictine life, and, second, the conversion of England to the Catholic faith. In the immediate historical context and in the theological understanding prevalent at the time, the only means by which this latter objective could be pursued was to send monk-priests to England as single individuals in order to administer the sacraments and make conversions. At that time the essential and only carrier of the Congregation's missionary impetus was a priestly one. All the monks were required to take the oath obliging them to be ready and willing to go on the mission if they were sent. The martyr monks died and were honoured because of this explicitly sacerdotal work, and their proud claim was to be the descendants of St Augustine of Canterbury and those missionary monks who first converted the Anglo-Saxon countries. Indeed it may well have been the conviction that this link with St Augustine made the Benedictines the order most likely to convert England again which attracted our founders to them.

In more tolerant times when the monasteries themselves returned to England there was the possibility of an interpretation of the monastic mission that would be different from the hitherto predominantly sacerdotal one. But the English Benedictine Congregation chose to make only minor modifications in its seventeenth-century missionary model, such as were necessary to work in with the settled parochial system of the restored Catholic Church in England.

The constitutional disputes at the end of the nineteenth century are usually construed as the coming to a head of the tension between the missionary and the monastic elements of the Congregation under the challenge of the general monastic revival throughout Europe which marked that era. Without going into the details of this controversy it is evident that the issue was how the past tradition should be interpreted in new and changed circumstances. The antagonists agreed in conceiving this issue more or less in the following terms: was the English Benedictine Congregation in the last analysis a seventeenth-century missionary order which had taken on a Benedictine colouring? Or was it a congregation of monks originating in the Middle Ages and forced by the necessity of responding to an urgent contemporary need to adopt certain 'unBenedictine' features in Counter-Reformation times?

Our interest in this controversy is not in the questions which were being debated, but in the assumptions which were taken for granted by both sides. The missionary tendency, it was agreed, was to be identified with 'the missions'; that is, with priestly work on the parishes. Such work was predominantly the provision of the sacraments, although in many cases it also entailed the planting and nurturing of local Catholic communities in places where none existed before. The final solution of this controversy – the distribution of the parishes, formerly the responsibility of the Congregation as a whole, between the newly constituted and independent abbeys – left still almost unchanged the manner in which the missionary character of the Congregation was to be manifested.

Today the question is posed to us again, because of the Church's call for the self-examination of all religious orders with a view to renewal, because of the changing world in which we are required to keep a missionary presence in accordance with the authentic traditions of our Congregation and because of the broader frontiers of the priesthood which Vatican II has recovered from the earliest Christian sources.

The monastic mission *as a whole* requires continual reappraisal. This clearly goes deeper than 'the future of the parishes and the schools'; it covers the whole life and work of each community. One of the criteria for renewal laid down in *Perfectae Caritatis* is response to contemporary needs, and it may be plausibly argued that there are many 'signs of the times' which point to a deep hunger for something that would require a closer convergence of our missionary and monastic tendencies than has ever been the case so far. The central problem today is not the conversion of Protestant England to Catholicism; it is a question of basic evangelization in an unbelieving world. Yet this world is also one in which disenchantment with the uniformity of technological affluence is breeding a desire to experience the transcendent and to search for the authentic inner self. It is perhaps as a mission for this sort of world that new ways of monastic living are to be sought which combine the shared God-centredness of a closely knit community with an openness to the needs and aspirations of the world around it. Such a radical response to the 'signs of the times' is not only justified in terms of present-day needs; it also reflects a genuine fidelity to tradition which goes deeper than the mechanical continuation of inherited institutions. And to understand aright our monastic mission will help to enlighten and revitalize the understanding of our priesthood.

17
Hospitality

Words such as 'community', 'sharing', 'openness', 'reconciliation', 'acceptance' have occurred frequently in earlier chapters to evoke the quality of life which should flow from the binding together in Christ of the members of a monastic community. But these things are not specifically monastic; they belong to the fulness of human and Christian living, and all men need them. Even though some measure of withdrawal from secular involvements is needed to keep the community's life strong and deep, life of its nature tends to overflow, to communicate itself, and to grow by being shared.

From the earliest days of Christian monasticism monks and nuns have made provision for welcoming travellers and pilgrims. In ages when there were few inns, a monastery might be the only shelter for these people. Today many other establishments cater for the bodily needs of travellers, yet the number of guests in monasteries increases. They are in search of a depth and quality of human life and an experience of God which are hard to find in a fragmented society. This chapter examines the ideal and tradition of monastic hospitality, the contemporary conditions which create a particular need for it, and the practical means by which the need can be met.

The modern search for community as the background to monastic hospitality

The contemporary behavioural sciences have shed considerable light on the various ways in which man is positively and negatively conditioned by his personal and material environment. Attention both in the arts and in the social sciences has shifted from the nineteenth-century emphasis on the isolated individual to a concern for the individual's need for belonging, for friendship, for community. Whereas emphasis in the arts was formerly on alienated man, man described as rootless and impotent,[1] more recent artists have seemed to sense that art itself could be an important factor in reversing the trend towards total impersonality and could present man with a vision that would disclose the superficiality of a life geared to consumption and provide him with a revolutionary alternative.

Sociology has attempted a reasoned explanation of what the artist has been exposing in man's experience. Where once the theme was the individual triumphant over the narrowness of the tribe, the goal is now triumph over uprootedness, loneliness, and alienation, by the achievement of some sort of fellowship. The ideal of the self-sufficient self-stabilizing man is on the wane. The revolt against the village and other small communities has ended and belonging has replaced escape as an important value in man's life.

The industrial, technological, urban world has stimulated this re-examination of man and his institutions in terms of needs which that world does not in itself meet. The problem is whether or not the anti-community factor can be eliminated, whether or not there can be true community in advanced industrial societies. Lewis Mumford summed up the human need behind what the artists and sociologists have explored:

> We need, in every part of the city, unity in which intelligent and co-operative behaviour can take the place of mass regulations, mass decisions, mass actions, imposed by ever remoter leaders and administrators. Small groups: small classes: small communities: institutions framed on a human scale, are essential to purposive behaviour in modern society. [2]

These aspirations have found practical application in the planning and construction of environments in the various 'new cities' which may be far more conducive to human community than present urban areas. But the problem is one of a mentality which the capitalist system has spawned. [3]

It is consciously against such an existence and its sources, above all a particular economic system, that a new communitarian way of life is being evolved by those in deepest rebellion against the institutions and institutionalization of advanced industrial societies. Recent years have seen many people, most of them young, leaving the larger society and attempting to form various kinds of communities. They reject the possibility of working within the given economic, social and political structures and finding there a life in which belonging is basic.

The new communities are of various kinds. Their number and growth indicate that they cannot be passed over in any attempt to come to grips with the drive for belonging that exists in the contemporary world. Of course intentional communities are nothing new in the West. For the most part they have been associated with intense religious movements such as monasticism and the free churches of the sixteenth century. But whereas in earlier days these communities represented alternatives to the more or less tightly-knit societies of their time, today they are alternatives to the experience of no community at all.

Such thought and experiments in community point to the seriousness and depth of the question. If nothing else, the developing fact of communal life has taken dissatisfaction with impersonal existence out of the realm of theory. These new ways of life have already had their effect on other levels of society where people are experimenting with new ways of communicating, attesting to the widespread need for relating to those with whom one lives and works. Throughout the secular world, people are seeking new life-styles which provide for community. They are being selective about the aspects of technological society which they take into their communal experience.

It is against this background that the apostolate of monastic hospitality must be viewed today, for it is out of the modern technological world that most of our guests come. Usually they come not simply for food and shelter, not simply for an experience of Christian prayer, but for an experience of Christian humanism in the fullest and richest sense of that term. Having read about the theory of community in general and possibly religious community in particular, they want to see how that theory is put into practice. They are sensitive to the effects that this experience has on the people who value it so highly as to commit themselves to it for life. The drawback of many new types of community living is that they disintegrate for lack of stable intention on the part of the members or realism in dealing with internal psychological tensions or external pressures. Furthermore the members of such communities tend to come from one age group. Experience of monastic communities where stability, realism, and a variety of age groups are prominent features may show a way to overcome these weaknesses. Certainly the varied needs and complex questions that we are apt to find in our guests today can be a great help in stimulating us to recover what is best in our tradition of monastic hospitality and to renew this apostolate without sacrificing our essential monastic character. Like the modern artists, sociologists, and humanistic psychologists, we too can provide our guests with a vision of life quite different from that offered by contemporary technological society. In the measure that a monastic community is allowing the reconciling power of Christ, which transcends differences of age, social status, nationality, and opinion, to be the living bond of unity among its own members, in that measure will it also be able to offer to its guests an experience of unity and peace.

Traditional understanding of hospitality

Hospitality is not just another apostolate taken up by monks, nor is it merely part of the work that flows from their life-style. Rather it is an essential component of the Judeo-Christian tradition, and therefore also of monasticism.

a) Hospitality in the biblical tradition

In the ancient world the exercise of hospitality usually had religious overtones, and readiness to offer it was for the Greeks a criterion which distinguished civilized people from barbarians.[4] In the biblical tradition hospitality is both a work of mercy and a witness to faith. The visitor who asks for the shelter he needs[5] reminds Israel of her former condition as an enslaved stranger,[6] and also of her present condition as a traveller on the earth.[7] The visitor needs to be welcomed and treated with love in the name of the God who loves him.[8] There is thus a double recognition: under one aspect God's people will always be wanderers and pilgrims; under another God's people must offer the traveller hospitality. The eager and religious welcome of which Abraham is the model[9] and which is approved by Christ[10] is a work of fraternal charity which makes the Christian aware of his debt to others.[11]

At the Last Judgement Jesus will reveal to everyone the mystery of this hospitality. Through and in the visitor Christ himself is welcomed or sent away,[12] recognized or unrecognized, just as when he came to his own people. It was not only at his birth that there was no room for him in the inn;[13] it was right to the end of his life that the world did not recognize him and his own did not receive him.[14] Those who believe in him receive his ambassadors in his name,[15] as well as all men, even the most humble.[16] They see in every visitor not only an ambassador of the Lord, an 'angel',[17] but also the Lord himself.

Against this background it is easy to see why the victory of faith in a man is frequently portrayed in the imagery of hospitality, of welcoming the stranger into one's home. One of the best examples is that of Abraham who welcomed the three strangers by the oaks of Mamre.

345

Abraham had experienced love; he had been called and his spirit had been regaled with glowing promises; he was a free man. But he was also a troubled man who had grown very old and was constantly preoccupied with the emptiness in his life where his son should have been. This is not the kind of situation that would incline a person to reach out for the new and the different. Rather one would tend to shrink and retire. Yet the hospitality of Abraham for the three strangers is prompt and lavish.[18] The strangers turn out to be the messengers from God who announce the birth of Abraham's long-awaited son. The point is that Abraham deliberately and painfully opened his life to the unprogrammed and uncontrollable presence of the stranger. And the result was nothing less than new life for a very old man.

Nor is it any accident that the strangers who came to Abraham's tent were agents of God, for God is the ultimate stranger, the great Other One. He is radically outside the human order of things; he is sovereign, free, unpredictable, largely unknown, potentially the most threatening of all beings, yet the one most able to bring man new life.

The coming of Jesus has not changed this. God still comes in large measure as the stranger. Luke's account of the journey to Emmaus is relevant here. 'That very day two of them were going to a village named Emmaus. While they were talking and discussing together, Jesus himself drew near and went with them. But their eyes were kept from recognizing him.'[19] Only in the breaking of the bread of hospitality did that day of confusion and despair become a day of peace and joy.

Hence far from treating the visitor as a debtor or as unwelcome, to be mistrusted and made the subject of murmuring,[20] every Christian[21] must see in the one knocking at his door[22] the Son of God who has come with his Father to establish his dwelling with men.[23] These divine visitors will in turn introduce the man who receives them into their own home, not as a guest but as a child of the house.[24] Happy will the watchful servants be who open the door to the master when he knocks at the time of the parousia. He will reverse the roles and manifest the mystery of hospitality by serving at table and sharing his meal.[25]

b) Post-apostolic and early monastic tradition

In the post-apostolic period there is clear evidence that Christians took the biblical teaching on hospitality seriously. Clement of Rome praised the Corinthians for their hospitality,[26] and Aristides maintained that all who were truly Christian practised the virtue.[27] Ignatius of Antioch insisted on the presence of Christ in guests[28] and praised hospitality as a sign of gratitude to Christ. Cyprian appointed a priest to take over the care of poor strangers during his absence,[29] while John Chrysostom boasted that the community of Antioch took care of three thousand widows, strangers, and sick people daily.[30] By the fourth century special buildings were constructed for the lodging of pilgrims and strangers, as well as for foundlings, orphans, the aged, and the sick. Since hospitality was looked upon as an important duty of the bishop,[31] St Basil founded a special village near Caesarea for the care of indigents. In many cases the task of caring for such people was delegated to deacons.

Christian hospitality was also one of the characteristic traits of the early cenobites and hermits. Pachomius had a special guest house erected near the portal, just inside the monastic enclosure, for male visitors; very probably outside the cloister walls, but likewise near the portal, stood the hospice for women. The early monks developed various styles of association with their guests which gave their hospitality a distinctly religious character. St Benedict knew of the usages in this matter that were already well established, and some of them he adopted in his Rule.

c) Hospitality in the Rule of St Benedict

In the Rule, as in the earlier monastic tradition, the principal apostolic work in which the monks are to engage is the practice of the works of mercy within the monastery itself. The Rule is particularly concerned about those who are in need of special consideration because of youth, old age, or sickness.[32] But the exercise of charity is not limited to the members of the community; it extends to outsiders as well. In Chapter 53 St Benedict makes provision for the reception of guests. He supposes that there will always be guests in the monastery and is clearly pleased that this is so. He is prepared to go to almost any inconvenience to take proper care of guests, even allowing the breaking of the night silence[33] and the superior's fast.[34] However, he takes prudent measures to ensure that the frequent reception of guests shall not unduly disturb the order and quiet of the monastery and the regular observance.

The reason for his concern that guests shall be properly cared for is a religious one: like the sick, they represent Christ. St Benedict refers specifically to the gospel text, 'I was a stranger and you took me in',[35] and he reminds his monks that Christ will repeat these words to them on the last day. Hence the porter is to welcome guests at the door,[36] the cellarer must see that they are not neglected,[37] and a monk who is filled with the fear of God is to look after them.[38] The Rule emphasizes that the care of guests is to have a distinctively religious character: they are to share in prayer, the kiss of peace, and *lectio divina*. In a very practical and effective way, then, the Rule provides for both the temporal and the spiritual welfare of visitors to the monastery.

Hospitality in our monasteries today

The exercise of monastic hospitality today must be guided by the two basic principles stressed by St Benedict: (1) that of seeing Christ in all who come to the monastery, and (2) that of preserving the peace of the community. If these principles are observed, it should be possible for the guests to find Christ in the monastic community and to have an experience of unity and peace.

a) The type of guests who will come

The Rule makes particular mention of three kinds of guests who will come to the monastery: (1) members of the household of the faith, (2) pilgrims, (3) the poor. This is still a fair description, even though the membership of each class is somewhat different today.

1. Members of the household of the faith

Catholics have come regularly to our monasteries for retreats, for spiritual direction, and for the celebration of the monastic liturgy. In an age when effective spiritual directors are sometimes hard to come by, when traditional retreat houses have often been converted into centres for theological and pastoral renewal and when dignified liturgy is somewhat rare in parish churches, the number of devout Catholics who visit our monasteries is apt to increase. Catholics from parishes served by our monks are also frequent visitors. All these are in a special way deserving of our hospitality. Some who come will undoubtedly be confused and disturbed by recent developments in the Church, but an experience of a monastic community that has remained faithful and at peace in spite of change can be reassuring to those who are anxious and perplexed.

In some monasteries the sharing of monastic life with lay people has taken a more stable and permanent form through the establishment of a lay community alongside the monastic community. Men and women belonging to this type of lay community, while retaining their professional work, lead a genuine common life among themselves, sharing their prayer, goods, and ideas. At the same time they share to a considerable extent in the worship and life of the monastic community; they may make some form of temporary commitment, accept a disciplined way of life, and be enriched by theological and spiritual instruction provided by the monks. Where a monastic community has the necessary resources, this kind of venture can become a very significant apostolate of hospitality, and at the same time a means of keeping the monks attuned to the needs and aspirations of lay people who are thoughtful and purposeful.

Since many of the communities in our Congregation conduct schools, it is to be expected that a considerable proportion of our guests will be associated with the school in one way or another. The boys, teachers, and other members of the staff are regarded as part of the extended family, yet it is possible for them to spend a good deal of time in proximity to the monastery and the monks without coming to know much about monasticism itself. Their lives, as also the lives of the boys' parents and others who make contact through the school, may be considerably enriched by an experience of the life and prayer of the monks.

One of the most fruitful meeting-points between a monastery and the modern world is continuing friendship with the old boys of its school, who bring people in trouble and others who encounter in the monastery a totally new way of life. Some of these may be university students in search of a quiet place to reflect, study, and pray. The pace of their daily lives is often frantic and the psychological and social pressures intense. The quiet, peaceful atmosphere of the monastery and friendly relations with the monks may be very helpful in restoring balance to their lives. These and other types of guest may need time and peace to see their problems in true perspective and to recover a sense of wholeness.

The accelerated pace of human mobility and social communication has contributed to the breaking-down of many barriers among men and encouraged an ecumenical spirit. As a result there has been a marked increase in the number of non-Catholic guests in our monasteries. The result has often been enriching for both the monks and the guests. The experience has prompted a willingness to affirm worth outside one's own tradition and has revealed the limitations of outlook to which those whose contacts have been chiefly restricted to Western Catholics are liable. Within such an enlarged horizon monasteries have discovered a positive role in the development of Christian unity.

There is already a firm basis for a monastic apostolate in the field of ecumenism. Monastic orders have much in common with the Eastern Churches because of the eastern origin of monasticism. Both share a deep appreciation for the liturgy, an emphasis on personal prayer and contemplation, and a yearning for silence and peace.[39] Although there is less background for association with Protestants and Jews, recent years have seen a revival of monasticism among Protestants, and Judaism has witnessed a growing interest in community life among the kibbutzim.

A number of non-Christian religions, such as Hinduism and Buddhism, have a rich monastic tradition. A discovery of what we have in common has occasioned visits by guests from these religions. Informal contacts, as well as more highly organized discussions among specialists representing diverse forms of monasticism, have prompted a sense of fellowship and a better understanding of what religion is basically all about. They can help us to simplify our monasticism and regain a proper perspective in which we are better able to see institutionalized structures as subservient to the monk's response to the living God.

Whether received individually or in organized groups for conferences, religious men who are welcomed in an environment of true Christian charity and in the best tradition of monastic hospitality should be helped to enter more readily into that meeting of minds and hearts which is the goal of religious men in search of unity.

2. Strangers and pilgrims

From the earliest times monasteries have cared for pilgrims who stop for a night or two and then pass on their way. Some monasteries have themselves become centres of pilgrimage. To this day they continue to attract large groups of people who come for spiritual renewal.[40] St Benedict singles out the pilgrims for special honour. He was obviously aware that it is easy for monastic communities to behave towards the less privileged among their guests with an air of patronage, easy for them to be selective, and easy to be ruled by considerations of class. This is the reason why he attaches so much importance to the need for filling offices in the community with deeply religious men. He knows that if officials are swayed in their judgements about guests by material and worldly considerations, the religious life of the community as well as the religious apostolate to guests will be in danger.

St Benedict devotes a special chapter of the Rule to the reception of pilgrim monks. In an age when monks are often sent away for study or for conferences, requests frequently come to our monasteries for hospitality over an extended period of time. It can certainly be advantageous for a monk if he can pursue his education while living in a monastic context. Likewise, at a time when organizational and ideological changes are taking place in our monasteries, some monks become unsettled or perhaps find that their religious vocation is in jeopardy. They are often helped by residence in another community for an extended period of time. In these and similar cases, the Rule speaks for itself.[41]

An important group in the population and among the guests in our monasteries is that of idealists who are 'on the way' not geographically but spiritually, intellectually, and humanly. They may include people in search of community. In many instances such guests are disillusioned by the 'establishment'; they often gravitate towards our monasteries because they believe that monks have consciously and deliberately adopted a mode of life which is marginal with respect to the rest of society.[42] They see us living at a certain distance from the rest of society so as to be free from its imperatives and its domination, but nevertheless open to its needs and willing to discuss its problems. They are likely to be very critical of monks if they discover that the monastery is closely identified with a certain wealthy class of people and thus identified by implication with an ideology and attitude based on a reactionary view of social reality. These guests are usually intellectuals who tend to have broad perspectives. They are usually aware of the problems of the underprivileged and have attempted in their own way to alleviate them. At the same time they are usually deeply interested in religious matters and are involved in the project of self-discovery on a spiritual level.

Although the reactions of these idealists may sometimes be wrong or biased, they are close to us in many ways and interested in our way of life. They come to our monasteries with very keen and alert curiosity; they want to know if we have something they can respect. If they find that we are simply uninformed, narrow-minded, rigid, pious individuals who identify blindly with the secular value-systems which they see as stupid and decadent, they are apt to reject us too as totally irrelevant. If we are to relate to these people and be a source of meaning for them, they must find in our monasteries people of depth and simplicity who have acquired the values of monasticism by living them and who are open to the social questions of the present time.

Among the values of monasticism are an experience of prayer and contemplation, a vital celebration of community liturgy, a deep awareness and acceptance of the eschatological message of the gospel, and a measure of personal silence and solitude which will vary from monk to monk. These traditional values must be expressed in such a way that they speak to today's world.

Openness to the social questions of the present time means not just information about current events but rather a personal communication with others who are recognized as like-minded and with whom we can share ideas and projects fruitfully even though they may not be Christian believers. It implies the ability to learn from exchanges with people of other religious, intellectual, and cultural traditions. It is certainly very difficult to combine real monastic depth and experience with openness to the living intellectual and cultural forces of our time, but it seems imperative that both of these be realized within our monasteries if we are to attract new vocations and communicate with the growing number of young people who identify with the 'counter-culture'. By hospitality we may also 'pre-evangelize' some of these pilgrims in search of truth and life.

3. The poor

The oppression and sufferings of people everywhere and the debasement which affluence can bring to human life make it imperative that individual monks and the community as a whole live in true simplicity, sharing their goods with the less fortunate. In spite of today's highly developed social agencies, many poor people continue to live in our midst. They often come to our monasteries looking for help. Although the care of the poor is normally the specific concern of the officials in the monastery, the initial contact is often made with other monks. Our response on these occasions should be one of Christian courtesy and concern as we seek help from the proper officials. In providing for all our guests, but for the poor especially, we must be careful lest they be scandalized by the opulence of our monastic tables or the décor of our houses.

Among the tools of good works St Benedict lists the relief of the poor and the clothing of the naked. Poverty should not be identified solely with material want; it can be spiritual, intellectual, emotional, and cultural as well. The dull are part of today's poor; so are the lonely.

b) The type of guests to be invited

Depending on their personal and material resources, monasteries may seek to enlarge their apostolate of hospitality by inviting various types of guests to the monastery. St Benedict is insistent on the wise and responsible use of the monastery's goods.[43] In line with his directives, the monastery plant and equipment may often be made available to outsiders. The school playing fields, swimming pool, and gymnasium may be offered to neighbouring children. The monastic library and conference rooms may be opened to outsiders. Frequently various members of the community have special talents and training that can be used in setting up and conducting programmes such as summer camps for the under-privileged and schools for the under-achievers. Obviously there are risks involved in opening up the monastery property to outsiders, but provided we use discretion in our decisions it seems to be a calculated risk we should take.

Our monasteries can also render a special service of hospitality to the diocesan bishops and clergy. Unfortunately relations between regulars and seculars are often strained and characterized by mutual suspicion. Although the diocesan clergy may come to our monasteries for their annual retreats, their visits tend to be confined to these more formal occasions. Contacts may be improved and co-operation strengthened by the extension of our hospitality. It is commonly recognized that diocesan priests often suffer from excessive loneliness; hence they sometimes find celibacy a very heavy burden. If they are invited to the monastery on a more informal basis, they may find considerable support and encouragement as they pray and take their meals and recreate with the monks. Sharing in monastic manual labour may also be a welcome change from the routine of parish life. Likewise secular and religious priests who have been hurt by the 'establishment' may be helped considerably by the offer of our hospitality during the time of their difficulties. Similarly, monasteries of nuns can easily welcome sisters from active congregations, who because of the professional demands of their work are in special need of peace and silence, and are particularly able to benefit from sharing the life of a monastic community.

Because of the intellectual resources and the organizational talents that exist among our monks, our houses may make a special contribution to the life and development of the Church by sponsoring conferences and seminars of various kinds. Not only may outsiders be invited to these conferences, but they may also be asked to deliver papers in order to share their ideas with the monks and the other participants.

It often seems that the people who could possibly profit most from our monastic life do not know about our existence. If this is so, it makes sense for us to publicize our existence and to let it be known that we are open to guests. For example, we can advise the university or military chaplains of our willingness to receive students and military personnel.

Since our guest facilities are usually somewhat limited, it is often not possible for the houses of monks to offer much hospitality to women. But our monks should be sensitive to the changes that have taken place in the understanding of woman's role in the Church and in the world, and make a special effort to provide adequate guest facilities for women. In a special way they should be made to feel at home in our liturgy and should be able to obtain spiritual direction from the monks if they so desire.

c) The guest master

St Benedict stipulates that a prudent man who fears God should be put in charge of the guest house.[44] In view of the diverse kinds of guest that come to our monasteries and the complex problems they often have, the guest master should be a wise, open-minded, sensitive man, capable of discerning problems that the guests may have, and able to decide when a guest is not good for the community or the monastery not helpful for a guest. Above all he should be a kind and patient man. His job demands a certain degree of efficiency so that rooms may be properly prepared and correspondence promptly answered. Sometimes the guest master is the only monk that a guest gets to know. It is important, therefore, that he be a deeply religious man who relates easily to different kinds of people and is capable of giving spiritual direction.

Although the job of guest master is normally assigned to one man, it is really the whole community which is responsible for monastic hospitality, especially when the number of guests is large. St Benedict ruled that only the monks authorized to care for guests might speak to them, other members of the community being obliged to greet them and then pass on. This is an instance where the situation has totally changed today; it could be a real lack of charity to take refuge in this passage of the Rule when Christ in the person of a guest is waiting to be talked to. It is also important that telephone calls be courteously and efficiently received and messages promptly delivered. It is, after all, the whole community that shapes the values in which most of our guests are interested – liturgy, prayer, silence, order and peace, and the experience of community itself.

d) Guests who want to be monks for a time

It is generally recognized that many young people find it very difficult to make a lifelong commitment. They frequently want a great diversity of experiences rather than a unified experience over a long period of time. Hence young people sometimes come to the monastery and ask to be allowed to live the life of a monk for a certain length of time but have no immediate intention of binding themselves to the community for life. Communities which have tried this experiment with a limited number of young men have found it a worthwhile experience. The lives of the guests have often been deeply enriched and stabilized, and the community too has been strengthened by the presence of these young men who bring new life and insights to the monks. Should a community take in such guests, it is free to terminate the arrangement if this is deemed necessary for the community or good for the guest. However, this does seem to be a form of monastic hospitality which is worth pursuing today.

e) Other questions to be considered in monastic hospitality

In this whole matter of guests various difficulties are bound to be encountered. For example, our monastic schedule often conflicts with the timelessness of some of our guests. Hence the basic monastic horarium should be made available and clearly explained to guests so that the monks will not be unduly disturbed by their comings and goings. Likewise, if people who have special problems are invited to the monastery as guests, we should remember that special training is often required to deal with these problems. Although we may be motivated by the best intentions, the extension of our hospitality to certain guests may be good neither for them nor for the community. Furthermore, in their dealings with guests monks should maintain a certain discretion about internal community affairs out of loyalty to the brethren and concern for the security and good name of the community.

Each community has to decide on the degree to which guests are to be involved in the life of the community. Privacy and relative freedom from disturbance are certainly necessary to the community if it is to be faithful to its traditions and to maintain the specific monastic values that the guests are seeking. The rules of enclosure exist for this purpose. However, if they are too rigid they can impede a community in the exercise of true monastic hospitality. On account of their stricter enclosure the nuns of the EBC are especially sensitive to this problem. It must be remembered that most visitors to monasteries of enclosed nuns are seeking, and expecting, a different kind of welcome from that provided by the many congregations of active sisters, and that enclosed nuns can often relate to their guests in a different way; nevertheless the rules of enclosure should not obstruct them in warmly welcoming and caring for guests.

Sometimes guests may be disturbing to the community in a good sense. Like the pilgrim monks of whom St Benedict speaks they may be helpful in pointing out deficiencies in the community. By the questions they ask and the comments they make we may be shaken out of our lethargy and complacency and stimulated to re-evaluate our life and apostolate. If monks are good for guests, guests are also good for monks.

In determining our monastic policy concerning guests, then, several basic questions must be asked: Are guests interested in us? Are we interested in them? Do they see Christ in us? Do we see Christ in them?

18
Autonomy of the Monasteries

Most of the religious orders and congregations which have arisen in the Church since the medieval period are centralized: it is obvious that any large body of men or women dedicated to a particular form of service needs strong central co-ordination to achieve its purpose efficiently. Benedictines stand out as being, from an organizational point of view, incurably untidy. For them the essential unit and source of initiative is not the order, nor the province, but the monastery. A monk is not normally liable to be transferred, nor are the monasteries subject to any strong central government in most matters. The relative freedom of each community makes for healthy monastic development, but a delicate balance is needed if this autonomy is not to lead to isolation and weakness. There must be opportunities for contact, and for the mutual encouragement, inspiration, and support which communities need for vigorous life. There must also be some possibility of collaboration.

This book is an instance of the pooled efforts of various communities in the EBC. Its final chapter examines the roots and development of monastic autonomy and the means by which the right relationship of the monasteries to the Congregation can be ensured. A healthy system of autonomy may have a special contribution to make in an age when, in reaction to many pressures towards centralization and a uniform technological culture, people are becoming aware of the need to save the creative kernel in local traditions.

The basis of Benedictine autonomy

Benedictine monasticism has always been characterized by a spirit of pluralism. Throughout its history there has been a diversity of traditions, but they have generally been marked by a unity of spirit and by a basic fidelity to the Rule. St Benedict undoubtedly foresaw that his Rule would be adopted in monasteries other than his own; but for centuries

357

there was no organizational bond between the various monasteries that observed it. St Benedict certainly did not found an 'order' as St Francis and St Dominic founded 'orders'. He simply wrote a rule which came to be observed all over Europe because of its intrinsic excellence and flexibility.[1]

St Benedict's Rule envisages no confederation of monks beyond the individual monastery. The Rule itself, rather than a specific legislator or governmental structure, was to be the fundamental norm of monastic life. For the purpose of maintaining religious discipline, however, monasteries have from time to time gathered into congregations with common constitutions and an abbot president who has limited powers of visitation and legislation. In some congregations the bond between the various houses is relatively close; in other cases it is loose. But in no case is there any juridical structure bringing the various congregations together into an order in the strict sense, and there is no superior general with jurisdiction over all the monks in the world.[2]

If one compares the observances and even the orientations of the various Benedictine congregations today, considerable differences are apparent. What is true of the whole confederation is also verified in the individual monasteries of the English Benedictine Congregation. The Rule itself suggests the main reasons which justify the diversity of its particular application: diversity of God's gifts,[3] of temperaments,[4] of climate,[5] and of monastic works,[6] and above all the diversity in the particular charisms of the abbot which enable him to interpret and apply the Rule.[7] Differences of local culture, and more especially the pressures of historical developments in various countries, have also powerfully contributed to the differentiation of monasticism. This diversity of form was ratified by the Second Vatican Council[8] and was reaffirmed by Pope Paul VI in his discourse to the Congress of Abbots on 30 September 1966.[9]

a) The role of the abbot

It is above all the autonomy of each monastery which distinguishes the Benedictine confederation from the various orders in the Church today. This autonomy is essential to Benedictine life and is the consequence of a number of constitutive elements in the Rule. In the first place, autonomy is founded on the special role of the abbot in the community.[10] The abbot is meant to have a much more enduring relationship with his monks, and his responsibilities towards them are much more extensive, than is usual for the superior in other religious communities. The abbot is the keystone of St Benedict's monastery. As Christ's special representative in the community he is a source of unity for his monks. He is responsible not only for the temporalities of the monastery but above all for the spiritual formation of his monks. Whereas the relationship of many major superiors to their religious is often confined to official visitations and the assignment of duties, the Rule gives every indication that the abbot is to be an influence operating on the lives of his monks throughout the ordinary day's routine. Because of the nature of his office and the extent of his jurisdiction, canon law recognizes the abbot as the canonical ordinary for all his monks.[11]

b) The vow of obedience

Another basis for monastic autonomy is the vow of obedience.[12] Because of the unique role of the abbot in the monastery, the Benedictine vow of obedience is qualitatively different from that taken by other religious. In most religious communities superiors are frequently changed, so that an individual's relationship with a particular superior usually does not extend over a long period of time. In such a case obedience tends to be determined by official appointments and extensive juridical constitutions. For a Benedictine, obedience is meant to be personal. The abbot is in a real sense the servant of his monks. He is to lead them to God, not in his own way or at his own pace but in the way God wishes for each. The Rule states clearly that the strengths and weaknesses of each monk should be taken into account.[13] Hence Benedictine obedience is a personal response made by each monk to the person of a particular abbot. The monk's relationship to the abbot is one of a responsible son towards his father. The abbot's office has no meaning apart from his monks; he is abbot only of and for the sake of a particular community of monks. His relationship to his monks is further qualified by the fact that they have freely elected him to be their abbot. Hence the abbot's authority and the monk's vow of obedience are complementary and correlative; both exist for the religious development of the individual monks and the community as a whole.[14]

c) The co-responsibility of all monks

Although the monastery is not a religious democracy, the Rule provides for extensive co-operation between the abbot and his monks.[15]

Whenever anything of importance is to be decided the abbot is to seek counsel from all his monks, whose advice has serious value because of their lifelong commitment to that particular community. Similarly when lesser matters are in question, the council is to be consulted.[16] As in providing for the election of the abbot by the community, so also in the matter of giving counsel to the abbot, the Rule manifests a firm faith in human nature and also in each monastic community. Most legislators have devised a system of checks and balances to safeguard superiors from interference and subjects from the consequences of human weakness, but St Benedict preferred to legislate on broad lines which point to the ideal and leave it possible for the ideal to be realized.[17] In this way he challenged the monastic community to be responsible for its own development and destiny and precluded undue interference from outside the monastery.

d) Stability within a community

Another distinguishing quality of Benedictine obedience is that it is meant to extend not only to the abbot but also to the brethren.[18] The monks believe that in the context of a specific community God will reveal his word and his will. Since they vow stability in a particular community until death, they undertake a special loyalty to the community in a spirit of fraternal charity that is no abstract ideal but one which demands a daily acceptance and support of the brethren. Because of the close and enduring bond which prevails among the monks of a particular house, the monastery manifests a settled type of life that is not apparent in religious houses where the members are more mobile and transient.[19]

As a result of the central place of the abbot in the community, the distinctive quality of the vow of obedience, the co-responsibility which all the monks bear for the community, and the vow of lifelong stability, the monastery is characterized by a certain independence and self-sufficiency that are neither possible nor perhaps desirable in other religious communities today. Hence to be true to the Rule, Benedictine monasteries must enjoy a real autonomy which gives them their proper identity and is essential to the religious development of both the individual monks and the community as a whole in the spirit of St Benedict.

The historical background to monastic autonomy

It is not known precisely when the monks living under the Rule began to call themselves 'Benedictines', a name which tended to align them with the centralized orders such as the Cistercians and Franciscans. But before the thirteenth century Benedictines, apart from those in the Cluniac system and other special reforming movements, had no form of centralized government controlling the monasteries and imposing uniformity on them.[20] Each monastery was free to respond to the demands made upon it by its social, economic, and religious environment. Nevertheless this pluralism was kept from degenerating into mere heterogeneity by the common inspiration of the Rule, which not only established in essential matters an objective way of life but also provided criteria by which adaptations to the environment could be assessed. Above all it was the common spirituality inspired by the Rule which united the various monasteries.

However, the dangers of isolation have always been real. Because there was no authority structure to ensure correction and support among individual monasteries, decadence tended to be widespread. Few abbeys escaped moral decline. Moreover, failure to gain new members had disastrous effects on the liturgy, intellectual life, and external influence of the communities.[21] Those seeking to effect a reform had recourse especially to a Cistercian institution, the general chapter.[22] Innocent III (1198–1216) prescribed general chapters, restored free abbatial elections. and insisted on poverty and control of finances.[23] The Fourth Lateran Council in 1215 prescribed that monastic communities should be grouped into chapters with a system of regular visitations.[24] The first Benedictines to implement the Lateran decrees were the English monks, so that the present English Congregation ranks as the oldest Benedictine congregation.[25] Honorius III (1216–27) required annual chapters,[26] and Gregory IX (1227–41) extended the powers of visitators.[27] Other councils, papal legates, and local bishops also sought to raise the moral tone of the monasteries.[28] These vigorous attempts at renewal were not entirely successful because they did not always show due consideration for the autonomy of the individual houses.

In 1336 Benedict XII undertook a further monastic reform by gathering all the monasteries into thirty-two provinces. He prescribed a triennial chapter and visitation in each, and demanded a raising of the intellectual level of the communities.[29] This legislation remained for two centuries, but there was no effective organ of enforcement.[30]

The fifteenth century saw the rise of a new institution, the congregation, which more efficaciously guaranteed a regular observance of monastic discipline and warded off the threats of external interference represented by the commendatory system. Luigi Barbo (d. 1443), who became abbot of St Justina at Padua in 1408, restored regular discipline in his community. Recruits were so numerous that he founded new monasteries and reformed existing ones, all of which were joined in a congregation in 1419. The local superiors were appointed for a limited term, and authority was concentrated in the annual general chapter. All monks made their profession for the congregation, and the chapter could move them from one monastery to another. All the monasteries of Italy and Sicily eventually joined this congregation which became known as the Cassinese Congregation after the accession of Monte Cassino in 1504.[31] The reform movement adopted in this congregation was implemented in the monasteries of other countries as well.[32]

However, with the spread of Protestantism in the sixteenth century many of the Benedictine monasteries were destroyed. The English monastic communities were dissolved by Henry VIII and their property was confiscated. During the years of persecution that followed, Englishmen who wished to be monks had to make their profession in communities on the Continent. English monks lived in Continental monasteries or in various residences such as those at Douai and Dieulouard. Some English monks joined the Valladolid and Cassinese Congregations, but in 1619 Paul V united all of them in an English Congregation,[33] which from 1623 onwards also included nuns.

The Council of Trent (1545–63) legislated for the restoration and maintenance of monastic discipline, defined the conditions for admission and profession, the choosing of superiors, and the administration of property. It ordered all monasteries to unite in congregations with triennial chapters and visitations.[34] Hence the congregational system became ecclesiastical law, enforced by the Holy See and exempt from local episcopal authority.[35]

By the year 1700, Benedictine monasticism was again in a generally healthy state, thanks to the congregational system. The eighteenth century, however, witnessed another decline and the extinction of various monasteries under the attack of the Enlightenment, the French Revolution, and secularization.[36] Despite the Prussian *Kulturkampf* and the further suppression of monasteries in Portugal, Spain, Italy, and

Switzerland, the nineteenth century was an age of vigorous renewal and expansion. This monastic revival was expressed in the form of highly centralized groupings such as the Solesmes Congregation and the Congregation of the Primitive Observance.[37] In England, however, this revival aspired towards the establishment of autonomous abbeys and the subjection of the missions into the individual houses, so that the provincial system in the English Congregation was brought to an end.[38]

In 1888 Pope Leo XIII revived the College of Saint Anselm in Rome, originally founded in 1687 by the Cassinese Congregation. He stipulated that the college should not belong to any one congregation but that it should serve as an international college for monks of all congregations.[39] In 1893 he created the office of abbot primate to head the confederated Benedictine congregations.[40] On 21 March 1952, Pius XII approved the *Lex Propria* governing the Confederation.[41] Substantial changes were made in the government of the Confederation and of the College of Saint Anselm at the Congress of Abbots in 1967.[42] Although many Benedictines orginally resisted the establishment of the office of abbot primate,[43] experience has shown that his moral authority has been a source of encouragement to the individual congregations and monasteries, and the office itself has been an effective agency through which the values of monasticism have been represented before the Holy See. Since the abbot primate's authority is moral rather than disciplinary, his office in no way interferes with the individual communities and their relations with the Holy See.[44]

As history has shown, there are definite limits to the diversity of observances which may be tolerated within the unity of Benedictine monasticism. These limits are difficult to define exactly; although continuing renewal is implied by the dynamic quality of the vow of Conversion, it is the responsibility of each monastery and each congregation to discern the exact forms which its own renewal should take. Hence it is in accord with the character of Benedictine life that the primary responsibility for implementing conciliar directives for the renewal of religious life, where these are applicable to monasticism, should rest with each community under its abbot.[45]

Practical considerations

a) The relationship between the monasteries and the congregation

Although each monastery of our Congregation must be regarded as an autonomous community which should be left free to develop its own life according to the diversity of the gifts of God, the separate traditions that rightly belong to it, and the work which it has legitimately undertaken, nevertheless our monasteries do comprise a single Congregation. This is bound by constitutions based on a particular interpretation of the Rule and is informed by a wisdom and tradition which are the endowment derived from its long history. The same history has clearly demonstrated that true autonomy requires a wider framework and constitutional structures for its existence and preservation.

The proper balance between the monasteries and the Congregation is safeguarded by a right application of the principle of subsidiarity,[46] which will avoid over-centralization of government and a too rigid uniformity of practice, yet will afford to the monasteries the necessary means of co-operation and mutual help in all matters concerning their spiritual and temporal welfare and especially in the preservation of regular monastic discipline. The aim of our Congregation is to leave each monastery its own jurisdiction and administration, while enabling all to co-operate in the promotion of monastic life.

Throughout the history of the Congregation co-operation has been important as a means of strength and unity and as an exercise of the collective responsibility of the whole Congregation for each of the monasteries. This co-operation should be exercised not only in General Chapter but at every level, especially through meetings of those concerned with liturgy, studies, the constitutions, and other monastic matters, and through the contacts between the juniors during their studies in theology and at the universities. In this way the resources of the Congregation in persons and projects, in ideas and aspirations, will be developed and deployed to the best advantage of all the monks and nuns and also of the Church and the world. The English Benedictine Congregation is fortunate in that it comprises both monks and nuns, so that the communities of men and those of women can derive great spiritual and practical benefit from contact and collaboration with each other.

One of the goals of the Congregation is to foster the right kind of autonomy within our monasteries. True autonomy implies an openness to one another on the part of the communities. It implies that each community in fulfilling its responsibility to keep abreast of current developments in the biblical, liturgical, doctrinal, pastoral, ecumenical, and social fields is nevertheless free to adopt them in accordance with its own tradition.[47] But autonomy must be distinguished from inbreeding, isolationism, complacency, and competitiveness, all of which may develop in a community if it does not see its identity and mission in terms of the larger community of the Church and the world. Congregational structures exist, then, not only to support the various communities but also to challenge them to realize the potential of the individual monks and monasteries. Throughout its history monasticism has been plagued by mediocrity. Communities are tempted, especially when they are well-endowed economically, to develop a spirit of smugness, closed-mindedness, and even arrogance. Since our horizons tend to shrink, congregational structures can be helpful in opening up communities not only to the needs of others but also to the spiritual, intellectual, and cultural resources of others. Similarly, the Congregation itself should be open to the exchange of ideas and assistance with monks and houses of other congregations and with other monastic and religious orders.

b) The president and officials of the congregation

In the constitutions of any Benedictine congregation it is crucial that the nature of the president's office and the position and powers that he holds be so defined as not to interfere with the autonomy of the monasteries or the jurisdiction of the abbots. On this point the Code of Canon Law has clearly stated that 'the superior of a monastic congregation does not have all the power and jurisdiction which the common law gives to major superiors; but this power and jurisdiction are to be gathered from the constitutions of the congregation and the particular decrees of the Holy See'.[48] Although the constitutions of the various Benedictine congregations safeguard the essential independence of the individual abbeys and the authority of the abbots, nevertheless the degree of authority given to the president varies considerably from one congregation to another.[49]

In the English Benedictine Congregation the president's powers are quite limited because the autonomy of each monastery is a value held in very high esteem within the Congregation. Since the qualities to be looked for in the abbot president are monastic experience, wisdom, good judgement, and a sensitivity to the distinct traditions of each monastery and the unique characteristics of its abbot and monks, there would seem to be no reason why the president must be a ruling abbot. It would be possible to have a president who has been a ruling superior but is now freed from the responsibilities of ruling a community of his own so that he has more time to be at the service of the Congregation and each of the communities.

At the regular General Chapter the president appoints an assistant from among the ruling abbots, and the Chapter elects a second assistant. Together they constitute the president's council and perform jointly with him certain acts assigned by the Code of Canon Law to the central governing body of other religious orders. Within the Congregation there are also certain officials who are elected by the General Chapter because of their competence in areas which touch on the life of the whole Congregation. They serve as advisers to the president and his council and also to the individual abbots. Through their expertise and service they are meant to foster the development of the Congregation and the various communities, but like the president and his council they may not infringe the autonomy of the communities or the jurisdiction of the abbots.

c) Visitations

The practical working of St Benedict's concept of the government of the monastery depends to a great extent on the community and the personality of the abbot. On account of human weakness certain safeguards have been devised to secure the most satisfactory working of the system. Of these the earliest and most important is the visitation.

The first, and for many centuries the only, visitator was the bishop of the local diocese. He was the natural visitator since the monasteries were diocesan institutions without any juridical bond with other monasteries.[50] Furthermore, the foundation for episcopal visitation is within the Rule itself. In Chapter 64 St Benedict stipulates that in the event of an unworthy or incompetent abbot being elected by the monks, it is the duty of the bishop to quash the election and appoint a worthy abbot. Similarly, in Chapter 62, the Rule maintains that the bishop of the diocese should be asked to intervene in the case of a priest who proves refractory. It would be a natural extension of such episcopal interventions for him to step in if disorder or abuses should develop in the monastery.

The position of the bishop as canonical visitator of the monasteries in his diocese was recognized at a very early date. The Council of Chalcedon placed the monks under the control of the bishops, as did many other councils of the West.[51] Naturally, difficulties arose on the part of both monks and bishops. As pope, St Gregory the Great often mediated in such disputes.[52] There was a natural tendency on the part of the monks to secure independence of episcopal control. St Columbanus contested the bishops' rights,[53] and the Venerable Bede wrote with satisfaction of a privilege which St Benet Biscop had obtained from Pope Agatho whereby his monastery at Wearmouth was 'made safe and free from every kind of external interference for ever'.[54]

It was a natural development that the bishop's visitation should not be limited to occasions of crisis in the community calling for drastic measures, but should take place periodically to make sure that things were going well. When the Fourth Lateran Council made provision for triennial visitations of Benedictine monasteries by Benedictine visitators acting in the name of the Holy See, monasteries became subject to a double system of visitation.[55] The practice continued in the English Congregation until the dissolution. When the congregational system of visitations developed on the Continent and was approved by the Council of Trent, it brought about the general exemption of Benedictine houses and a system of visitation whereby the president of the congregation or visitators appointed by the General Chapter are the ordinary visitators.[56]

In our Congregation the abbot president must carry out a visitation of each monastery once every four years. His powers and responsibilities are considerable while the visitation is in progress, since he must form an overall judgement about the temporal and spiritual welfare of the monastery. In no sense may he interfere with the autonomy of a community; but coming from outside he may be aware of strengths and weaknesses in monastic observance which are unnoticed by the community. As history has often shown, the visitator can in some cases be an important agent in saving a community which is about to collapse.

It must be admitted, however, that the autonomous system, while benefiting the growth and life of a flourishing community, limits the possibility of assisting a declining community. Although the means of renewal can be made available to communities, in the last analysis it is the task of the community itself to implement them, a task which cannot be imposed from without.

d) Constitutions

The constitutions of a congregation provide both a limitation on the discretionary power of the abbot and a safeguard for the maintenance of discipline in each monastery. The purpose of the constitutions is to make clear the distinction between the disciplinary and doctrinal elements of the Rule. They help to show in which cases the Rule is to be followed in its spirit rather than its letter, and in which cases the letter is to be regarded as the necessary guarantee of the spirit.

Such codes of ordinances date back to the *Capitulare Monasticum* enacted at the general congress of abbots of the Carolingian Empire held at Aachen in 817 under the influence of St Benedict of Aniane. A similar effort to bring about a uniform observance was the formulation of the *Regularis Concordia* issued about a century and a half later under the influence of St Dunstan and imposed on the English abbeys by royal authority. An aspect of the system of provincial chapters set up by the Fourth Lateran Council was that the regulations decided upon by the chapter had to be observed in all the monasteries of the province. In compliance with this decree a code of English statutes was issued for the monasteries in 1225. Finally, when the congregational system was established, each congregation had to draw up a set of constitutions or declarations which the abbots had to follow just as St Benedict tells them to follow the Rule itself.

In the monastic revival following the Council of Trent the constitutions of the new congregations reflected two schools of thought within Benedictine monasticism. The one school wanted a strict centrally controlled union under an abbot general, severely limiting the authority of the local abbots. It rejected local stability, so that stability was vowed not to the monastery but to the congregation, with the result that a monk could be transferred from house to house. The adherents of this school had the support of the Roman curia which sought a stricter supervision of the individual religious institutes in the Church and was progressively centralizing Church government in general. The other school defended the autonomy of the individual monastery and stability within a local community. The adherents of this view had the Rule and centuries of Benedictine history on their side.[57]

When the English Congregation was re-established in the seventeenth century its initial constitutions reflected the trend towards centralization. This orientation, however, was abandoned when the Congregation gave up the provincial system at the beginning of the twentieth century.

It was the fashion of constitutions drawn up in the seventeenth century to regulate the lives of the monks in great detail, deciding such things as the quantity and quality of food, the horarium, the type of clothes to be worn, and the furniture to be used. Recent editions of EBC constitutions have rightly respected the autonomy of each house in these matters. Experience has shown that it is desirable to set some broad limitations on the power of the abbot, but it must be admitted that the more general the nature of constitutions, the more in conformity they are with the mind of St Benedict. The Rule expressly gives the abbot the right to regulate the life of the monastery in matters of food, drink, horarium, and clothing; hence the constitutions should not derogate from the abbot's powers in this regard. Nor should the constitutions consist of moral exhortations, since the abbot is the primary teacher and spiritual leader in the monastery. In a real sense the constitutions should be based on the collective wisdom and experience of the congregation, but they should always recognize that the wisdom is expressed in a special way in the life of each monastery. Hence the constitutions should be primarily concerned with the structure and operation of each congregation and the application of general legislation emanating from the Holy See to the individual monasteries.

Ecclesiae Sanctae, the *Motu Proprio* implementing Vatican II's decree on the Adaptation and Renewal of Religious Life, dealt specifically with the revision of constitutions in accordance with the conciliar documents.[58] In the application of these directives it must be kept in mind that St Benedict's Rule is the basic spiritual and disciplinary document for monastic life; constitutions play a very secondary role in the life of our communities. However, the *Motu Proprio* specifically called for a clear statement of the evangelical and theological principles of the religious life of each institute and its relationship with the Church. In addition to this statement of the theology of religious life, it called for a statement of the juridical norms which define the character and purpose of the religious institute, and its means of attaining its goals. Finally, the apostolic letter directed that those norms which have no enduring value because of changing situations, or which correspond with mere local usages, should be excluded from the fundamental constitutions and set down in books of customs.

The application of these norms to our Congregation indicates that there is need for a statement of the theology of monastic life as understood in the EBC and also for a clear and concise set of juridical norms which flow from the theological statement and are consistent with its principles. These juridical norms should be applicable to the Congregation as a whole and to each of the monasteries, but they should not unnecessarily infringe the autonomy of each house and the jurisdiction of each abbot. Each monastery should be free to formulate its own customary as it sees fit.

e) Exemption

Because of the autonomy of a Benedictine monastery, and more specifically because of the nature of the abbatial role, the vow of obedience, and the cenobitic character of monastic life, the community is exempt from the ordinary jurisdiction of the local bishop in matters, religious or secular, relating to its internal development. The law of the Church concerning the exemption of religious has been quite stable for the last four hundred years. This indicates that it has generally not been a source of discontent or disagreement.

Prior to the Council of Trent, the history of exemption fell into two periods. Until the twelfth century, exemption was a general condition for the establishment and development of the monasteries. From the twelfth century until Trent it was a source of widespread contention because the privileges granted to monks were so extensive that they seriously curtailed the authority of the local bishops. To alleviate this tension the Council of Trent inaugurated a reform which, while not reducing the privileges of the regulars concerning the inner life of their communities, nevertheless restored the authority of the bishops in matters of pastoral ministry and public ecclesiastical order.[59] Following the Tridentine tradition, the legislation in the Code of Canon Law concerning exemption may be summarized under two headings:

(1) In so far as religious are involved in pastoral ministry, they are subject to the local bishop.

(2) In matters of religious life, they are subject immediately to the Holy See.[60]

Unfortunately, religious communities and diocesan authorities have sometimes been looked upon as distinct powers which must be kept in balance by a clearly delineated list of rights and responsibilities. Too often there is a failure to understand that the religious life is a charism of the Spirit which always works within and under the authority of the Church. Religious institutes are not meant to be power structures distinct from the governmental structures of the Church nor are they meant to be readily available sources of manpower at the disposition of diocesan authorities.[61] Consequently, monks should not strive to have more 'exemptions' than are necessary to safeguard their free monastic development and to foster their proper activities; likewise, diocesan authorities should respect the unique role of monks in the Church, a role which is distinct from the apostolic ministry which they may perform.

Exemption exists to foster peace and good order in the activities of an institute and in the lives of its members. This is explicitly stated in Vatican II's decree on the Pastoral Office of Bishops:

> The privilege of exemption, by which religious are called to the service of the Supreme Pontiff or other ecclesiastical authority and are withdrawn from the jurisdiction of bishops, applies chiefly to the internal order of their communities, so that in them all things may be more aptly co-ordinated and the growth and depth of religious life better served.[62]

From what has been said about the autonomy of a monastic community it follows that the notion of exemption as described in the conciliar decree is really essential to the life of a Benedictine abbey. Although the Code of Canon Law and the conciliar decree speak of exemption as a privilege, it is in fact not so much a privilege as a condition basic to the nature and well-being of monastic life. Consequently it is applicable to the whole community, including the novices. Canonical commentators are in general agreement that it is also applicable by the provisions of common law to postulants, oblates, and those who regularly live with the monastic community. This would include the school boys and staff whom we have regularly considered to be part of the monastic family.[63]

One of the areas of monastic life where exemption is especially necessary today is the monastic liturgy. A monastic community celebrates the liturgy not simply because it is imposed by ecclesiastical law but above all because the community is by its nature and by its Rule a praying community. As such, monastic communities have traditionally developed their own rites and liturgical customs according to their proper gifts and needs. A sound esteem for this tradition should be maintained. The formulation and the application of much liturgical law have recently been placed in the hands of competent territorial authorities, but it cannot be expected that the local bishops, engaged as they are almost exclusively in pastoral ministry, will readily understand the proper needs of a monastic community or provide for such needs through legislation. The Consilium for the Implementation of the

Constitution on the Sacred Liturgy ruled that there should be a competent authority with due jurisdiction within the monastic institute to provide for these needs:

> The aim of the Consilium is the revision, restoration and reform of the Roman liturgy. It is concerned directly with the Roman Rite. With other rites, including the Cistercian, it concerns itself only indirectly, in so far as the principle and norms actuated in the revision of the Roman Rite can be a guide for other rites. But a true and proper reform must be prepared and executed only by those immediately concerned, that is, by the monastic institutes, through those organs which the Major Superiors deem opportune.[64]

The Constitution on the Sacred Liturgy explicitly extended many faculties to all ordinaries, including monastic superiors.[65] Furthermore the decree on the Bishops' Pastoral Office and the Apostolic Letter implementing that decree made explicit provisions for particular liturgical customs and rites:

> The proper rite which religious legitimately use for their community alone, their manner of reciting the divine office in choir and the religious observances pertaining to the special end of their institute are to remain intact.[66]

If the monastic community is responsible for a parish or if the monks engage in pastoral activity outside the monastery, exemption is not applicable to this pastoral work. If the liturgy is celebrated primarily for the laity other than the community, the monks are bound to observe in their churches and also in their public and semi-public oratories those laws and decrees that are issued by the local ordinary according to the general law of the Church concerning the public exercise of worship.[67] If the liturgy celebrated in such churches and oratories is primarily for the monastic community, exemption applies.

The Code of Canon Law has explicitly granted jurisdiction to the abbot in areas touching the internal life of his community.[68] Such legislation clearly indicates that whenever the good of the monastic community or of an individual monk is at stake, the Church grants the monastic superior the authority and the jurisdiction he needs. As the spiritual leader and teacher of his monks, the abbot is above all responsible for the monastic liturgy and the proclamation of the word of God in its various forms. In this sense he shares in the authoritative teaching office of the Church. As a major superior confirmed in office by the Holy See, the abbot must have that degree of exemption from other ecclesiastical superiors which is necessary to carry out his duties effectively. Hence exemption not only serves the good of the monastic community, but in facilitating the development of the monastery it also serves the good of the whole Church.

Conclusion

The positive influence which Benedictines have had on the Church and the world throughout the centuries has not been that of a centralized body, but that of scattered communities attempting to live a deep spiritual life, sensitive to the needs of the environment in which they have found themselves, but nevertheless regulating their response to that environment by the discipline, spirituality, and temperament created by the Rule. This has all been possible because of the autonomy of each monastery, a characteristic which is essential to Benedictines and one which must be preserved at the present time when there are strong pressures towards centralization.

NOTES

▶▼◀

SELECT BIBLIOGRAPHY

▶▼◀

INDEX

Notes

References to the psalms give the Hebrew numbering first, followed by the Vulgate numbering in brackets. It should be noted that *The Psalms, A New Translation*, the version quoted throughout, uses the Vulgate numbering. Details of the RB, Documents of Vatican II, and biblical versions used appear in the List of Abbreviations on pp. xix–xx. Where no translation is cited, the authors have given their own version.

INTRODUCTION

1. A review of some of those proposed down to 1961 is given by B. Calati: 'La questione monastica nella letteratura di carattere teorico degli ultimi trent'anni', in C. Vagaggini, *Problemi e orientamenti di spiritualità monastica, biblica e liturgica* (Rome, Edizioni Paoline, 1961), pp. 339–497; cf. also M. Sheridan, 'Towards a Contemporary Self-Definition of Monasticism', in *American Benedictine Review*, vol. xix, 4 (December 1968), pp. 452–82.

2. Matt. 19.12.

3. If comparisons are made between the calling of the monk and that of the Christian layman it is usually better to speak in terms of different grace or different means than to use such comparatives as 'better' or 'higher'. But for a discussion of the senses in which the evangelical counsels can be called a 'better way' without derogation to the vocation of all Christians to holiness and perfect charity, see K. Rahner, 'The Status of Christians under the Evangelical Counsels and in the World', in *Theological Investigations*, vol. 8 (Darton, Longman & Todd 1971), pp. 159–63. He sums up as follows: 'The statement "the evangelical counsels are the 'better way'"' . . . is not an assertion that those who practise them have reached a higher stage of perfection. For the sole measure of the degree of perfection which the individual achieves is in all cases the depths of his love for God and his neighbour. This statement refers rather to the fact that the counsels are "means" (an objectivation and a making manifest) of faith and love (a) *relatively speaking* in their reference to the individual called to follow them. Here a contrast is established between his situation under the counsels and the situation which would be his if *he as an individual* were to refuse them; (b) *absolutely speaking* to the extent that they alone, considered as a renunciation and a practising of the passion of Christ himself, can be said to have the character of an objectivation and manifestation of faith and love (not only as preached but as assumed and lived). Here there is a contrast between the way of life prescribed by the counsels and the other

377

"material" for a Christianity that is lived to the full, which is capable of being integrated into this fulness of Christian life because, as having a positive existence in this world, it is the material in which the Christian can express his affirmation to the world. But even when it does this it cannot make manifest the "transcendence" of grace and faith' (op. cit., p. 163).

4. Cf. Thomas Merton, *The Asian Journal of Thomas Merton* (New Directions Book 1973), Appendix iii, pp. 305 ff, to which this Introduction is indebted.

5. This was the case not only where such a perspective might inevitably be expected to have priority, as in the Constitution *Lumen Gentium* which devotes an entire chapter to religious, but also – and this is especially evident when its final version is compared with the original draft – in the decree *Perfectae Caritatis* which one might have expected to treat of religious in their own right.

6. 'The counsels are a divine gift which the Church has received from her Lord and which she ever preserves with the help of his grace' (*LG* ed. Abbott-Gallagher 43).

7. *SC* 2; 6; 7; 83–5.

8. RB Prol. 124–7: '*Processu* vero conversationis et fidei . . . *curritur* via mandatorum Dei'; cf. RB 73, where monastic life is described as a progress from 'initium conversationis' to 'perfectionem conversationis'.

9. It should be admitted that some writers maintain that extra-Christian 'monasticism' is improperly so called, and that only western minds put it into the same category as Christian monasticism; e.g. A. de Vogüé in *Downside Review*, vol. 92, no. 307, p. 117, n. 38: '"Monk", "monachism", "monastic" are in fact Christian words. To talk of "Buddhist monks" or of "Monks of Qumran" is to recognize in these Buddhists and in these Jews a certain similarity to those who are called monks in the Christian world. The point of reference is Christian monasticism.'

10. The foundation of the Kurisumala Ashram in Kerala, South India, under Dom Bede Griffiths is the best-known example.

11. T. Merton, op. cit., p. 317.

12. *PC* 2. These correspond to Newman's two basic conditions for the faithful development of Christian doctrine: (1) it will be truly faithful '. . . if it retains one and the same type, the same principles, the same organization; if its beginnings anticipate its subsequent phases and its later phenomena protect and subserve its earlier'; and (2) it will be truly a development 'if it has a power of assimilation and revival, and a vigorous action from first to last' (*Essay on the Development of Christian Doctrine*, ch. 5).

13. GS passim.

14. Pascal, *Pensées*, vii. 553.

THE MYSTERY OF THE CHURCH

1. 1 John 4.16.
2. RSV Col. 1.26.

3. Cf. Eph. 2.4–5; 1 John 3.1.

4. John 11.52.

5. Phil. 2.6–9.

6. Cf. Rom. 4.24; 8.11; 10.9; 1 Cor. 6.14; 2 Cor. 4.14; 13.4; Gal. 1.1; Eph. 1.20.

7. Rom. 5.5; 8.14–16.

8. Eph. 1.14.

9. Eph. 1.6, 12, 14.

10. John 17.1–5.

11. Heb. 9.11–24.

12. *LG* (ed. Abbott-Gallagher) 1.

13. Cf. Karl Rahner, *The Christian of the Future* (New York, Herder & Herder, 1967), p. 83; M. Sheridan, 'Towards a Contemporary Self-Definition of Monasticism', in *American Benedictine Review*, vol. xix, 4 (December 1968), pp. 473 ff.

14. M.-J. le Guillou, 'The Theology of the Church', in *Sacramentum Mundi*, vol. 1 (Burns & Oates 1968), p. 319.

15. *LG* 3; 4; 48.

16. 1 John 5.6–8.

17. 1 Cor. 15.45.

18. John 19.30.

19. John 20.21–3.

20. Acts 2.

21. 2 Cor. 5.14.

22. Eph. 4.13.

23. 1 Cor. 12.4 ff; Eph. 4.4–16.

24. Cf. Rom. 12.5.

25. 1 Cor. 3.16 ff; 6.19; Eph. 2.21 ff; John 2.21; cf. Rev. 21–2.

26. Rom. 6.

27. 1 Cor. 6.15–20.

28. 1 Cor. 10.16 ff.

29. Cf. 1 Cor. 11.26.

30. *LG* 8.

31. Rom. 8.1–4; Gal. 4.6.

32. John 7.39. John V. Taylor in *The Go-Between God*, SCM Press 1972, refers to the suggestion of R. P. C. Hanson that this verse might better be rendered 'it was not yet Spirit', as we might say, 'it was not yet spring'. Bishop Taylor comments: 'That is exactly how it must have appeared to anyone looking back from the end of that prodigious first century. There had never been anything like it before, and it had all stemmed from Jesus' (op. cit., p. 85).

33. Cf. Eph. 1.13.

34. Cf. 1 John 2.20, 27; 3.24; 4.13.
35. Rom. 8.23, William Barclay's translation.
36. Cf. Col. 1.15–20; 2.9 ff.
37. Eph. 4.15 ff.
38. Eph. 5.25–32.
39. *LG* 9; cf. Exod. 19.5; 23.22; Deut. 7.6; 14.2; 26.18.
40. Cf. Mark 2.9–11; Matt. 1.21; Luke 1.77; 7.49 f; 1 Tim. 1.15; Rom. 5.9; John 12.47; 1 Cor. 5.5.
41. 1 Cor. 11.25.
42. Rom. 8.14; Gal. 4.6.
43. 2 Cor. 3.6; Rom. 7.6; 1 Pet. 1.9 ff; cf. Ezek. 37.14–28.
44. Cf. 1 Cor. 1.26–9; 2 Cor. 12.9 ff.
45. *LG* 48; cf. Acts 3.21; Eph. 1.10; Col. 1.20; 2 Pet. 3.10–13.
46. *LG* 48.
47. *LG* 5.
48. Luke 22.30; cf. 1 Cor. 11.26.
49. Cf. Col. 1.20; Eph. 1.10; 1 Cor. 15.24.

THE MISSION AND RELATIONSHIP OF THE CHURCH TO THE WORLD

1. Mark 16.15.
2. John 17.22 f.
3. There is another authentically Christian sense of the phrase 'separation from the world' which is not relevant to the argument of the present passage but is considered in Chapter 7, 'Freedom and Availability for God'; namely, the renunciation, in response to a personal charism, of certain genuine human fulfilments such as marriage, in view of what for the individual concerned is the higher good of following Christ more closely. It need hardly be said that such renunciation implies an affirmation of the goodness and validity of these human fulfilments, and does not imply that other Christians who follow Christ through the experience of, e.g., marriage are 'denying a broader horizon than that of this life'.
4. For a fuller account of the ideas summarized here and throughout this chapter see J. B. Metz, *Theology of the World*, Burns & Oates/Herder & Herder 1969; J. Moltmann, *The Theology of Hope*, SCM Press 1967; and other works by these authors. The 'political theology' of which they are leading exponents seeks to avoid providing theological support for existing power-structures, and aims at supplying a critical corrective to any exclusive relegation of faith to the private sphere. It emphasizes the political dimension of faith by refusing to limit 'political' life to the formal relations between the individual and the state (e.g. the periodic casting of a vote), regarding everything embraced by the term 'society' as political. Thus the basic realities apprehended by faith, such as grace, redemption,

sin, and salvation, are seen to be operative within the full historical process. The Church is regarded as an institution of social criticism in the sense that it must work for the growth of an overall political order which is an 'order of freedom'.

THE RULE

1. Some scholars prefer a tripartite classification, analysing the contents of the Rule under the headings (*a*) spiritual, (*b*) essential-structural, (*c*) accidental-structural. This perspective is not incompatible with that adopted in the present chapter. But the difference between the two is this: the twofold scheme implicitly admits that there may be essential structural continuities between St Benedict's monasteries and our own, but does not commit itself to any *a priori* assertion as to what the continuities must be; the threefold scheme, in claiming that there is a category of essential-structural elements, lays itself open to the challenge of indicating what they are, and herein lies the difficulty. It is not easy to draw up a list of such elements that would command general agreement, or to see what should be the criterion for selecting them, for to take as a criterion St Benedict's degree of insistence on this or that particular point is to attribute to him something like omniscience; he lays heavy stress, for example, on the duty of saying the whole psalter once a week, yet many monasteries today have departed from this practice, and certainly without forfeiting their Benedictine identity. Something like the following might seem to be a fairly non-controversial statement of essentially structural elements: stable, celibate, community life under an abbot, in which the spirit inculcated by St Benedict can find practical expression in obedience, prayer, work, mutual service, and community of goods. But the vast untidy history of Benedictine monasticism provides instances not only of individual monks but of whole communities and even congregations functioning and flourishing for long periods without exhibiting certain features which might *a priori* have been deemed structurally essential; the EBC, for instance, existed for generations without abbots. If too many items are declared structurally essential, then category (*c*) will consist only of a few relatively trivial matters, the contingent character of which is hardly disputed; and, further, the more closely delimited is the area of changeable elements by the formal classification we adopt, the less freedom and manoeuvring room is left for monks to face the future and the demands of real life with confidence in their vocation, intelligence and courage. When an individual monk who has a mature understanding of obedience and a good relationship with his superior is given a complex and delicate assignment in conditions far removed from those familiar to the superior, he knows that he is trusted to confront the situation and use his initiative and common sense. He does not have to be anxiously looking back over his shoulder all the time at a list of immutable instructions; rather, he honestly and faithfully interprets the mind of his superior, whose particular directives were intended as guidelines. The analogy is valid for our relationship with St Benedict. Pluralism is an accepted principle in Benedictine life; it can apply to differences between individuals within a

community, to differences between communitites within a congregation and to differences between congregations. At least between different congregations there is likely to be imperfect agreement about which items are to be regarded as structurally essential. Only the living charism of the monks and nuns called to Benedictine life, in touch with tradition and subject to the general guidance of the Church, can decide. The page of contents of this book is a list of the empirical realities which *de facto* characterize the life of the EBC; no claim is made that it must necessarily coincide at all points with a list of structurally essential elements acceptable to all Benedictines. For these reasons the twofold classification adopted in the text has been preferred, as making possible a more nuanced approach to the task of distinguishing essential embodiment of the ideal from historically conditioned expressions of it, while at the same time emphasizing the essentially incarnate nature of the ideal, whether we are thinking of St Benedict's world or of our own.

2. G. C. Colombas, *S. Benito, Su Vida y su Regla*, 2nd edn. (Madrid, Biblioteca de Autores Cristianos, 1968), p. 276; A. Veilleux, 'The Interpretation of a Monastic Rule', in *The Cistercian Spirit* (Shannon, Cistercian Studies, 1970), pp. 55 ff.

3. RB 1.3.

4. Cf. Cassian, '. . . cenobitarum qui scilicet in congregatione pariter consistentes unius senioris judicio gubernantur' (Conf. 18.4).

5. See A. de Vogüé, *La Communauté et l'Abbé dans la Règle de Saint Benoît* (Paris 1960), p. 60; idem, 'Sub Regula uel Abbate' in *Rule and Life*, ed. M. Basil Pennington (Spencer, Mass., Cistercian Publications, 1971), pp. 21–63; G. C. Colombas, op. cit., p. 91.

6. RB (McCann) 1.15–25.

7. De Vogüé, op. cit., p. 68.

8. RB (McCann) 3.16.

9. RB (McCann) 3.22; cf. 64.51; 65.41 (for the prior); 60.4, 20; 62.8 (for priests in the monastery).

10. RB 58.21.

11. RB 58.27.

12. RB 73.3, 22. In this he contrasts strikingly with the Rule of the Master which claims to be a complete code of righteousness.

13. LG 40; Matt. 5.48.

14. RB 73, title.

15. RB Prol. 1, 21, 52, 85, 92. 'Gospel' should be understood here in a very broad sense, to include the Old Testament too as understood in the light of the gospel.

16. RB Prol. 31; cf. 7.212; 49.15.

17. See J. Dupont, *Mariage et Divorce dans l'Évangile* (Paris, Desclée de Brouwer, 1959), pp. 202–7; S. Legasse, *L'Appel du Riche, Contribution à l'Étude des Fondements Scripturaires de l'État Religieux* (Paris, Beauchesne, 1966), pp. 113–83; A. M. Denis, *Ascèse et Vie Chrétienne* in *RSPT* xlvii

(1963), pp. 606–18; Q. Quesnell, 'Made themselves Eunuchs for the Kingdom of Heaven' in *CBQ* xxx (1968), pp. 335–58. But cf. J. Galot, 'Le fondement évangélique du voeu religieux de pauvreté', in *Gregorianum* 56/3 (1975), pp. 441–67.

18. RB 33.11; 34.1.
19. See Tillard, 'Le Fondement Évangélique de la Vie Religieuse', in *NRT* xci (1969), p. 939 for examples.
20. *PC* (ed. Abbott-Gallagher) 2a.
21. Prol. 31; 7.212. See many other examples in E. von Severus, 'La Structure Charismatique Fondementale de la Communauté', in *Collectanea Cisterciensia* xxxv (1973), pp. 203 ff.
22. 1 Cor. 12.7.
23. Rom. 12.6; 1 Cor. 12.4.
24. RB 40.1; 2.90 ff.
25. RB 1.5–13.
26. John 3.8; Acts 10.45; see also Rosemary Haughton, *The Transformation of Man* (Geoffrey Chapman 1967), pp. 227–37.
27. RB 58.3.
28. RB 18.63; 40.10; 55.1–4.
29. RB (McCann) 64.69.
30. H. B. Workman, *The Evolution of the Monastic Ideal* (Charles N. Kelly 1913), p. 148.
31. RB Prol. 22.
32. RB Prol. 54.
33. Athanasius, *Vita Antonii*, 2 (*PG* 26.842–4).
34. *Confessions* viii. 12, 15.
35. Celano I, c. ix.
36. Cf. Chapter 8, 'Vocation and Growth in Community', n. 44.
37. RB Prol. 10 ff., 46, 78, 108; 4.46; 5.46; 20.10.
38. John 14.15.
39. RB 5; 7.100, 209; 63.31.
40. RB 18.73; 40.14; 49.1.
41. RB 73.3–6. See the conclusions drawn by A. Borias from the proofs that there were successive layers in RB: 'Benoît envisage son oeuvre avec vitalité. Elle n'a rien de figé une fois pour toutes. Elle est toujours en création. . . . Pour faire face à une situation imprévue, pour résoudre de nouveaux problèmes, Benoît ajoute ici telles prescriptions, là il remanie son texte, toujours avec la plus grande liberté et le souci de correspondre à la réalité. L'attitude de Benoît par rapport à son oeuvre n'a rien de fixiste; elle est évolutive et s'efforce de s'adapter au réel' (A. Borias, 'Couches Rédactionelles dans la Règle Bénédictine', in *Revue Bénédictine* 85 (1975), pp. 38–56. The quotation is from p. 55.)
42. *AAS*, liv (1962), p. 792.

43. RB 28.4; 30.6; 56.1;. 59. In some respects St Benedict's Rule, when compared with those of his predecessors, seems even to have been a regression, e.g. in the reintroduction of a common dormitory after individual cells had become quite common (RB 22). His regulations for infant oblates were also a backward step, compared with the practice of Fathers and Councils of the previous century, cf. de Vogüé, *La Règle de Saint Benoît* (Paris, Éditions du Cerf, 1972), in collection *Sources Chrétiennes*, vol. v, p. 696; vol. vi, p. 1358. 'St Benedict's Rule is generally better than all the others, but not always', judges Dom Jean Leclercq in 'Autour de la Règle de Saint Benoît', in *Collectanea Cisterciensia* xxxvii (1975), p. 169.

44. But cf. Mark Sheridan, 'Towards a Contemporary Self-Definition of Monasticism', *American Benedictine Review* xx (1969), pp. 464 ff.

45. RB 73.10; cf. Prol. 22, 53, 85, 93.

46. *PC* 2; 6. See also C. Augrain, 'Les Sources Bibliques du Prologue de la Règle' in *Collectanea Cisterciensia* xxii (1960), pp. 3–10; S. Pawlovski, *Die biblischen Grundlagen der Regula S. Benedicti* (Vienna, Herder, 1965), pp. 7 ff; and especially A. de Vogüé, 'Per Ducatum Evangelii' in *Collectanea Cisterciensia* xxxv (1973), pp. 186–98, who shows that comparison with the Rule of the Master reveals a far greater number of gospel texts, omitted by St Benedict but determining a great deal of his legislation.

47. De Vogüé, *La Règle de Saint Benoît*, vol. iv, p. 94.

48. See P. Miquel, 'Trois Caractères de la Règle de S. Benoît', in *Collectanea Cisterciensia* xxxi (1969), pp. 265 ff.

49. On slavery, 2.49, 54; on the relations of old and young, 3.7; 63.13; on the value of manual labour, 48.1; repudiating class distinctions, 53.33.

50. *PC* 2b.

51. Dom de Vogüé sees 'the vow of *conversatio morum secundum regulam S. Benedicti* as a promise to live according to monastic tradition, using the Rule as a guide to understand that monastic tradition' ('Sub Regula uel Abbate', p. 64); ibid., pp. 55 ff., 'The image [of the monastic life of the first centuries] which it reflects is not complete, certainly, but it would be difficult to find a Latin document which would be as representative as is the Rule of Benedict. . . . Of considerable amplitude when one compares it to the majority of its sisters, it is relatively complete and organic, very rare qualities among the ancient rules.' He points out that a written rule had two different functions: it was a real rule for the author's contemporaries, but a monument of monastic tradition for later generations. We enter into communion with this monastic tradition through the Rule of St Benedict. To acknowledge this is not to depreciate it but to define its value for us. Compare also idem, *La Règle de Saint Benoît*, vol. i, p. 39: 'Le grand mérite de Benoît a été sans doute de réunir ces deux courants cénobitiques, l'un, plus individuel, qui lui venait d'Égypte à travers Cassien et le Maître, l'autre, plus communautaire, qui découlait d'Augustin.' Cf. also C. Peifer, 'According to the Rule', in *Monastic Studies* 5 (1968), p. 28.

52. *PC* 3.

53. For example, the etiquette which St Benedict requires to be observed in the reception of guests is today clearly obsolete. Nevertheless it demonstrates the spirit of monastic hospitality in a way which is still relevant, showing that guests are to be considered as members of the community, sharing its common life, spiritual reading, and prayer. For other examples see 'The Relevance of the Rule Today', by Ambrose Wathen in *American Benedictine Review* xix (1968), pp. 234–53.

54. *UR* (ed. Abbott-Gallagher) 11.

COMMUNITY: INTRODUCTION

1. Cf. Chapter 8, 'Vocation and Growth in Community', and Chapter 9, 'Stability'.
2. Cf. Chapter 3, 'The Mission and Relationship of the Church to the world', pp. 32–3.
3. Cf. Chapter 2, 'The Mystery of the Church'.
4. Prov. 8.22–36; Sir. 24.3–22; Wisd. 7.22–9.18.
5. Prov. 8.31; Wisd. 7.27.
6. Isa. 55.11; Ps. 147.15, 18; Wisd. 18.15.
7. John 1.1–18; Col. 1.15–20; cf. 1 Cor. 1.24.
8. RSV 1 John 1.3.
9. Cf. Acts 2.44 ff.; 4.32 ff.
10. Cf. Basil, *Reg. Fus.* vii; *Reg. Brev.* lxxxv; Augustine, *Letter* 211, 5.
11. Cf. Introduction, pp. 1–10.
12. John 17.22.
13. Gal. 4.6; cf. Rom. 8.15 ff.
14. Rom. 15.7; Eph. 4.2, 32; cf. Phil. 3.9.
15. RB 27; 28.
16. Ibid.
17. E.g. Mark 2.3 ff.
18. RB 72.7 ff. 'Good zeal' might sometimes be translated 'active concern'.
19. RB 13.24–31.
20. RB 4.89 ff.
21. RB 71.10–18.
22. Rom. 8.32.
23. Cf. Luke 15.22 ff., John 21.15–17.
24. Cf. B. J. F. Lonergan, *Method in Theology*, 2nd edn (Darton, Longman & Todd 1973), pp. 356 ff: 'Common meaning calls for a common field of experience and, when that is lacking, people get out of touch. It calls for common or complementary ways of understanding and, when they are lacking, people begin to misunderstand, to distrust, to suspect, to fear, to resort to violence. It calls for common judgements and, when they are lacking, people reside in different worlds. It calls for common values,

goals, policies and, when they are lacking, people operate at cross-purposes.'

25. Exod. 19.5 ff; 24.7 ff; cf. Deut. 5.1; 6.4, 20; Jer. 31.10.
26. Acts 2.41 ff.
27. RB Prol., and Chapters 5; 6; 73, etc.
28. RB 33.
29. RB 43.
30. RB 23; cf. 30.
31. Rom. 1.12; Eph. 4.11–16; 1 Cor. 12.7 ff; 14.12.
32. Cf. 2 Cor. 7.6 ff.
33. GS 25; 32; 39; 41; 42; 1 Thess. 4.9–12.
34. Acts 1.8.
35. Cf. John 14.17, 21–3; Phil. 4.7; Col. 3.12–17; 1 John 4.13, etc.
36. LG 48–51.

COMMUNICATION AND CO-RESPONSIBILITY

1. 1 Cor. 12.13.
2. 2 Cor. 13.14.
3. The principles mentioned here all have a basis in the New Testament. The balance between solidarity and pluralism received classic expression in St Paul's doctrine of the diversity-within-unity of the members of the Body: cf. 1 Cor. 12.4–31; Rom. 12.4–8; Eph. 4.1–16. A brief statement on authority within the Christian community is found in Heb. 13.17, but the concept of authority as service underlies many New Testament texts and will be considered expressly in the following chapter. Christ's example in delegating something of his own power and mission to Peter and the apostles (Matt. 16.18 ff; 18.18; John 21.15–17) and his continuous entrusting of his saving work to the Church down the ages, are a model for the principle of subsidiarity, which was a prominent theme also in the Encyclical *Mater et Magistra* by Pope John XXIII.
4. RB 67.
5. Cf. RB 50.
6. Cf. Chapter 14, 'Shared Prayer'.
7. For the history of this institution in cenobitism, see A. de Vogüé, *La Communauté et l'Abbé dans la Règle de Saint Benoît*, pp. 187–206.
8. RM 2. The matter is dealt with simply in an appendix to the Master's treatise on the abbot.
9. RB 3.
10. Sir. 32.24 (19). St Basil appeals to the same text, *Reg. Fus.* xlviii.
11. Deans, RB 21; senpectae, RB 27.5 ff; spiritual seniors, RB 46.11–14; novice master, RB 58.11 ff.
12. RB 64.25; Matt. 13.52; cf. Chapter 6, 'The Abbot', pp. 83, 92.
13. Rom. 1.12.

14. Dom Augustine Baker's famous advice is pertinent, although he is not speaking about this kind of disagreement precisely. It is given in his chapter 'How to Obtain Light in Doubtful Cases' (*Holy Wisdom*, Burns & Oates, Orchard Books, 1964, First Treatise, Second Section, ch. 7). In seeking to know the divine will by prayer, he says: 'Let not the person make the subject and business of his recollection to be the framing a direct prayer about the matter; neither let him in his prayer entertain any discoursing, debating thoughts in his imagination or understanding about it, as if he had an intention to account that to be God's will which by such discourse seemed most probable. (1) Because, by such proceedings, our prayers, which should be pure and internal in spirit, will be turned into a distracting meditation upon an external affair, and so the mind comes to be filled with sensible images, and passions perhaps will be raised. (2) Because by so doing we incur the danger of being seduced, by mistaking our own imagination or perhaps natural inclination for the divine light and motion, whereas such divine light is most effectually and securely, yea, and seldom otherwise, obtained than when the imagination is quiet and the soul in a profound recollection in spirit. (3) Because such discoursing in time of prayer is anything else but prayer, being little more than human consideration and examination of the matter, the which, if at all, ought to be dispatched before prayer' (loc. cit., pp. 85 ff). Similarly, 'in all cases of such like nature, the purpose and resolution is seldom to be made in the very time of our recollections; both because . . . the thinking on such matters is not the proper subject of prayer, but is very distractive; and likewise because the internal illustrations and motions of God's Spirit are better perceived after prayer, when the soul, having been recollected, doth reflect on them' (ibid., p. 92).

15. Christ spoke of the Kingdom of God on earth as a field where wheat and weeds are growing together. The servants are anxious to pull up the weeds at once, even before they are readily distinguishable, as human beings are often impatient to get rid of ambiguities. The Master of the harvest prefers to wait.

16. Eph. 4.12–16.

17. 1 John 3.14.

18. E.g. on saying the whole psalter, RB 18.70; on wine RB 40.13–15; on reading the Fathers, RB 73.14–18.

19. It is possible that St Benedict's 72nd Chapter, as also his view of authority, community, obedience, and service, was influenced by the thought of Pope St Clement's *Letter to the Corinthians*.

20. RB 34.9 ff; 40.23–5.

21. RB 1.34; cf. Qoh. 3.7.

22. The important question of friendships in monastic life is dealt with more fully in Chapter 9, 'Celibacy'.

THE ABBOT

1. RB 2. In thirty-eight out of the seventy-three chapters the abbot's

judgement or ruling is referred to by St Benedict; on at least ten occasions there are reminders of the burden placed on the abbot's conscience, and throughout the Rule the abbot is mentioned over 130 times.

2. Such words as *sapiens, sobrius, non turbulentus, timens Deum, sicut pater, sollicitus* are used at different times of the cellarer, novice master, guest master, and prior as well as of the abbot who is explicitly told to rule by the example of his deeds rather than by words (RB 2.30–45).

3. In this section much use has been made of the article by Dom Armand Veilleux in *Monastic Studies* 6 (1968): 'The Abbatial Office in Cenobitic Life'.

4. Cf. J. Gribomont, 'Saint Basile', in *Théologie de la vie monastique* (Études publiées sous la direction de la Faculté de Théologie S.J. de Lyon-Fourvière, Aubier 1961), p. 109.

5. St Pachomius's dying words to his brethren were: 'Behold, I am going to the Lord who created us all; since he has brought us all together so that we might do his will, you must decide together whom you wish to have as your father.'

6. Cf. G. Bardy, 'Didascale', in *Catholicisme*, iii, col. 749.

7. Cf. A. de Vogüé, 'Monachisme et Église dans la pensée de Cassien', in *Théologie de la vie monastique*, p. 238.

8. Cf. de Vogüé, ibid.

9. The Master repeatedly applies Luke 10.16, 'He who hears you hears me, he who despises you despises me', to the teaching authority of the monastic superior. Underlying his thought is the ancient conviction which inspired early cenobitism that the monastic community is *ecclesiola in Ecclesia*; but an inspiration which was in the traditions of Basil and Pachomius well balanced with an understanding of the monastic community's relationship to the local church and its bishop has been exaggerated in the Rule of the Master. The high claims made for the abbot are justified by the Master in terms of a fanciful exegesis of 1 Cor. 12.28; Eph. 4.11: in honour of the Trinity the Lord has established three grades of teachers in his Church, and these are to be understood as a chronological succession; there are first the prophets, then the apostles, then the teachers (cf. RM 1.82). In the time of God the Father (old covenant) the prophets taught God's people; in the time of the Son (new covenant) the apostles taught; but now is the time of the Holy Spirit, the time of waiting for the parousia, when the teachers have succeeded to this office and are Christ's representatives.

10. On the Master's development of this analogy, see B. Jaspert, '"Stellvertreter Christi" bei Aponius, einem unbekannten "Magister" und Benedikt von Nursia', in *Zeitschrift für Theologie und Kirche* 71 (1974) 3, pp. 291–324.

11. RM 73.

12. RB 2.3–7. The idea of Christ as *Father* is unfamiliar to modern spirituality but has some basis in revelation: Christ as Second Adam is father to the new race of men, and the litany of titles in Isa. 9.6, traditionally recognized as messianic, calls the child who is born to us 'Eternal Father'. The idea is

very prominent in the Rule of the Master; see A. de Vogüé, 'The Fatherhood of Christ', in *Monastic Studies* 5 (Easter 1968), pp. 45–57.

13. RB 49.24 ff; 67.15–19.

14. RB 3.22–4.

15. RB 41.10–13.

16. RB 2. Cf. C. Butler, *Benedictine Monachism* (Longmans, Green & Co. 1919), p. 190: 'The abbot's responsibility is as great as his power. Untrammelled power in the abbot's hands and undivided responsibility on his shoulders, this is St Benedict's idea. . . .'

17. RB 64.40–50.

18. RB 36; 37; 48.56–60.

19. RB 64.22 ff.

20. RB 68.

21. RB 64.24 ff.

22. RB 2; 55; 63; 64; etc.

23. RB 3.

24. The Rule of the Master (2.30 ff.) expects the abbot to blend the love of a mother with that of a father: 'He shall show to all his disciples and sons the qualities of both parents together, being a mother in his equal love for all, and a father to them by his reasonable tenderness (*mensurata pietate*).' St Benedict did not reproduce this passage, but its spirit is akin to his concept of the love the abbot should have for the brethren.

25. Cf. Chapter 9, 'Obedience', Introduction.

26. RM Ths. 17; RB Prol. 53 ff.

27. Cf. Jaspert, art. cit., pp. 320–22.

28. RB 64.

29. RB 27.5 ff.

30. RB 46.11 ff.

31. Cf. Chapter 2, 'The Mystery of the Church', pp. 21–4. On *koinonia*, cf. 1 John 1.3; Acts 4.32–5; 2.44–7.

32. Cf. 'Community': Introduction, pp. 58–9; Chapter 5, 'Communication and Co-responsibility', p. 70.

33. John 13.1–15; Mark 10.42–5.

34. Cf. Rom. 12.4–8; 1 Cor. 12.27 ff; Eph. 4.11–16; 1 Thess. 5.12 ff.

35. Cf. Chapter 9, 'Obedience'.

36. Cf. 1 John 4.20; 3.17.

37. RB 5.2 ff, 21–7; 71.1.

38. Since Vatican II the Pope's position as Vicar of Christ has been seen very much in the context of collegiality. Similarly the priest is Christ's representative in a way which, even though his priesthood is different in kind, is best understood in the context of the priesthood of the People of God. By analogy it can be said that since the Rule of St Benedict is penetrated with the idea that *everyone* – the brethren, the poor, the sick, the

guests – is a sacrament of Christ, the abbot's quality as Christ's representative must be understood in a way that does not obliterate but rather focuses all these other modes of Christ's presence. The abbot's charism is personal, but only makes sense within the community.

39. RB 5.38.
40. RB 64.3 ff.
41. The same considerations apply to the election of a conventual prior.
42. Rom. 8.29.
43. RB 3.22; cf 64.51.
44. RB 3.16–18; cf. Chapter 4, 'The Rule', p. 47.
45. Cf. Rembert Weakland, 'L'abbé dans une société démocratique', in *Collectanea Cisterciensia* xxxi (1969, 2), p. 106.
46. RB 3.
47. Luke 12.49.
48. 1 Cor. 12.10; 1 John 4.1.
49. RB 64.29–37.
50. RB 27.5–9; 28.13 ff.
51. Gal. 5.1; cf. Rom. 6.16–18.
52. Jas. 3.18.
53. RB 2.12 ff: 'There will be an examination of both matters at the dread judgement of God: of the abbot's teaching and of the disciples' obedience . . . and if every effort on the shepherd's part has been spent on a turbulent and disobedient flock, and all care lavished in the attempt to cure its vicious ways, the shepherd will be acquitted. . . .'

FREEDOM AND AVAILABILITY FOR GOD

1. Gen. 5.24; cf. 6.9 (Noah).
2. K. Rahner, *Nature and Grace* (Sheed & Ward 1963), p. 36.
3. Gen. 12.1.
4. Cf. Exod. 19.4–6; Deut. 14.2, etc.
5. Ps. 63 (62).1, in *The Psalms, A New Translation*, Collins, Fontana 1967.
6. Exod. 14.11; 16.2; Ps. 78 (77), etc.
7. Deut. 8.2–5.
8. E.g. Jer. 2.2 ff.
9. 1 Kings 19; cf. Hos. 2.16–25.
10. Jer. 16.2–9.
11. Mark 1.12.
12. Luke 6.12; Mark 6.46; Luke 9.28.
13. Mark 6.31–4.
14. RSV John 12.32.
15. Isa. 53.10–12; Mark 14.24.
16. Heb. 10.20.

17. Mark 3.27.
18. JB John 17.19.
19. John 14.26; 15.26; 16.13–15.
20. John 20.21.
21. JB 1 Pet. 2.9.
22. E.g. Acts 4.31.
23. Heb. 4.16.
24. 1 John 3.21.
25. Eph. 2.18.
26. 1 Cor. 7.20 ff. The preceding paragraph is indebted to a talk given at Spode House by Fr Robert Murray, S.J., on Freedom in the New Testament.
27. Gal. 1.17.
28. NEB Acts 13.2.
29. Cassian, *Conferences* 1.4, 5, 6, 8.
30. Cassian, ibid., 9.2, 6.
31. Cassian, ibid., 10.6.
32. Cf. *LG* 44.
33. RB 66; 67.
34. RB Prol. passim.
35. RB 4.99–101.
36. RB 58.
37. RB 4.66–9.
38. RB (Bolton) 49.4–10.
39. RB 52.6–9. The sources of St Benedict's doctrine of 'pure and intent' prayer are the two conferences attributed by Cassian to Abbot Isaac, see *Conferences* 9 and 10. This point is brought out clearly in C. Butler, *Benedictine Monachism* (Longmans, Green & Co. 1919), pp. 61 ff.
40. RB 7, first rung.
41. Cf. RB 33.
42. RSV 2 Cor. 3.17; cf. RB 7.202–13.
43. RB Prol. 129–31.
44. RB 4.22.
45. *LG*, Chapter 7.
46. RB 4.52 ff; 5.2–6; 49.18 ff.
47. RB 6.
48. Cf. RB 5.
49. RB 52.7 f.
50. Cf. Chapter 15, 'Work'.
51. T. Merton, Preface to J. Leclercq, *Alone With God*, Hodder & Stoughton 1962.
52. Cf. *Statement on Benedictine Life* by the Congress of Abbots, 1967, 33.d.

53. Cf. M. Buber, 'Dialogue', in *Between Man and Man* (Collins, Fontana 1961), p. 51: 'Collectivity is not a binding but a bundling together: individuals packed together, with only as much life from man to man as will inflame the marching step. . . . But community, growing community . . . is the being no longer side by side but *with* one another of a multitude of persons. And this multitude, though it also moves towards one goal, yet experiences everywhere a turning to, a dynamic feeling of, the others, a flowing from *I* to *Thou*. Community is where community happens. Collectivity is based on an organised atrophy of personal existence, community on its increase and confirmation in life lived towards one another. The modern zeal for collectivity is a flight from community's testing and consecration of the person. . . .'

54. Cf. *LG* 46.

55. RB Prol. 116 ff.

56. RB 53.30–32; cf. Chapter 17, 'Hospitality'.

57. On the concept of marginality, cf. Chapter 9, 'Celibacy', pp. 176–8.

58. Cf. M. Sheridan, 'Flight from or Challenge to the World?', in *American Benedictine Review* XXI.3 (Sept. 1970).

59. Cf. Amos 8.11; Deut. 8.3.

60. RSV Rom. 12.2.

61. *DV* 8. Quoted from Harrington and Walsh, *Vatican II on Revelation*. Dublin, Gill, 1967.

62. JB Heb. 11.27.

VOCATION AND GROWTH IN COMMUNITY

1. Exod. 3; Isa. 6.
2. RSV Jgs 6.11–14.
3. Ezek. 1–2.
4. Hos. 1–3.
5. RSV Gen. 12.1.
6. Amos 7.14 f.
7. Mark 1.16–19; 2.14.
8. Isa. 6.5.
9. JB Isa. 6.8.
10. Jer. 1.
11. RSV Jonah 1.3, 14–16; 3.1–2.
12. Isa. 40.3–8; 55.10 ff. The literary form of the Old Testament vocation stories has been analysed by N. Habel, 'The Form and Significance of the Call Narratives' in *ZAW* 77 (1965), pp. 297–323; cf. G. Meagher, 'The Prophetic Call Narrative', in *Irish Theological Quarterly* XXXIX, 2 (1972), pp. 164–77. Habel distinguishes six characteristic elements: (1) the divine confrontation; (2) the introductory word; (3) the commission; (4) the objection; (5) the reassurance; (6) the sign. He notes also that in the stories

concerning Moses, Gideon, Isaiah, Jeremiah, and Second Isaiah there is no indication that the experience was an ecstatic one. The man called appears to be in full possession of his faculties and asks pertinent questions.

13. John 1.38 ff.

14. RSV Luke 5.8.

15. Cf. 1 Cor. 15.8.

16. RSV Gal. 1.1.

17. Cf. Gal. 1.15.

18. Jer. 1.5; Isa. 49.1.

19. Mark 3.14.

20. RSV John 15.15 ff.

21. RSV Deut. 7.7.

22. Mark 3.14.

23. RSV Mark 10.21. Contrast Mark 5.18 ff., the story of one who wanted to follow Christ in this particular way, but was not called to do so.

24. RSV Exod. 3.11.

25. RSV Judg. 6.15 ff. This phrase runs like a refrain through Old and New Testaments. Other examples of God's promise to 'be with' someone include Gen. 26.24 (to Isaac); Jos. 1.5 (to Joshua); Jer. 1.8 (to Jeremiah); Ps. 91 (90).15 (to the man who calls on the Lord); Deut. 20.1; and Isa. 41.10; 43.2–5 (to Israel whom Yahweh saves); Luke 1.28 (to Mary); Acts 18.10 (to Paul); Matt. 28.20 (to the Church). The Paraclete will 'be with' the Christian (John 14.16 ff.); the Holy Trinity will 'make their home with him' (John 14.23). 'Immanuel' is the first and last word of the gospel of grace, cf. Rev. 21.3.

26. Jer. 15.10 ff., 15–21.

27. RSV Amos 3.8.

28. RSV Jer. 20.9.

29. RSV 1 Cor. 9.16.

30. Cf. Gal. 5.13.

31. Cf. Isa. 41.8.

32. Cf. Phil. 3.5–14.

33. Cf. 1 Thess. 2.12, quoted in RB Prol. 55.

34. RSV Rev. 2.17.

35. RSV Rom. 1.1–7.

36. Cf. Isa. 51.1 ff.

37. Cf. Luke 9.35.

38. Cf. John 10.36; Isa. 49.6.

39. Mark 8.33.

40. Heb. 5.8.

41. RSV 1 Cor. 1.26–8.

42. Cf. Col. 1.15; Eph. 4.13.

43. Cf. Robert C. Leslie, *Jesus and Logotherapy*, Nashville, Abingdon Press, 1965; Abraham H. Maslow, *Religions, Values and Peak Experiences*, Columbus, Ohio State University Press, 1964; F. Goble, *The Third Force*, New York, Pocket Books, 1971.

44. Just as there is a distinct literary form for the narratives of the prophetic call (see note 12 above), so tradition tends to provide certain classic types of story about the vocation of monks. The clearest seem to be: (1) A man listens to Scripture being read and has an inner certainty that some passage is addressed directly to himself, e.g. Antony (cf. Athanasius, *Life of Antony*, 2–3). (2) He becomes aware of his vocation in some moment of personal crisis. For St John Gualbert it was a crucial moral decision, for St Sylvester the experience of looking into an open grave, for Augustine Baker a situation of extreme danger crossing a river (see Serenus Cressy, *Life of Father Augustine Baker*, ch. 1). The existential shock is the means chosen by God to make the call clear. (3) The influence of some man of God is instrumental, e.g. B. Maurus Scott was influenced by St John Roberts (cf. B. Camm, *Nine Martyr Monks* (Burns & Oates 1931), pp. 192 ff., B. Philip Powell by Fr Augustine Baker, ibid., pp. 318–20). These stories are difficult to evaluate because in some cases there is no clear-cut distinction between conversion from a life of sin and vocation (cf. Augustine, *Confessions* 8.12), and we cannot know how far legend has been coloured by the memory of prophetic texts.

45. RB 58.

46. The word 'growth' has been preferred to 'formation' in this chapter in order to exclude the idea that training means the imposition of a corpus of readymade traditions and nothing else. It should rather include an education which makes it possible for each to give what he has to give.

47. RB 3.7 ff.

48. RB 61.7–11.

49. RB 58.16–18.

50. The following topics are more fully dealt with later in the book: *Opus Dei* in Chapter 11, 'Obedience' in Chapter 9, 'Conversion and Asceticism' in Chapter 9; but they are considered here from the special angle of the newcomer to monastic life.

51. Cf. I. Hausherr, 'Opus Dei', in *Monastic Studies* 11 (1975), pp. 181–204; A. de Vogüé, 'Prayer in the Rule of St Benedict', in *Monastic Studies* 7 (1969), p. 125.

52. Cf. RB Prol.1–3; 5.13–15.

53. RB passim, especially 7.91–8.

54. RB 7, especially third and fourth rungs.

55. Cf. Chapter 6, 'The Abbot', pp. 86 ff: Chapter 9, 'Obedience', pp. 197 ff.

56. Rom. 6.10.

57. Cf. RB 2.6 ff.

58. Cf. 2 Cor. 5.15.

59. The song of the blessed is, 'Amen, alleluia'; cf. Rev. 19.4.

60. RB 5.
61. RB 7.104–33.
62. RB 2.87–96; the reference is to the abbot but it can be more widely applied.
63. RB 71.10–18.
64. RB 7.150 ff.
65. RB 7.106 ff.
66. RB 7.8.
67. Cf. RB Prol. 129–31.
68. Cf. *Renovationis Causam* 18.
69. St Benedict prescribes a waiting period of four or five days outside the door, followed by a few days in the guest house before the applicant is admitted to the novitiate (RB 58.1–9). In modern conditions with swift travel this might be represented by a much longer period.
70. Cf. Mark 8.35.
71. Cf. Chapter 5, 'Communication and Co-responsibility', p. 75; Chapter 9, 'Celibacy', pp. 180–81, 184.
72. Both 'open' and 'closed' novitiates have a point here: with the former the range of friendships can be wider for the novice, with the latter the friendships formed between novices may be deep and lifelong.
73. Cf. Chapter 6, 'The Abbot', pp. 91 ff.
74. Cf. RB 27.5 ff; Chapter 6, 'The Abbot', p. 83.

COMMITMENT TO GOD IN THE COMMUNITY: INTRODUCTION

1. Canon 1307.
2. On alienation, see Chapter 2, 'The Mystery of the Church', pp. 18, 19.
3. Shakespeare, *Sonnet 116*.
4. Cf. G. Lafont, 'The Institution of Religious Celibacy', from *The Future of the Religious Life*, ed. Peter Huizing and William Bassett (*Concilium* vol. 97/1974), pp. 57 ff: 'A promise made to him [God] does not, as it were, leave him unscathed. Whatever language we choose to say it in, the Christian message implies that there is a history of God. The question of knowing how exactly God is affected by our decisions as men is as difficult as that of knowing how he is affected by the act of Creation and the manifestation of Revelation, but the problems of language do not annul the truth of the fact. The promise . . . is not a decision without an opposite number, or to which the opposite number is impassive, in the sense this word has for us. . . . The impassivity of God is passionate. Thus he accepts the promise. Thus the promise made to the living God and accepted by him creates a relational structure between God and man. . . .'
5. Cf. 1 Cor. 12–13.
6. This is not to equate solemn vows with temporary commitment but rather

to emphasize that the Spirit cannot be restricted to any institutional form. The analogy with marriage is helpful but must not be overplayed. Marriage is of its essence a commitment to a human person; if it fails, there cannot be sufficient reason for going beyond him or her to another person. In the case of monastic profession the commitment is first of all to God, union with whom in love is man's ultimate destiny; the commitment to monastic life is the means to this end. There can therefore always be a tension, and this is perhaps part of the reason why the Church in recent centuries has claimed the power to dispense from even solemn vows, but not to permit divorce and remarriage.

7. Gabriel Marcel, *Creative Fidelity* (New York, Farrar, Strauss & Giroux, 1964), pp. 166 ff.

STABILITY

1. RB 58; 60; 61.

2. RB 58 passim; 4.100 ff; Prol. 127–31.

3. RB (Bolton) 7.106–10; cf. Matt. 10.22.

4. In dealing with the novice's perseverance in Chapter 58 St Benedict makes 'perseverance in stability' (*de stabilitate sua perseverentiam*) the object of the candidate's preliminary promise at the beginning of his probation, and obedience the object of the promise he makes at the end of it, this obedience connoting stability (*si . . . promiserit se omnia custodire et cuncta sibi imperata servare, tunc suscipiatur . . . sciens . . . quod ei ex illa die non liceat egredi de monasterio, nec collum excutere de sub iugo regulae . . .*). Clearly, in St Benedict's mind stability and persevering obedience were two aspects of the same promise. Later monastic tradition, on the basis of St Benedict's description of the novice's profession which follows, distinguished stability and obedience into separate vows, along with *conversatio morum* which makes its appearance in the same account of the profession. This distinction is certainly legitimate, but to attribute it to St Benedict is to over-schematize his thought. Cf. Chapter 9, 'Conversion and Asceticism', note 2, pp. 397–8.

5. Cf. Code of Canon Law, canons 572–86, 632–6, 637–45.

6. RB 58.33–7, 67–72.

7. E.g. (1) departure to make new foundations: Benet Biscop, Boniface, Bernard; (2) appointment of a monk of one monastery to be abbot of another, or archbishop: Odo, Anselm; (3) breakaway to found a more observant monastery or order: Robert, Alberic, Stephen Harding, Richard of York (first abbot of Fountains), Robert of Newminster.

8. RSV Luke 9.23.

9. RB Prol. 124–31.

10. 2 Cor. 1.18–20.

11. Cf. RB 61.

12. Cf. RB 1. But he also shows great consideration for unstable monks, cf. RB 29.

13. Gabriel Marcel, *Man against Mass Society*, trans. G. S. Fraser (Chicago, Henry Regnery Co., 1969), p. 93. The reader may be struck by the obvious contrast between the principles set out in this chapter about man's need for rootedness, and the gospel invitation to leave all in order to follow Christ. There is a paradox here which cannot be eliminated, as is often the case when two aspects of Christian life are contrasted and their reconciliation is not immediately evident. But certain comments can be made:
(1) Idolization of the place is a possible temptation for Benedicines. The Introduction to this section on the vows, p. 134, mentioned the danger of idolatry in religious life whenever some structure intended to support man's response to God attracts to itself the unconditional love and reverence due to God alone. A special form of this danger may arise in the case of Benedictine monasteries where the beauty and peace, the associations, memories, and atmosphere, the whole *genius loci*, can have a powerful effect on both community and guests.
(2) As (non-idolatrous) stability is a virtue for monks, so mobility and detachment from place and particular community are virtues for most modern religious. Both are valid expressions of Christian response to grace. No single order or way of life can reflect the whole reality of Christ; the Church is called to do so, in its measure, through these complementary charisms.
(3) Some kind of authentic love and attachment are the necessary presupposition for authentic detachment. Christian detachment is not to be confused with psychological rootlessness, and it is in relation to the latter that Benedictine stability may offer its witness, as this chapter goes on to show.

14. This is not to deny the value of occasional absences or foreign travel. It has already been stated that stability is not to be identified with so rigid an interpretation of enclosure that all travel would be a violation of stability. A stable monk, like any well-rooted person, is in the best position to enjoy and profit from an occasional change of scene.

15. On the *differences* between monastic and marital commitments, see the Introduction to this section on the vows, note 6, p. 396.

16. Cf. Acts 2.42–7; 4.32.

17. Cf. Eph. 2.14; John 17.21, 23.

CONVERSION AND ASCETICISM

1. Thus Dom John Chapman, after examining the meanings of *conversatio* in Latin monastic texts from the fourth to the sixth century, settled for the translation 'monasticity of behaviour'. He held that the best paraphrase for RB 58.39 ff. would be: 'Let him promise to live as a monk should live'; cf. J. Chapman, *Saint Benedict and the Sixth Century* (Sheed & Ward 1929), pp. 224–5.

2. See the comprehensive study by Dom Ambrose Wathen, 'Conversatio and Stability in the Rule of Benedict', in *Monastic Studies* 11 (1975), pp. 1–44. The writer surveys the interpretations of modern commentators and the

usage of these words by RB's sources and RB itself, showing the interpenetration of the notions of stability, *conversatio*, and obedience. He shows that 'Stability includes the ideas of perseverance, firmness and steadfastness in decision, fidelity and obedience to monastic routine and tradition, the dispossession of all personal property (poverty) in a life of radical dependence upon the community resources, life in fellowship in a given monastery, i.e. in a determined place. *Conversatio* refers to a life of communion with brothers which is determined by tradition, i.e. the Scriptures and monastic fathers. This pattern of life . . . includes mutual support, hospitality, the *opus Dei*, fasting, chastity, and poverty, for such actions are the external manifestations of the monk's faith. Faith and *conversatio* are synonyms. When they are used together then *conversatio* looks primarily to the external manifestation of this faith, and faith looks primarily to the internal reality that is manifest in the behavior. Sometimes *conversatio* refers to the unit of internal-external behavior. In any case the totality of the monk's life is dynamic; it is a unified process that moves from past sins into present virtues and future glory. . . . Stability has the nuance of fidelity and perseverance, and this is related primarily to persons, not primarily to place. By this promise the monk is associated with a particular community and its life-style (*conversatio*), obediently responding to all that this demands. *Conversatio* is then a term that looks to life, its activities and the energy it demands. Synonyms of *conversatio* are life, observance, discipline or what could be called life-style, behavior patterns, routine. . . . Ultimately, stability, *conversatio morum* and obedience are inseparable for the monk who lives according to the Benedictine Rule. No one of these terms does justice to the total view of the commitment the monk makes to Christ in the Benedictine monastic way of life. All three are necessary and add their own nuance . . .' (art. cit., pp. 43–4).

3. In fact St Benedict seems to play down this sense, twice changing RM's *conversio* or *converti* to *conversatio*; see Wathen, art. cit., pp. 28–9. The Master took a more unfavourable view of secular life.

4. RB Prol. 4 ff.

5. So Thomas Merton, '*Conversio morum* is turning toward God in monastic ascesis and good works and implies the refusal to "turn back" to the works of the world or to negligence' ('Conversatio Morum', in *Cistercian Studies*, vol. 1, 1966.2, p. 136). It should be mentioned that some authors have held that so far from being equivalents, the two terms are so dissimilar in meaning that to discuss the vow of *conversatio morum* in terms of conversion is misleading; cf. Dom Ambrose Wathen, art. cit. But the prevailing view is that there is at least a continuity of meaning between them.

6. Cf. Isa. 1.11–20; 30.15–18; Mic. 6.6–8; Jer. 7.3, 28; Amos 5.21–5; Hos. 6.1–6.

7. Jer. 24.7; 31.31–4.

8. Mark 1.2–8 p.

9. Mark 1.15; cf. also Matt. 4.17.

10. Cf. Mark 2.13–17; Matt. 9.9–13; Luke 5.27–32.
11. Cf. Mark 10.21–5; Luke 18.9–14.
12. Cf. Acts 11.18.
13. Acts 5.31.
14. Cf. 1 Thess. 1.9; Gal. 4.9; Rom. 6.3 ff; 9.30; John 5.24; 11.25; 6.40; 12.46; 3.16; 6.47.
15. Cf. Acts 2.38; SC 7.
16. Cf. Col. 3.5–10; Eph. 4.20–24; AG 13.
17. Cf. Mark 8.34–8, a key passage for the understanding of conversion.
18. There are many echoes of them in the Rule, especially in Chapter 4 and in Chapter 7, 4th rung.
19. Cf. RB 4.1–3, 23, 'To love the Lord God with all one's heart, all one's soul, and all one's strength. Then, to love one's neighbour as oneself. . . . To prefer absolutely nothing to the love of Christ.'
20. Cf. 2 Cor. 3.4–18.
21. RB 34.9–11; 40.23–5, etc.
22. NEB Phil. 3.13 ff.
23. Cf. 1 Tim. 6.16.
24. Cf. Heb. 11.1.
25. Cf. Job 38–42; Rom. 11.33–6.
26. RB 49.
27. RB 46.
28. Phil. 2.7.
29. Cf. 1 Pet. 2.24; Rom. 8.3.
30. RSV Heb. 12.2.
31. JB Col. 2.14.
32. JB Mark 8.34 ff.
33. Cf. Heb. 11.10, 13–16.

CELIBACY

1. A remark made by a French Dominican at the time of Vatican II, quoted by Ida Friederike Görres in *Is Celibacy Outdated?* Cork, Mercier Press, 1965.
2. For an account of the aspects of Existentialism most pertinent to questions of Christian vocation, see Ignace Lepp, *The Christian Philosophy of Existence*. Dublin, Gill, 1965.
3. Cf. Introduction to Chapter 9, pp. 128–36.
4. 'Sexist' (parallel to 'racist') here means that type of male dominance whether in marriage or outside it which excludes real inter-personality. The ethic of 'liberated sexual personalism', which also affects the understanding of marriage, does not necessarily rule out celibacy altogether. In a context of apocalyptic risk or prophetic witness celibacy is allowed to have meaning, but in its institutionalized form it is held to be a

residual neurosis bequeathed by the anti-sexual strain in early Christianity, and removed by the very fact of its institutionalization from the situation of prophetic insecurity which alone gave (or gives) it validity. For a statement of these views, see the very questionable article by Rosemary Ruether, 'The Ethic of Celibacy', in *Commonweal* (2 February 1973), pp. 390–94.

5. *GS* 48–52; *LG* 40–42.

6. Cf. Chapter 4, 'The Rule', p. 56.

7. Dom de Vogüé, however, thinks that this item is an erratic block, which may have been introduced by the Master into the list provided by his source; cf. A. de Vogüé, *La Règle de Saint Benoît*, iv (Paris, Éditions du Cerf, 1971), p. 163, n. 143.

8. Cassian, *Inst.* 2.3; cf. *Conf.* 24.23; Basil, *Reg. Fus.* 8, cf. 41.

9. RB 4.23.

10. RB Prol.125 ff.

11. RB 20.5, 6, 8; 49.4; cf. 52.6–9. Compare also Chapter 7, 'Freedom and Availability for God', p. 99; Chapter 12, 'Lectio Divina', p. 268 and also later pages in the present chapter.

12. Gen. 1.1 – 2.4a.

13. Gen. 1.27.

14. Gen. 1.28; cf. 9.1.

15. Gen. 2.4b–25.

16. Interestingly, it is usually the J account which is quoted in the New Testament as a basis for a discussion of sexuality, cf. Mark 10.7 p; 1 Cor. 6.16; Eph. 5.31. The P statement about mankind being created male and female is also quoted, Mark 10.6 p, but not the P command to increase and multiply.

17. In the opinion of some exegetes, however, the Yahwist may have described it in sexual terms. He had no information on the nature of man's earliest rebellion, but may well have used for his vivid and psychologically perceptive account the colours provided by Canaanite fertility cults, which in their divinization of sexuality represented for him an epitome of man's disobedience to the Creator. Nowhere in Scripture is it suggested that sexual sins are necessarily the most culpable of man's attempts to defy God. But it is understandable that sin may be the most shame-producing in that dimension where fallen man is at grips with the deepest and most powerful forces of his nature.

18. Gen. 4.1.

19. Gen. 3.15.

20. Cf. Gen. 12–18 passim; 25.21; 1 Sam. 1–2; Luke 1.7.

21. Prov. 30.19.

22. Prov. 31.10–31.

23. According to the exegesis assumed here, the Song of Songs is a collection of human love-songs, religious already at its own level as praise of God who created human sexual love, but subsequently interpreted as typifying

the love between Yahweh and Israel. Some exegetes, however, believe that the poems are allegorical in their original literal sense, being intended from their composition as descriptions of the relationship between Yahweh and his people.

24. Cf. Hos. 1–3; Jer. 2.2; 3.1, 6–12; Ezek. 16; 23; Isa. 50.1; 54.6–8; 62.4 ff; Matt. 22.1–14; 25.1–13; 1 Cor. 6.15–17; 2 Cor. 11.2; Eph. 5.25–33; John 3.29; Rev. 19.7 ff; 21.2.

25. RSV Rom. 8.3.

26. Cf. 2 Cor. 5.21.

27. RSV Rom. 8.3.

28. Gen. 2.7.

29. 1 Cor. 15.45.

30. Cf. Rom. 8.11, 19–23.

31. Eph. 5.21–33.

32. Judg. 11.34–39.

33. So when a man saw his children and grandchildren unto the fourth generation, he could die in peace (Job 42.16; Ps. 128 (127).6); the Levirate law sought to prevent a childless man's name being blotted out from Israel (Deut, 25.5 ff.); Absalom set up a pillar as a memorial to his name because he had no son (2 Sam. 18.18).

34. Cf. von Allmen, *Theological Dictionary of the Bible*, Lutterworth Press, 1958, s.v. 'Virginity': 'In the New Testament marriage ceases to be a means of ensuring survival beyond death. . . . Procreation is no longer the primary end (in fact, the New Testament never connects the sexual act with procreation). . . . To die a virgin is no longer a catastrophe. . . . Virginity and celibacy are held in honour in a manner unknown in the Old Covenant. . . . It can no longer be said without reservation that "It is not good for a man to be alone".' For one who is a member of the Body of Christ solitude can never be absolute.

35. Jer. 16.1–4.

36. So L. Legrand, *The Biblical Doctrine of Virginity* (Sheed & Ward 1963), p. 34: 'Man's primary duty is no more to continue the human species. It is on the contrary to free himself from a fleeting world which has already lost its substance.'

37. 1 Cor. 7.32–4. On this Karl Barth remarked: 'The very thing which confers on marriage a new consecration and meaning also enables us to understand and appreciate abstention from marriage as a possibility, a way, a matter of special gift and vocation. . . . Marriage, for Paul, was not a universally obligatory and binding order of creation. The Christian enters marriage not on the basis of a natural necessity, but on that of a special spiritual gift and vocation. To deny the possibility of not marrying and to make marriage a universal obligation deprives it of its only meaning for the Christian' (*Church Dogmatics*, vol. iii, T. & T. Clark 1936 onwards, pp. 144 ff.).

38. Paul's preoccupation with freedom is similar to that of Luke, who twice

adds a wife to the list of commitments that may have to be avoided by Christ's disciples, and ranks marriage along with possessions as a possible distraction from the Kingdom: Luke 14.26; 18.29; cf. 14.20.

39. 'I wish that all of you were as I am myself. But everyone has his own special gift from God' (1 Cor. 7.7; cf. 7.8–9).

40. Matt. 13.44–6.

41. Cf. Mark 10.29 ('for my sake and for the gospel') and Matt. 19.29 ('for my name's sake') with Luke 18.29 ('for the sake of the kingdom of God').

42. This interpretation of the eunuchs logion follows that of J. Blinzler, 'Eisin eunuchoi. Zur Auslegung von Matt. 19.12' in ZNW 48 (1957), pp. 254–70. Other exegetes are more impressed by the presumed intention of the evangelist in attaching this pericope to vv. 3–9, and hold that the eunuchs logion must be interpreted in function of the preceding statements of Jesus on the indissolubility of marriage. So according to Zahn (Das Evangelium des Mattäus, 4th edn., 1922, pp. 592 ff.) Jesus's argument would be an a fortiori: 'If some give up marriage altogether, is it too much to ask that married people separated from their partners should refrain from remarriage?' But other scholars who regard vv. 3–12 as an intentional unity deny any reference to voluntary celibacy in the eunuchs saying. Just as there are physical eunuchs incapable of marriage, so the abandoned Christian husband or wife is incapable of remarriage, not because of a physical defect but 'because of the Kingdom'. On this interpretation, see J. Dupont, Mariage et divorce dans l'évangile (Paris, Desclée de Brouwer, 1959), pp. 161–222; also Q. Quesnell, 'Made Themselves Eunuchs for the Kingdom of Heaven' in CBQ xxx.3 (July 1968), pp. 335–58. That not all understand this but only 'those to whom it is given' means not that our Lord's teaching on the indissolubility of marriage is optional, but that the high ideal of marital fidelity he puts forward is incomprehensible and impossible outside the gift of grace. What it could entail in terms of self-sacrificing love is suggested by Eph. 5.25 ff., as Quesnell points out. It should be noted that if this latter interpretation is accepted we have no formal gospel text recommending celibacy. That Paul when speaking of celibacy insisted that he was only giving his own opinion, having no command from the Lord (1 Cor. 7.25), proves nothing either way, as Paul may not have known the eunuchs saying.

43. Cf. G. Lafont, 'The Institution of Religious Celibacy', in Concilium, New Ser., vols. 7, 8, no. 10 (Sept.–Oct. 1974), p. 55.

44. Cf. Mark 3.34–5 p.

45. RSV John 15.14 ff.

46. Gal. 3.28.

47. Cf. John 11.52; Eph. 1.10; Col. 1.15–20.

48. On this, see Arturo Paoli, Freedom to be Free (Maryknoll, New York, Orbis Books, 1973), pp. 105 ff.

49. Cf. RSV 2 Cor. 4.7; 12.7; Rom. 8.38 f.

50. See the thought-provoking study by Sandra M. Schneiders, 'Non-

Marriage for the Sake of the Kingdom', in *Widening the Dialogue*. *Reflection on 'Evangelica Testificatio'*, published by the Canadian Religious Conference, Ottawa, and the Leadership Conference of Women Religious (Washington 1974), pp. 125–97. This essay considers the two types under the names 'celibacy' and 'virginity' respectively, and establishes their existence in the first three centuries of Christianity.

51. This argument may throw some light on the virginity of Jesus, but does it say anything about celibacy for anyone else? Yes, because although his natural sonship of the Father is unique and non-imitable it is the ground of our adoptive sonship, and his relationship to the Father is a reality in which he explicitly desired us to share. A kind of 'theocentric virginity' has already been mentioned, the vocation of those who feel it existentially impossible to choose otherwise, because of an existing relationship.

52. Rabbinic references in Blinzler, art. cit., nn. 48–52. Blinzler conjectures that a confrontation between Jesus and the Pharisees who charged him with neglecting the duty may have been the *Sitz im Leben Jesu* of the eunuchs logion.

53. 'The Human-not-quite-Human', in D. L. Sayers, *Unpopular Opinions* (Gollancz 1946), pp. 121–2.

54. Luke 7.36–50.

55. John 20.11–18.

56. John 8.3–11.

57. Temporary continence was required by the Old Testament as a preparation for certain cultic acts, cf. Exod. 19.15; 1 Sam. 21.5. This did not imply a disparagement of sexuality but a withdrawal from all 'profane' engagements before entering on the sacred. But it has only slight relevance for the understanding of Christian virginity.

58. 1 Cor. 6.19.

59. RSV Rom. 12.1.

60. *Letter to Polycarp* 5.2. On this, S. Schneiders comments: 'It is Ignatius' concept of martyrdom as perfect assimilation to the Lord which justifies the assertion that, when he speaks of virginity as an honouring of the flesh of the Lord, he is most likely not speaking of a merely external imitation of Jesus' way of life but of the same type of interior assimilation, mystical identification with Christ' (art. cit., p. 147).

61. 2 Cor. 4.10 ff.

62. Mark 12.24 ff.

63. John 17.3.

64. Matt. 24.45–51; cf. 24.42–4.

65. Matt. 25.1–12.

66. See Chapter 9, 'Obedience', Introduction.

67. Eph. 5.25–30.

68. This chapter is primarily concerned with monastic celibacy, so the question of clerical celibacy as such need not detain us. The latter is a

reflection of monastic celibacy, historically later and not universal (since the lower clergy in the Eastern Churches can be married). For a monk-priest celibacy flows from his monastic vocation and from his privilege of sacrifice as a member of the priestly people of God, rather than directly from his ministerial priesthood, even though in pastoral situations he may experience the advantages of a celibacy that enables him to enter into the lives of many people, in the same way as any other priest does.

69. See ST 2–2. 152.1; cf. ibid., a.3.

70. On this, see B. Häring, *The Law of Christ*, vol. 3 (Cork, Mercier Press, 1967), pp. 380–81.

71. 'And at the end the Lord will be left alone with the woman. And then he will stand erect and look upon this prostitute, his bride, and ask her, "Woman, where are your accusers? Has no one condemned you?" And she will answer with inexpressible repentance and humility, "No one, Lord." And she will be astonished and almost dismayed that no one has done so. But the Lord will come close to her and say, "Then neither shall I condemn you. . . . My bride, my holy Church".' (K. Rahner, 'The Church of Sinners', in *Theological Investigations*, vi, Darton, Longman & Todd, 1969, p. 269).

72. *Consilium ad Exsequendam Constitutionem de Sacra Liturgia*, 15 August 1968.

73. As long as these points are clear to all concerned, this is a good policy. But it does not dispose of all difficulties. There is a considerable middle ground between the fully public and the entirely private in the sexual life of many young people, and therefore there may be danger of misunderstanding on the part of family and friends. There is also the possibility of psychological conflict in the candidate.

74. There are certain ways forward, particularly since the dissociation of the *Consecratio Virginis* from solemn profession is now possible. One is to provide for flexibility in the profession rite, so that the junior can freely choose between (a) solemn profession alone, and (b) the mixed rite of solemn profession combined with consecration, without an option for the former carrying any kind of stigma. Another is to let all make solemn profession with nothing added, and allow the *Consecratio Virginis* later as an optional extra.

75. J. Dillersberger, *Wer es fassen kann* (Salzburg, Otto Müller, 1933), p. 54, quoted in Häring, op. cit., p. 391.

76. Antiphon 'O sacrum convivium' from the office of Corpus Christi by St Thomas.

77. Eph. 5.29.

78. A. Hastings, *The Faces of God: Essays on Church and Society* (Geoffrey Chapman 1975), p. 21.

79. Ibid., p. 18.

80. See Chapter 9, 'Poverty and Sharing of Goods', last section of chapter, 'Monastic Poverty Today'.

81. Denziger-Schonmetzer (1967) 1810.

82. Explicitly in *GS* 48–52, implicitly in the teaching of *LG* 40–42 on the universal call to holiness. It is noteworthy that in *PC* 12 the Council reaffirmed that celibacy for the kingdom is to be esteemed as a surpassing gift of grace, but did not cite Trent even in a footnote.

83. Cf. A. Gelin, *The Poor of Yahweh* (Collegeville, The Liturgical Press, 1964), especially pp. 91–8.

84. Cf. n. 21 above.

85. Cf. the variant reading in John 1.13 'who was (singular) born not of blood or the will of the flesh or of man, but of God . . .'; and K. Rahner, *Mary Mother of the Lord* (Herder-Nelson 1962), p. 68: 'He . . . willed to become man in such a way that it would be clear from the very manner of his coming that his origin is not of this earth, from the inner forces of this world, not even from the noblest and holiest human love, but wholly from on high. . . .'

86. Rom. 4.18–25.

87. K. Rahner, 'Virginitas in Partu', in *Theological Investigations* iv (Darton, Longman & Todd 1966), p. 159.

88. Cf. Luke 1.48 with Phil. 2.5–11.

89. It is vital to distinguish between repression, which is a blind, unconscious, desperate mechanism triggered by pre-rational fear, and control or rational suppression, which is a free and intelligent act or series of acts, motivated by some higher love, compatible with full acceptance of one's sexual nature and gradually growing into part of a human life-style. Suppression in this sense is not dangerous; repression is.

90. A man who has not wholly faced and accepted his own sexuality cannot relate in a Christlike way to women. If he is a Christian trying to live for God, and especially if he is a celibate, he will tend to regard any woman to whom he gets too close as a threat. So the immature, non-integrated celibate either takes refuge in shyness, awkwardness, and withdrawal, or else he converts the adult man–woman relationship which he feels he cannot handle into one which he thinks more tractable and less dangerous, namely a father–child relationship. So he treats the woman like a child, perhaps with joviality, heartiness, and paternalism. Of course, this can be just as much her fault. A similar distortion is possible for women, especially nuns, in relating to priests. Nuns are often tempted to mother a priest, to surround him with vast quantities of food and other comforts, and announce that Father is tired and must not be disturbed. This can be perfectly good, motivated by genuine charity and at times very necessary; for if a priest is unwell or exhausted he probably needs a woman to look after him. There can also be a vocation to spiritual motherhood, of which the obvious example is Our Lady's relationship to St John. But if a nun has only two ways of relating to a priest, the attitude of a little girl looking up to Father and the mother-role, she is falling short. (Of course, this may be just as much his fault.) The highest thing she can do is to call out Christ in him.

91. Many young people develop through a homosexual phase to healthy

heterosexuality. While they are in the former it is pastorally important not to close doors on them.

92. Gal. 5.22 ff.

93. Cf. 1 Cor. 3.1–3 where Paul tells the (baptized) Corinthians that they are still 'fleshly' and proves it not by listing what we would call 'sins of the flesh' but by pointing to their jealousy and factiousness.

94. Rom. 8.9–11.

95. Tradition reports this of St Seraphim of Sarov.

96. E.g. St Maximus the Confessor, De Ambiguis, PG 91.1305 ff.; cf. Vladimir Lossky, The Mystical Theology of the Eastern Church (James Clarke & Co. 1957), pp. 109 ff.

97. In the discussion of the New Testament passage on eunuchs on p. 163 above, it was maintained that overwhelming joy in the gift of the Kingdom is the source of the decision for celibacy. This interpretation seems the strongest at the level of New Testament exegesis and that of the experience of the first disciples. But in the lives of many of us things may happen in the reverse order. Some people undertake monastic life and celibacy in an ascetical and fairly moralistic spirit, and subsequently grow towards a fuller experience of joy and freedom.

98. On sexual integration, see D. Goergen, The Sexual Celibate (SPCK 1976), pp. 51 ff., especially his remarks on Abraham Maslow's category of 'self-actualizing' persons, pp. 59–64. (Fr Goergen's book contains many excellent insights but needs to be used with caution.) For an imaginative description of the power of sexual energies mobilized for spiritual love, see C. S. Lewis, The Great Divorce (Geoffrey Bles 1946), pp. 89–95. For suggestions on the mystery of masculinity and femininity at a higher level than we know, see C. S. Lewis, That Hideous Strength (Bodley Head 1945), pp. 389–91.

99. Matt. 5.8; cf. 6.22.

100. Cf. PL 195.670.

101. Ibid., col. 666.

102. Ibid., col. 661.

103. Ibid., col. 691.

104. Ibid., col. 663 and 671.

105. Ibid., col. 690.

106. See the excellent remarks on this by Fr Herbert McCabe, O.P., in the editorial of New Blackfriars, vol. 56, no. 658 (March 1975), pp. 98 ff.

107. 'All our relationships are sexual in the broadest sense of the word. . . . I approach every relationship with my own personality, which in fact is a sexual personality. This does not mean that it is only sexual, but it does mean that my sexuality is involved. I approach life as a man differentiated from a woman or as a woman differentiated from a man. . . . Every affective relationship involves some sexuality. Although friendships are not best described in sexual terms, they involve the totality of our person.

There is more to friendship than our sexuality, but we cannot deny that sexuality enters into friendship . . .' (D. Goergen, op. cit., pp. 77 ff).

108. *ST* 2–2. 142.1. In so far, naturally, as it is a consequence of intemperate choice and not of temperament.

109. Or vice versa. It is tedious to repeat 'he or she', 'himself or herself' continually, but the same is true for women in this matter of heterosexual friendships.

110. That prayer, faith, and experience of God are closely related to celibate life was stressed in a joint declaration by the Dutch Major Religious Superiors in 1969: 'The motive for consecrated celibacy . . . is to be sought in a personal experience of God. . . . One cannot choose the path of celibacy and remain within it unless one holds, however obscurely, to the conviction that God makes demands on us and that he is worth remaining celibate for. In a world where faith is opposed, it is not surprising that there is also a crisis of prayer and celibacy. Prayer and chastity are related, for in both cases there is question of an attitude of loving attention to him who revealed himself to this world and revealed himself to us. Thus without prayer there can be no lasting celibacy.' (Quoted by Mr David Goodall in *The Tablet*, 9 October 1976, p. 975).

111. John 15.1–8.

OBEDIENCE

1. See especially the lucid account of them in de Vogüé, *La Communauté et l'Abbé dans la Règle de Saint Benoît*, pp. 266–88.

2. Cassian, *Inst.* 4.9; RM 1; 2; 11; 14; etc. Cf. Chapter 6 above, 'The Abbot', pp. 77–9.

3. *Inst.* Preface: 8; 1.2; 2.2–6; 7.7–18; *Conf.* 18.5; 21.29–30. This is a myth in the sense that it is historically indefensible, but also in the sense that it has all the power of a myth.

4. The Master cites Luke 10.16 many times, e.g. RM 1.89; 7.6, 68; 10.51.

5. For this perspective on obedience, see Cassian, *Inst.* 4.8; RM Thp 34 ff.; 10.42–4, 49. John 6.38 and Matt. 26.39 are cited by Cassian, *Conf.* 24.26; and by the Master RM Ths 117–26, etc. For Phil. 2.8, see Cassian, *Conf.* 19.6; *Inst.* 12.28; and in the Master RM 10.49, etc.

6. Cassian, *Inst.* 4.24, 25, etc.

7. See L.-T. Lefort, *S. Pachomii vita boharica scripta* (Louvain, CSCO 107, 1936), p. 15, 9–25; idem: *Les Vies coptes de Saint Pachôme et de ses premiers successeurs* (Louvain, Bibliothèque du Museon, 16; Publications Universitaires, 1943) S (1), p. 3, 12–32; S (3), p. 65, 31–3; also the *Third Catechesis of Theodore*, passim; and the *Liber Orsiesii*, 23, 50; for both of these last, see Lefort, *Oeuvres de S. Pachôme et de ses disciples*, Louvain 1956. Cf. also Armand Veilleux, *La Liturgie dans le cénobitisme pachômien* (Rome, Studia Anselmiana, 1968), p. 171.

8. *Inst.* 5.4. Similarly, St Benedict thought of the hermit-monk as one who went out from the community well armed after his long probation, RB 1.6–13.

9. *Conf.* 19.6.
10. Cf. Chapter, 'The Abbot', pp. 91–3.
11. John 4.34.
12. John 6.38.
13. John 12.23, 27; 13.31 ff; 17.1.
14. Cf. C. F. D. Moule, 'The Manhood of Jesus in the New Testament' in *Christ, Faith and History*, ed. Sykes and Clayton, Cambridge University Press 1972. This is only one interpretation of a disputed text, but related though different ideas about the crucifixion of Jesus as a 'trinitarian event' are powerfully expressed by J. Moltmann in *The Crucified God*, SCM Press 1974, especially pp. 241–9; e.g. 'The Son suffers in his love, being forsaken by the Father as he dies. The Father suffers in his love the grief of the death of the Son. In that case, whatever proceeds from the event between the Father and the Son must be understood as the spirit of the surrender of the Father and the Son, as the spirit which creates love for forsaken men, as the spirit which brings the dead alive. It is the unconditioned and therefore boundless love which proceeds from the grief of the Father and the dying of the Son and reaches forsaken men in order to create in them the possibility and the force of new life. . . . Here we have interpreted the event of the cross in trinitarian terms as an event concerned with a relationship between persons in which these persons constitute themselves in their relationship with each other. . . . What is in question in the relationship of Christ to his Father is not his divinity and humanity and their relationship to each other but the total, personal aspect of the Sonship of Jesus. . . .' (Moltmann, op. cit., p. 245). Another text which implies this mystery of the revelation of God-likeness in the loving will of Jesus to suffer and be emptied in obedience is 2 Cor. 8.9: 'Though he was rich, he became poor for your sake, that by his poverty you might become rich' (on this see Chapter 9, 'Poverty and Sharing of Goods', pp. 209–11). Even at the end of the Philippians hymn, the exaltation of Jesus is seen as something divinely unselfish; he is confessed as Lord 'to the glory of God the Father'. And in 1 Cor. 15.24 he hands over the Kingdom to his Father.
15. John 8.50; cf. 8.54.
16. John 18.37.
17. Matt. 23.12; Luke 14.11; 18.14.
18. Cf. E. Manning, 'Une catéchèse baptismale devient Prologue de la Règle du Maître', in *Revue Mabillon* 52 (1962), pp. 61–73; de Vogüé, *La Règle de Saint Benoît*, iv (Paris, Éditions du Cerf, 1971), pp. 42–9.
19. RB 7, third rung.
20. RB 5.41–8.
21. RB Prol. 2; cf. JB Prov. 4.23, 'More than all else, keep watch over your heart, since there are the well-springs of life.'
22. *ST* 2–2. 186. 8; 5.
23. RB 5.2 ff.
24. RB 71.

25. RSV Phil. 2.1, 5.

26. RB (Bolton) 7, first rung: 'We are forbidden to do our own will, when Scripture tells us: Turn away from your own will. So too we ask God in our prayer that his will may be done in us.'

27. RB 20; 52.4–9; cf. 4.66–8.

28. 1 Cor. 1.18, 25.

29. Cf. Heb. 5.8 ff.

30. RB 7, fourth rung; cf. Rom. 8.37.

31. RB 31.31–41; 36.5–10; 54.10 ff.

32. 1 Sam. 15.22; Mark 12.33.

33. RB 58.38 ff.

34. Cf. RSV Heb. 10.5–10.

35. John 7.39; 12.32; cf. 1 Cor. 15.45. So the instrument of Christ's obedience becomes the instrument for the giving of the Spirit. Christ's obedience was the inner principle of the redemption, cf. Heb. 5.8 f.

36. Cf. A. Storr, *The Integrity of the Personality* (Penguin Books 1968), p. 44: 'It is difficult for those who have been reared in the odour of sanctity to perceive that an undue submissiveness is as culpable as an undue assertiveness. . . .'

37. Rom. 16.26.

38. Cf. RB 1.2 ff; and perspective (a) in the Introduction to the present chapter.

39. RB 7.167.

40. Cf. Gal. 3.19–22; 5.4–6.

41. Cf. Chapter 4 above, 'The Rule', pp. 48–51.

42. Cf. John 17.23.

43. RB 2.3–7; 63.29–32; cf. Chapter 6 above, 'The Abbot', pp. 79–82, 86–93.

44. RB 64.8–19.

45. Rom. 12.10; RB 72.

46. RB 65.

47. *Statement on Benedictine Life*, 36. d.

48. RB 5.

49. RB 68; 3.

50. Rainer Maria Rilke, *Duino Elegies*, trans. J. B. Leishman and Stephen Spender (Hogarth Press 1968), First Elegy.

51. 1 Cor. 7.22; cf. Rom. 6.17 f; Philem. 16.

52. Constantinople iii, Denziger 557–8 (292–3); cf. *ST* 3. 18. 5 ad 2: 'In friendship there is agreement of will, in that each takes account of the wishes of his friends in what he himself desires.'

53. Cf. RSV John 8.32: 'If you continue in my word, you are truly my disciples, and you will know the truth, and the truth will make you free.'

54. RSV 2 Cor. 9.7; RB 5.40.
55. Ezek. 11.19 ff; 36.26; cf. Ps. 51 (50).10.
56. Ezek. 11.19 ff; Jer. 31.33; Rom. 7.6; 8.2, 14 ff.
57. On this concept of 'heart', cf. Chapter 13, 'Personal Prayer', n. 64.

POVERTY AND SHARING OF GOODS

1. Cf. E. F. Schumacher, *Small is Beautiful*, Abacus 1974 (original publishers: Blond & Briggs). Speaking of Keynes the author remarks: 'Economic progress, he counselled, is obtainable only if we employ those powerful human drives of selfishness, which religion and traditional wisdom universally call upon us to resist. The modern economy is propelled by a frenzy of greed and indulges in an orgy of envy, and these are not accidental features but the very causes of its expansionist success. The question is whether such causes can be effective for long or whether they carry within themselves the seeds of destruction. If Keynes says that "foul is useful and fair is not", he propounds a statement of fact which may be true or false; or it may look true in the short run and turn out to be false in the longer run. Which is it?' (op. cit., pp. 24 ff). Schumacher goes on to demonstrate its falsity and destructiveness. It is fair to add that Keynes thought of this inversion of values as a short-term expedient to lead us out of the tunnel of economic necessity into daylight, cf. ibid., p. 19.
2. Cf. A. Gelin, *The Poor of Yahweh*, Collegeville, The Liturgical Press, 1964.
3. Cf. Ps. 1.3 ff; 37 (36) passim.
4. Prov. 19.1, 22; 28.6; Qoh 4.13.
5. Cf. Prov. 6.6–11; 10.4 ff; 13.18; 21.17.
6. Cf. Job 24.2–12.
7. Cf. Ezek. 22.29; Amos 8.4–6; Hos. 12.8; Mic. 2.2; Isa. 5.8; 10.1–4; Jer. 22.13–17; 34.8–22; Neh. 5.1–13; also Amos 5.7.
8. RSV Exod. 22.27. Cf. also Exod. 20.15 ff; 22.21–6; 23.6; Deut. 15.1–15; 24.10–15; 26.12.
9. Isa. 11.4; Ps. 72 (71).2 ff.
10. Phil. 2.5–11; cf. 2 Cor. 8.9.
11. Cf. J. B. Metz, *Poverty of Spirit* (Glen Rock 1968), pp. 13–20.
12. John 13.12, 15.
13. Matt. 5.3; Luke 6.20; 4.18; cf. Jas. 2.5.
14. Cf. Luke 2.7; Matt. 13.55; 8.20; 27.35.
15. Matt. 11.28–30.
16. John 6.27; Luke 6.21; cf. Matt. 11.1–6.
17. Cf. K. Rahner, 'The Theology of Poverty', in *Theological Investigations* viii (Darton, Longman & Todd 1971), pp. 182–3.
18. Cf. Mark 10.25 p; Matt. 13.22; Luke 1.53; 6.24; Matt. 6. 19–24.

19. Cf. Mark 14.3–9; Luke 8.2 ff.
20. Matt. 25. 31–46; cf. Luke 18.9–14, 15–17; Mark 10.17–22.
21. Mark 4.19 p.
22. Luke 16.19; 12.15–21.
23. Luke 12.33 ff.
24. Cf. John 12.6.
25. Rahner, art. cit., p. 184; cf. Luke 8.2; 19.1–10; 7.36 ff.; 10.38 ff.
26. John 2.1–11.
27. Luke 5.29.
28. Matt. 8.20.
29. Cf. Mark 10.21 p.
30. Rahner, art. cit., p. 185.
31. Cf. 2 Cor. 8.20; 11.8; Acts 21.24; 28.30.
32. 1 Cor. 9.17 ff; Phil. 4.11 ff; 2 Cor. 11.27. Cf. also Matt. 10.8.
33. Cf. Acts 4.32; 2.44–47; 2 Cor. 8–9.
34. Cf. 1 John 3.17; 2 Cor. 8.9.
35. *Dialogues*, Book II, Prologue.
36. RB 58.14 ff; 5.2 ff.
37. Cf. RB 58.58–63.
38. RB 33; 54.
39. RB 2.97–107.
40. RB (McCann) 57.18 ff.
41. RB 53; 36.
42. RB 57.11–15.
43. RB 39; 40; 55; cf. 7.148–55.
44. Cf. René Dubos, 'Franciscan Conservation versus Benedictine Stewardship', in *A God Within* (New York, Charles Scribner's Sons, 1972), pp. 153–74.
45. Ibid., p. 169; cf. also Lynn White, *Machina ex Deo* (Cambridge, Mass., MIT Press, 1968), p. 65.
46. Cf. *PC* 13; *Evangelica Testificatio* (Apostolic Exhortation of Pope Paul VI on Religious Life, 1971), 16–22 (*AAS* lxiii, pp. 497–526).
47. Matt. 6.21.
48. T. Cullinan, *If the Eye be Sound* (Slough, St Paul Publications, 1975), p. 23.
49. Cf. *GS* 63; *Evangelica Testificatio* 17.
50. JB Rev. 3.17.
51. Thomas Merton, *Contemplation in a World of Action* (George Allen & Unwin 1971), p. 220.
52. RB 53.30–33; cf. also Jas. 2.2–7.
53. St Benedict seems to think of acute poverty in a community as an abnormal situation, though he is ambiguous about it, since he recognizes that 'then

they are truly monks' when they live by the labour of their hands under the pressure of necessity (RB 48.18–21).

54. Cf. Chapter 15, 'Work', section on 'Work and poverty'.

55. Matt. 10.8.

56. This is not to deny the need, pointed out in Chapter 7, 'Freedom and Availability for God', and Chapter 15, 'Work', for periods of leisure and silence if a monk is to be truly human and to grow in awareness and prayer. But there is a difference between providing for this need and habitually hugging one's time to oneself.

WORD OF GOD: INTRODUCTION

1. Rom. 4.17.

2. Amos 4.12.

3. RSV Isa. 48.18.

4. Cf. Ps. 136 (135).

5. Cf. Jer. 31.31–4; Ezek. 36.26 ff; 37.

6. Cf. Isa. 55.10 ff; Ps. 107 (106).20; Wisd. 18.14 ff.

7. Luke 2.15, see the Greek. Cf. 2.19, 51.

8. John 15.3.

9. John 15.11.

10. John 9 passim; cf. 3.21.

11. Cf. John 15.22; 3.18; Mark 4.12.

12. RSV Isa. 1.3; 42.19.

13. Ps. 40 (39).6.

14. Cf. Luke 24.27, 44–6; Acts 1.3.

15. St Justin and the other second-century Apologists seized on the Johannine doctrine of the Logos and tried to find a rapprochement with the Stoic belief in an immanent word, developing the idea of a 'seminal word' throughout creation.

16. Cf. Acts 14.16 f.

17. Cf. John 1.9.

18. John 16.14.

19. Acts 2.37.

20. Qahal. Cf. Deut. 4.10; 9.10; 18.16.

21. Ek-klesia.

22. Cf. 2 Cor. 1.19 ff.

23. Josef Pieper, Leisure the Basis of Culture, tr. Alexander Dru (Faber & Faber 1952), p. 52.

24. ST 2–2.35.4. See also the wonderful description by Cassian (Inst. 10.1–3) of the monk whose peace and joy are eaten away by acedia, in PL 49.365–9.

25. Pieper, op. cit., p. 49.

26. Cf. Col. 3.15 ff., which makes peace (itself the gift of God) the prerequisite for the abundant dwelling of God's word among us.

27. RSV Isa. 43.1.

28. Jas. 1.23.

EUCHARIST

1. Cf. J. H. Newman, *Essay on the Development of Christian Doctrine*, ch. 5, where Newman presents seven 'Notes' or principles whereby genuine developments can be distinguished from corruptions.

2. Cf. *The General Instruction of the Roman Missal*, especially ch. iv, no. 76: 'All the presbyters who are not bound to celebrate individually for the pastoral care of the faithful should concelebrate at the conventual or community Mass if possible.'

3. Cf. the four Eucharistic Prayers of the Roman Missal, e.g. 'Let your Spirit come down upon these gifts to make them holy so that they may become for us the body and blood of our Lord Jesus Christ. . . . May all of us who share in the body and blood of Christ be brought together in unity by the Holy Spirit' (Euch. Prayer ii).

4. Cf. the constant references in the four Roman Canons and in the Anglican Series iii Eucharist to the paschal mystery and the expectation of Christ's future coming.

5. Cf. the 1971 Anglican-Roman Catholic Statement on the Eucharist, 5.

6. RB 71: 'That the Brethren be Obedient to One Another'.

7. The practice favoured in the text is based on the belief that the solidarity of the monastic community is the primary unity, which each monk-priest is mainly concerned to build up. The distinction which needs to be visibly expressed is that between the eucharistic President (who manifests his priestly function outwardly) and the eucharistic assembly of which all, ordained or not, are members. Others, however, equally concerned for the unity of the monastic family and not in favour of a return to private Masses, attach great importance to the visible exercise of their priestly function by all, since this is a real communication in grace and in the Spirit, and as such an indispensable contribution to the building up of a largely priestly community which for its life and work needs the fullest support that all its members can give. This chapter takes an option in favour of what seems to be the more probable future direction of the liturgy, but it is fair to point out that both views exist.

8. Cf. RSV Matt. 5.23 ff., 'So if you are offering your gift at the altar, and there remember that your brother has something against you, leave your gift there before the altar and go; first be reconciled to your brother, and then come and offer your gift.'

OPUS DEI

1. 1 Tim. 2.5; 1 Cor. 8.6. Cf. *General Instruction on the Liturgy of the Hours* (hereafter *IGLH*), 6.

2. Heb. 7.25.
3. Col. 1.17.
4. *LG* 16.
5. Heb. 5.5 ff.
6. Cf. *IGLH*, 7.
7. RSV Acts 1.14.
8. JB Acts 2.42.
9. Col. 1.16; 1 Cor. 3.22 ff; 6.12; Acts 10.15.
10. Luke 18.1; 1 Thess. 5.17.
11. In this section use has been made of the articles 'Prayer in the Rule of St Benedict' by A. de Vogüé, in *Monastic Studies* 7 (1969); and 'L'Office Divin' by P. Salmon in *Lex Orandi* 27 (1959).
12. St John Chrysostom (*PG* 55.157–8).
13. Pachomius, *Reg.* 5.7.12; Cassian, *Inst.* 2.12–14.
14. RB 52.1 ff.
15. RB 16.10–12.
16. RB 20.10 ff.
17. RB 9.27.
18. J. Jungmann, *Pastoral Liturgy* (Challoner Publications 1962), pp. 92 ff.; J. D. Crichton, 'A Historical Sketch of the Roman Liturgy', in *True Worship*, ed. Lancelot Sheppard (Baltimore, The Helicon Press; Darton, Longman & Todd, 1963), pp. 72 ff.; B. Neunheuser, 'Possibilities and Limits of Liturgical Spontaneity', in *Monastic Studies* 8, Spring 1972.
19. Jungmann, op. cit. p. 90.
20. Ibid., p. 92.
21. *SC* 21.
22. *IGLH*, 273.
23. RB 50.
24. This title has been preferred because it is the exact equivalent of the Latin prototype *Liturgia Horarum*, and because it is the title of the English version prepared by the International Commission on English in the Liturgy, New York, Catholic Book Publishing Co., 1975. In England the Latin original is represented by *The Divine Office*, Collins 1974.
25. *IGLH*, 28.
26. 'Communities of monks, nuns, . . . represent the Church at prayer in a special way' (*IGLH*, 24).
27. Even this distinction is liable to give a false impression, since it could seem to imply a reification of the *Liturgy of the Hours* as recited by the clergy, as opposed to the expression of the life of a praying community.
28. Cf. de Vogüé, art. cit., p. 117: 'Those who limit their prayer to the hours must never forget that this is not an end but a means, not an ideal or a law descended from heaven, but a wise and humble human attempt to respond to the call of Christ and guard against human weakness.' Dom de Vogüé is

not here referring to making up in private offices from which one has been absent, but the principle is relevant.

29. J. Leclercq, 'Vérité et Continuité', a paper read at a conference in France in 1968 on the theme 'The Office in Today's Communities', reported in *American Benedictine Review* xix.4, December 1968.

30. Pius XII, Apostolic Constitution *Sponsa Christi* (*AAS* xxxxiii, pp. 13–14); also his broadcast address, *Audience Invisible*, in 1958 (*AAS* l, pp. 575–6); cf. *PC* 13.

31. *IGLH*, 164.

32. Ps. 33 (32).3.

33. Cf. Augustine Baker, *Holy Wisdom*, Treatise iii, sect. 1, ch. 3.

34. John 12.3.

35. RB 11.16, 30–32; 17.13–15; 18.62–75; cf. Chapter 4 above, 'The Rule', p. 50.

36. Cf. *Inst.* 4.36; *Conf.* 10.11.

37. Ibid.

38. Cassian, *Conf.* 9.26.

39. RB 19.12.

40. Ps. 58 (57).7, 11, in *The Psalms, A New Translation*.

41. Ps. 137 (136).8 ff., op. cit.

42. RSV 2 Tim. 3.16.

43. Song of Songs 8.6.

44. John 12.31.

45. RB Prol. 53 ff.

46. Rom. 15.4; cf. 1 Cor. 10.11.

47. RB 7. 210–13.

48. RB 9.21–3.

49. JB Sir. 2.15, 17.

50. RB 7, first rung.

51. RB (McCann) 4.56 ff.

52. RB 5.1–11.

53. RB 66.9 ff.

54. RB 19; 20; 52.

55. Cf. RB 4.50–55.

56. Cf. RB 19.

57. Cf. Isa. 55.9.

58. *SC* 10.

59. Cf. Chapter 8, 'Vocation and Growth in Community', n. 51.

60. Ps. 33 (32). 11, in *The Psalms, A New Translation*; cf. Entrance Song for Mass of the Sacred Heart.

LECTIO DIVINA

1. Isa. 30.8; Jer. 30.2; 36.2; Ezek. 43.11.
2. 1 Cor. 4.6.
3. Luke 24.27, 32, 44 ff; John 20.31; Acts 3.18, 24; 8.35; 17.2, 11; 18.28; 28.23. Cf. Matt. 22.29.
4. 1 Cor. 2.10–16; 2 Cor. 3.12–18.
5. John 5.39; 20.31.
6. Matt. 13.23; John 14.21; 15.3, 7.
7. St Thomas Aquinas, *ST* 2–2. 180. 3, ad 4. See also M. Lace, 'The Intrinsic Criterion of Divine Authorship', in *Downside Review* (LXXXIV, 1966), pp. 45 ff.
8. Marshall McLuhan, *The Gutenberg Galaxy* (Routledge & Kegan Paul 1962), pp. 5 ff.
9. Idem, *The Medium is the Message* (Penguin Books 1967), pp. 61, 122. Cf. ibid., p. 63: 'Ours is a brand-new world of allatonceness. "Time" has ceased, "space" has vanished. We now live in a global village . . . a simultaneous happening.'
10. Idem, *The Gutenberg Galaxy*, p. 89.
11. This latter expression first appeared in the treatise of Bartolomeo Ricci, S.J., *Instruttione di meditare*, Rome 1600, and then became current in other Jesuit authors (see article 'Lectio Divina' in *Dictionnaire de Spiritualité*, vol. ix, col. 494.
12. EBC Constitutions of 1931. Declarations 37, 93.
13. See F. Vanderbroucke, 'La *Lectio Divina* Aujourd'hui', in *Collectanea Cisterciensia* 32 (1970), p. 256.
14. A. de Vogüé: *La Règle de Saint Benoît*, vol. v, p. 598 (in *Sources Chrétiennes*). Cf. idem, ibid., pp. 599 ff: 'Pour le Maître il semble que le choix des heures les plus propices à l'activité manuelle soit la considération déterminante dans la fixation de l'emploi du temps . . . pour autant que les intentions de Benoît se laissent deviner, les aménagements de son horaire paraissent calculés d'abord du point de vue de la lecture. Celle-ci reçoit une part de temps meilleure que dans la RM, soit en durée, soit en qualité.' St Benedict is also conspicuous among monastic legislators for his pronounced interest in the choice of readings (see de Vogüé, *La Règle*, vol. i, p. 39).
15. St Augustine, *Sermo* 17: 'Dei servum sine intermissione legere, orare et operari oportet.' For Athanasius, Jerome, and Evagrius Ponticus requiring from the monk assiduous contact with the Bible, see G. Colombas, 'La Biblia en la Espiritualidad del Monacato Primitivo', in *Yermo* (I, 1963), pp. 1 ff. Cassian in *Conf.* 14.13 demands 'divinae legis sancta et incessabilis ruminatio'. Evagrius Ponticus urges: 'Let the rising sun find you with the Bible in your hand' (*PG* 40.128 3a). His master Origen's assiduity in studying the Scriptures was not even interrupted by meals (see D. Gorce: *La Lectio Divina* (Paris, Wépion-sur-Meuse, Monastère du Mont-Vièrge, 1925), p. 135). Guy de Chartreuse urged 'sedula Scripturarum cum animi intentione inspectio' (*PL* 40.997).

16. For Origen and Jerome see Gorce, op. cit. pp. 4 and 63. For Tertullian, Augustine, and Paulinus of Nola, ibid. pp. iii and 4. For St Benedict and St Caesar of Arles, see J. Leclercq, *L'Amour des Lettres et le Désir de Dieu* (Paris, Éditions du Cerf, 1957), p. 18. Cf. St Nilus (*Liber iv, Epist. i*): 'If you wish to have real compunction, do not read the works of profane authors, whether historical or rhetorical, and do not even think of the Old Testament, but read often the New, together with the Acts of the Martyrs, and the lives and examples of the ancient Fathers.' Cf. Origen: *In Exod. Hom. 12* in *PG* 9.143. St Benedict continues in this line, where the monastic life is almost identified with *lectio divina*, when to those for whom his little Rule shall have served its purpose he indicates the further reaches of the monastic life in terms of a number of books to be read and acted upon 'that we may travel by a straight road to our Creator' (RB 73.13).

17. Gorce, op. cit., p. 221. St Jerome made the Bible his code of education and forbade his lady pupils to continue studying profane letters, and even music. In the final chapter of his Rule St Benedict, it is true, recommends the Rule of St Basil and Cassian's Conferences alongside the Old and New Testaments and the Catholic Fathers. In this innovation he stands almost alone among contemporary legislators, but this should not be taken to mean that he was beginning the process of emancipating *lectio divina* from its biblical tutelage. For he shared the belief of his contemporaries that monastic rules merely set out in immediate practical terms what the Scriptures demand of a monk. Hermits also knew no other rule than the Scriptures. The recurrence in St Benedict's final chapter of the word *rectus* in connection with spiritual reading ('*rectissima* norma vitae humanae', 73.10; '*recto cursu*', 73.11), as also of *festinare* (73.5, 21), suggests that he envisaged a very direct relationship between this reading and man's last end, God. There are strong grounds too for believing that the *bibliotheca* from which each monk received a book to be read during Lent (48.36) meant not the library but the Bible in its various codices (see A. Mundo, ' "Bibliotheca", Bible et Lecture du Carême d'après Saint Benoît' in *Revue Bénédictine* (60), 1950, p. 65). St Basil especially does not claim in his Rule to be furnishing his disciples with legislative documents but simply with interpretations of the Bible (see G. Colombas, 'The Ancient Concept of Monastic Life', in *Monastic Studies* (2), 1964, p. 96. A similar very close association of them with the gospels may explain the Rule of the Master's recommendation of the reading of the Acts of the Martyrs (72.8). See also St Nilus, *Lib. iv, Epist. 1*).

18. See Augustine, *De Doctrina Christiana* (*PL* 34.89–90); Cassiodorus, *Institutiones* (ed. Mynors, Oxford University Press 1937), pp. 89 ff. Also Hugh of St Victor's *Didascalion*.

19. Leclercq, op. cit., p. 71, quoting Jerome.

20. *DV* 10.

21. See J. Mattoso, 'A "Lectio Divina" na alta Idada Media', in *Studia Monastica* (IX, 1967), p. 185.

22. RB 2.30–33, 63; 64.24. See also D. Chitty, *The Desert a City* (Oxford University Press 1966), p. 26, for the practice of Pachomius's successors.

23. See A. M. Mundo, 'Las Reglas del s. VI y la "Lectio Divina"', in *Studia Monastica* (IX, 1967), p. 239.

24. See F. Resch: *La Doctrine Ascétique des Premiers Maîtres Égyptiens du IVe Siècle* (Paris, Beauchesne, 1931), p. 165. For the economics of *lectio divina*, see A. Altisent, 'Libros y Economia en los Monasterios en la Edad Media', in *Yermo* (IV, 1966), p. 1.

25. RB 48.36, 'accipiant omnes *singulos* codices'; 48.13, 'aut forte qui voluerit legere sibi, sic legat ut alium non inquietat'.

26. Athanasius: 'In the words of Scriputure we encounter the Lord whose presence the demons find unbearable', in Colombas, op. cit. (*Yermo*, II, 1964), p. 14. Jerome: 'We eat his flesh and blood in the divine Eucharist, but also in the reading of the Scriptures', quoted by M. Evdokimov in 'La Lecture Orthodoxe des Écritures' in *Amitié* (1972), p. 14. For a comparison between the Bible and the Eucharist, see C. Charlier, *The Christian Approach to the Bible* (Sands 1958), p. 297.

27. Rom. 15.4; 1 Cor. 2.9-13; RB Prol. 22-35; St Gregory the Great, *In Ezechielem* 1, 8; *Epist.* v, 46; St Francis de Sales, *Introduction to the Devout Life*, part ii, ch. 16.

28. E.g. Prologue. 23, 'excitante nos Scriptura ac dicente'; 26: 'divina cotidie clamans . . . nos admonet vox dicens'; 63: 'audiamus Dominum respondentem et ostendentem nobis viam'.

29. Prologue. 22-91. St Cyprian coined the formula which became classic in subsequent writers: 'Sit tibi vel oratio assidua vel lectio, nunc cum Deo loquere, nunc Deus tecum' (*Epist.* i. 15; *PL* 4.221 b). The Constitution *Dei Verbum* of Vatican II describes the reading of the Scriptures as 'colloquium inter Deum et homines' (25). Cf. G. Morin, *The Ideal of the Monastic Life* (R. and T. Washbourne 1914), p. 130: 'Before a man undertakes to traffic with God, he must borrow the material from him.'

30. St Jerome, *Epist.* 22 *ad Eustochium* (*CSEL* 54, p. 178); St Odilo (*PL* 184.475-84); St Isidore of Seville (*Sent.* iii. 8, no. 2 in *PL* 83.679). Note too in RB 4.65 ff. how *oratio* immediately follows *lectio*. Cf. too Hugh of Mortaine, 'Legendo oro, orando contemplor' (MS Latin 3589, Paris).

31. L. Bouyer, *The Meaning of the Monastic Life* (Burns & Oates 1957), p. 168; J. Leclercq in *Dictionnaire de la Spiritualité* vol. iv, p. 194. A. Vööbus, *History of Asceticism in the Syrian Orient* (Louvain, CSCO, Subsidia, tome 14 1960), vol. 1, p. 147: Mesopotamiam monasticism sprang up independently of Egypt: 'In quest of the conditions and circumstances which may have evoked monasticism, the simplest assumption is that it could well have arisen in circles inspired by a devout perusal of the Scriptures.' Athanasius gave the early monks the title of 'philologoi', lovers of the word of God (*Life of Antony* 4, 44). Chrysostom had to combat in his sermons the conviction that lay people were exempt from studying the Scriptures because that was the speciality of the monk. For St Maximus the Confessor too the spiritual reading of the Scriptures was the principal occupation of the monk (see *Théologie de la Vie Monastique*, Paris, Aubier, 1961, p. 412). In the *Vita Prima* Pachomius addressed his disciples: 'Strive, brethren, to attain that whereunto you have been called: to meditate the Psalms and the lessons

from the rest of the Bible, especially the Gospel' (see *The Desert a City* by Derwas Chitty, p. 21).

32. RB 4.65, 'Lectiones sanctas *libenter* audire'. Conversely St Benedict (RB 48.42–4) defines the 'frater acediosus' as one who is not 'intentus lectioni', as does Cassian (*Inst.* 10.2). Cf. Matt. 13.18–23 p; Luke 6.47–9; 8.16–21; 11.27–8.

33. See Colombas, op. cit., p. 12; Resch, op. cit., p. 165: Pachomius required each novice to learn by heart twenty psalms and two epistles. (Gorce, op. cit., p. 73).

34. This may have been general practice in the ancient world, but it also shows the influence of liturgical proclamation of the word. See Augustine's surprise at Ambrose's silent reading in *Confessions* vi. 33; see also ibid. viii. 12, 29. *Meditatio* in early monasticism was a development of the 'soliloquy' of the philosophical schools; see Colombas, op. cit., p. 15.

35. Guy of Chartreuse:
    Lectio quasi solidum cibum apponit
    Meditatio masticat
    Oratio saporem acquirit
    Contemplatio est ipsa dulcedo.

36. See n. 33; cf. Athanasius, *Life of Antony* 3 (*PG* 26.845A).

37. Gorce, op. cit., pp. iii, 4 and 63. The *Regula Ferreoli* speaks of many works 'quibus saepe generat lectio divina fastidium'. St Nilus compared Scripture to the unattractive waters of the Jordan to which the prophet sent Naaman.

38. *Sent.* iii.40 (*PL* 80.896). Cf. Cassian (*Conf.* 14.11): 'As our mind is renewed by this study, so the face of the Scriptures also begins to be renewed. . . . The Scriptures appear to each man in proportion to his dispositions: earthly for the carnal man, divine for him who is spiritual.'

39. Bouyer, op. cit., p. 169. Cf. L. Blosius, *A Mirror for Monks* (Burns & Oates 1926), p. 23: 'For as a vessel which often receiveth water remains clean, although the water poured in be presently poured out again, so likewise, if spiritual doctrine often run through a well-willing mind, although it abide not there, nevertheless it makes and keeps the mind clean and pleasing to God.' That *lectio divina* was an exercise to be pursued for its own sake is further illustrated by the frequent references to the joys of savouring it, e.g. Arnold of Boheries, 'Si ad legendum accedat, non tam quaerat scientiam quam saporem' (*PL* 184.1175 b). See also G. M. Colombas, *El Monacato Primitivo* (Madrid, Biblioteca de Autores Cristianos 1975), vol. 2, p. 348.

40. 2 Cor. 3.18. Clement of Alexandria: 'When a man leaves his error to listen to the voice of Scripture, and to open his mind to the Truth, he is no longer a mere man. He has in some way become God' (*Stromata* vii.16).

41. Cassian, *Conf.* 10.11, 'Eundem namque recipientes cordis affectum quo quisque decantatus vel conscriptus est psalmus, velut auctores eius facti precedemus magis intellectum quam sequemur.' For the Scriptures as food, see St Gregory, *Moralia* vi.5; Jerome in Gorce (op. cit.), p. 339; RM 24.4–5.

42. *Conf.* 1.7. 'We must exercise ourselves in fasts, vigils, solitude, meditation on the Scriptures in order to obtain our immediate end – purity of heart,

which is charity.' Cf. Basil (*Ep.* 2. 3): 'The great way that leads to fulfilment of duty is the meditation of the sacred Scriptures.' In Pachomius's monastery the meditation of the Scriptures was the ascetic means *par excellence* of never losing sight of Christ (Gorce, op. cit., p. 79). The texts of Scripture were also held to be effective means of rebuffing the onslaughts of demons (Colombas, op. cit. (1964), p. 8). Also the Rule of the Master (15.19–27) prescribed special readings to help brothers afflicted with evil thoughts.

43. For Origen's notion of conversion in terms of turning all one's energies to the study of God's word, see Gorce, op. cit., p. 63. For Jerome manual labour was intended to provide his disciples with equilibrium in the midst of their reading (ibid., p. 160), fasting to be a means of self-purification for understanding the Scriptures (ibid., p. 173), enclosure and silence to enable them to concentrate while reading the Bible (ibid., pp. 136, 138). St Samson did penance to receive a better understanding of the Scriptures.

44. St Augustine (*De Doctrina Christiana* 1.39: 43): 'A man who is firm in faith, hope and charity has no need of the Scriptures – he has already attained the end for which the Scriptures were disposing him, the sanctification of his human nature.'

45. P. Grelot, *The Bible, Word of God* (New York, Desclée, 1968), p. 200. Cf. Colombas, *El Monacato Primitivo*, vol. 2, p. 357: 'Primitive monasticism, especially in its more erudite varieties, never conceived of any contemplation of God which did not take as its starting-point the reading, meditation and assimilation of the Scriptures by the monk.'

46. Jas. 1.23–5. 'A mirror in which we attain self-knowledge' (St Gregory, *Moralia* ii.1). 'The great way to discover our duty is to meditate on the inspired Scriptures . . . and the lives of the blessed ones which the Scriptures have transmitted to us are, as it were, living images of life according to God, proposed to us that we may imitate their good works' (St Basil: *Ep.* 2.3, in *PG* 32.228 bc).

47. In RB 73.6, if one may judge by his syntax and the order of his sentences, St Benedict seems to include Scripture in the wider class of *doctrina sanctorum Patrum*: it is for him part of the monk's spiritual ancestry.

48. See Colombas, op. cit., pp. 274–80.

49. Acts 2.44–7; 4.32–5. St Jerome: 'Monachus apostolicam vitam desiderat imitare' (*Hom.* 7.8; Cassian, *Conf.* 18; cf. G. Morin, op. cit., passim; for St Augustine see D. Sanchis, 'Pauvreté Monastique et Charité Fraternelle', in *Studia* Monastica (IV, 1962), p. 8.

50. See for examples Colombas, op. cit., pp. 163–4.

51. E.g. St Benedict's habit of juxtaposing or even combining texts of the Old and New Testaments and his consistent description of the psalmist as *propheta*. See Gorce, op. cit., p. 10, for St Jerome's notion of Christ's figure dominating the Old Testament. Cf. Luke 24.27.

52. A. M. Mundo, op. cit., p. 251.

53. Ibid., p. 252.

54. RB 73.9; 53.20.

55. See F. Murphy, '*Scienter nescius*: A Study of Monastic Culture' in *Downside Review* (LXXIX, 1961), pp. 245, 247.

56. It nevertheless remains true that determined and regular times for reading (*certis temporibus*) are not the juridical invention of a recent age, but were also insisted upon in primitive monasticism.

57. The Congregation of Valladolid has a privileged place among the formative influences on the English Benedictine Congregation, and its attitude towards *lectio divina* can be gauged from certain practical prescriptions of its greatest representative, the reforming abbot Cisneros: he held regular chapters in which all his monks had to render an account of their reading; the abbot felt himself responsible for providing his monks with help towards the understanding of their books, even if necessary having recourse outside the monastery; the purchase of books for *lectio divina* was to be regarded as the most necessary expense of the monastery. (See *Obras Completas*, ed. C. Barrault, Montserrat, Abadia de Montserrat 1965, vol. 2, pp. 519–22).

58. RB (McCann) 53.19 ff.

59. See St Benedict's receptivity to remarks made on his monastery by visiting priests and pilgrim monks, RB 61.8 ff.

60. Leclercq, op. cit., p. 71. The Maurist studies also evolved from their efforts to organize *lectio divina* (see F. Vanderbroucke, 'L'Esprit des Études dans la Congrégation de Saint-Maur', in *Los Monjes y los Estudios*, Poblet, Abadia de Poblet, 1963, p. 457).

61. Ibid., pp. 97 ff.

62. N. Ward, *The Use of Praying* (Epworth Press 1967), p. 111. Cf. Bede Griffiths, 'On Reading Novels', in *Pax* XLIV (Autumn 1954), pp. 124 ff: 'There is a limit to the amount that one can take in by way of spiritual reading. After a time abstract principles, having been fully assimilated, cease to exercise any further attraction, and the effort of consecutive discursive thought becomes almost intolerable. The mind no longer wants to discourse and reason; it wants the evidence of concrete experience.'

63. RB 48.37. Evagrius Ponticus acclaimed *lectio divina*, along with watching and prayers, as a means of discipline, leading to concentration. (See *Praktikos* 15.)

64. Augustine Baker in *Holy Wisdom* (First Treatise, sec. ii, ch. 3, pp. 58 ff. in Orchard Edn., Burns & Oates 1964) warns the seeker after God that if he selects the wrong reading, it may do more harm than good. Cf. St Francis de Sales, op. cit., p. 100. Francis Bacon, *Essays Civil and Moral* (J. Havilard, Hanna Barret & R. Whitaker 1625): 'Some books are to be tasted, others to be swallowed, and some few to be chewed and digested.'

65. See W. Johnston, S.J., 'The Mystical Reading of Scripture; Some Suggestions from Buddhism', in *Cistercian Studies* (VI, 1971), pp. 57 ff.

66. Jerome, *In Isaiam*, Prologue (*PL* 24.17 A).

421

PERSONAL PRAYER

1. *Confessions*, x.27.
2. *Pensées*, sect. vii.
3. J. H. Newman, *Apologia pro Vita Sua*, part VI (Collins, Fontana 1959), p. 278.
4. For another way of expressing the same idea, cf. Martin Jarrett-Kerr, C.R., on Gerard Manley Hopkins in *The Times*, 5 June 1971 (reproduced from *The Times* by permission). When we look into ourselves we find something unique. I find myself, 'my pleasures and pains, my powers and experiences, my deserts and guilt, my shame and sense of beauty, my dangers, hopes, fears, and all my fate, more important to myself than anything I see.' For when I look within, it is not only my mind which I discover, it is 'my self-being, that taste of myself, of I and me above all and in all things, which is more distinctive than the taste of ale or alum, more distinctive than the smell of walnut leaf or camphor, and is incommunicable by any means to another man (as when I was a child I used to ask myself: What must it be to be someone else?)'. We find, he says, that there is nothing else in nature like this: 'Nothing explains it or resembles it, except so far as this, that other men to themselves have the same feeling.' But where should this 'selfhood' come from? It cannot have been developed or evolved from 'the vastness of the world', but can only have been the work of 'one of finer or higher pitch' than itself . . . this individuality cannot be explained by 'form, quantity, and so on', but only by the divine will.

This penetration into man's being not only inspires Hopkins's poetry but is most clearly expressed by it:

As kingfishers catch fire, dragonflies draw flame;
As tumbled over rim in roundly wells
Stones ring; like each tucked string tells, each hung bell's
Bow swung finds tongue to fling out broad its name;
Each mortal thing does one thing and the same:
Deals out that being indoors each one dwells:
Selves – goes itself; *myself* it speaks and spells,
Crying *What I do is me: for that I came*. ('As Kingfishers Catch Fire', in *The Poems of Gerard Manley Hopkins*, 4th edn., ed. W. H. Gardner and N. H. MacKenzie, Oxford 1967. Published by arrangement with the Society of Jesus).

5. Cf. Matt. 5.8.
6. Jer. 8.7.
7. On this, cf. B. J. F. Lonergan, *Method in Theology*, 2nd edn. (Darton, Longman & Todd 1973), p. 103. The question of God 'rises out of our conscious intentionality, out of the *a priori* structured drive that promotes us from experiencing to the effort to understand, from understanding to the effort to judge truly, from judging to the effort to choose rightly. In the measure that we advert to our own questioning and proceed to question it, there arises the question of God. . . . The question of God, then, lies within

man's horizon. Man's transcendental subjectivity is mutilated or abolished, unless he is stretching forth towards the intelligible, the unconditioned, the good of value. The reach, not of his attainment, but of his intending is unrestricted. There lies within his horizon a region for the divine, a shrine for ultimate holiness. It cannot be ignored. The atheist may pronounce it empty. The agnostic may urge that he finds his investigation has been inconclusive. The contemporary humanist will refuse to allow the question to arise. But their negations presuppose the spark in our clod, our native orientation to the divine.'

8. John 1.46. Faith does not rest on the wisdom of men but on the power of God (1 Cor. 2.5). It is impossible by human effort *alone* to 'see for oneself'; Nathanael required help from Jesus (John 1.47–9). This incident might be taken as illustrative of the whole process whereby man comes into contact with God: a right disposition and readiness to come and see; further enlightenment received; the seeing which unites; the promise of greater things (John 1.50).

9. P. Tillich, *The New Being* (New York, Charles Scribner's Sons, 1955), p. 128.

10. Cf. Rom. 8.28; Eph. 4.1; 2 Tim. 1.9; 1 Pet. 2.21, etc. The call is capable of being heard by all, otherwise there would be no point in the command to preach to all nations (Matt. 28.19).

11. Cf. Chapter 7, 'Freedom and Availability for God', p. 95.

12. Phil. 2.13.

13. Cf. John 3.8.

14. T. Merton, *The Climate of Monastic Prayer* (Kalamazoo, Michigan, Cistercian Studies, 1969), p. 58.

15. Cf. Mark 4.26–9.

16. Cf. Col. 3.3 ff.

17. John 14.16; 4.10, 23; Luke 11.13 (especially if compared with Matt. 7.11). The importance of the Spirit's action in prayer can be seen from Matt 4.1 (led by the Spirit); Luke 1.15; 2.27; John 1.32; 3.5; 14.26; Acts 9.17; 10.44; Rom. 8.26 ff; 1 Cor. 6.19; Gal. 5.25; Eph. 1.13; 2.22; 1 Thess. 4.8; 2 Tim. 1.14.

18. Cf. Chapter 7, 'Freedom and Availability for God', p. 99; Chapter 9, 'Celibacy', pp. 165–6; Chapter 12, '*Lectio Divina*', p. 268.

19. Luke 9.29, 35; 3.21 ff.; Mark 14.36.

20. Rom. 8.14–17; Gal. 2.20; 4.6.

21. Ps. 36(35).10.

22. 2 Pet. 1.4.

23. Cf. Eph. 5.2.

24. Col. 1.18.

25. Rom. 6.4; Eph. 4.4 ff.

26. RSV Rom. 12.5.

27. Eph. 4.12.

28. Col. 1.24.
29. NEB 2 Tim. 2.10.
30. John 17.1–3.
31. Cf. Chapter 9, 'Conversion and Asceticism', pp. 148 ff.
32. John 15.2.
33. RSV John 14.13.
34. Cf. Mark 3.31–5; Luke 11.27 ff.; John 2.1–11; 19.25–7.
35. Luke 1.29, 34; 2.33, 50.
36. Luke 2.19, 51.
37. Cf. Matt. 1.19.
38. Luke 11.28.
39. Luke 1.39 ff.
40. John 19.26 ff.
41. RB Prol. 52, 125, 46 ff.
42. RB 4.56 ff.
43. RB 7.42 ff.
44. RB 7.46.
45. RB 19.1–5.
46. T. Merton, op. cit., p. 153.
47. RB Prol. 106–9.
48. RB 20.8.
49. RB 4.66.
50. RB 4.11 ff., 32 ff., 35 ff., 46 ff., 58–60, 88; also ch. 7, rungs 1–4, etc.
51. RB 35.25–37.
52. RB 38.4–11.
53. RB 58.57.
54. RB 27.11 ff., 44.
55. RB 63.29 ff.
56. RB 66.8.
57. RB 67.1–5.
58. RB 28.13–16.
59. RB 47.8 ff.; 38.29; 19.12; 22.17 f.; 43.3.
60. Cf. Chapter 3, 'The Mission and Relationship of the Church to the World', p. 30.
61. RB 52; 49.8 ff., 12.
62. RB (Bolton) 20.4–9.
63. RB (Bolton) 52.6–9. Thomas Merton, commenting on this, says, 'The concept of "the heart" . . . refers to the deepest psychological ground of one's personality, the inner sanctuary where self-awareness goes beyond analytical reflection and opens out into the metaphysical and theological confrontation with the Abyss of the unknown yet present – one who is

"more intimate to us than we are to ourselves"' (op. cit., p. 48. The closing phrase is adapted from St Augustine's *Confessions*).

64. See *The Spiritual Letters of Dom John Chapman*, ed. Hudleston (Sheed & Ward 1959), especially p. 293.
65. Merton, op. cit., p. 65.
66. RSV Rom. 8.26.
67. Tillich, op. cit., p. 135.
68. JB Heb. 5.7.
69. Cf. Rom. 8.17.
70. Eph. 5.2; cf. *AG* 40.
71. 2 Cor. 3.6.
72. Luke 18.1; 21.36.
73. Cf. John 10.10.
74. Prayer of 'giving thanks', John 11.41; 6.11 (= Mark 6.41); Mark 8.6; Luke 22.19.
75. Luke 6.12.
76. Luke 22.44, and the whole scene.
77. NEB Eph. 6.18.
78. John 5.24; 6.47; 17.3; cf. 3.15 ff., 36; 6.40; 7.38; 11.25; 20.31.
79. Eph. 4.13.
80. Cf. John 14.6 ff., 17; 17.25 ff.

SHARED PRAYER

1. *Shared Prayer*: a leaflet by Fr Bohdan Kosicki and Fr George Kosicki (unpublished).
2. Luke 2.19, 51; 1.35, 46 ff.
3. Mark 3.14.
4. E.g. Mark 6.32; Luke 9.1; Mark 9.2, 30 ff.; John 1.38 ff.
5. RSV Acts 1.14.
6. JB Acts 2.46 ff.; cf. Acts 4.21; 21.20.
7. JB Acts 4.29 ff.; cf. 4.23–31.
8. RSV Acts 12.5, 12.
9. JB Acts 16.25.
10. JB Acts 20.36–8.
11. JB Acts 15.12; cf. 21.17–20.
12. RSV Acts 11.17 ff.
13. JB 1 Cor. 14.26.
14. JB Col. 3.16 ff.
15. JB Eph. 5.19 ff.
16. JB 1 Thess. 5.16–20.

17. *SC* (ed. Abbott-Gallagher) 1.
18. RB (Bolton) 19.1–3.
19. JB Matt. 18.20; cf. preceding verse.
20. Edward O'Connor, C.S.C., *The Pentecostal Movement in the Catholic Church* (Notre Dame, Indiana, Ave Maria Press 1971), p. 32.
21. Léon Joseph, Cardinal Suenens, *A New Pentecost?* (Darton, Longman & Todd 1975), pp. 111, 113.
22. O'Connor, op. cit., p. 34.
23. See especially Pope Paul's allocution to the International Charismatic Conference in 1975 (*AAS* lxvii, pp. 364–8).
24. *Statement on Benedictine Life* by the Congress of Abbots in 1967, no. 15.
25. 1 Cor. 12.7; cf. the whole of chapters 12–14.
26. Matt. 7.7.
27. JB Matt. 11.28.
28. JB Eph. 4.2 f.
29. Matt. 7.20.
30. RB (Bolton) 13.28–31.
31. Cf. Mark 16.18; Luke 9.1 ff.; 10.9; John 14.12. See also F. MacNutt, *Healing*, Notre Dame, Indiana, Ave Maria Press, 1974; M. Scanlan, *Inner Healing*, New York, Paulist Press, 1974.
32. JB Acts 5.38 ff.

WORK

1. Cf. M.-D. Chenu, *The Theology of Work*, Dublin 1963, especially ch. 1: 'Towards a Theology of Work' and Appendix: 'The Relationship between Man and Nature according to St Maximus'.
2. RSV Eph. 2.10.
3. Cf. *GS* 67: 'Work proceeds immediately from the person, who puts his seal on the things of nature and subjects them to his will.'
4. Cf. *GS* (ed. Abbott-Gallagher) 67: 'It is ordinarily by his labour that a man supports himself and his family, is joined to his fellow-men and serves them, and is enabled to exercise genuine charity and be a partner in the work of bringing God's creation to perfection. Indeed, we hold that by offering his labour to God a man becomes associated with the redemptive work itself of Jesus Christ, who conferred an eminent dignity on labour when at Nazareth he worked with his own hands.'
5. Gen. 1.31–2.3.
6. St Thomas, *De Potentia*, q. 3, a. 4, Ad horum autem. . . ; cf. John 9.4; *GS* 33; 34; *AA* 7.
7. *GS* (ed. Abbott-Gallagher) 39. Even here we depend totally on the support of God for the success of our work: 'If the Lord does not build the house, in vain do its builders labour' (Ps. 127(126).1, in *The Psalms, A New Translation*, cf. *GS* 34; 57).

426

8. Exod. 20.8–11. The Sabbath is not an obligation to be rigidly imposed on men as though any external observance could in itself bring about our fulfilment; cf. Mark 2.27.
9. Gen. 1.28; cf. GS 34; 57.
10. GS (ed. Abbott-Gallagher) 35: 'A man is more precious for what he is than for what he has.' Cf. GS 9; 67.
11. GS (ed. Abbott-Gallagher) 37; 1 Cor. 3.22 ff.; cf. 2 Cor. 6.10.
12. Cf. Gen. 3.17–19.
13. John 17.4.
14. Heb. 2.10.
15. Heb. 5.8 ff.
16. Cf. Chapter 9, 'Conversion and Asceticism', pp. 149 ff.
17. RB 48; cf. C. Butler, Benedictine Monachism (Longmans, Green & Co. 1919), ch. 17.
18. Cf. also GS 43; St Augustine, De opere monachorum 18 (PL 40.565–6).
19. RB (McCann) 48. 18–21; cf. 1 Thess. 4.11; 2 Thess. 3.10–12; Acts 18.3; 20.33–5.
20. RB 48.1.
21. Cf. GS 57; 61.
22. Cf. St Augustine, De opere monachorum 17 (PL 40.564–5).
23. RB (McCann) 35.1–5.
24. Cf. 2 Thess. 3.6–12; GS 67; PC 13.
25. Cf. Chapter 5, 'Communication and Co-responsibility', pp. 66, 70.
26. Cf. ibid., pp. 70 ff.; Chapter 6, 'The Abbot', pp. 90–92; Chapter 9, 'Obedience', pp. 201–2.
27. RSV 2 Cor. 9.7.
28. 'When we state that man realizes his potential in prolonging the work of creation through his labour, we mean that by virtue of this fact he places himself inside a process of saving history. Building the earthly city is not a simple stage of "humanization" or "pre-evangelization", as the theology of a few years ago used to have it; it is integrating oneself fully in a saving process that embraces all mankind' (Gustavo Gutiérrez, Liberación, opción de la iglesia en la decada del 70 [Bogota 1970], vol. I, p. 49; quoted by Hugo Assmann, Theology for a Nomad Church [Maryknoll, New York, Orbis Books, 1976], p. 68).
29. Mark 8.34 p.
30. Col. 1.24. Cf. Chapter 9, 'Conversion and Asceticism', pp. 150–52.
31. GS (ed. Abbott-Gallagher) 35: 'The norm of human activity is this, that in accord with the divine plan and will, it should harmonize with the genuine good of the human race, and allow men as individuals and as members of society to pursue their total vocation and fulfil it.' GS 17: 'Man's dignity demands that he act according to a knowing and free choice. Such a choice is personally motivated and prompted from within. It does not result from

427

blind internal impulse nor from mere external pressure.' *Statement on Benedictine Life*, Appendix 2.D, 'Personalism': monks want 'to be able to realize themselves by the full and legitimate development of their personal capabilities, to be treated as human beings – adult, free, and responsible, and to be able to act with initiative'.

32. RB 64.40–50.
33. Cf. RSV Gen. 29.20: 'Jacob served seven years for Rachel, and they seemed to him but a few days because of the love he had for her.'
34. Cf. Chapter 7, 'Freedom and Availability for God', p. 105.
35. Cf. Chapter 9, 'Poverty and Sharing of Goods', pp. 218–20.
36. Cf. Luke 17.10; RB 57.2–7.
37. Cf. Chapter 3, 'The Mission and Relationship of the Church to the World', pp. 36–8.
38. Cf. RB 57.15–19.
39. Job 28.20 ff., Wisd. 7–9.
40. Cf. John 1.1–18.
41. RSV 1 Cor. 2.10.
42. *The Public Schools Commission, First Report* (HMSO 1968), vol. 2, p. 178.
43. 1 Cor. 3.9; cf. C. Spicq, *Saint Paul, Les Épîtres Pastorales* (Paris, Gabalda, 4th edn, 1969), pp. 595–9, Excursus v, 'Une théologie de l'apostolat'.
44. Eph. 4.11 ff.
45. 1 Pet. 4.10.

MONASTICISM AND THE PRIESTHOOD

1. LG 10; AA 2; 1 Pet. 2.9; Rev. 5.10; also St Augustine, 'Sicut omnes christos dicimus propter mysticum chrisma, sic omnes sacerdotes quoniam membra sunt unius sacerdotis' (*De Civ. Dei* 20.10, PL 41.676). In this reassertion Vatican II had been anticipated by the encyclical *Mediator Dei* (1947). Trent had failed to meet the Reformers' challenge on this point, but that Council's silence should not be construed as a repudiation of this doctrine *in se*.
2. Heb. 3.14; 4.14.
3. See T. W. Manson's addresses to the Free Church Federal Council published in *Ministry and Priesthood, Christ's and Ours* (Epworth Press 1958), p. 40: 'Bishop Kirk described the priesthood of all believers as "the decisive formula of all non-episcopal Christendom". Certainly it has been one of the great rallying-cries of Free Churchmanship. But it may be suspected that some who use it most often and most emphatically mean by it something more like "the priesthood of no believer whatsoever" or "the non-priesthood of all believers".'
4. For St Irenaeus all Christ's earthly activity was sacerdotal in character since it was all directed towards leading men in exile and under condemnation back to God and to the inheritance man had lost by sin. Irenaeus thus justified Christ's work on the Sabbath when priestly works were allowed

(*Adv. Haeres.* iv.8, 2); cf. J. Lecuyer, *Le Sacerdoce dans le mystère du Christ* (Paris, Éditions du Cerf, 1957), p. 23. See also A. George, 'Le Sacerdoce de la Nouvelle Alliance dans la Pensée de Jésus', in *La Tradition Sacerdotale* (Le Puy, Éditions Xavier Mappus, 1959), pp. 68 ff., for the reasons for interpreting the Presentation in the Temple, the Baptism of Jesus, and his Cleansing of the Temple as manifestations of his priesthood.

5. *LG* 10. Henceforth in this chapter the word 'priest' will mean 'ministerial priest' in accordance with normal usage, although this is misleading in that it suggests a radical dichotomy between priests and laity; for 'priests' are also members of the 'laos', the people of God who in turn have the priestly qualities already mentioned.

6. See St Thomas Aquinas, *Sent.* IV, d.xviii, q. I, *art.* I, *sol.* II, (*ad primum*).

7. 'Each of the seven sacraments is the manifestation of some element which belongs to the nature of the Church as the sacrament of Christ. The ordained minister, because of the sacramental character which he has received . . . is a telling and permanent witness to the dependence of the Church on Christ and to his influence over it, whereby it is he, and he alone, who transforms and renews it in the Spirit' (D. N. Power, *Ministers of Christ and his Church* [Geoffrey Chapman 1969], p. 175).

8. *PO* 4; *LG* 28; *SC* 10. This is clearest in the case of bishops who possess the fulness of the priesthood and are the persons in whom priesthood is most itself. Their office is essentially pastoral and apostolic, not bound exclusively to the Eucharist.

9. Matt. 28.19 ff. shows the conferring on the apostles of Christ's threefold power of sanctifying, governing, and teaching.

10. Vatican II never spoke of a priest in the singular, always in the plural. See also G. H. Luttenberger, 'The Priest as a Member of a Ministerial College. The Development of the Church's Ministerial Structure from A.D. 96 to 300', in *Recherches de théologie ancienne et médiévale* (xliii) (1976), pp. 5–63.

11. *CD* 34 asserts that religious clergy in a real sense form part of the diocesan presbyterium in so far as they too have a share in the apostolate under the bishop.

12. St John Chrysostom taught that a priest because of his consecration must be 'detached from everything, even more so than the monks who live on the mountains'; i.e. the priest must live like a monk in the world (*De Sacerdotio* vi.4).

13. *LG* 28; 31; 41; *AG* 16; 20; 39; *CD* 34; *PO* 13. For the amendment in question, see the *Modi* on the Schema for *PO* (1965), pp. 74 ff., its discussion in 'La Vie Contemplative et le Monachisme d'après Vatican II' by Jean Leclerq in *Gregorianum* (xlvii), 1966, no. 3, p. 511, where he uses the rejection of this amendment as a basis for his plea for a non-sacerdotal contemplative monasticism, and the disputation of his position and of his interpretation of that amendment by G. Frenaud, 'La Vie Monastique et le Sacerdoce' in *Gregorianum* (xlviii), 1967, no. 3, pp. 588 ff.

14. J. Winandy in 'Priest and Hermit' in *Monastic Studies* (8), 1972, pp. 119–32,

upholds the 'indifferentiation' of the priesthood in relation to its concrete occupations. (See also *Cistercian Studies* 1976.2, p. 261.)

15. See David Knowles, *The Religious Orders in England*, vol. iii (Cambridge University Press 1959), pp. 445–6.

16. See Cassian's injunction that monks should flee women and bishops in *Inst.* 2.18.

17. Regular clergy are also related to the college of bishops and form with them 'one single priesthood' (*CD* 28; cf. 34–5). 'Religious orders do not in themselves constitute particular churches, and the relations of religious to their particular diocese take precedence over all monastic autonomy and exemption' (K. Mörsdorf in H. Vorgrimler, *Commentary on the Documents of Vatican II*, vol. ii [Burns & Oates 1969], p. 267); cf. Chapter 18, 'Autonomy'.

18. 1 Tim. 2.5 ff; Rom. 3.25.

19. Cf. John 4.23.

20. See Lecuyer, op. cit., p. 294.

21. But it is as a priest with his hands raised in blessing that Luke depicts Christ ascending to heaven (Luke 24.50; Acts 3.26). And the office is also implicit in all Christ's claims to be the new Temple, the centre of the new worship of God he would inaugurate.

22. Eph. 2.20–22 shows Christ's mediatorship with cultic overtones which specify that mediatorship as sacerdotal.

23. Mark 10.45; Eph. 5.2; Heb. 9.13 ff.

24. B. C. Butler, *A Time to Speak* (Mayhew McCrimmon 1972), p. 146.

25. Mic. 3.11; Jer. 18.18; Lev. 10.10 f; Ezek. 7.26; 22.26; 44.23; cf. Deut. 33.8–10 where the order in which the priestly functions and privileges are set out is: (1) the custody and operation of the apparatus for obtaining oracles by means of the sacred lot; (2) the custody, interpretation, and application of the Torah of Yahweh; (3) certain sacrificial functions. 'Priests were from the first, and most conspicuously in the earlier periods, recipients, organs of revelation' (G. Buchanan Gray, *Sacrifice in the Old Testament* [Oxford University Press 1925], p. 200). The priests of Israel thus contrasted with those of adjoining Near Eastern countries whose ministry was purely cultic. See also L. Leloir, 'Valeurs permanentes du sacerdoce lévitique' in *NRT* (xcii) 1970, pp. 246–66.

26. Mark 10.45; 14.24; Rom. 3.25; Eph. 5.2; 1 John 2.2; 4.10.

27. According to A. Feuillet, *The Priesthood of Christ and his Ministers* (Garden City, New York, Doubleday Books, 1975), John 17 is designed on the same plan as the Jewish liturgy for the Day of Atonement. Then the High Priest made atonement successively for himself, for his family (which was equivalent to saying 'for the priesthood') and for the entire chosen people (Lev. 16). Feuillet interprets the foot-washing as the preparation of the Twelve for their consecration as priests, a ceremony also transposed from initiation into the Aaronic priesthood (Lev. 16.4; Exod. 29.4; 40.12). In Christ's words, 'You have no share with me' (John 13.8) he sees a formula

used in the Old Testament only in connection with Levites. Christ's baptism too would have been his high priestly act of purification, not for himself but for others with whom he sought the fullest possible solidarity (Luke 3.21).

28. John 17.21.

29. So *eucharistēsas* and *eulogēsas* are not only a formula of thanksgiving but express the joyful and enduring proclamation of the *mirabilia Dei*; cf. 1 Cor. 11.26 (*La Tradition Sacerdotale*, p. 252).

30. 1 Sam. 16.13–15; 1 Kings 19.16; Exod. 29.7; 40.12–15; Lev. 8.12.

31. This threefold designation of Christ is by no mean exhaustive. Numerous other titles are used by the gospels in order to express the richness of the mission of Christ, as also of the commission he hands on.

32. RSV Heb. 6.20; cf. Acts 3.15; 5.31.

33. Also, according to St Augustine, it was because the priesthood after the order of Melchizedek is for ever; God will not repent of it as he did of the priesthood according to the order of Aaron.

34. Heb. 1.1–13; 2.18; 4.15.

35. Rom. 12.1–5 shows that the 'living sacrifice' offered by the faithful has the purpose of building up the community as the Body of Christ.

36. Rom. 12.1 (beginning a lengthy list, 12.1—15.12, of works of charity); Phil. 2.17; 4.18; Heb. 13.16. St Ignatius of Antioch describes the whole process of his martyrdom in sacrificial and even eucharistic terms, and gives many other instances of a spiritualization of the cult (*Rom.* 2.2; 4.1, 2; *Eph.* 8.1).

37. B. C. Butler, op. cit., p. 146.

38. Exod. 19.6; Isa. 61.6; Rev. 5.10.

39. This danger was not altogether avoided, and several Christian writers depicted the Christian priesthood as a lineal descendant of that of Aaron (see R. Murray, 'Christianity's "Yes" to Priesthood' in *The Christian Priesthood, 9th Downside Symposium*, eds. N. Lash and J. Rhymer [Darton, Longman & Todd 1970], pp. 31–5).

40. See Manson, op. cit., pp. 67 ff., finding very frequent instances in Tertullian: *Ad Nat.* 1.7; *De Praescript.* 41; *De Virg. Vel.* 9; *De Bapt.* 17; Hippolytus: *Apostolic Tradition* 1.3, 4; Cyprian in *Epist.* 5; 63; 69; *Didascalia* 9. It is taken for granted in Origen: *Hom. in Jos.* 2; 7; 9. See also J. Moingt, 'Caractère et ministère sacerdotale', in *Recherches de Science Religieuse* (56), 1968, no. 4, p. 569.

41. J. A. T. Robinson, 'Christianity's "No" to Priesthood', in *The Christian Priesthood* (see n. 39), p. 13.

42. 2 Cor. 3.6 connects 'the ministers of the new covenant' very closely with the Spirit. The Christian ministry is not simply an ontological participation in the priesthood of Christ, but a communion in the Spirit who consecrated Jesus's human nature for the priesthood.

43. Cf. 2 Cor. 4.5.

44. JB John 17.17.

45. RSV John 10.36, 'whom the Father consecrated and sent into the world'; cf. John 20.21 ff.

46. The priest represents not only Christ to his people, but also his people to Christ. The apostles were originally called 'the Twelve' because they thus represent the whole People of God. Exod. 28.9–11, 17–21 shows that the symbol of the unity of Israel's tribes comes from priestly as well as from prophetic circles. At the *Hanc igitur* the priest is acting as the symbolic representative of the liturgical assembly. But at the Consecration, when repeating the gestures and words of Christ, the priest appears as the representative of Christ, to assemble, sanctify, and nourish the Church and bring it with him to his Father in praise.

47. Many of the Fathers (e.g. St Gregory Nazianzen) define the priest not by any speciality, such as to celebrate Mass or to preach, but by a comprehensive activity which includes all the ministries which render a priest 'a maker of Christians', 'a maker of the sons of God'. (See Y. Congar, 'Le Sacerdoce du Nouveau Testament', in *Les Prêtres: Décrets 'Presbyterorum Ordinis' et 'Optatam Totius'*, vol. 68 in coll. *Unam Sanctam*, Paris, Éditions du Cerf, 1968.)

48. See R. E. Brown, *Priest and Bishop, Biblical Reflections*, Geoffrey Chapman 1971. But see also a criticism of this analysis in R. J. Dillon, 'Biblical Approaches to the Priesthood', in *Worship*, October 1972, pp. 454–72.

49. John 15.14 ff; Matt. 6.24; Luke 9.62.

50. The strenuous labours of the apostle can be gauged from the three metaphors Paul uses for them: soldiers, athletes, industrious farmers (C. Spicq, *Les Épîtres Pastorales* [Paris, Gabalda, 1969], pp. 350, 740 ff.).

51. 2 Cor. 4.5; 1 Cor. 9.19.

52. 1 Cor. 1.17; Matt. 28.19; Rom. 10.15.

53. 1 Cor. 11.26; Acts 20.7–11.

54. Phil. 2.17; Rom. 15.15–18; 1 Cor. 3.16 ff.; 9.13 ff.; 2 Cor. 2.15 ff. It is unlikely that this language is, as some have maintained, borrowed from pagan rather than from biblical usage, even if the sacrificial terminology used to describe his martyrdom by St Ignatius of Antioch (cf. n. 36 above) is more clearly Christian: 'ground by the teeth of the beasts to be found the pure bread of Christ'; then he will be 'a sacrificial victim for God' (*Rom.* 4.1, 2).

55. See Rom. 5.1–11 for Christ's ministry of reconciliation; 2 Cor. 5.18–20 for that of the apostles.

56. In the *Didache* (11.3) both the apostles and the prophets are mentioned as classes who are always itinerant.

57. 2 Cor. 10,8; 13.10.

58. 1 Tim. 3.2–6; Titus 1.9.

59. 1 Tim. 3.4 ff.; 1 Pet. 5.2–4; cf. 1 Clem. 54.1; 57.1.

60. Hippolytus, *Apostolic Tradition* viii. See J. Lecuyer, 'Épiscopat et

presbytérat dans les écrits d'Hippolyte de Rome', in *Recherches de Science Religieuse* (61) 1968, pp. 30–50.

61. In the primitive Church government was the first purpose of ordination. This was not just the empowering of the ordained minister to posit specific acts, the aspect which received the emphasis in later medieval ordination rites; rather it entrusted the recipient with a permanent responsibility for the community. The functions followed from this responsibility (Power, op. cit., pp. 167, 175).

62. This conclusion is already implicit in 1 Cor. 10.14–21 where the Last Supper is opposed to the sacrifice offered to demons. A similar parallelism with the sacrifices of Israel underlies 1 Cor. 9.13 ff. If the Last Supper was a paschal meal it would have been thought of as an integral part of the paschal sacrifice, and its sacrificial nature is implicit in the term 'the cup of the new covenant', since a covenant presupposed a sacrifice (cf. R. de Vaux, *Ancient Israel, its Life and Institutions* [Darton, Longman & Todd 1961], p. 453). The *Didache* (14) asserts that the Eucharist is the sacrifice of the Gentiles mentioned in Mal. 1.12. So does Justin (*Dial.* 116–17) and Irenaeus (*Adv. Haer.* iv.29, 5 ff.). But it is also found as early as Ignatius of Antioch (*Magn.* 6; *Trall.* 7; *Philad.* 4). It was difficult for the Jewish Christians to conceive of the Presidents of the Eucharist as 'priests', since in their tradition the priests had officiated at the sacrifices *prior* to the sacrificial meal over which the father presided (see J. M. Tillard, 'What Priesthood has the Ministry?' in *One in Christ* [ix], 1973, no. 3, p. 256), and the Church's counterpart to these bloody sacrifices was accomplished in the flesh of Jesus.

63. The only time in the New Testament that a eucharistic celebration is described, it is presided over by Paul who alone preaches and breaks the bread (Acts 20.7–12). This passage also shows the natural connection between breaking the bread and the work of preaching. 1 Clem. 40 insists that only those should offer the sacrifices 'whom God has determined'. Ignatius specifies this officer (*Phil.* 4) as the bishop and his assistants. See also *Smyrn.* 8.

64. They were often called *sacerdotes secundi ordinis* to make it clear that they were the delegates of the bishop. See P. M. Gy, 'Notes on the Early Terminology of the Christian Priesthood', in *The Sacrament of Holy Orders* (Aquin Press 1962), pp. 109–10.

65. Discipleship was the beginning of the apostolate and remained its permanent presupposition. 1 Pet. 5.1 shows that the apostles sometimes thought of themselves as presbyters too. The New Testament uses the same basic vocabulary to describe both the apostles and the ministers designated by them: St Paul uses compound words prefixed with *sun*, e.g. *sundoulos, sunergos, sustratiotēs*, to describe his associates. In Acts 13.1 ff. prophets and teachers in Antioch are said to *leitourgein*. In the *Didache* 13.3 also *archiereus* is applied to the prophets as a reason why they should receive the first-fruits, and they too are said to *eucharistein* (10.7).

66. See J. Moingt, 'Caractère et ministère' (see n. 40 above), pp. 566 ff.

67. Denziger 957.
68. Denziger 960, quoting Song of Songs 6.3.
69. St Ignatius of Antioch also stresses the fundamental unity of hierarchical authority. Nothing must be done in the Church without the bishop, but Christians must be subject also to the presbyterium, which was a Senate, a Sanhedrin, not only of collaborators with the bishop, but also of counsellors who can give their views both on the execution of the bishop's decisions and even in the preparation of them (*Phil.* 4.1; *Trall.* 13.2; *Magn.* 6.1; *Smyrn.* 8.1).
70. The Tridentine theology of the episcopate also suffered from the failure to consider *organically* the relations between the different degrees of holy orders. Because of Trent's definition of the priesthood, the episcopate was considered to be a sort of inflation of the priesthood; when post-Tridentine theologians discussed the priesthood, they took the simple priest as their point of departure so that the bishop was viewed as a priest with certain special powers, instead of taking the bishop as the primordial priest. Trent placed a much greater difference between bishops and priests in the juridical than in the sacramental order.
71. Cf. Vatican II where the point of departure was the apostolic nature of the Church, the mission of the whole People of God. The visible priesthood is no longer justified, as at Trent, solely by reference to a visible sacrifice (cf. Denziger 957), but by the visibility of the whole nature of the Church.
72. See J. D. Crichton, 'Church and Ministry from the Council of Trent to the First Vatican Council', in *The Christian Priesthood* (see n. 39 above), pp. 127–63.
73. 'In all cases a new peace was created for man through the sacrifice and renewal of harmony [with God]. But man could only be in harmony with God when he was "whole". The sacrifice removed whatever was wasting his integrity, whatever was called sin' (J. Pedersen, *Israel, Its Life and Culture* [Oxford University Press 1959], vol. iii–iv, p. 359). Also: 'In the sacrifice all the threads of life are gathered together; renewed life springs from it, because the blessing is recreated in it, and its effects are felt in all the forces of life, in the world of God, the world of man and the world of nature' (ibid., p. 323).
74. See St Augustine's definition of sacrifice: 'Verum sacrificium est omne opus quod agitur ut sancta societate inhaereamus Deo' (*De Civ. Dei* 10.6, 'De vero perfectoque sacrificio'). Also: 'Hoc est sacrificium Christianorum: multi unum corpus in Christo; . . . totum sacrificium ipsi nos sumus; . . . tota ipsa redempta civitas, hoc est congregatio societasque sanctorum, universale sacrificium offeratur Deo per sacerdotem magnum qui etiam semetipsum obtulit in passione pro nobis, ut tanti capitis corpus essemus' (ibid., *PL* 41.283–4).
75. Heb. 3.1 ff., 14; 1 Cor. 4.2.
76. Prol. 129 ff.
77. Rom. 12.1.
78. Col. 1.24.

HOSPITALITY

1. E.g. the dramas of Arthur Miller, the novels of Albert Camus, along with much contemporary work in music, poetry, painting, and the plastic arts, as well as newer art-forms such as film-making, have expressed various degrees of hope and despair for rootless modern man. Writers such as Orwell and Huxley, with their visions of what will come of our society, have testified to the disappearance of true community among men.

2. *The Culture of the Cities* (New York, Harcourt Brace Inc., 1938), pp. 475–6.

3. Cf. Erich Fromm's analysis of the loneliness of modern western man: 'While everybody tries to be as close as possible to the rest, everybody remains utterly alone, pervaded by the deep sense of insecurity, anxiety and guilt which always results when human separateness cannot be overcome' (*The Art of Loving* [Unwin Books 1962], p. 64).

4. Cf. Paschal Botz, 'The Challenge of Hospitality', in *Benedictines* xxviii.3–4 (1973), pp. 69–78.

5. Prov. 27.8; Sir. 29.21.

6. Lev. 19.33 f.; cf. Exod. 22.21; Acts 7.6.

7. Ps. 39(38).12 ff.; cf. Heb. 11.13.

8. Deut. 10.18 ff.

9. Gen. 18.1 ff.

10. Luke 7.44 ff.

11. Rom. 12.13; 15.7.

12. Matt. 25.35, 43.

13. Luke 2.7.

14. John 1.9–11.

15. John 13.20; cf. Matt. 10.40.

16. Luke 9.48 p.

17. Gen. 19.1 ff. The Old Testament provides a few instances of horror at hospitality refused or the ill-treatment of guests, e.g. this story of Sodom and Judg. 19.

18. Gen. 18.2–8.

19. RSV Luke 24.13–16.

20. Sir. 29.24–28; 11.34; 1 Pet. 4.9.

21. 1 Tim. 5.10.

22. Rev. 3.20.

23. John 14.23.

24. John 14.2 ff.; Eph. 2.19.

25. Luke 12.37; Rev. 3.20.

26. 1 Clem. 1.2.

27. *Apol.* 15.15, 7.

28. *Ad Eph.* 6.1.

29. *Epist.* 7.
30. *Hom. in Matt.* 66.3.
31. *Didasc.* 2.58.6; Synod of Elvira, ch. 25; Synod of Arles, ch. 9; Synod of Antioch, ch. 9.
32. RB 37; 36.
33. RB 42.23.
34. RB 53.21 ff.
35. Matt. 25.35; cf. RB 53.3.
36. RB 66.7–10.
37. RB 31.15.
38. RB 53.47–50.
39. Cf. *UR* 15.
40. Perhaps this is due not to historical accident but to something in the nature of monasticism. The idea of the monk as a pilgrim is very ancient and prominent especially in Celtic monastic tradition. It may partly explain why pilgrims gravitate towards monasteries.
41. RB 61.
42. The ideas in this section of the chapter are derived especially from Thomas Merton, *Contemplation in a World of Action* (George Allen and Unwin 1971), pp. 222–5.
43. RB 32; 57; 31.19 ff.
44. RB 53.47–50, and the whole chapter.

AUTONOMY OF THE MONASTERIES

1. Cf. Aelred Sillem, 'The Benedictine Paradox', *Monastic Studies* 6 (1968), pp. 73–5.
2. *Lex Propria Confoederationis Benedictinae a Congressu Abbatum anno 1970 revisa et ad experimentum approbata*, no. 1; cf. also David Knowles, *The Benedictines* (St Leo, Florida, The Abbey Press, 1962), pp. 21–2.
3. RB 34; 40.1–3, 7–9.
4. RB 34; 72.7 ff.
5. RB 40.10–13; 41.4 f.; 55.1–4.
6. RB 48; 57.
7. RB 64.
8. *PC* 9.
9. *AAS* lviii, pp. 884–9.
10. RB 2; 64.
11. Code of Canon Law, canons 198.1; 488.8.
12. RB 5.
13. RB 2; 64.
14. Knowles, op. cit., p. 18.

15. RB 3.
16. RB 3.26–8.
17. Knowles, op. cit., p. 21.
18. RB 71.
19. Cf. J. McMurry, 'Monastic Stability', *Cistercian Studies*, 1 (1966.2), pp. 223–4.
20. Cuthbert Butler, *Benedictine Monachism* (Longmans, Green & Co. 1919), pp. 239–40.
21. Stephanus Hilpisch, *Benedictines through Changing Centuries* (Collegeville, St John's Abbey Press, 1958), pp. 43–5.
22. A. G. Biggs, 'Benedictines', in *New Catholic Encyclopedia*, vol. 2, p. 293.
23. Hilpisch, op. cit., p. 82.
24. Butler, op. cit., p. 240.
25. Hilpisch, op. cit., p. 83.
26. Biggs, art. cit., p. 293.
27. Ibid.
28. Butler, op. cit., pp. 240–41.
29. Hilpisch, loc. cit.
30. Ibid.
31. Ibid., pp. 93–4.
32. Ibid., pp. 94–9.
33. Ibid., pp. 105–6.
34. Session Twenty-Five, *Canons and Decrees of the Council of Trent*, Original Text with English Translation by H. J. Schroeder (St Louis, B. Herder Book Co., 1941), pp. 485–99.
35. Biggs, art. cit., p. 294.
36. Ibid.
37. Butler, op. cit., pp. 249–51.
38. Ibid., pp. 245–6.
39. *Lex Propria* no. 126.
40. Hilpisch, op. cit., p. 130.
41. *AAS* xliv, pp. 520–22.
42. Cf. *Lex Propria*, nos. 24–125; 126–59.
43. Butler, op. cit., pp. 260–62.
44. Cf. *Lex Propria*, nos. 74–125.
45. *Ecclesiae Sanctae*, Norms for the Implementation of the Decree *PC*, no. 1; cf. also *Acta Congressus Abbatum ac Priorum Conventualium Congregationum Confoederatarum O.S.B. in Aedibus S. Anselmi de Urbe, Duplici Sessione Celebrati* (1966–7), p. 9.
46. Cf. Encyclical Letter of Pope John XXIII, *Pacem in Terris*, *AAS* lv, p. 294.
47. *PC* 2 (2).

48. Canon 501.3.
49. Butler, op. cit., pp. 253–6.
50. Ibid., p. 218.
51. Canon viii, *Disciplinary Decrees of the General Councils*, Text, Translation and Commentary by H. J. Schroeder (St Louis, B. Herder Book Co., 1937), p. 520.
52. Butler, op. cit., p. 219.
53. Ibid.
54. Bede: *Lives of the Holy Abbots of Wearmouth and Jarrow*, Book I (*PL* 94.717).
55. Butler, op. cit., p. 220.
56. Ibid.
57. Hilpisch, op. cit., pp. 106–7.
58. *Ecclesiae Sanctae*, Norms for the Implementation of the Decree *PC*, nos. 12–14.
59. Cf. C. J. van der Poel, 'Exemption and Institutes of Pontifical Law' in *The Jurist*, vol. xxv, no. 4 (October 1965), p. 439; Basil Pennington, 'Monastic Autonomy', in *Cistercian Studies*, vol. 3, 1968.1, p. 28.
60. Cf. canons 615–17.
61. Van der Poel, art. cit., p. 443.
62. *CD* (ed. Abbott-Gallagher) 35.3.
63. Cf. Coronata: *Institutiones iuris canonici*, i (Turin 1939), no. 623; Abbo-Hannon, *The Sacred Canons*, i (St. Louis, B. Herder Book Co., 1952), pp. 637–8.
64. A. Bugnini, C. M., Secretary, *Consilium ad Exsequendam Constitutionem de Sacra Liturgia*, Prot. n. 134/67, 27 January 1967, as quoted in Pennington, art. cit., p. 48.
65. Cf. *SC* 22.2; 36.3; 39; 40 (1); 44; 63 (b); 77; 101.1; 110; 120; 128.
66. *Ecclesiae Sanctae*, i, no. 26.
67. Ibid.
68. Cf. canons 1245.3; 1516.3; 806.2; 822.4; 47; 15; 81.

Select Bibliography

de Vogüé, A., *La Règle de Saint Benoît*. 7 vols. in ser. *Sources Chrétiennes*. Paris, Éditions du Cerf 1972–7.

de Vogüé, A., *La Communauté et l'Abbé dans la Règle de Saint Benoît*. Paris, Desclée de Brouwer 1961.

Delatte, Paul, *The Rule of St Benedict, A Commentary*. Burns & Oates 1921.

Herwegen, I., *Sinn und Geist der Benediktinerregel*. Einsiedeln, Benziger 1944.

Steidle, B., *The Rule of St Benedict*, English trans. U. J. Schnitzhofer. Holy Cross Abbey, Canon City, Colorado 1967.

van Zeller, H., *The Holy Rule. Notes on St Benedict's Legislation for Monks*. Sheed & Ward 1959.

Colombas, Garcia M., *San Benito, Su Vida y Su Regla*, 2nd edn. Madrid, Biblioteca de Autores Cristianos 1968.

Colombas, Garcia M., *El Monacato Primitivo*. 2 vols. Madrid, Biblioteca de Autores Cristianos 1974, 1975.

Veilleux, A., *La Liturgie dans le cénobitisme pachômien au quatrième siècle*, vol. lvii in collection *Studia Anselmiana*. Rome, Herder 1968.

Chitty, Derwas J., *The Desert a City. An Introduction to the Study of Egyptian and Palestinian Monasticism under the Christian Empire*. Basil Blackwell 1966.

Knowles, David, *From Pachomius to Ignatius. A Study in the Constitutional History of the Religious Orders*. Clarendon Press 1966.

Knowles, David, *Christian Monasticism*. Weidenfeld & Nicolson 1969.

Butler, Cuthbert, *Benedictine Monachism. Studies in Benedictine Life and Rule*, reprinted with a new Foreword by Dom David Knowles,

BIBLIOGRAPHY

Cambridge ('Speculum Historiale', 42 Lyndewoode Road), 1961. 1st edn. Longmans, Green 1919.

Théologie de la Vie Monastique. Études sur la Tradition Patristique. Paris, Aubier 1961.

Cousin, P., *Précis d'Histoire Monastique.* Paris, Bloud & Gay 1956.

Schmitz, P., *Histoire de l'Ordre de Saint Benoît.* 7 vols. Maredsous 1942.

Knowles, David, *The Monastic Order in England,* 2nd edn. Cambridge University Press 1963.

Knowles, David, *The Religious Orders in England,* vols, i–iii. Cambridge University Press 1948–59.

Vagaggini, C., *Problemi e orientamenti di spiritualità monastica, biblica e liturgica.* Rome, Edizioni Paoline 1961.

Vagaggini, C., Penco, G., and others, *La Preghiera nella Bibbia e nella tradizione patristica e monastica.* Rome, Edizioni Paoline 1964.

van Zeller, H., *The Benedictine Nun. Her Story and Aim.* Dublin, Helicon 1965.

Marmion, Columba, *Le Christ, idéal du moine.* Maredsous 1922. English trans. *Christ, the Ideal of the Monk.* Sands 1926.

Peifer, C. J., *Monastic Spirituality.* New York, Sheed & Ward 1966.

Bouyer, Louis, *Le Sens de la Vie Monastique.* Paris, Brepols 1950. English trans. *The Meaning of the Monastic Life.* Burns & Oates 1955.

Cary-Elwes, Columba, *Monastic Renewal.* New York, Herder 1967.

du Roy, O., *Moines Aujourd'hui.* Paris, Épi 1972.

Leclercq, J., *Le Défi de la Vie Contemplative.* Gembloux, Duculot 1970.

Merton, T., *Contemplation in a World of Action.* Allen & Unwin 1971.

Tillard, J. M., *Les Religieux au Cœur de l'Église.* Paris, Éditions du Cerf 1969.

Tillard, J. M., and Congar, Y., *L'Adaptation et la Renovation de la Vie Religieuse. Decret 'Perfectae Caritatis',* vol. 62 in collection *Unam Sanctam.* Paris, Éditions du Cerf 1968.

Pellicia, G., and Rocca, G., *Dizionario degli Istituti di Perfezione.* 3 vols. so far printed. Rome, Edizioni Paoline 1973 ff.

Index

Major themes are in bold type.

Receptivity 136, 166, 179, 223

Reconciliation 18–19; in community life 151; 276; shared prayer and 299; 336

Recreation 56, 152

Religious 9, 48, 135, 219, 370–71

Religious experience 297

Renunciation 3, 51, 149, 150, 158, 170, 178, 205, 211

Repentance 25, 26; in RB 101; in community life 151; and prayer 283; sacrament of 336

Reverence 53, 216

Rule of St Benedict (RB) 37; characteristics of the 46–51, 211, 245; its place in history 51–4; hospitality in 347–8

Rule of the Master 46, 50, 53, 69, 76, 79, 90, 157, 193, 263, 265

Sacrament 3, 4, 19; notion of 20–21; Christ s. of God 20; Church s. of Christ 21; sacraments build Body of Christ 22; 28; *opus Dei* as s. of monastic life 259–60

Sacred Liturgy, Constitution on the 233, 260, 372

Sacrifice 19, 48, 167, 169–70, 187, 196–7, 279, 328, 336

Salvation 4, 20–21, 27, 31, 59

Sarabaites 47

Sayers, Dorothy (quoted) 168–9

Schools 37, 311, 312–14, 349

Second Vatican Council (Vatican II) 4, 5, 7, 8, 9, 13, 20, 44, 52, 54, 56, 58, 154, 177, 214, 232, 233, 236, 247, 252, 258, 292, 319, 322, 324, 330, 333, 335, 337, 341, 358, 369, 371

Self-denial 149, 151, 177

Sermon on the Mount 34, 148

Service 26, 51, 56, 211, 303, 306

Sexuality 56, 156–7, 159–62, 173–4, 176–8

Sexual love 15, 166, 173–4, 176–8

Sharing 8, 33, 59, 60, 63–5, 70–71, 94; of goods 205, 218–20, 309

Silence 3, 8, 49, 64, 102, 104, 143, 284, 292, 309, 350

Simplicity 220, 283, 309, 351

Sin, sinfulness 30, 31, 145, 146, 150, 161, 195

Solidarity 66, 71

Solitude 8, 95, 99, 100, 105, 309

Sonship, our adoptive 18, 19, 25, 60, 87, 103, 189, 243, 278

Spirit, the Holy 13, 14; gift of S. marks new era 19; forms Body of Christ 21–5, 59; forms community as S. of communication 30–31; promptings of the 36; 46; RB subordinate to 48–9; gives freedom 101; leads to mature celibacy 183; leads to mature obedience 203; inspires prayer 277–8; experience of the 287; monastic life a charism of 292

Spirituality 145, 232, 270, 294, 335

Stability 5; personal 51; in a community 134–5, 149, 191, 198, 234, 360; legal 138

Studies 37, 125, 304

Subsidiarity 66

Suffering 16, 25, 30, 138, 150, 170, 279

Synoptic gospels 27, 327

Taius of Saragossa 267

Tensions 65, 72, 106, 107, 237

Theology 8–10, 32, 36, 45; contemplative 109; post-Tridentine 109; 156, 157, 159, 174, 233; ascetical 270; of religious life 369

Theology, monastic 8–10; its place in renewal 8–9, 36; its service to Church 108–9

Thomas, St 185, 226

Tillich, Paul (quoted) 276, 284

Tradition 6; process of communication between generations 15, 54; needs to be reappropriated by each generation 34, 36; RB as monument of 52–3
Trent, Council of 177, 230, 247–8, 334–5, 362, 367, 368, 370
Trust 63, 132–3, 299
Truth 15, 32, 75, 102, 352

Unity of Christians 28, 49, 60, 64, 87, 305, 345, 349

Vatican II *see* Second Vatican Council
Virginity 34, 56, 154, 162, 167; the example of Jesus 167–9; sacrificial aspect of 169–70; as an eschatological value 170–72; motivation for 172–5
Visitations 366–7
Vocation 110–27; and response 110–12; common features in v. narratives 112–14; and service to others 114; to monastic life 115–20; and growth in community 120–27
Vows 66, 101; made to God 129; human possibility of lifelong vowing 129; compatibility with

personal growth 129–30; 170; vow of obedience 196–7, 359; relation to Eucharist 241

Witness 4, 6, 26, 33, 36, 142, 259
Word of God 24, 54, 63, 64, 161, 242; addresses man throughout history 245–6; receptivity to 252; listened to and preached by monastic community 257–8; 274; listening to 282, 296
Work 67, 187, 301–17; theological context of 301–2; integration 304; pluralism in 304; in relation to monastic life 304–9; as duty 304–5; unity and co-operation in 305; and the individual 306–7; and leisure 308–9; and poverty 309–10; in relation to those outside monastery 310–12; present forms of w. in the EBC 312–17. *See also* Leisure
World 6, 13; characteristics of the modern w. 13–16, 35; mission of Church in the 16, 26, 27–36; Christian understanding of the 29–31; critical transformation of the 32–5, 58; monastery and 36–8; *fuga mundi* 106–7
Worship 6, 20, 258–9

CISTERCIAN PUBLICATIONS INC.
Kalamazoo, Michigan

TITLES LISTING

THE CISTERCIAN FATHERS SERIES

Texts and Studies in the Monastic Tradition

* Temporarily out of print

† Fortbcoming

* *Temporarily out of print*   † *Forthcoming*